RANDOM
HOUSE
LARGE
PRINT

ZERO FAIL

ZERO FAIL

THE RISE AND FALL OF THE SECRET SERVICE

CAROL LEONNIG

RANDOM HOUSE
LARGE PRINT

Cover design: Tyler Comrie and Greg Mollica
Cover photograph: Jabin Botsford/
The Washington Post via Getty Images

The Library of Congress has established a
Cataloging-in-Publication record for this title.

ISBN: 978-0-593-41412-5

www.penguinrandomhouse.com/large-print-format-books

FIRST LARGE PRINT EDITION

Printed in the United States of America

10 9 8 7 6 5 4 3 2 1

This Large Print edition published in accord
with the standards of the N.A.V.H.

FOR MY HUSBAND, JOHN,
AND MY DAUGHTERS,
ELISE AND MOLLY

AUTHOR'S NOTE

When I began reporting on the United States Secret Service in 2012, this unique law enforcement agency was rocked by what seemed like the most humiliating scandal in its modern history: A dozen agents and officers stood accused of turning a presidential trip to a South American resort town into a kind of Vegas bachelor party, complete with heavy drinking and prostitutes. At the time, the misconduct shocked the country precisely because the men and women of the Secret Service had for so long been synonymous with tireless and selfless vigilance, a band of patriots willing to take a bullet to protect America's democracy.

But as I reported more deeply, I learned of a more worrisome scandal than these **Mad Men**–style antics: This long-revered agency was not living up to its most solemn duty—to keep the president safe.

Agents and officers gave me a guided tour, showing me step by step how the Secret Service was becoming a paper tiger, weakened by arrogant, insular leadership, promotions based on loyalty rather than capability, years of slim budgets, and outdated technology. With their help, I decided to dig deeper still to understand how this had happened and to chart the previous five decades of the proud Secret Service. How had it recovered from the assassination of President Kennedy, rebuilt its security force to be the envy of the world, and later begun a slow slide that had worried and angered its frontline workers?

An important note about my purpose: Some Secret Service leaders and alumni have vowed to attack my work, claiming that I seek to embarrass their venerable institution and highlight its blemishes. But it is for the Secret Service's front line and its future that I write these hard truths. I am in awe of the agents and officers who pull together for their critical common purpose, and what they still accomplish every day under considerable strain. They toil on, often without thanks, proper support, or a proactive strategy from above. I write because they deserve better.

This book is based on hundreds of hours of interviews with more than 180 people, including current and former Secret Service agents, officers, and directors, cabinet members, advisers, and senior government officials in eight previous presidential administrations, and members of Congress and their staff, as well as other witnesses to the events described herein. I spoke with Secret Service staff who worked a heartbeat from the president and in far-flung field offices, and with the equally dedicated members of their families. Most of the people who cooperated in my research agreed to speak candidly on condition of anonymity, either to protect their careers or because they feared retaliation from the agency and alumni who seek to tamp down bad news and burnish the agency's brand. Many shared their experiences in a background capacity, allowing me to use their information as long as I protected their identities and did not attribute details to them by name.

I am an objective journalist dedicated to sharing the truth with the public, and here I have aimed to provide an account that is as close to the full truth as I could determine based on rigorous reporting. Scenes you read in this book are reconstructed from firsthand accounts and, whenever possible, corroborated by multiple sources. They are also vetted by my review of internal government reports and memos. While there is a tendency to discount the words of anonymous sources, many of the people who spoke to me in confidence also submitted to rigorous fact checking and shared with me contemporaneous notes, calendars, and correspondence to buttress their accounts. Dialogue cannot always be exact, but it is based here on multiple people's memories of events. In a few instances, different sources disagreed about substantive elements, and when necessary, I note that, acknowledging that different narrators can remember events differently.

This book is an outgrowth of my reporting for **The Washington Post**. Some of the episodes you read in **Zero Fail** began with stories I wrote for the newspaper, often with the help of my wise colleagues. The majority of the scenes, dialogue, and quotations are original to my book, however, and based on the extensive reporting I conducted exclusively for this project.

This historical account benefited significantly from contemporaneous news reports in **The Washington Post** and other publications. I also relied on a handful of compelling books covering specific periods, including some written by former agents who recognized that their experiences are indeed the stuff of history. I credit key information gleaned from those accounts, either with a direct reference in the narrative or in the endnotes.

PROLOGUE

On the evening of March 30, 1981, an eight-year-old boy in Norfolk, Virginia, sat glued to his family's living room TV. Earlier that day, John Hinckley, Jr., had attempted to assassinate Ronald Reagan outside the Washington Hilton. But as CBS News played the scene in a slow-motion loop, the boy's focus wasn't on the president. It was on the man who entered the frame.

Over and over again, the boy watched in amazement as this square-jawed man in a light gray suit turned toward the gunfire and fell to the ground, clutching his stomach. **By taking a bullet for the president**, the newsman said, **Tim McCarthy probably saved his life**. At that moment, young Brad Gable (not his real name) knew exactly what he wanted to do when he grew up:

He would be a Secret Service agent.

Now, thirty years later, Gable had indeed fulfilled that mission. He was a member of the Secret Service's Counter Assault Team, or CAT. In the constellation of presidential protection, CAT arguably has the most dangerous assignment. When most people think of the Secret Service, they picture the suited agents who cover and evacuate the president in moments of danger. The heavily armed CAT force has a different mission: Run toward whatever gunfire or explosion threatens the president and neutralize it. The team's credo reflects the only two fates they believe await any attacker who crosses them: "Dead or Arrested."

Gable was proud of the career he had chosen. Among his colleagues, he was respected for the pure patriotism driving him and for his intense focus on operational details. So why, in the late summer of 2012, as he sat in a restaurant near Fort Bragg, North Carolina, did he suddenly feel like throwing up?

Gable and his fellow agents had come to a mom-and-pop restaurant with a group of Delta Force members who were overseeing the CAT team's annual training. Gable's squad had drilled for almost a week with these steely Special Forces operators, playing out mock assassination attempts and blind attacks to learn how to shield themselves and their buddies in close-quarters combat.

After a dinner of ribs, steaks, and wings, Gable sat back for some beers and small talk with one of

9/11's faceless heroes, a Delta Force sergeant major I'll call John. Gable liked John's no-bullshit style. He had real battlefield experience—two weeks after the 9/11 attacks, he'd been part of the raid on Mullah Omar's Kandahar compound, but he didn't crow about it—which instantly earned Gable's trust and respect.

On his second beer, Gable felt loose enough to ask John a question that had been on his mind: "After teaching so many operators and law enforcement agents, what do you think of the Secret Service's overall readiness?" The sergeant major demurred, so Gable pressed him.

"Seriously, how would you rate us?"

"Look," John said. "I feel sorry for you guys. The Service has really let you down. You'll never be able to stop a real attack."

It wasn't the answer Gable had hoped for, and as he listened to John dissect the Service's outdated equipment and spotty training, his stomach grew queasy. Deep down, he knew how ill-equipped and out of date the Secret Service was, but hearing it articulated by someone he respected made it impossible to deny. His mind drifted to all the times he had seen the Service drop the ball—most recently, a 2010 trip to Mumbai with President Obama, in which his unit had narrowly avoided a major international incident after nearly killing an unidentified gunman who turned out to be a local police officer. Scenarios like these were dress rehearsals for a real attack on the president, and in his five years with CAT, he had seen the Service fail so many of them.

Gable was now faced with a brutal truth: Increasingly, the Secret Service was fulfilling its Zero Fail mission based not on its skills, people, training, or technology, but on dumb luck. How long would it be before that luck ran out? Gable wasn't alone. He knew other dedicated agents who felt a growing sense of disillusionment, especially with the agency's leadership. But fear of repercussions had kept them silent. Until the stakes got too high.

I'VE BEEN COVERING the Secret Service since 2012, starting with my reporting on "Hookergate," the scandal in which agents brought prostitutes to their hotel rooms while making arrangements for President Obama's visit to Cartagena, Colombia— and which gave me my first glimpse into the Service's deeper institutional problems. In the years since, however, many agents have expressed concerns to me about the agency's ability to guard the presidents, their families, and other key government officials. They describe an organization stretched too thin, drowning in new missions, and fraught with security risks brought on by a fundamental mistrust between rank-and-file agents and leadership.

These agents have rejected the Service's code of silence in favor of the higher good of sounding an

alarm. They came to me hoping that an investigative reporter at **The Washington Post** could bring
attention to their concerns, shame the leaders who
had failed them, and help right the ship. To tell
their complete story, I conducted and reviewed
hundreds of interviews with agents, officers, directors, lawmakers, presidents, and their staffs. I read
through thousands of documents, including presidential archives as well as internal Secret Service
reports, investigation files, and security reviews that
have never been shared publicly. What I discovered
was a rich, complicated story—of bravery and
venality, heroism and incompetence—that America
cannot and should not turn away from.

This book isn't an academic history. My intent
here is to focus on the rise and entirely avoidable fall
of the Secret Service over the last sixty years, from
Kennedy to Trump. We sometimes forget that this
proud, largely invisible force stands between the
president and all attackers. By protecting the president, they protect democracy. And while the agency
once stood for dedication and perfection in the face
of impossible odds, it now finds itself in a state of
unprecedented peril.

In these pages, I attempt to paint the portrait of
an agency marked by a unique set of contradictions:
An ever-shifting and murky mission coupled with
impossible expectations to meet it. A rigid management structure that inspires discipline while also
inciting resentment and rebellion. An organization

whose performance standards are far higher—and whose morale and personal conduct standards are, at times, far lower—than those of any other federal agency. A working battalion whose members often sacrifice a normal life and push themselves to exhaustion to deliver on a near-impossible mission, slaving for some leaders who look after themselves first and fail to make the bold choices that could help support their corps.

My goal is to offer a behind-the-scenes look at an organization saddled with a never-ending struggle to improve its reputation, boost its resources, and raise its morale. In perhaps the ultimate irony, I present an agency that seems to improve only in the wake of the thing it is sworn to prevent: tragedy.

In the last six decades, the Secret Service has grown from three hundred agents and a $5 million budget to seven thousand agents, officers, and other staff and a budget of over $2.2 billion. Its mission has expanded as well. Instead of protecting one leader, the agency now shields his extended family, many of his deputies, and even his political opponents. It focuses not just on stopping a bullet but also on blocking a drone carrying poison gas, a cyberattack throttling the nation's energy grid, and any threat to a stadium of spectators watching the Super Bowl. This kind of mission growth could prove challenging to any organization. But the Service hasn't just suffered growing pains. By its own staff's measures, the agency's standards and capacity to fulfill its core assignment have been slipping for years, raising several crucial questions:

How did the Secret Service go from an elite, hardworking band of patriots vowing to do whatever it takes to protect future presidents in the wake of JFK's assassination, to a frat boy culture of infighting, indulgence, and obsolescence?

How did the Service go from a close-knit group that prided itself on a nonpartisan "the people elect 'em, we protect 'em" attitude, to an organization that is used by presidents for craven political means and feels it must acquiesce to stay in favor?

And finally, how did the Service go from an institution that inspired and captured the imagination of an eight-year-old boy in Norfolk, Virginia, to an organization that can't hire people fast enough to fill its departures, and that for three years running had recently been ranked as the most hated place to work in the federal government?

Zero Fail chronicles this deterioration across decades, leadership changes, and game-changing world events. But while the agency has suffered many embarrassing failures along the way, it must be noted that no president has been killed on its watch since John F. Kennedy. Many committed men and women who stand on rope lines and scour crowds looking for the subtlest signs of danger have been tested repeatedly, and at least by their own sense of duty, they have proved themselves true to their motto: "Worthy of Trust and Confidence."

Sadly, their organization can't stop an assassin with stubborn devotion alone.

Writing this book helped me see how the Service's decline has been decades in the making, but it also helped me appreciate the many agents who keep their rounds despite the disorder and haphazard management swirling around them. Every day, these public servants, whom Eisenhower dubbed "soldiers out of uniform," brave cold and wet at the White House gates and endure mind-numbing boredom guarding convention center stairwells and hotel hallways. They sweat through their under-shirts and socks standing for hours at back-to-back campaign rallies. They maintain for hours, for days, the kind of hypervigilance that would exhaust a normal person after just ten minutes.

I also came to appreciate how the Secret Service was born out of a fundamental tension that lies at the heart of American democracy: symbolism versus security. The weight that rests on their shoulders became palpable for me when some agents recounted their introduction to presidential protection from a standout leader of President Clinton's detail. Special agent in charge Larry Cockell had begun their tute-lage by sharing the obituary for the agent who drove President Kennedy's limousine the day he was killed, and who had initially slowed the car at the sound of the first shot. The opening line of the death notice called out the agent's role in a tragedy that would define his life.

"You are now part of an agency responsible for the life of the president and the stability of our democracy," Cockell told them, the agents recalled. "This is what failure looks like. I can't succeed unless you succeed. Unless we all pull together, we all fail. I expect you to be focused and invested in this and accountable at all times, and if you think there is any obstacle to you doing this, then I ask that you leave the detail today."

America wants to project the image of being free and open, "of the people." As recently as 1881, sixteen years after Lincoln's assassination and fresh off James Garfield's, the country rejected the idea of a presidential security force because it smacked of "royals" hiding behind an imperial guard. Despite the inherent dangers, Bill Clinton and JFK continually subverted their detail agents to get closer to their adoring fans—the latter famously ditching his detail to go for a swim at a public beach in California. Reagan's handlers engaged in a heated debate with the Service over the optics of using metal detectors at the president's first public appearance after the attempt on his life. Even internally, agents have nearly come to blows over such issues, including whether long guns on the White House roof would create the impression that the leader of the free world lives in a military compound.

A rare success in marrying these two competing impulses came at Barack Obama's victory speech on the night of November 4, 2008, when more than 71 million prime-time TV viewers watched a joyous, almost spontaneous-looking event in Chicago's Grant Park celebrating the election of America's first Black president. Invisible to the cameras: the fact that the airspace had been declared a no-fly zone, and that two enormous sheets of bulletproof glass flanked the president-elect to thwart would-be snipers. In both practical and symbolic terms, the scene communicated everything you need to know about what the Service is routinely expected to achieve.

Zero Fail touches on this loftier story, but the history it recounts is ultimately more personal. This book is about the current and former agents, officers, and administrative staff in this secretive fraternity who chose to share their stories with me. I will be forever grateful to them for risking their careers—not because they wanted to share tantalizing gossip about presidents and their families, but because they know that the Service is broken and needs fixing. By telling their story, they hope to revive the Service they love. They deserve a public commitment to rebuilding their agency so they're not left toiling in constant fear of failure, not to mention constant risk of personal harm.

America, its presidents and its citizens, have taken the Secret Service for granted in the past, too often with tragic results.

CONTENTS

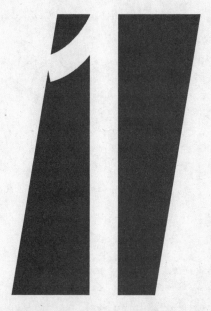

THE TRAGEDY THAT BIRTHED
A NEW SECRET SERVICE

KENNEDY TO NIXON (1963-1974)

CHAPTER 1

PROTECTING LANCER

Win Lawson felt his chest puff out a little this particular day in Buffalo, his shoulders hiking his lanky frame just a little taller and straighter. Proud. Yep, he could admit it to himself. Win Lawson, the shy, quiet worrier, felt proud.

The thirty-four-year-old had grown up in a no-stoplight town along the banks of Lake Erie that few outside upstate New York had ever heard of: Portland, New York. The community, about sixty miles south of Buffalo, was best known for its chilly lake air, vineyards and apple farms, and families as hardy as the crops they tended.

Lawson, the son of an elementary school teacher and a local banker, had left for college the summer after high school. He got his degree, married a fraternity brother's sister, and joined an Army intelligence unit as the Korean War began.

Now, a dozen years later, on this fall day in 1962, Lawson had returned to his home turf in a prestigious new role: He was an agent with the Secret Service, assigned to protect the president of the United States.

Nearly two hundred thousand people spilled across Buffalo's largest downtown square, angling for a glimpse of the most famous man on earth, John Fitzgerald Kennedy. And Win Lawson stood beside him.

Kennedy visited Buffalo on October 14, 1962, the day of the city's beloved Polish heritage parade. Seeing the crowds eight deep on the limo route, Lawson thought: **Polish or not, all of upstate New York has turned out today to see their dashing president.**

Lawson and the seven other members of the president's detail had a job that required every ounce of their concentration: Safeguard Kennedy from start to finish of the trip. They shadowed him as he stepped off Air Force One, as he stood waving from his limo the last half mile of the parade, and now finally as he addressed the enormous crowd in the city's center—Niagara Square.

That inner ring of detail agents kept a unique vigil that relied largely on sensory instinct and coiled muscles. When "the Boss"—their informal name for the president—stepped on the platform stage, his detail trained their eyes and ears on the crowd for any odd duck, strange movement, or person with hands stuffed in their pockets. When Kennedy was shaking hands, as he loved to do, detail agents flanked him on either side, watching those outstretched hands for any sign of danger. Their duty: to put their body between the president and a gun, knife, or any other threat.

Standing at the base of the wooden stage in front of City Hall, Lawson rotated his head from left to right, scanning the square, a human periscope rolling over endless heads, faces, and arms, alert to any sign of danger.

For this visit, Lawson had the added duty of serving as the Secret Service's chief of security planning. He had arrived three days earlier to assess the safety of every step the president would take on the visit, an elaborate choreography known as "the advance." He had chosen which streets to block off for the motorcade, how close crowds could stand, and what perimeter posts local cops and motorcycle escorts would man.

But Lawson's meticulous planning didn't change the laws of physics: He and his fellow agents were ultimately insignificant dots in the swirling mass of people pouring into the square.

Cheers went up as Kennedy told the crowd they had kept Poland in their hearts and urged them to pray that her people might one day live free of Communist rule. "And as the old song says, 'As long as you live, Poland lives,'" Kennedy continued. Thundering applause filled the square. Kennedy smiled at how long he had to wait before he could say the next line.

Kennedy was winning hearts, and—his political aides hoped—votes. To help Democrats win congressional seats that November, the White House wanted as many voters as possible to see the president. Secret Service agents privately disapproved of how close Kennedy wanted to get to his public, but they didn't have the power to override him. Still, the agents knew that the longer the parade route and the more hand-shaking at rope lines, the greater the chances that something bad could happen.

Hard as it was to believe that the president needed protecting from the cheering masses in Niagara Square, Lawson and the detail had to assume at all times that an enemy lurked within the throng. Kennedy may have been handsome, rich, and devilishly charming, but plenty of people in the country despised him. A select few wanted him dead.

The forty-three-year-old politician threatened the status quo. He was the first Catholic to win the presidency, a shock for an older generation that considered Protestants the nation's nobility. Many Americans were also deeply unsettled by Kennedy's insistence that Black people deserved to study in the same schools, use the same bathrooms, and eat in the same restaurants as whites.

A few weeks after Kennedy won the 1960 election, Richard Pavlick, a retired seventy-three-year-old postal worker with a history of mental problems and rants against Catholics, loaded the trunk of his Buick with seven sticks of dynamite. He drove from his native New Hampshire to Palm Beach, where the president-elect was staying before his inauguration. Pavlick plotted to blow up Kennedy by ramming his car as he left to attend mass, but he scrapped the plan when he saw Kennedy's wife and children walking by his side. Palm Beach police arrested him a few days later, based on a tip from a worried colleague who pieced together that Pavlick had been stalking Kennedy.

In Kennedy's first six weeks as president, the White House received three times the average number of letters threatening violence against the president. "We are sick of the dirty black Catholics," read one anonymous letter postmarked from Los Angeles. "The next bomb will be for you, Mr. Kennedy."

The agents who made up the president's White House detail privately feared for Kennedy's safety. And not just because their job naturally bred paranoia. To the public, President Kennedy was a dashing, cerebral leader with a picture-perfect family. In private, Kennedy's Secret Service agents saw a man courting danger.

Kennedy kept up an unrelenting pace compared to his predecessors, and it pushed his detail close to exhaustion. He was also extremely reckless with his own personal safety. His actions made some of his protectors uneasy and a few quite angry. The agents on his detail liked the new president personally, but professionally, he was their toughest assignment yet.

When Kennedy moved his young family into the White House in January 1961, the Service was so small it resembled a modest city police force more than a federal agency. The Service's top official was even called Chief. The agency ran on a $5 million budget and employed just over three hundred agents, the majority of whom were stationed in field offices spread across fifty states. Just thirty-four agents were assigned to the White House detail— the arm that protected the president. They typically worked in six-man teams around the president, rotating in eight-hour shifts.

These agents—all men, and most of them from working-class backgrounds—had grown up in the shadow of World War II and possessed a keen sense of duty to country. The typical hire was an athletic, straitlaced college graduate in his late twenties or early thirties who served in the military or worked for a local police department.

New agents were always sent first to a field office, but "keepers" were summoned to the White House for a tryout on the detail within one or two years. The Service struck a deal with the federal government to bypass the federal hiring pool and instead hire any agent the chief wanted. As part of the agreement, the Secret Service had to put these relatively junior agents on the president's detail within two years if the Service wanted to keep them on the job.

The agents received no specialized protection training, but learned on the job from experienced colleagues on the detail. "That's how the Secret Service worked. They got you started, they paired you with someone good," said Tim McIntyre, a former Kennedy detail agent. "The Service had a policy of allocating assignments to you and expecting you to respond. When you're posted at various spots, it could be anyplace. It could be in an auditorium. They don't have time to spend to explain a whole lot to you. They expect you to pick up the ball and run with it."

The work of an agent, standing watch at a fixed post, was grueling—even boring. But working alongside the affable, debonair Kennedy gave the job a special cachet. And unlike the general before him, this president made an effort to get to know his agents and greeted them by name. His glamorous life, which included regular sightings of Frank Sinatra, Marilyn Monroe, and the queen of England, sprinkled a little stardust on his security team. Agents relished standing next to history.

"I'd go down to the LBJ ranch, I'd be working the midnight shift. I'd be standing under one of those big oak trees out in front. And it'd be two in the morning, and it'd be cold," Lawson grimaced, recalling one assignment. "You'd think, 'What in the world am I doing here? You know I'm a college graduate and here I am almost like on guard duty in the middle of the night and so far away. I've been away from home, it's over Christmas,' whatever.

"Then maybe two weeks later, you'd go to an event you couldn't **buy** your way into. I was at Cape Canaveral . . . for the first moonshot. I was there when they took off," he said. "You think, 'My gosh, I'm a guy from a little town in western New York and look what I've just been witness to.'"

The Polish heritage parade was one of those days for Lawson. After the parade was over, the president of the United States hopped into his open-topped limousine and left Buffalo, all without incident.

Then, as he'd prearranged, Lawson met his parents and brother at the Niagara Falls airstrip parking lot and quickly placed them in a choice spot on the fence line. He knew the president would shake hands there before boarding his plane for the return flight to Washington. Kennedy loved this part of his public outings best: the face-to-face greetings with voters who'd waited for hours to welcome him.

As the president neared Lawson's family, Lawson stood behind his left shoulder and nodded quickly at his parents. Lawson's shift leader, Floyd Boring, paused at their section of fence.

"Mr. President," Boring said, "this is Agent Lawson's family."

Ever gracious, the president beamed. He shook hands with Lawson's brother and father and thanked them for Win's service. Lawson's mother, wearing one of her best day dresses and a pillbox hat decorated with pink and lavender flowers, thrust her right hand toward him with a determined look.

"I am sorry for how busy we have been keeping your son," Kennedy said, grasping the mother's pale white arm. And then came that Kennedy trademark: his whip-fast humor. "He must be doing a pretty good job, because nobody has shot me yet," the president deadpanned.

BIZARRELY, A STARK reminder of the many dangers that shadow the president of the United States on his daily outings had been staring the Kennedy detail in the face that day in Buffalo. McKinley Monument rose like a white finger from the center of the square—President Kennedy was looking directly at the monument as he spoke. The city had built this marble obelisk as a kind of apology to William McKinley, the twenty-fifth president, who had been assassinated there by an unemployed recluse in 1901. His death had prompted the creation of the modern Secret Service. An assassin's bullet fired at the start of the century had brought Lawson and his fellow agents to the very posts where they now stood.

Leon Czolgosz, the son of Polish immigrants who settled in Detroit, had lived in brutal poverty most of his life. He had worked in glass and steel factories since he was a teenager, following his mother's death when he was ten. By the age of twenty-eight, he had been without a job for several years due to the economic crash of 1893. Sick with a respiratory illness, he went to live on his father's farm and grew increasingly isolated and bitter about what he considered the social injustice of America's capitalist system. He read the leaflets of socialist and anarchist groups, and he believed the government was helping rich business owners exploit America's lower classes and ignoring their poverty. After attending the speech of the famous American anarchist Emma Goldman in Cleveland in May 1901, he learned that another anarchist had shot and killed King Umberto I of Italy several months earlier. He took this crime as his inspiration. The assassin explained he had to commit a bold act to call attention to the plight of the common man.

In September, Czolgosz traveled to Buffalo and shot McKinley in a receiving line at the 1901 World's Fair.

Members of Congress were shocked at the time at how easily McKinley had been killed, and chastened that the country had now lost three presidents to assassination in thirty-six years, after Presidents Lincoln and Garfield. Congress soon ordered the Secret Service, a small federal law enforcement team then primarily in charge of combating counterfeiters and check forgers, to secure the president's safety from that point on. But Congress added this mission to the Service on the fly—hastily and without a cohesive strategy.

It was in a similar slapdash, reactionary rush that the Secret Service had been born, in the spring of

1865. President Lincoln and his Treasury secretary were still trying to recover from the brazen escape of a mass counterfeiter, Pete McCartney, and his return to a lucrative life of crime. The Civil War had just ended, which was a cause for great celebration, but the scourge of counterfeiting continued to destabilize the recovering nation's fragile economy. During much of the war, states had issued their own paper money, a confusing array that made it difficult for merchants and bankers to keep track of the variations and easy for counterfeiters to pass forgeries. In 1862, the Treasury had begun issuing federal currency in notes worth $1 to $1,000. They were known as greenbacks because of the green print on the back of the bill. But counterfeiters adapted and quickly copied the seal of federal currency by making their own printing plates. Federal bankers estimated that one-third to one-half of the paper currency floating through the country in 1865 was fake.

For years, McCartney had been an especially talented thorn in the U.S. Treasury's side. He was an intelligent, soft-spoken man who might have inherited the Illinois farm of his father, but instead as a teenager he took a job working for an engraver, William Johnson. Johnson was secretly the head of a counterfeiting clan that was based in Lawrence, Indiana. And in Pete McCartney, Johnson saw a natural. The young man had a keen eye for detail and shading and was a gifted draftsman and printer. On top of that, he was handsome and genial. Starting in the 1840s, Johnson groomed McCartney to be a master forger.

By the opening of the Civil War, McCartney was a wealthy man with his own counterfeiting crew based in Indianapolis and a matchless skill at printing fake banknotes. He plotted to take advantage of wartime inflation, when the volume of currency flow would make it less likely that merchants would spot his fakes. He flooded Indiana with phony $10 and $20 bills and kept the mounting change. By summer of 1864, McCartney and his crew were believed to have printed and passed $100,000 in fake greenbacks, an amount equivalent to $1.5 million in today's dollars.

With his greenback scheme, McCartney had earned his sobriquet, King of the Coney Man, but also earned a target on his back. Treasury agents, led by a gruff government investigator and former cavalry officer named William P. Wood, stepped up their investigations of both the Johnson and McCartney crews. Wood led a dual raid that summer of 1864 that captured McCartney in the Indianapolis post office and snatched up members of the Johnson gang in Lawrence. They hauled their prisoners onto a train bound for Washington, but McCartney was determined not to go. After nightfall, at a moment when the guards were looking in another direction, McCartney ran with the chains still binding his arms and legs and leaped off the rear platform of the train as it chugged along the tracks at 35 miles per hour. Wood halted the train and arranged a search party, but the agents could not find their man.

The escape led to embarrassing headlines in the news, and more grumbling inside the Lincoln administration about the continued threat of counterfeit dollars weakening the U.S. financial system. President Lincoln soon called for a commission to address the problem.

Treasury Secretary Hugh McCulloch had an idea for a permanent fix: creating a "regular permanent force whose job it [would] be to put these counterfeiters out of business." He suggested forming a special unit within the Treasury Department to track down, arrest, and prosecute them.

But Lincoln would not live to put McCulloch's idea into action. On the night of April 14, 1865, Lincoln went with his wife, Mary, to see the play **Our American Cousin** at Ford's Theatre in downtown Washington. The president had received numerous death threats, and his aides had succeeded, after years of prodding, to get him to accept that he needed a bodyguard. A team of four police officers borrowed from the local department took turns accompanying him on his travels out in public. But his police officer the night of the play was the weakest of the group, well known for drinking and falling asleep on the job. He left the passageway of the president's box so he could watch the play, then strolled across the street to the Star Saloon to have a drink. John Wilkes Booth, an actor and Confederate sympathizer who had heard of the president's upcoming visit to the theater, stepped behind Lincoln in his box to the left of the stage and shot him in the head. The president died after sunrise the next morning.

OVER THE YEARS, a myth grew that Lincoln had signed legislation to create the Secret Service at a meeting with McCulloch earlier on the very same day he was fatally shot. It's a story rich with irony, but also an apocryphal one. It is possible, however, that Lincoln had given his general endorsement for the idea. Some historians believe that McCulloch offered his proposal to combat counterfeiters when he met with Lincoln that afternoon, and that Lincoln liked what his Treasury secretary outlined and generally encouraged him to proceed. Some hotly dispute that any such discussion took place at all.

Whatever Lincoln and McCulloch discussed that afternoon, the country changed that night. The president's assassination at Ford's Theatre led to a massive manhunt by agents who tried to chase down his killer. His murder also spurred a deeper, month-long investigation to find potential co-conspirators, with an interesting detective playing a central role. William Wood, the lanky, gruff Treasury Department investigator who had chased down McCartney and lost him, was assigned to help investigate Lincoln's murder. Wood had made a name for himself as a celebrated cavalry officer in the Mexican-American War and then joined the Treasury Department and become an expert in catching counterfeiters. He had a reputation as something of a swashbuckler and was known to use brutal techniques to get suspects to rat on one another. In the Lincoln administration, he was appointed the superinten- dent of the Old Capitol Prison used to hold and question Confederate spies and traitors. But still the Treasury Department often tasked Wood with spe- cial investigative assignments as the need arose.

Twelve days after the shooting, agents of the War Department found and killed John Wilkes Booth in a Port Royal, Virginia, barn. The government agents' mission then turned to a new question in which Wood would play a key role: determining whether Booth's plot might have been part of a larger Confederate conspiracy, possibly directed by Confederate president Jefferson Davis. Wood first captured and questioned Dr. Samuel Mudd, then interrogated the rest of the suspected co-conspirators at his prison. That June, four were condemned to death.

On July 5, 1865, Wood was sworn in as the first chief of the Secret Service Division of the Treasury Department by Secretary McCulloch. Ten other men—called "operatives"—joined his team and agreed to give up whatever hours in a day were necessary for the job, for a salary not to exceed $3 a day. The Secret Service was created on the fly, without any detailed paperwork spelling out its duties. Future presidents and Congresses would tack new assignments onto the Secret Service's mission in the same way.

The Secret Service was a unique government institution at the time—and accordingly was viewed with some measure of suspicion. Few law enforcement agencies existed in the federal government at that point, partly because of the young democracy's continued resistance to anything that resembled European institutions or centralized bureaucracies that could invade the citizenry's privacy and liberty. But within two years, Lincoln's successor, President Andrew Johnson, decided this team of investigators could be useful in rooting out other problems vexing the country. In 1867, the Secret Service was newly charged with "detecting persons perpetrating frauds against the government." This power would later allow the Service to investigate criminal acts by a large swath of suspects. This broad new mandate was very much to the liking of the Secret Service's second chief, Hiram C. Whitley.

Whitley took the oath of office in 1869 and almost immediately began reorganizing the Service on the model of a professional bureaucracy and imposing some of the military order he absorbed from his time as a Union officer. The imposing

six-foot-ten chief, a former investigator of boot-
leggers, appointed a deputy chief and series of
midlevel managers to oversee his team of twenty
agents. He thinned from the ranks some ex-
criminals who had become informers and then
operatives, and began efforts to recruit cleaner-
cut agents. Whitley issued a series of new rules for
agents in order to try to curb conflicts and misconduct, demanded daily reports from agents that
documented their hour-by-hour movements and
expenses, and created a promotion system based on
arrests and prosecutions. He also branched out into
other investigations that he considered high priorities: bank robberies, mail heists, bootlegging and
gambling rings, illegal smuggling, and more. He
viewed the expansion of the Service's mandate as a
way to heighten the Service's value to the government, and his own power in the administration.

That power would lead Congress to turn to
Whitley when violence erupted in the South at
the hands of the white-robed Ku Klux Klan. The
Service's investigation of the KKK began in 1871,
shortly after Congress issued a resolution condemn-
ing the organization and their lynchings. President
Grant's attorney general ordered Whitley to dispatch
eight new agents to the KKK investigation. For the
next three years, they shadowed Klan leaders across
the South, from North Carolina to Florida, and
prosecuted more than five hundred people involved
in Klan activities, with more turning themselves in.

But that honorable work, and much of the Secret Service's reputation, came under fire when Chief Whitley became embroiled in scandal in 1874. During the course of an investigation of some local officials accused of skimming federal funds in the District of Columbia, several accounting ledgers—key evidence in the case—were stolen from the safe of the local U.S. attorney. Cooperating witnesses accused Whitley of helping provide the suspects in the case with a trusty burglar who could pick the safe for them. Whitley admitted no wrongdoing and insisted the claims were bogus, but the Treasury secretary at the time insisted he resign for the good of the Service. He did so in September 1874.

The scandal badly diminished the Service's clout for the next decade. In 1880, the division absorbed a 40 percent cut to its budget and a broad investigation by the solicitor general. Congress also added a rider that restricted the agency to its single original mission: combating counterfeiters. At its height, the agency had had 47 operatives, but by 1880, it fell to 25 men on average.

The dramatic cuts in the Service's funding and reach came just before another national crisis. Sixteen years after Lincoln's assassination, another president was felled.

On July 2, 1881, President James Garfield hurried with his aides to the Baltimore and Potomac Railroad station in downtown Washington, where he prepared to board a train for a summer vacation at the New Jersey seashore. Charles Guiteau, who felt he had helped Garfield win the election and was angry the president never offered him a position in his administration, was waiting in the crowd. He had read of the president's plans in the newspaper. He shot him twice at point-blank range—in the arm and back. The president lingered in recovery for months, but he died in September from slow blood poisoning and ultimately a massive heart attack.

It may seem surprising now, but after Garfield's death neither Congress nor the administration moved to establish a permanent protective force for the president. Both Lincoln's and Garfield's assassinations had spurred talk in Congress of increasing security for the president, but Americans and their politicians remained politically allergic to anything that smacked of a "royal guard." Instead, White House aides persuaded presidents, many of them reluctant, to have a few local police officers shadow them on their travels in public.

When the Secret Service finally entered the business of protecting presidents, it was in an unofficial capacity, done without permission. In the spring of 1894, then Secret Service director William Hazen grew concerned upon hearing from his operatives in Colorado that some gamblers and anarchists there had made death threats against President Grover Cleveland. He instructed two of his men to report to the White House immediately to safeguard the president indefinitely. Only a handful of people in the division were aware of this clandestine, informal protective duty.

Later that summer, the First Lady was at the family's retreat in Buzzard's Bay, Massachusetts, and heard a rumor about a plot to kidnap her family. She was aware of Hazen's informal protection of her husband. Now frantic, she contacted Hazen directly and sought his help in protecting their New England home. He sent three agents to stand by for the rest of the season. The president returned from a trip and quietly accepted the extra protection for his worried wife. For the next few years, the Clevelands, Hazen, and a few of his men concealed the secret: They had been using agents for a purpose that was not authorized by Congress or the government, and that some would argue was expressly forbidden.

Once this secret arrangement was revealed after William McKinley became president, Hazen was demoted and accused of misusing federal funds. However, the same year, after the start of the Spanish-American War, the Secret Service won permission on an emergency basis to assign four of its agents to guard McKinley. After the war, that emergency authority lapsed, but a few agents continued to travel with the president. When McKinley was assassinated while greeting visitors at the Pan-American Exposition in Buffalo, New York, in 1901, there was actually an agent traveling with him who was supposed to stand by his side, but he agreed to move farther away when the president of the exposition asked to stand next to the president for the public greeting.

It was only after McKinley's death—the third president assassinated within thirty-six years—that Congress finally agreed to create a permanent security force for the president's safety. Lawmakers formally assigned the Secret Service to take on this protective role full-time. It would take five more years, until 1906, for Congress to properly authorize the funds to pay for the two-man shifts that shadowed the president around the clock.

For the first half of the twentieth century, the Service's dual mission of protecting money and presidents kept it busy. This small Treasury division continued to invest most of its time in fighting counterfeiters, and lawmakers had assumed the White House guard role would represent a small fraction of the Service's workload. But the man-hours for presidential security steadily grew. Two world wars and a series of assassinations in Europe led the Service to increase the number of agents on the security detail to ensure assassins could not carry out their plots. The agents imposed new restrictions on their leaders' movements as well.

Theodore Roosevelt, the first president to have Secret Service protection, called his new agents "a very small but very necessary thorn in the flesh." Of course, he didn't put much stock in their abilities.

He told his friend Henry Cabot Lodge in the same letter that they would "not be the least use" if a serious assassin wanted to kill him. But the next time a sitting president faced gunfire, the Secret Service officers who manned the White House campus, then called the White House police, and the agents on his security detail proved their worth.

During the fall of 1950, when the White House was under renovation, President Harry S. Truman was temporarily decamped to the nearby Blair House. On the afternoon of November 1, two Puerto Rican nationalists learned Truman's location and determined they would try to shoot their way into Blair House to kill him. The would-be assassins, Oscar Collazo, thirty-six, and Griselio Torresola, twenty-five, hoped to draw attention to the cause of separating the island from the United States. They walked up from Pennsylvania Avenue from opposite directions, Torresola from the west, Collazo from the east.

Secret Service agent Floyd Boring, who would later become a top leader of President Kennedy's detail, was on duty in the east security booth near the front door of Blair House. His colleague, officer Leslie Coffelt of the White House police, was in a west side security booth and turned around to see a man with a gun coming his way.

"The president was upstairs, having a nap before he was due to go to Arlington to lay a wreath," Boring explained later. "We were outside on the steps when two gentlemen came up and one pulled out a gun and aimed it at me. I heard it snap, and I pulled out my gun and shot back. Then everybody was shooting."

Leaving the east security booth, Boring and another officer drew their pistols and opened fire on Collazo. One bullet pierced Collazo's chest, and he fell onto the front steps. Secret Service agent Stewart Stout, who was on Truman's detail, heard the shots outside and pulled a submachine gun from a gun cabinet. Truman had woken at the sound of gunfire and gone to the window. A guard outside saw the president's head and yelled at Truman: "Get back! Get back!"

Outside, Torresola pointed his Luger at Coffelt and shot him twice in the chest and once in the abdomen. Coffelt slid down to the floor of the booth. Torresola shot at two more officers, jumped a hedge, and headed toward the entrance of the house.

But Coffelt wasn't finished. He pulled himself to his feet and aimed his revolver at Torresola's head. He fired, and the would-be assassin fell dead on the paved walkway. With that, Coffelt collapsed again into his booth.

Several agents and officers had been hit and survived. Coffelt was rushed to surgery but died four hours later, the first and still only Secret Service officer to die while protecting a president.

In public, Truman seemed unfazed. "A president has to expect such things," he told reporters in a briefing the day after the shooting.

As a captain in World War I, Truman had seen soldiers die on his orders, but in private he seemed moved in a different way by Coffelt's death. He told Coffelt's widow and friends that he was heartbroken; Coffelt had been one of the best-liked guards at the White House. He wrote a private note to his secretary of state saying the death was "a most unnecessary happening" and "the people who really got hurt were wonderful men." He had taken a daily walk around downtown Washington accompanied by his agents since his first day in office. Each time his anxious detail had tried to talk him out of it, he had rebuffed their concerns. Now he acquiesced.

"Because two crackpots or crazy men tried to shoot me a few days ago my good and efficient guards are nervous," he wrote a few days later. "So I'm trying to be as helpful as I can."

Coffelt's sister, Mildred Good, heard the news of her brother's death on the radio in their hometown in the Shenandoah Mountains. She said he had always felt proud to be part of the corps entrusted with the president's safety and realized that any Secret Service officer or agent might one day be called upon to give their life for his.

"You know," she said, "he loved his job, he wouldn't have chosen any other way to go. I am sure he had no regrets."

CHAPTER 2

TEMPTING THE DEVIL

In his first year in office, 1961, John Kennedy quickly broke all records for the number of presidential trips outside the White House—and he never slowed down. It was not lost on the president and his advisers that he had won an extremely tight election at least in part because of his telegenic good looks. The White House knew its best political weapon was getting Kennedy and his vibrant, handsome family seen by the public as much as possible.

Kennedy's weekly travel was a shock to the Secret Service's system, after a string of older, conservative presidents who had been happy to stay put in the White House for weeks at a time. The added trips forced his detail agents to routinely work double shifts, so they often missed sleep and days off. In the busiest times, Service supervisors cut a few men from trips, just to have enough people ready for the next trip.

By the end of the summer of 1963, the Kennedy glamor had begun to dull for many agents. Two and a half years of tailing Kennedy on his frequent jaunts around the globe had left the detail burned out and exhausted. That summer, a handful of detail agents including Win Lawson traveled with Kennedy in back-to-back diplomacy trips to Germany, Ireland, the United Kingdom, and Italy. Just eight men formed a ring about the nation's leader, using their bodies to keep back the crushing crowds who tried to leap onto Kennedy's limousine.

KENNEDY DERIDED THE idle jet-setter class who decamped to resorts for wine-soaked lunches, but his life resembled theirs at times. There were few seasons he wasn't weekending somewhere posh, or at one of his family retreats. He sometimes joined his wife at their 166-acre estate outside Middleburg, Virginia, where the First Lady hoped to create a relaxed playground for her children. Depending on the season, he also spent weekends at his family's compound on Cape Cod or his father's estate in Palm Beach. "We were like ducks," agent Larry Newman joked of the detail. "Hyannis Port every summer, Palm Beach in the winter."

Thirty-four detail agents were not nearly enough to both plan security for all the upcoming places Kennedy would visit and shield him when he arrived. During busy periods, detail members hopscotched their own shadows. They flanked Kennedy all day in one city, flew late that night to a second city to plan the advance for a visit a week later, then flew back as quickly as possible to accompany the president for a trip to a third destination.

"It got to be so busy on the road, we were all working double shifts as the norm," said former detail agent Jerry Blaine. That meant agents traveling with the president would work the day shift, rising at around 6 A.M. and reporting for duty around 8 A.M., and then work most of the evening shift until 9 or 10 P.M. They were lucky to eat a bag of peanuts or a cold sandwich for dinner, knock back a scotch or a beer, and then fall into their hotel beds by 11 P.M. or midnight. To keep the Service from busting its budget, the agents had to double-bunk in hotel rooms. "And you just hoped and prayed the guy you bunked with didn't snore," said detail agent Tim McIntyre.

When the agents did return to Washington, it was often only long enough for a day with their wives and children. Wives grew accustomed to their husbands showing up just to drop off dirty clothes and grab clean ones for the next trip. "I traveled over three hundred days a year," said Paul Landis, a detail agent who first protected the Kennedy children and later was assigned to Mrs. Kennedy. "I didn't mind it. I was single. But most of the guys were married. I don't know how anybody at that time could have been married and done this job."

Secret Service chief James Rowley, a New York Irishman and twenty-two-year veteran of the White House detail, knew his agents desperately needed reinforcements to keep up with the new, more active "Boss." Though he was grateful to Kennedy, a fellow Irishman, for choosing him to lead the agency shortly after taking office, Rowley could see that his men were now critically overworked.

Rowley had tried twice to beef up the White House detail since Kennedy's arrival—and largely failed. In the spring of 1962, the chief asked the White House and Congress for 58 additional agents and a $1 million increase in his total budget, a 19 percent increase for his modest force. Congressional appropriators, who had doubled the White House detail after the 1950 attempt on Truman's life a decade earlier, gave Rowley half his request. He got 30 more agents.

In the spring of 1963, Rowley again requested additional agents—35 this time—to help him comply with the very recent 1962 law requiring full-time protection for the vice president. This time Congress rejected the request completely.

But congressional resistance wasn't Rowley's only obstacle. The president himself wanted less protection. While Kennedy was always cordial to his agents, he resented the limits they tried to place on his ability to interact with the public. Kennedy regularly bounded headlong into crowds of strangers to shake hands, ignoring the Secret Service's script without even a nod to his detail. As he told his detail leaders many times, he couldn't very well be a politician without meeting the people.

His spontaneity had frequently crossed the line. On a lazy mid-August weekend in 1962, President Kennedy made front-page news by slipping his dedicated bodyguards in broad daylight. The prank endeared him to his public. But it left his detail furious and red-faced, and it set Chief Rowley on edge. For anyone who cared to look more closely, the incident highlighted a recklessness in Kennedy that some in the Secret Service had been trying to discreetly contain.

The incident occurred in Santa Monica, California, where Kennedy had flown for a bachelor weekend at his brother-in-law Peter Lawford's ocean-front mansion. Lounging in a chaise by Lawford's pool on Sunday, August 19, the president got the idea to stroll off the Lawford property and across the wide public beach for a quick swim in the ocean.

Dozens of beachgoers loped toward the president as soon as they spotted him. Some jumped up from their towels, yelling, "It's the president!"

Kennedy realized he'd have to move more quickly to get to the surf before being surrounded. He awkwardly tugged his blue polo shirt off over his shoulders and picked up his pace before diving into the waves.

A few excited spectators jumped into the water after Kennedy. Kennedy's detail agents, most of whom were standing guard at Lawford's front door—facing away from the beach—heard the commotion and raced to the shore. They soon found the leader of the free world swimming laps about a hundred yards out.

"The Secret Service and FBI were beside themselves," said Bill Beebe, a news photographer who captured the scene that day.

The shift leader radioed for a municipal patrol boat to motor near the president as he swam. The agents waited about ten minutes as the president finished his laps and returned to shore. Then four of them stepped into the surf to form a pie-shaped barrier between Kennedy and the nearly one thousand spectators who by that time had swarmed over to this small patch of beach.

"Oh, no, I can't believe it," Kennedy said, laughing, as he saw the news photographer standing in the water and snapping photos of him.

With dripping pant legs and shoes full of water, Kennedy's agents returned the grinning president to the security of Lawford's backyard. Kennedy plunked himself back down in his chaise longue as Lawford and White House aide David Powers followed.

"That was the best swim I've had in months," he said.

Within fifteen minutes, Kennedy's press secretary, Pierre Salinger, called the **Los Angeles Times** to try to persuade the editor not to run any photographs of the president in swim trunks. No luck. Beebe's photograph—of a dripping Kennedy exchanging a smile with a beaming, trim wife and mother in a polka-dot bikini—covered more than half of the **Times**'s front page the next day. The headline read KENNEDY CAPS VISIT WITH DIP IN PACIFIC.

The shift leader and his agents fumed at the embarrassment of their charge slipping into a crowd and an ocean without their noticing, and the many disasters that could have befallen the president if there had been one nut job on the beach. Yet no one in the Secret Service, not even Chief Rowley, had the nerve to confront the president about his little unscripted caper.

When the Kennedy entourage returned to Washington, however, Salinger gently suggested to the president that he think of his own safety and avoid going into crowds without his agents. But Kennedy dismissed the idea that anyone, including the Secret Service, could keep him from a determined assassin. "If anyone is crazy enough to want to kill a president of the United States, he can do it," Kennedy told his spokesman. "All he must be prepared to do is give his life for the president's."

Kennedy often used humor to try to slough off the tension his agents felt about his safety. Vice President Johnson had just threatened to fire a well-liked agent in a fit of pique over his helicopter's arriving to take him away from Eleanor Roosevelt's funeral a few minutes later than he wanted. Kennedy joked with his detail that now he finally understood why they were so overprotective with him: "You guys don't want anything to ever happen to me, because then you'd have to work for Johnson."

But alone in the residence, Kennedy confided to his wife that one part of this scenario genuinely disturbed him, too: "Oh, God, can you ever imagine what would happen to the country if Lyndon was president?"

ALL AGENTS KNEW that discretion was part of their duty. They weren't supposed to share the inner workings of the White House or the private moments they witnessed between the president and his family. Kennedy's agents had to keep some darker secrets as well.

"In the White House, it's a little like Vegas," said Joseph Paolella, one of the agents on Kennedy's detail. "What happens in the White House stays in the White House.

"I'm not an angel. . . . I'm not a priest. I wouldn't want someone following me around and reporting everything I did. To have a president be comfortable, they have to rely on the Secret Service. Imagine every step you made, there was someone following you and sharing that information. If we can't trust the Secret Service to keep secrets, who the hell can we trust?"

Only Rowley and some members of his detail knew it, but Kennedy gave his protective squad the slip on several late nights in Washington. He headed off the White House complex incognito, ducking into an unmarked car with his brother or a friend and returning in the wee hours of the morning.

Agents could guess the reason, but Rowley and his team worried. For several hours, the Secret Service didn't know where the president of the United States was.

Kennedy courted this sort of danger, trying to feed a seemingly insatiable appetite for sexual conquest, but members of his detail feared that within the sea of random women he met for trysts, one would try to blackmail, poison, or kill him.

When agent Tim McIntyre joined the detail on a tryout in the summer of 1963, he was welcomed by collegial agents and supervisors offering to help him learn the ropes. But a surprise came when a shift leader pulled him aside on an evening shift. "You're going to see a lot of shit around here," supervisor Emory Roberts told McIntyre. "Stuff with the president. Just forget about it. Keep it to yourself. Don't even talk to your wife."

McIntyre tried to make light of the president's sexual dalliances at first, joking with other agents, "What happens if one bites him?" But eventually he stood witness to a steady parade of secretaries, starlets, and even prostitutes escorted to the president's bedroom—in hotels and in his private residence. The Secret Service agents, who scrutinized the background of anyone who met privately with the president, weren't allowed to so much as ask the women's names.

The night shift became accustomed to random female visitors arriving at the president's private quarters, often on the arm of longtime Kennedy aide and friend David Powers. Afternoon shift members who were about to go off duty at 10 P.M. gave their shift leaders a discreet and terse status report on Kennedy's nighttime guests.

"As we were about to go off shift, we'd explain, 'So-and-so brought in a blonde,'" a former detail agent said. "Or, 'Just so you know, boss, there are two guests in the room.'"

"You wanted to tell the midnight shift the situation," the former detail member said. "The point of it was, if [the woman] didn't come out by about 4 A.M., you were going to start to worry."

Agents on Kennedy's detail were torn. They admired so much about the president. "He was truly a special guy," said Paolella. "Whether it was the queen of England or the housemaid, he would treat them the same way." But several felt embarrassed—and even grew resentful—at being asked to enable such brazen behavior and relax their own standards for security. U.S. intelligence officials warned that Cuban and Soviet operatives hoped to blackmail or even kill the president. Agents on the detail privately theorized that the best way to infiltrate the White House would be to send a good-looking young woman.

"We were in the middle of the Cold War, for Christ's sake," Newman said. "We **anguished** over the possibility of that happening. We were instructed, nobody was to go in that door, but the job was not done. Because we failed. We had to acquiesce to a form of behavior that was dangerous—not to us, but to the country and to the protection of the president."

"We took an oath. . . . Nobody goes into his office unless we clear them. Then there we are watching Dave Powers bring some women up to the suite and just walk right in."

Like Newman, Anthony Sherman, another former detail member, admired Kennedy's charm and political courage. But the president's devil-may-care attitude struck him as disrespectful to his office.

The last straw for Sherman came on a June 1963 trip to Honolulu. Kennedy traveled there to speak at a conference of mayors and tour the USS **Arizona** battleship memorial in Pearl Harbor. The president's entourage, including Sherman and the rest of the detail, arrived the night before the conference. After Hawaiian dignitaries greeted Kennedy at the airport with leis of colorful flowers, his motorcade sped him toward his resting place for the night. A Marine officer who oversaw the nearby naval base had arranged a guesthouse for the president's stay. Ten minutes after Kennedy entered, a White House aide drove up with two young women who walked directly into the house, past Sherman, who was guarding the front door. The hosting officer turned to Sherman with a puzzled look.

"Who are they?" the naval base's officer asked, staring at the women.

Sherman stopped a second to think, ashamed at the lie forming in his head. "They're secretaries," Sherman replied. "I assume there is some work the president wants done this evening."

The colonel stared back, not smiling. Sherman could tell he didn't buy that story.

"We protected the president in many different ways," Sherman told ABC News in 1997. "But the Honolulu episode made me angry. This is the president of the United States. I'm not a holier-than-thou guy, but he just should not be doing this in public like this."

What was a dedicated Secret Service agent to do? Waiting together in hotel hallways and airport tarmacs, members of the detail quietly shared their worst fears. The president's personal life and decisions were not their business. But if his risk taking endangered his life, wasn't it automatically their business?

To keep true to the agency's motto—"Worthy of Trust and Confidence"—agents decided to follow shift leader Emory Roberts's advice. They kept their mouths shut.

EARLY ON TUESDAY, November 12, Win Lawson's wife, Barbara, drove him from their modest Alexandria home to the White House, with their two young children in the back of the family sedan. He was heading to Dallas for ten days to handle the advance for Kennedy's upcoming visit there. He would miss his son Jeff's fifth birthday. He would have to skip spending time with their just-adopted baby girl Andrea, the peaceful bonding of the nighttime bottle feedings.

The summer and early fall of 1963 had been a busy one for the detail. And now the White House had ordered up a doozy of a travel schedule for November. After trips up and down the East Coast in the early part of the month, Kennedy would sweep through Florida and Texas just before Thanksgiving. Kennedy needed to win these two large states. Because of the contentious civil rights agenda, these were the only Southern states they believed he could win, so his aides chose them for the unofficial launch of Kennedy's reelection campaign. Lawson shook his head at the schedule that lay before the detail: twenty-two stops in nine cities, all in less than a week.

Jerry Behn, the leader of Kennedy's detail, had chosen Lawson, one of his most meticulous advance men, to handle the planning for Dallas. The city had been openly hostile to Kennedy. Local conservatives had distributed a mock Wanted poster with his picture. A month earlier, protesters there had spat on and struck his visiting ambassador.

Lawson was all business. He didn't drink. He didn't chase women. He was known to sleeplessly check and recheck his security blueprint late into the night before the president's arrival. In one of his first advance assignments, Lawson had insisted that the chief judge in Binghamton, New York, shutter his courthouse on the day Nixon was visiting. Lawson had learned court staff were inviting friends to watch Nixon's speech from higher floors in their building. Lawson felt strongly that people looming over Nixon's head posed a security risk. The judge agreed.

As he had done before leaving for each advance location, Lawson checked in the Service's Protective Research Section on November 8. Better known as PRS, this tiny office kept an index of approximately four hundred individuals across the country that investigators felt posed a true threat to the president. Lawson wanted the names of anyone in the index based in the Dallas area. Oddly, for a sizable city, no names came up. He checked again the morning of November 12 to see if there was any updated information. None.

Around noon that Tuesday, Lawson climbed aboard a military charter plane with six other advance agents from the detail. All were bound for different cities in Texas. As they flew south, the protective research office that Lawson had just visited got an urgent call. Agents had gotten wind of what sounded like a plot to kill the president.

THAT TUESDAY MORNING, November 12, Miami special agent Robert Jamison couldn't tell whether the

Georgia Klansman on the police tape recording was exaggerating or telling the truth. But his claim on the tape was unnerving. The man said he knew of a plan in the works to assassinate President Kennedy.

Joseph Milteer, a wealthy organizer of white supremacist groups, had been on a road trip through the South and visited his childhood friend in his Miami apartment the previous weekend. He didn't know that his friend was a police informant working undercover to infiltrate the Klan—and recording their chat.

Milteer had gotten to know some notoriously violent Klan leaders whom police suspected in a recent series of bombings and murders. Police had hoped their informant, William Somersett, could get his old friend Milteer talking about the Birmingham, Alabama, church bombing in mid-September that had killed four Black girls between the ages of eleven and fourteen. Milteer was friendly with their lead suspect at the time: Jack Brown, the Imperial Wizard of the Tennessee-based Dixie Klan.

Milteer wasn't specific about the church bombing. He was much more specific when their conversation turned to the president's pending visit to Miami.

"I think Kennedy is coming here November eighteenth to make some kind of speech," Somersett said. "Well, he'll have a thousand bodyguards, don't worry about that."

"The more bodyguards he has, the more easier it is to get him," Milteer replied.

"What?" Somersett asked.

"The more bodyguards he has, the easier it is to get him," Milteer repeated.

"Well, how in the hell do you figure would be the best way to get him?" Somersett asked.

"From an office building with a high-powered rifle," Milteer said.

"They are really going to try to kill him?" Somersett asked later.

"Oh, yeah," Milteer said. "It is in the working."

Milteer said Brown was the most likely one to kill Kennedy. He said Brown had also been shadowing civil rights leader Dr. Martin Luther King, Jr., in hopes of taking him out.

"He followed him for miles and miles, and couldn't get close enough to him," Milteer said.

"Hitting this Kennedy is going to be a hard proposition," Somersett said. "I believe you may have figured out a way to get him, the office building and all that. I don't know how them Secret Service agents cover all them office buildings everywhere he is going. Do you know whether they do that or not?"

Milteer gave an accurate explanation of why an advance agent like Lawson would not check nearby buildings.

"Well, if they have any suspicion, they do that, of course," he said. "But without suspicion, chances are that they wouldn't."

He was right. Given the Secret Service's small

size, it was impossible to check the hundreds of buildings along any motorcade route. If there was a reason to suspect a specific problem, or a structure was very close, buildings could be checked or shuttered, as Lawson had done in Binghamton. But otherwise, the agents would do nothing about the buildings they passed.

That Tuesday morning, Jamison and his boss, the special agent in charge of the Miami office, conferred about the tape recording. Then they called the head of protective research, Robert Bouck.

Bouck was widely admired in the Service as a clever investigator and a natural leader. He had become fascinated with electronic surveillance and was dubbed the Service's "electronics genius." In 1962, at Kennedy's request, Bouck installed a secret tape recording system in the Oval Office. An author before he became president, Kennedy wanted to keep a record of important discussions and events in the White House, most likely for writing a memoir.

After hearing about the threat, Bouck had to tread carefully. Normally, he would send agents to interview Milteer, but that would blow the informant's cover. Instead, Bouck instructed Jamison to write up a "confidential" report about the suspected plot and alert the advance agent handling Kennedy's upcoming visit to Miami. He told Jamison to share the report with just four other field offices—Atlanta, Nashville, Indianapolis, and Philadelphia. Agents there would discreetly check on the homes and whereabouts of extremist friends Milteer had mentioned.

Lawson landed in Dallas on November 12 and the next day met with local police to map a route for the president and First Lady's motorcade—from their landing at Love Field to his luncheon speech at the Trade Mart. Lawson knew he had to take Kennedy down Main Street through the busy downtown. "If a president or a vice president is going through a town or a city, it is to be seen and for people to see them," Lawson said. "Often it's arranged so they're going around noontime or suppertime. Why is that? People are coming out of the office buildings. You have a built-in crowd. If you take someone to a downtown area that has a lot of office buildings, a lot of stores. That's one reason we came downtown. . . . The White House wanted people to see the president. The most people were going to be downtown. That route almost had to be what it was."

So Lawson worked with police to map and block each intersection, meticulously choreographing a dizzying set of plans. For the Love Field arrival, for example, he stationed officers on rooftops of buildings immediately overlooking the tarmac receiving area. He scattered plainclothes police throughout the surrounding spectators. For the motorcade, he requested motorcycle escorts to form a buffer alongside the presidential limousine. He asked police to clear overpasses and bridges the motorcade would pass to keep people a safe distance from the president's car.

He didn't know what headquarters had learned from their Miami and Chicago field agents—threats of high-powered rifles along the motorcade ride.

"No, I never heard that," he said. "I would have remembered."

CHAPTER 3

THREE SHOTS IN DALLAS

On Monday, November 18, 1963, the president woke in his father's sprawling Mediterranean-style beachfront estate in Palm Beach after a work weekend, headed with his detail to the airport, and boarded Air Force One, bound for Tampa. It was the first stop on a weeklong publicity tour through Florida and Texas.

Kennedy hoped a string of appearances in both these states would help secure him a second term in the White House. His aides were ecstatic that the First Lady—withdrawn and depressed since the death of her prematurely born baby son that summer—had decided to join him for the Texas portion of the trip.

"You're going to draw the biggest crowds ever," spokesman Pierre Salinger told Kennedy. "Going with Mrs. Kennedy will be terrific."

The agents of Kennedy's detail hoped for what

they always hoped for on a trip away from the White House: no trouble. But they began the trip already exhausted from the last several months of heavy travel, which also forced them to rely on skeleton crews and some junior agents working the shifts around the president. They skimped on advances, sending one lone agent to some cities instead of two.

Still, the detail agents remained stoic. They figured if they just gutted it out the next five days, they could get the Boss from Palm Beach to Tampa to Miami to Washington to San Antonio to Houston to Fort Worth to Dallas to Austin to Vice President Johnson's ranch and safely home again. They didn't see then that the chinks in their armor had been multiplying. By this point, a very large hole had opened, leaving them vulnerable to attack.

IT WAS 11:24 A.M. on November 18, 1963. The president and his entourage touched down in his plane, AF 26000, at MacDill Air Force Base. So began the busiest travel week the Secret Service had tackled in Kennedy's term. The Boss was scheduled to make twenty-two public stops spread over three activity-crammed days on the road.

The president stepped spryly across the tarmac, appearing rested and carefree that Monday morning. Kennedy wore a custom-made gray suit and flashed his celebrity grin. With his head and shoulders high, he waved to the cheering crowd lined up near the air base officers' mess.

Shift leader Emory Roberts walked a few paces behind the president and squinted into the hot late-morning sun. At six foot one, with a pale complexion and jet-black hair slicked back with hair cream, Roberts bore a resemblance to the stone-serious Joe Friday from **Dragnet**. After several years as a Maryland state trooper and two decades in the Secret Service, it was hard to rattle him. But agents fondly called him either Father Roberts or Mother Hen, because he took pains to guide newer agents through their assignments.

This morning, Roberts fretted a little about the president too. Would Kennedy balk at having agents directly behind him during the long limo ride through Tampa? The president had chafed at agents' standing between him and a handshake. He good-naturedly complained when the detail tried to keep him dozens of yards from the crowds who wanted to greet him. "If I don't mingle with the people, I couldn't get elected dogcatcher," he told another shift leader.

The thirty-four agents assigned to protect Kennedy and the First Family had chalked up an unhealthy streak of days working double shifts that year. Eleven of the most experienced detail members were unavailable to spell their co-workers; they were busy crafting advance security plans in other Florida and Texas cities Kennedy planned to visit.

Roberts, who worked straight through the weekend with Kennedy in Palm Beach, knew the protective layer he could put around the president in Tampa was thin: just twelve agents. Yet huge crowds, upward of 125,000, were expected. Kennedy and his entourage planned to travel twenty-eight miles on the motorcade route, the longest of Kennedy's time in office.

Motorcades always stressed the detail. Jumbled crowds of excited spectators could seem harmless—but then someone would invariably lurch toward the slow-moving limo, hoping to get closer. Or, far worse: The happy throng could camouflage a lurking assassin.

The Tampa advance agent, Jerry Blaine, told Roberts he was worried about that long route. Blaine was focused on the risks posed by several groups in Florida. The mob had a considerable presence in Tampa, and the Kennedy administration had declared war on organized crime. Cuban activists based in the area—those who opposed and those who supported Fidel Castro's regime—were threatening to use a presidential visit to make a public splash. Some of them were furious about Kennedy's failure to fully support Cubans who had joined in the failed Bay of Pigs invasion.

Blaine recommended that two agents ride on the rear steps attached to the back of the limo for the whole ride. The follow-up car, an open-topped 1955 Cadillac sedan loaded with armed agents and even an assault rifle, was the nerve center for shielding the president on these slow parades. Four agents rode standing on the follow-up cars' side running boards so they could dash to the president if a stranger got too close. The two agents on the front of the follow-up car's running boards typically ran forward and jumped onto the back of the limo at riskier moments in the ride. They moved onto the limo at times when the president was more exposed: when thick crowds forced the motorcade to slow down, or when motorcycle cops didn't have room on the street to ride alongside the limo.

After greeting a crowd of thousands of military personnel, families, and spectators gathered on the airstrip at MacDill Air Force Base, inspecting the honor guard, and then eating a quick lunch, the president and a few agents hopped a helicopter for a speech at nearby Al Lopez Field. Roberts's eyes went wide when they landed. It looked like a Beatles concert. Women screamed upon seeing the president, and people clambered over the stadium fence to avoid the long lines. A crowd of roughly ten thousand swarmed the five-thousand-seat stadium.

After the speech, Kennedy and two local congressmen took their seats in his open-air Lincoln Continental for the long ride through the city. Several times on the route, Kennedy grabbed on to a wide roll bar specially added to his interior car door. He stood, waved, and tried to lock eyes with voters.

Now and again the president turned back toward

the dark outlines of two agents looming behind his shoulders. Chuck Zboril and Don Lawton stood on the rear steps on the tail of his limo, as Blaine had suggested, and held on to handles installed on the trunk. When the crowds thinned on Grand Central Avenue, the president bent forward to speak to trip supervisor Floyd Boring in the front seat. "Floyd, have the Ivy League charlatans drop back to the follow-up car," Kennedy said dryly.

Boring paused at the word "charlatan." He figured Kennedy, whom the Service had code-named Lancer, had made up his own teasing code name for his working-class bodyguards in their business suits. He radioed the instruction nearly verbatim to Roberts in the follow-up car: "Lancer requests the Ivy League charlatans drop back to your location."

Roberts whistled to his agents, and once the limo slowed, they clambered back onto the follow-up car's running boards. When the motorcade reached the local armory, Kennedy explained more to Boring: "It's excessive, Floyd. And it's giving the wrong impression to the people. Tell them to stay on the follow-up car. We've got an election coming up. The whole point is for me to be accessible to the people."

From Tampa, they headed to Miami for a fast-paced three-hour visit: greeting the crowd at the airport, a chopper ride to a beachside hotel, and a dinner speech. They returned the president safely to the White House at around midnight.

On the flight back to Washington, Blaine puzzled over two competing worries. First, had he ticked off the president by putting the agents on the limo? Then again, didn't moving them farther away leave the Boss vulnerable?

Sitting together on the plane, Boring told Blaine not to worry. Kennedy had thanked Blaine for the successful visit. Plus, they all had more assignments to tackle. Texas was coming up quickly.

"Forget it, Jer," Boring told Blaine. "He told you, you did a fine job in Tampa. Now let's try to get some rest. You think today was a long day, you should see the schedule we've got for Texas."

THE AGENTS ON Roberts's shift rose before daybreak in their own homes the morning of Thursday, November 21, headed back to the White House for the ride together to Andrews, and then flew with the Kennedys and the Johnsons to San Antonio, arriving around noon. Over the next twelve hours, they covered more than five hundred miles of Texas by ground and air. They hit downtown San Antonio for a luncheon speech and motorcade, then lifted off for Houston for another motorcade and a dinner speech. Air Force One flew its last leg of the day, to Fort Worth, where the Kennedys and their entourage would stay overnight before spending the next day in Dallas and the weekend at Johnson's ranch outside Austin.

The First Couple drew adoring crowds everywhere they set foot, but it still surprised newly
arrived detail agent Tim McIntyre to glance out the
plane window at Carswell Air Force Base as it taxied
to a stop. A crowd of three hundred people waited
excitedly in the drizzly dark night, waving from the
airstrip fence and hoping to catch sight of America's
most famous couple.

Hundreds were crowded outside the Beaux
Arts–style Hotel Texas when the Kennedy motorcade pulled up to the entrance at 11:45 P.M. It was
absolutely not the welcome the weary agents were
looking for. The president could not help but shake
hands despite the late hour. After about five minutes, his detail got him and his wife securely tucked
into suite 850.

Shortly after midnight, Roberts's day shift could
finally go off duty. The agents were ravenous. Their
last meal had been a light lunch twelve hours earlier
on the plane ride from Washington.

Bone-tired, room key in hand, the twenty-six-
year-old McIntyre did the math. He had been on
duty for twenty-three hours, and that day, he and
his workmates had jogged or walked more than ten
miles. The father of four wasn't entirely sure where
he'd slept the night before. Maybe Miami? Maybe
Washington? He padded down the hall to his room.
Then, seeing a familiar shift leader heading the
same way, he realized he had drawn the short straw:
McIntyre was sharing a room with Roberts, the

detail's legendary snorer. "We didn't get a heckuva lot of sleep," McIntyre recalled. "I probably got around six [hours]. The next morning of course we have to get up and do it again."

But some got far less rest that night. Nine Kennedy detail agents headed to the Fort Worth Press Club in a nearby hotel, which reporters said was staying open late to serve light dinner and drinks for the traveling press. The sandwiches were all gone by the time the agents arrived, though, so they joined reporters for a few scotch and sodas and glasses of beer. Sometime after 1 A.M., press club president Cal Sutton told the group he had to shut down the party. It was against the law for the club to serve alcohol after midnight. So a reporter in the group called over to the Cellar, a legendary and slightly scandalous nightspot, and reached manager Richard Mackie. Could he bring over some fellow reporters, some Secret Service agents, and some White House people who were in town with the president?

Led by CBS News cub reporter Bob Schieffer and other members of the press, nine agents went on to the Cellar. Four of them—Clint Hill, Jack Ready, Glen Bennett, and Paul Landis—were scheduled to report for duty first thing the next morning. The men found a curious, dimly lit bar that was part gentlemen's club, part beatnik coffee house. It was unlike any other bar they had seen in Washington. Some of the waitresses wore the skimpiest of outfits, more like bras and panties than clothes. The Cellar didn't have a license to sell alcohol, but its owners kept hard liquor behind the bar and often served free "specials"—grain alcohol in fruit juices and other mixers—to friends. For club owner Pat Kirkwood, a wiry daredevil who wore cowboy apparel, those "friends" included anyone he felt might be useful to him: "all pretty girls, all reporters, all cops." He and Mackie personally welcomed their Washington guests a little before 2 A.M. and showed them to a few open tables.

The waitresses brought agents Hill and Landis a couple of yellow-colored drinks. "What's this?" Hill asked.

"A Salty Dick," came the reply.

The agent could taste sour fruit, maybe grapefruit. Hill wasn't sure if the other swirling fluid was imitation alcohol or what, but it didn't matter. The taste didn't improve with more swigs, so he didn't finish it. Landis had two.

In the course of the night, three agents on the midnight shift took breaks from securing the stuffy hotel hallway outside the president's suite to check out the Cellar too. Kirkwood heard some agents giggling about leaving their posts. "The firemen are guarding the president over at the Hotel Texas!" one said to a roar of laughter.

Hill headed back to the hotel around 2:45 A.M., and Ready and Bennett followed close behind at around three. Landis, who was single, ended up talking late into the night with a woman in the club, and left around five.

Secret Service regulations prohibited White House detail agents from drinking "intoxicating liquor of any kind" on the road. After all, they could be called for duty at any time when the president was traveling. But the rule was roundly ignored, in favor of letting grown men use their own judgment.

"Sometimes you'd come off a long day like that, you can't go to sleep right away anyway," Hill recalled. "There was no party. We were just trying to unwind."

WHEN THE AGENTS of the White House detail reported for duty in the Hotel Texas lobby at 8 A.M. that Friday, several members were very short on sleep. That was fairly normal. The abnormal part was how many experienced players the team was missing. All told, eleven veterans on the detail were on other assignments that week—all handling advances for the flurry of Florida and Texas stops instead. Ten more experienced hands had recently rotated off the job. Detail members who started with Kennedy's inauguration had won promotions to supervisory roles or secured transfers to other jobs. The most senior man on the detail—the person who had shadowed Kennedy on every public trip since his election—happened to be taking his first "vacation" from the road in four years that week too.

The detail's affable leader, Special Agent in Charge Jerry Behn, decided his seasoned deputies could handle the Florida-Texas trip. On the Friday that Kennedy planned to visit Dallas, Behn planned on a short day in the office to catch up on paperwork.

The president rose after 7 A.M. in his hotel suite, put on a dark suit, and headed, agents in tow, to speak to a crowd gathered outside. The locals clapped and cheered, but a few seemed disappointed that the First Lady hadn't joined him. "Mrs. Kennedy is organizing herself," the president explained. "It takes her longer, but, of course, she looks better than we do when she does it." Walking back in the hotel foyer, however, the president turned sternly to the nearest agent at his side: "Get Mrs. Kennedy down here, please."

Clint Hill, the head of the First Lady's detail, beat a quick path upstairs to collect Mrs. Kennedy. He found her in her suite putting on her gloves and escorted her briskly to the hotel banquet hall. There, two thousand members and guests at the Fort Worth Chamber of Commerce breakfast gave a standing ovation as the First Lady joined her husband on the dais.

A little after 11:20 A.M., the couple and their entourage boarded Air Force One for the thirteen-minute flight from the Carswell Air Force Base to Love Field in Dallas. They could have driven the thirty-five miles from Fort Worth, but Kennedy's aides wanted the television stations and newspapers to run plenty of pictures of a delighted Dallas welcoming their president as he disembarked from the newly designed Air Force One.

Here the strain that the detail was under showed itself more plainly as agents went to man their motorcade positions. Paul Landis, Hill's deputy on Jackie Kennedy's detail, walked down the ramp of the backup plane concerned he had the wrong assignment. He had been surprised when Roberts told him he was supposed to ride on the running boards of the follow-up car behind the president's limo. He'd never done that before. Landis, an amiable ham, kidded agent Sam Kinney, the follow-up car driver, as they both stood next to his car: "Hey, Sam," he said, feigning confusion and swiveling his head right and left. "I'm supposed to be in the follow-up car. Do you know where it is?"

Landis chuckled at his own joke. But still, he was concerned. He walked over to Lawson near the fence to double-check he had the correct assignment.

"Yep, that's right," Lawson told him.

Landis wasn't the only new guy assigned to the follow-up car either. Tim McIntyre had just finished his first full week as a permanent detail agent, after working several shifts on a temporary basis. Newly transferred from Spokane, he would ride the rear running board on the left side, behind the First Lady and behind Hill. Glen A. Bennett, on loan from the Protective Research Section at headquarters, was supposed to ride in the rear seat of the follow-up car. So was George Hickey, a driver agent who normally worked behind the wheel rather than behind a gun.

Other than shift leader Roberts, there was only one agent in the follow-up car who had spent more than a year protecting President Kennedy. That was Jack Ready, who was assigned to ride the boards, directly behind Kennedy, in front of Landis.

An impromptu crowd of two thousand pressed up to the fence around the Love Field perimeter, clapping and calling out to the Kennedys. The couple accepted the gifts of their receiving party when they reached the bottom of the plane's ramp-like stairs. A framed charcoal drawing for him, a bouquet of red roses for her. The president saw the faces at the fence and handed the gifts to Landis. Without a word, he was off with Jackie to shake all the outstretched hands.

Agents moved alongside the couple down the fence for a few minutes, then Lawson signaled it was time to go. They guided Governor John Connally and his wife to their small jump seats in the president's open-air limousine, and then helped the Kennedys into the long back row. Their Irish-born limo driver, fifty-four-year-old agent Bill Greer, pulled out slowly for the ride to Dallas. He drove through a wide break in the airport fence that Lawson had specifically arranged be cut for the president's visit.

Hill and Ready, old hands, would normally jump on the back of the limo's rear steps. But Roberts had warned the agents about the president's firm request in Tampa. As Kennedy had requested,

Ready did not ride on the limo steps behind him that day.

Hill wasn't keen on the president's request. As Mrs. Kennedy's longtime shadow, he felt his duty was to her. Hill hopped onto the limo behind the First Lady when he felt the limo put her too close to the crowds, which was often that day. Greer frequently steered to the left side of the roadway to give the president more buffer on the right. It put Mrs. Kennedy within two arm's lengths of spectators.

Crowds stood four and five people deep along the Main Street route. **The Dallas Morning News** that morning had outlined the specific streets the president's motorcade would travel, which some claimed a local politician leaked in order to bring people out.

The crowds thinned as the limo neared the turn into Dealey Plaza, a grassy rise between a few tall buildings and an on-ramp to the Dallas freeway. Hill hopped off the limo and returned to the follow-up car running board, expecting they would soon speed up on the freeway.

Arnold and Barbara Rowland, a young couple, had waited here—on the slope near the freeway— for the Kennedys to pass. A few moments before the cars arrived, Arnold Rowland looked up at a brick office building across the on-ramp and saw something striking. In a large window archway near the building's top floor, a man stood with a rifle resting on his shoulder.

The husband nudged his wife and pointed out what he thought was a Secret Service agent. "It must be a security man guarding the motorcade," he said.

Then the lead car of the motorcade came into view. Agent Greer cut his speed to 5 or 10 mph to make the turns—right onto Houston, then left onto Elm. As the cars descended toward the freeway, Hill heard an explosive crack behind his right shoulder. He saw the president raise his hands to either side of his throat. Someone had shot the president.

I knew I should have been on the back of the car! Hill thought. His body could have kept the assassin from getting a clean shot.

But Hill appeared to be the only agent who immediately connected that first sound to an attack on the president. Landis and Ready, the two agents on the right-side running boards, turned to look back over their right shoulders, scanning the spectators and buildings for the source of the sound.

"What was it?" Ready yelled. "A firecracker?"

"I don't know. I don't see any smoke," Landis said.

What the hell was that? McIntyre thought as he also swiveled his head to look behind him.

Roy Kellerman, forty-eight, the ranking supervisor on the Dallas trip, turned around in his right front passenger seat to look back into the rear of the limo. He couldn't immediately figure the source of the noise. Greer, the driver, thought maybe a motorcycle had backfired. He reflexively pulled his foot off the gas. Some police escorts on motorcycles thought they saw the limo's brake lights flash red. Whatever the reason, the limousine slowed as Greer awaited instructions from Kellerman.

Looking back, Kellerman heard the unmistakable Boston accent of the president: "My God, I am hit."

Kellerman saw the president's hands clutching his neck. The senior supervisor paused just a few seconds, trying to figure out what was happening. A second shot rang out.

Hill didn't hear it. With the first shot, he had jumped off the follow-up car and was now running for the back of the limo. He stumbled, then grabbed hold of the trunk handle. A third shot rang out, which Hill not only heard but felt. The right side of the president's head exploded, a pinkish spray rising up near his ear, and he slumped over on his left side onto his wife.

Mrs. Kennedy wailed, "Oh my God, Jack! Jack! What are they doing to you?"

Landis hadn't connected the first two shots to the president. But he turned back in time to see the impact of the third. The sound was sickening, he thought. Like someone had shot into a melon for target practice. "I saw pieces of flesh and blood flying through the air and the president slumped out of sight towards Mrs. Kennedy," Landis later said.

Kellerman, now flecked with that blood and bits of the president's flesh, instantly grabbed for his radio mike and yelled at Greer, "Step on it. We are hit." He shouted into the radio, hoping it reached the detail agent in the vice president's car: "Have Dagger cover Volunteer!"

Greer punched the accelerator hard. Kellerman would later say of that moment, "We just literally jumped out of the God damn road."

Shift leader Emory Roberts, who watched Hill's heroic dash for the trunk, saw the bloody spray around Kennedy's head. To his right, Ready moved to jump off the running board and sprint to the limo, but Roberts called him back. He feared it would be dangerous at this speed and not much help anyway.

"Halfback to Lawson," Roberts called on the car radio to the advance agent in the lead car. "The president has been hit. Escort us to the nearest hospital. Fast."

Agent George Hickey grabbed the AR-15 assault rifle from the rear floorboards. He stood up, scanning the sky to the rear of the motorcade, readying for another attack. But the attack had already come and gone.

Hill, with his feet on the rear steps of the accelerating limo and his hands holding tight to the upright handles on the trunk, found Mrs. Kennedy inexplicably coming in his direction. Standing on the bloodied backseat cushions, she stretched her torso and right arm out over the car's trunk. She looked blankly, straight through Hill. She reached out to retrieve something on the shiny black metal of the trunk's lid—a small chunk of her husband's brain and skull.

Hill pressed the First Lady back into her seat and spread his body across the back of the wide convertible to shield the couple.

Only six or seven seconds had passed since Hill heard the first shot. Peering down into the limo, he saw blood, as well as gray and white bits of flesh and brain, splattered over the backseat, Mrs. Kennedy, and the Connallys. The governor, the back of his shirt inked with blood, had fallen over from his waist onto his wife. Until that moment, Hill hadn't realized the governor had been shot too.

The president was slumped lifeless on his left side on his wife's lap, his gaze fixed. Hill could see Kennedy's brain through a golf-ball-sized hole in the right side of his head. A small piece of skull with hair still attached sat on the car floor.

Hill looked back to his brethren in the follow-up car, his face contorted with anguish. He shook his head back and forth and gave his teammates a thumbs-down sign. Hill felt sure the president was dead or close to it.

"They got him. They got him," Roberts shouted into the air.

The shift leader leaned toward McIntyre: "You and Bennett take over Johnson as soon as we stop."

Vice President Johnson couldn't see a thing. He was flattened on the floor of his limousine, under his lead detail agent. At the sound of the first or second shot, Rufus Youngblood yelled "Get down!" at the vice president. He clambered over the seat divider, from the front to the back, and threw his 185 pounds on top of Johnson.

A motorcycle escort officer pulled alongside Lawson, a passenger in the unmarked lead car, and yelled, "The president's been shot!"

Like an echo, Lawson then heard Kellerman call out on the radio: "We're hit. Get us to the nearest hospital."

It can happen all the time, Lawson thought as his driver, Dallas Police Chief Curry sped toward Parkland Memorial Hospital. **My God, it did happen.**

JUST MOMENTS LATER, a young woman's voice came over the paging system in Parkland Memorial Hospital's first-floor cafeteria. She was summoning Parkland's chief of surgery: "Dr. Tom Shires, stat."

Ron Jones, a thirty-year-old surgical resident eating lunch, knew Shires was at a conference in Galveston. The overhead pager then began calling out the names of other surgeons to respond immediately.

What is going on? he wondered. He walked over to answer the wall phone and asked the operator.

"Dr. Jones, the president's been shot and they're

bringing him to the emergency room," she gasped. "They need doctors right away."

Jones told his fellow doctor, Malcolm Perry. They dashed out of the cafeteria and hurried down the back steps toward the emergency room bay. A whine of sirens grew closer and louder.

An abbreviated part of the president's motorcade zoomed up to Parkland's emergency bay door at about 12:35 P.M. Some of the other cars, including the press, had continued to the Trade Mart, not knowing where the lead car and limo had gone. Kellerman hopped out of the limo's front seat and told his agents to get stretchers quickly.

Vice President Johnson and his wife scrambled out of their Lincoln convertible. Lady Bird saw a flash of raspberry out of the corner of her eye—it was Mrs. Kennedy curled protectively over her husband. Agent Youngblood hurried the Johnsons inside the hospital entrance and asked the first nurse he saw to find him a secure room.

Roberts walked to the rear of the presidential limousine. The gentle "Father Roberts" took one look at Kennedy and concluded he would not likely survive. "I am going to Johnson," he told Kellerman.

Some detail members rushed back with the hospital's long collapsible metal carts on wheels. Agents Hill and Landis asked Mrs. Kennedy to come out of the car so they could help the president. She shook her head. "No! I want to stay with him!" she said.

Hill opened the left rear door and stepped into

the limo on her side. The son who had been so fiercely protective of his deaf mother seemed to instinctively sense how to protect this shocked and fragile woman. He took his suit jacket and covered the president's head. Then he took Mrs. Kennedy's arm. She let him lead her out.

"We need to help your husband, Mrs. Kennedy," he said.

Hill, Landis, Lawson, and a few other agents lifted the president onto a gurney and pushed him into tiny Trauma Room One, as the nurses directed them. Doctors and nurses swarmed around the patient and the agents exited quickly to give them room to work. Mrs. Kennedy opened her fist to give a doctor a piece of her husband's skull, which she had been clutching since the shooting. Hill found a chair for the First Lady to sit in just outside the emergency room door as more doctors arrived.

Kellerman, who was trained to stay by the president's side no matter what, asked Hill to get an open line to the White House and to keep it open. Hill found a phone and connected Kellerman to Jerry Behn in his East Wing office.

"Jerry, we have had an incident here in Dallas. The president, the governor have been shot," Kellerman said. "We are in the emergency room of the Parkland Memorial Hospital. Mark down the time."

Behn felt he'd been punched. Behn had traveled alongside Kennedy everywhere he went since his election in 1960 and they'd become close. The first trip he hadn't taken! Behn called out to his assistant, "Find Chief Rowley!"

In the hospital passageway, Kellerman handed the receiver back to Hill and returned to the trauma room. Then a White House operator cut into the open line. "The attorney general would like to speak with you," she told Hill.

Hill heard Robert F. Kennedy's unsteady voice asking the only thing to ask: "How bad is it?"

"It's about as bad as it can get," Hill replied. He didn't say that he felt sure Robert's brother was dead.

Meanwhile, in a hospital office commandeered for the vice president on another wing, Roberts told Johnson and his wife that the president was probably not going to survive. "We need to get out of Dallas as soon as possible," Roberts said. Johnson asked Roberts to check to see whether White House staff agreed he should leave.

In the trauma room, the attending surgeon, Dr. Perry, saw that the situation was dire. The patient lying on the metal cart was unconscious. He had lost a lot of blood, he had widely dilated pupils and a gaping head wound. **Most patients like this don't survive**, Perry thought. This patient, though, was the president. The medical team set to work to save him, performing a tracheotomy to try to get oxygen flowing to his brain while also working to stop the bleeding.

A minute later someone came out of the Kennedy trauma room gasping that the president was breathing.

Mrs. Kennedy stood up from her chair and cried out, "Do you mean he may live?"

The agents waited. No one answered.

Doctors called for nurses to bring an electro-cardiogram machine into the trauma room. Dr. Kemp Clark, the chief neurosurgeon, arrived as they were connecting Kennedy to the machine. He couldn't find a pulse in Kennedy's neck. Perry had begun giving the president closed-chest compressions to try to get his heart beating. Over five minutes, he roused a few feeble pulse beats, then nothing. The flat thin line on the machine didn't change. Kennedy had no heart activity.

"It's too late, Mac," Clark told Perry.

President Kennedy is dead, Clark announced to the room. It was 1 P.M.

With that, the agents found themselves in an awkward, foreign role. They were no longer protecting a man's life but helping carry out the rituals to mark his death.

Kellerman, his face drained, emerged from the trauma room. He walked up to Hill. "Clint, tell Jerry that this is not for release and not official," he said quietly, "but the Man is dead."

Hill looked down and nodded. He relayed the news to Behn, who now had Chief Rowley in his office. Hill urged Behn to call the attorney general and key family members so they wouldn't hear the news over the television or radio first.

Kennedy aide Dave Powers found agent George Hickey in the hallway and gave him a time-sensitive task. "Get a priest," he said. "Quickly."

Few agents knew it, but Mrs. Kennedy had instructed the hospital doctors not to pronounce her husband dead until a priest could administer last rites. When Father Oscar Huber arrived in the next ten minutes, he found Kennedy dead, covered by a white sheet. The priest was taken aback by Mrs. Kennedy's composure. He began to administer the last rites, knowing he would get no response from his penitent but unsure whether Kennedy's soul had yet left his body. In Latin, he quietly recited the final words: "I absolve you from your sins in the name of the Father, and of the Son, and of the Holy Ghost. Amen."

Meanwhile, the Johnsons awaited word in the hospital office. Kennedy's detail shift leader, Emory Roberts, hurried in to tell Johnson, "The president is dead, sir." Johnson himself was now the president.

Roberts told Johnson he and his shift had to leave the hospital for Air Force One right away, and certainly before the White House confirmed Kennedy's death. Mrs. Kennedy would bring the president's body to join them on the plane as soon as possible. The Johnsons followed Roberts's advice, departing so quickly that they left one of Johnson's agents behind. In an unmarked car driven by Police Chief

Curry, Johnson flattened himself on the backseat below the windows at Youngblood's instruction. The men who had tried to protect Kennedy that day by riding in his follow-up car—Bennett, McIntyre, and Ready—now rode in an unmarked police sedan behind the new president in hiding.

Hill and Kellerman stayed behind with their original charges. Kenny O'Donnell, a Kennedy aide and friend, asked Hill to find a casket immediately. Hill had the closest mortuary send their best, a bronze-encased Britannia model.

At 1:36 P.M., assistant press secretary Mac Kilduff entered a nurses' classroom where reporters had swarmed to get an update on the president. The junior spokesman's eyes were red from tears, and he asked the clamoring press to give him a second to catch his breath. He started two or three times before he could get out the word "President."

"President John F. Kennedy died at approximately 1:00 CST today, here in Dallas," he began. "He died of a gunshot wound to the brain. I have no other details regarding the assassination of the president."

A few reporters gasped. They asked when and where Johnson would be sworn in. Then they ran through the hospital halls to grab an empty pay phone or beg for an office line to dictate their reports.

———

IN THE HOURS after Kennedy was pronounced dead, the president's protectors raced through new, unfamiliar tasks, so numb that they would forget some of what they did. Their immediate assignment was to commandeer an assortment of cars to rush the Washington visitors to Love Field to fly home. Kellerman and his team with the First Lady were delayed in leaving the hospital when the Dallas County medical examiner blocked them from taking the president's body, insisting that the law required they conduct an autopsy first, given that the president had been murdered. But Jackie Kennedy wasn't leaving without her husband, and President Johnson wasn't leaving without Jackie Kennedy. Kellerman cursed the doctor and snorted at the law, even after a local judge insisted the medical examiner was right. "We're removing it," he said. The agents loaded the casket into a hearse outside as Jackie Kennedy took her seat in the back row. A hospital functionary tapped on the driver's window, which the driver rolled down: "I'll meet you at the mortuary," the hospital official said. Kellerman replied, "Yes, sir." But the agents then directed that they drive the hearse and the Kennedys to the airport. The agents won the standoff, a small victory in a day of horrific loss.

They arrived to find that a flight steward and an agent had hacked out two rows of seats in the rear of Air Force One to make room for the casket. The agents carried Kennedy's coffin up the ramp, only to find that the entryway was too narrow for the elaborate Britannia. The agents broke the handles off the casket and scarred its sides while jamming it through. A federal judge, personally summoned by her friend Lyndon Johnson to the plane, swore him in as president at 2:38 P.M. Nine minutes later, at 2:47 P.M., Col. Jim Swindal lifted AF 26000 into the air, bound for Andrews Air Force Base. Mrs. Kennedy sat in the back next to her husband's coffin, joined by Kennedy's two closest friends on his staff as they offered one another sips of whiskey.

The detail agents slumped in their seats in the forward compartment. Most were silent. Landis, the youngest on the detail, broke down crying. He thought of the Kennedy children he'd spent so much time with.

Though Hill would eventually be considered a hero by generations of agents after him for his leap onto a moving car, on this plane ride he was racked by unremitting pangs of guilt that would continue to trouble him for most of the rest of his life: **If I'd only been on the rear steps of the car! I would have been close enough to get to him before the third shot,** he thought. **If only I'd been faster.**

Lawson, who had laid the security preparations for the day, wondered what might have happened if the rain hadn't quit: **If they had put the bubble top on, maybe the assassin would never have tried to shoot,** he thought.

It dawned on Lawson and the rest of the detail

that they now represented a historic marker for professional failure. "I'm the first agent in Secret Service history to lose a president," Lawson said aloud.

Greer, hysterical about his own failure to react when driving the president, had already confessed his sins to the First Lady. Back at Parkland Memorial Hospital, he cried into her shoulder. "Oh, Mrs. Kennedy, oh my God, oh my God. I didn't mean to do it. I didn't hear, I should have swerved the car, I couldn't help it," he told her. "Oh, Mrs. Kennedy . . . if only I had seen in time."

Greer's words stuck with Jackie in her coming year of grief. The shots echoing in the plaza, the bloody bits, and the desperate, pointless dash to the hospital replayed in her mind again and again. Though she would always be grateful to her agent Clint Hill, the widow nursed a private disappointment in the Secret Service.

Two weeks after her husband's funeral, Jackie complained to her personal secretary that some agents seemed ill prepared that day for precisely the kind of danger they should have been trained to tackle. **If only Greer had simply hit the gas when the first shot rang out,** she sighed.

"He might just as well have been Mrs. Shaw!" Mrs. Kennedy said bitterly, referring to John and Caroline's British nanny. "You should get yourself a good driver so that nothing happens to you."

CHAPTER 4

NO TIME TO GRIEVE

A stout, gentle-faced Irishman stood apart from the others on a cement tarmac, silently scanning the evening sky to the west of the military runway. James Joseph Rowley wore the trench coat of an unfussy workingman. His brown hair, frosted with gray, hinted at the twenty-five years he had spent in law enforcement. For twenty-three of them, he had been an agent with the U.S. Secret Service, protecting presidents all the way back to the Great Depression and Franklin Delano Roosevelt.

Everyone who waited at Andrews Air Force Base that evening—the secretaries from the White House, the young airmen preparing for Air Force One's evening return, the grim-faced lions of the cabinet and Congress—shared a similar numb grief. They had all lost their leader, the president. But failure magnified Rowley's mourning. A man he had admired, and a man who had entrusted Rowley with the job of leading the Secret Service, was dead. And he had died on Chief Rowley's watch.

Just two weeks before that grim evening, the fifty-five-year-old Rowley had run into a longtime friend, the journalist and historian Jim Bishop, not far from the White House. Rowley peppered Bishop with questions about his new book, **The Day Lincoln Was Shot**. The author was amused that Rowley seemed to have "studied the book more intensely than I had written it."

"I counted them," Rowley told Bishop. "Fifty odd coincidences that day caused the assassination. If just one of them had happened the other way . . ."

Now, almost a century after Lincoln's death, Rowley wondered about the small and large moments that might have gone another way in Dallas. A few dozen extra Secret Service agents would certainly have helped things. Over the last two years, the chief had pleaded with Congress to let him hire ninety-six more agents. But lawmakers had slashed his requests, sometimes with a sneer. Republican lawmakers questioned whether Rowley would use extra agents to help lead little Caroline Kennedy's ponies. Or perhaps, they offered, the agents were needed to organize the Kennedys' recreation as the family repaired to their "ancestral homes."

"Do you suppose I could get some Secret Service

men to tow me around if I wanted to water-ski?" Iowa Republican representative Harold Gross asked the chief in an Appropriations Committee hearing. Gross had been incensed by a glossy magazine picture of a Secret Service agent driving a boat while Mrs. Kennedy skied behind.

Even Vice President Johnson had been part of the effort to block Rowley from adding even thirty-five new agents. He privately urged lawmakers to repeal the law that gave him full-time protection. He simply didn't want to be the cause of adding staff and increasing spending and thus drawing voters' ire. Now Johnson was the president.

The president's plane touched down softly at just about 6 P.M. and taxied to a stop near the assembled crowd. A hatch on the side of the plane's silver hull opened. Rowley saw five agents, all of whom he had personally hired, holding a seven-hundred-pound bronze casket hip-high. Their chief stepped forward to help his agents struggling to place the casket on an awkward truck lift. The Service wanted the late president's body and his widow to disembark Air Force One with dignity.

Meanwhile, alone in the central aisle of the plane, the new president steamed. No agents or staff consulted him on how and when he wanted to exit the plane. Jackie and Bobby Kennedy and their staff and agents focused solely on the former president. As vice president, Johnson felt Kennedy had always kept him in the shadows. Now, after nearly four hours as president, Johnson still felt second string. This moment would bother him for a long time. "They paid no attention to me whatsoever," Johnson remarked later to his press secretary. He felt they had shown the new president no courtesy.

Kellerman and Hill accompanied Kennedy's body to Bethesda Naval Hospital for the autopsy. After a few minutes, Johnson deplaned and gave a short address. "We have suffered a loss that cannot be weighed," he said. "I know the world shares the sorrow that Mrs. Kennedy and her family bear. I will do my best. That's all I can do. I ask for your help—and God's."

A helicopter airlifted President Johnson to the White House, and he conferred about next steps with his aides. They found it odd that Johnson said almost nothing about the shooting in Dallas, except this: "Rufe did a very heroic thing today. He threw me on the floor of that car and threw himself on top of me."

Rowley also returned to the Executive Office Building. There he found agents and White House staffers from the Dallas trip in the foyer, wordlessly retrieving their suitcases. They moved like robots. "There were maybe seventy-five people in that room," said agent Larry Newman, who came over to check on his shell-shocked friends. "And there wasn't a sound. Nobody was going to ask 'Hey, how are you?' They were still absorbing and reeling."

Rowley told Jerry Behn to collect all the available

agents from the trip in his office. Once they arrived, the chief told the men they should each write an account of what they had seen and done in Texas immediately that night while the memories were still fresh. He told the men they were professionals who must continue to do the very best job. He told them they and the Service would not only survive this tragedy, but would even improve.

It was the first time he'd articulated it, but Rowley meant what he said. The agents were too numb to believe in anything just yet. Still, the chief's calm speech gave them their first moment of comfort. "There was no feeling that he blamed anyone or that the assassination could somehow have been prevented," agent Blaine said. "It was therapeutic for many of the men, and was the closest thing to counseling they would receive."

When alone with the shift supervisors, Rowley debated and reviewed everything that had gone wrong. He saw no reason to retraumatize the agents with those details that night.

A devout and stoic man, Rowley had spent a lifetime protecting people, starting with his widowed mother and younger siblings. It hurt to think history would remember him as the Secret Service chief who lost a president. That night he began, in small steps, crafting a fuller legacy. He determined he would protect his agents and, to be sure, himself. He would protect his beloved Secret Service by making a stronger one.

JAMES JOSEPH ROWLEY, Jr., grew up in a working-class Catholic parish in the Bronx, the firstborn son of Irish immigrants. His father, a city inspector, died when part of a deteriorating city bridge he was examining collapsed.

At the time, Rowley was seventeen. He and his younger brother were just finishing the school year and had been plotting a carefree summer. Instead, the eldest Rowley got a menial job after the funeral, taking over as the head of the house supporting his mother, younger brother, and sister. He worked during the day and finished his last year of high school attending night classes at Fordham Evening High School.

After getting his diploma, Rowley Junior took night classes again at a local Catholic college to earn his law degree. During the days, he worked as a messenger, a brokerage firm runner, and then a state banking assistant who helped defunct banks quickly sell off their assets in the Depression.

In 1936, his law degree landed him what many would consider a dream job: as an FBI agent. He got high marks for his investigations in the Charlotte field office. But his career was interrupted the next year, after he testified in a trial in Philadelphia. A judge asked him to speak up over the street noise coming in the open windows. The FBI director himself, J. Edgar Hoover, read a news clipping about the judge's request and fumed that any agent would appear mealymouthed or weak in court. He ordered his deputies to tell the young man to find another job.

Disappointed, Rowley applied elsewhere, and he soon had two offers: from a law firm and the Secret Service. He signed up as an agent in 1938 and joined President Roosevelt's detail the next year. His tireless work ethic showed. They put Rowley in charge of advances for Roosevelt's historic wartime meetings in Casablanca, Tehran, and Yalta. He rose quickly in supervisor jobs—as a shift leader on the Roosevelt detail, and then as the special agent in charge of Truman's detail.

But it was a newly arrived President Kennedy who entrusted Rowley with the Service's top job. The retiring chief gave the White House three names for possible replacements. Kennedy chose the one he knew best: a fellow Irish Catholic whose genial, direct style he had seen firsthand on the campaign trail. Kennedy chuckled remembering when Rowley was the far more important man in Washington. Agents had once blocked Kennedy from approaching President Eisenhower, and Rowley stepped in to vouch that the boyish Kennedy was actually a congressman. The president liked to tell the story of how they first met: Kennedy was campaigning in Brookline, Massachusetts, in 1948, when Rowley marched in and "pushed me aside to clear the way" for President Truman.

———

ROWLEY KNEW HE had to shore up the protective net his agents provided around the new president. But first he had to rally his broken men to stand guard for the riskiest public event of their careers.

Mrs. Kennedy set the tone. She refused to ride in what she called a "fat black Cadillac."

In the tower suite of Bethesda Naval Hospital late that Friday night, the former First Lady began planning her own vision for the funeral. She would walk with Jack's family and dignitaries behind her husband's horse-drawn coffin in a miles-long procession—from the Capitol to a downtown cathedral and then to his grave site across the Potomac River at Arlington National Cemetery.

Sargent Shriver, a brother-in-law who was helping to coordinate with the military on their funeral plans, got nowhere warning Jackie about her safety. She didn't care. He asked her to consider the world leaders who would feel compelled to walk with her, thereby placing themselves in danger.

"Nobody has to walk but me," she answered.

Chief Rowley was flabbergasted that Saturday morning to hear of her plans. Her idea would turn the new president and nineteen visiting heads of state into a phalanx of slow-moving targets, sitting ducks for another gunman. Rowley told Behn to ask Clint Hill to see if he could talk the resolute widow out of this unthinkable walk. "Please, Mrs.

Kennedy," Hill said when they met later that day in a study in the private residence, "won't you reconsider?"

Hill had been Mrs. Kennedy's most trusted protector, but also her smoking buddy, and someone with whom she shared laughs, secrets, and now the worst trauma of her life. She agreed to compromise. She would walk only the eight blocks from the White House to St. Matthew's Cathedral, where the requiem mass was to be performed.

Rowley asked Treasury secretary C. Douglas Dillon, his boss, to try to talk Johnson out of joining the walk. After a budget meeting, Dillon did share the chief's concerns. Johnson confided that he had initially decided that walking would be foolhardy. "But then Lady Bird told me I should do it," the president said.

Rowley summoned agents from across the country to Washington. Even though Mrs. Kennedy had agreed to a shortened walk, the Secret Service still had to safeguard dozens of VIPs—the Kennedy family, the president, the visiting prime ministers, presidents, and royalty—through two days of public mourning.

On Sunday, his agents, joined by a small army of military servicemen, monitored a crowd of more than a quarter million who filed behind the Kennedy family as the late president lay in state in the Capitol Rotunda. On Monday, the Kennedy family, the president and his family, and several heads of state walked from the White House to mass at St. Matthew's.

All weekend, Rowley had found it difficult to delegate. He combed over the plan for security checkpoints and the posts for White House police officers and special agents. On Sunday, the chief returned to an old role. As the black-veiled widow led the procession, Rowley walked on President Johnson's side, protecting his left flank.

The numb, sleep-deprived agents couldn't believe they were walking a little more than a mile down Seventeenth Street with an exposed president— three days after the previous president had been gunned down in front of them. The high-rise buildings created a cavern similar to Dallas's Main Street.

Hill clenched his jaw, fighting his emotions. His nerves could still register just one feeling: fear. Fear of the sound of gunfire. "But I knew it would be the longest mile I ever walked," he said.

ON THE MONDAY of the funeral mass, Drew Pearson, a well-known syndicated columnist in Washington, received a shocking tip: Kennedy's agents had been out drinking into the early morning hours before the Dallas trip. The tipster was a young **Fort Worth Star-Telegram** reporter, Thayer Waldo. He explained that his managing editor, Calvin Sutton, was president of the Fort Worth Press Club, which had served the agents drinks until they went to a notorious club called the Cellar. Pearson, whose "Merry-Go-Round" column often skewered politicians, started making calls.

"We need to get our stories together," Sutton told Pat Kirkwood, owner of the Cellar, in a phone call late Monday. "Because talk is already starting about the agents getting drunk."

Sutton asked the club owner to help cover for the agents, and Kirkwood agreed. He would just emphasize that his establishment didn't sell alcohol, which was technically true. Kirkwood wouldn't mention that he provided alcohol free to reporters, cops, women, and a host of other VIPs and friends.

Despite their efforts, Pearson felt he had confirmed enough about the agents' late night activities to run the story by the end of the week. On Saturday, November 30, Pearson hosted a radio show on NBC and revealed what he had learned. His column, published soon after, called for investigating the Secret Service agents:

Six Secret Service men charged with protecting the President were in the Fort Worth Press Club in the early morning of the day Kennedy was shot. Some of them remaining until 3 am. . . . They were drinking. . . . When they departed, three were reported en route to an all-night beatnik rendezvous "The Cellar."

Pearson argued that the agents could instead have stayed up late checking the empty buildings along the motorcade route, like the one where Oswald hid.

Rowley was reeling as his staffer told him about the radio report. He wasn't shocked that his men had had a few drinks at the end of a long travel day. But now a powerful journalist had all but charged his agents with negligence in the president's murder. To get on top of it, the next morning Rowley dispatched one of his inspectors to Fort Worth to begin interviewing witnesses. Rowley ordered every agent on the trip to write a memo explaining where they were on the night of November 21, what they drank, and when they had returned to their rooms.

The White House tried to help blunt the bad press. Spokesman Pierre Salinger called Pearson to complain on Sunday. He said the agents drinking in Fort Worth were probably not in charge of protecting Kennedy in the motorcade. Yet, when Pearson pressed for names, Salinger said he didn't know. "But it's terribly unfair to the men to come out with this story," Salinger said.

"I pointed out that I had praised the Secret Service over the years but that conditions had become lax," Pearson would later write. "Neither a locomotive engineer, a newspaperman, or a doctor could afford to drink before going on duty."

The inspector, Gerald McCann, gave his findings to Rowley on December 10 in a confidential report. McCann said no one he interviewed at the two clubs claimed to have seen the agents drunk the night before the Dallas visit. McCann noted that the Cellar did not even have a license to serve liquor.

The report sidestepped a less flattering reality. The club did serve liquor. "We didn't say anything, but those guys were bombed," Cellar manager Jimmy Hill told a **Star-Telegram** reporter in an interview nearly two decades later. "They were drinking pure Everclear."

Nine agents admitted going to the press club and the Cellar and having a few beers or drinks through the night, according to the memos Rowley asked for, though they said they believed they were only drinking fruit juice mixtures at the Cellar. They stayed out until between 2:45 and 5 A.M.

Four of them—Ready, Hill, Landis, and Bennett—were agents who had to report for duty at 8 A.M. They were all assigned to protect the president in Dallas by riding behind him in the follow-up car. Never did they imagine that a few hours winding down at the bar after a long day would be dissected in newspapers across the nation. Shame hung over the entire Service.

The timing of the Pearson column couldn't have been more painful for the Service. Many of the detail agents had been walking around like zombies, having already concluded that his assassination was their fault because of their failure to act quickly enough. But now Pearson gave the public a new and horrific reason to blame the agents for Kennedy's death: indulgent boozing. Rowley had hoped to help snap them out of their devastation by honoring two of his men for their unusual bravery that day.

On Tuesday afternoon, December 3, at Mrs. Kennedy's request, Dillon presented Hill with an award for exceptional bravery in Dallas. Hill, who had stared into the president's skull, felt no joy or pride in the decoration. He waited numbly for the ceremony to end.

The next day, December 4, Rowley joined President Johnson for a similar ceremony honoring Rufus Youngblood. Rowley beamed like a father in the pictures as the president greeted Youngblood's wife and called his detail agent "the most noble and most able public servant I have ever known." Rowley hoped this signaled a bond of trust building between his agency and the new president.

But another blow to the Service came in the papers that Sunday. One of their own, former chief U. E. Baughman, criticized the Service's performance in Dallas. In an interview with several journalists at his Alexandria, Virginia, home, Baughman said it appeared that agents had failed to follow protocol for checking buildings and hadn't responded properly when shots rang out. He questioned why Kellerman and the follow-up car agents didn't rush to shield the president, why the limo driver didn't immediately speed away, "and why that agent in the front seat didn't sort of cover [Kennedy] the way Rufus Youngblood did the vice president."

Rowley told his spokesman not to give any comment.

Jim Burke, a senior inspector assigned by Rowley to study the mistakes in Dallas, saw Chief Rowley one night in the halls of the Executive Office Building. He was walking and staring down at a clutch of documents in his hand.

The chief had been logging twelve-hour days every day since Dallas. No one in headquarters had seen him shed a tear. He hadn't snapped at his deputies, despite the intense pressure of the last several weeks. "Jim, how are you doing this?" Burke asked him in the hall. "How do you keep going?"

"I have to be fine," Rowley replied. "Everyone is watching me. All the agents are going to look at me as a signal. So I have to be fine. For them."

A WEEK AFTER Lee Harvey Oswald shot and killed Kennedy, President Johnson announced a blue-ribbon commission to investigate the assassination and the motives of the troubled former Marine. Johnson told the respected men whom he had pressured to serve on the panel—including four members of Congress, a former CIA director, and Earl Warren, the chief justice of the Supreme Court—that his first priority wasn't getting all the details. He wanted them to tamp down public fears about conspiracy theories that suggested the Russians or Cubans had had the president killed. The commission was tasked with answering two central questions: What led to Oswald's actions, and had he acted alone? The team was then also asked to examine why the Secret Service's protective shield had failed.

After the New Year, the commission's attorneys began to interview hundreds of agents, staffers, police, witnesses, gun experts, and others. The commission's chief counsel, Lee Rankin, consulted from time to time with Rowley about security issues his team discovered.

But Rowley wanted to beat the Warren Commission to the finish line with his own internal fixes, both short- and long-term. That month, he made some immediate changes to agent protocol, zeroing in on two systemic weaknesses that he knew had allowed Oswald to gun down the president.

First, the Service had far too few men to shield the president during exposed motorcades and public events. So Rowley brought experienced former detail agents back to Washington from their jobs as supervisors in field offices. Overnight he nearly doubled the manpower on the president's detail— from twenty-eight to fifty agents on any trip.

Secondly, Rowley instituted required checks on all buildings along presidential motorcade routes and the posting of additional men in the crowds. He still didn't have enough agents to accomplish this, however, so for the first five months of 1964,

Rowley "borrowed" 670 FBI agents, postal investigators, and other officers. They worked 9,500 hours on motorcade and crowd duty for the president's trips.

Rowley then began crafting a long-range reform he hoped to unveil for Congress's fall budget season. One step he later took led to one of the most significant advances in the Service's history: He consulted with IBM, asking the new computing technology company to help replace and update the Service's creaky system for identifying presidential threats.

Before visiting a city, agents flipped through a paper index of four hundred people who had been investigated by the FBI or local police and were deemed a credible potential danger to the president because of violent or antigovernment acts they had taken. The Service also kept brief background files on five thousand more people who might be—or might not be—threats to the president, based on their names being referred as potential trouble. This list of the Service's had a major weakness: It was somewhat random and woefully incomplete. Federal agencies and White House staff were asked to let the Service know if they came across someone who was making threats against the president. The White House sometimes forwarded a crank letter it received in which someone said hostile things about the president, and agents then added the author to their threat list. But the list was largely dependent on others to report. And not everyone felt compelled to flag potential threats. The CIA and FBI, for example, were supposed to share names of people they considered concerning but often did not. These databases were also paper-based and unwieldy to search before a visit. IBM had computerized millions of workers' pay information for the Social Security Administration. Now Rowley asked them if they could automate the Service's threat files too.

Rowley also began looking into the success of early tests of bulletproof vests, electroshock weapons, and pepper spray, searching for modern tools that the agency could deploy. And of course Rowley analyzed how many additional agents he needed to better shield the president. Because Kennedy's death had so shocked the country, Congress immediately reversed course. Lawmakers were now jumping over themselves to publicly pledge more money and staff for the Secret Service.

In early 1962, the chief had unsuccessfully sought enough agents to create a special "fourth shift" of the White House detail. By adding enough agents to create a fourth detail, the Service would be able to rotate agents off their draining protective assignment for a few weeks at a time. They would instead spend this dedicated period of time at headquarters to update their training, or take some essential days off.

In 1964, Rowley asked for the same thing again, politely calling this fourth shift "long overdue."

Republican representative Silvio Conte of Massachusetts had once been among the lawmakers blocking Rowley's push for more agents. With Kennedy's death, he became the Service's top advocate and Rowley's lifelong friend. "I think we fell far short of the mark in this country in providing the necessary protection for the president of the United States," Conte later explained. "And I think we've learned a lot. We went to town after that. . . . I pushed like the dickens. . . . We've come a long way, maybe we should have come a long way before that, but who knew?"

Conte also helped Rowley tell lawmakers in private what was indelicate to say in public: Kennedy had made the Secret Service's job a lot harder. "Isn't it true that the late president traveled around Washington sometimes at night without a Secret Service guard?" Conte asked Rowley in a closed House Appropriations meeting.

"Yes," Rowley replied, "but how could you protect a president who didn't want to be protected? There were a number of times when he slipped away from us at night. He didn't want us, and there wasn't a thing in the world we could do about it."

WHILE ROWLEY FOUGHT for the Service, President Johnson was fighting Rowley. Paranoid by nature, Johnson suspected that most detail agents remained loyal to the Kennedy family. He told his aides that the agents were "not deep thinkers" and that they were constantly talking behind his back.

Some agents did find Johnson shockingly coarse in comparison to Kennedy. He urinated in front of them, gave them orders while lying in bed or sitting on the toilet, and cussed them out when he was frustrated.

A confidential staff memo stoked Johnson's neuroses in January. It warned that agent morale was plummeting under Johnson and cited the high number of detail agents seeking transfers. Johnson's staff also suspected agents had leaked a gossipy tidbit to **Sports Illustrated**. The magazine accurately reported that Johnson threatened to shoot out the tires of his agents' follow-up car for driving too close and ruining his deer hunting.

"I think you better get all the men assigned to the White House detail together and tell them to quit their bellyaching," the president told Rowley in a call. "If they don't want to handle a president, I'll send up an amendment to get the FBI to do it."

Rowley stammered as Johnson said he'd be glad to "sever the connection" with the Service if the detail agents were so unhappy. "I'll ask Edgar Hoover to assign some men to go with me," Johnson said tersely before hanging up. "Let y'all go back to handling counterfeit."

Johnson had periodically threatened to have the FBI—the Secret Service's hated rival—take over the Secret Service's job, and he increased his threats that winter. The FBI owed its very existence to the Secret Service. In 1908, Congress had blocked Secret Service investigators from helping the Justice Department probe a series of fraudulent land grants that gave away valuable Western timberland to profiteers rather than settlers. The investigation had already taken down an Oregon senator and congressman. A few members were upset that their august body was being investigated, but many in Congress decried the notion of a "secret service" of detectives spying on Americans and feared this loan of private investigators could lead to abuse. But President Theodore Roosevelt, furious at Congress meddling with federal investigations, permanently transferred eight Secret Service agents to a new unit, which eventually became the FBI. In the years since its creation, though, the FBI had surpassed its mother agency in both annual budget and clout. The vast development of cities across the nation in the early 1900s had birthed a wave of crime, and the FBI became the enforcer for the rapidly growing country.

In early 1964, President Johnson shocked Rowley by ordering him to cut the number of agents on his detail. The president handed down his orders just as the Secret Service chief was pressing Congress to agree to let him hire at least a hundred more agents in the coming year. "I want less when I go into the campaign than you had before the assassination," Johnson told him.

Johnson's motivation was political showmanship. Days earlier, he had promised a budget with the lowest federal spending in years.

"I won't even go to the bathroom if I have to have more people," he told Rowley. "I'll just stay right behind these black gates."

The president grew even more hostile toward Rowley that year, accusing him of everything from "running a dictatorship" to "trying to get me killed." Johnson's erratic meddling played havoc with the Service's orderly hierarchy. He had installed Rufus Youngblood as his detail leader, and he soon began swearing him to secrecy about upcoming trips. The president also gave Youngblood final say on who served on the detail or got promoted. Johnson later tried to kick Hill, a Service hero, off the detail because he didn't trust anyone who had been that close to the Kennedys. Youngblood persuaded Johnson to give him a chance.

This palace intrigue further demoralized the Service "when it was going through a serious bout of cancer," agent Larry Newman said. "Rowley could not make a decision . . . without Youngblood signing off. It was like we had two leaders.

"People were talking about the FBI taking over," Newman added. "The press was saying the Service sucks. The field was in turmoil. Nobody knew what was going to happen. . . . And the Warren Commission report information was coming out."

————

ROWLEY TOOK ENDLESS abuse from his new president. But to the agents of the Secret Service, the chief was a hero. That feeling was only vindicated by how the quiet man they knew handled a contentious interview before the Warren Commission.

On June 18, Rowley arrived at the commission offices in a Capitol Hill row house to answer questions about the assassination. He knew the Service was going to absorb much of the blame in the report for failing to react quickly enough to the shooting. But he didn't realize how indignant the mild-mannered chairman, Chief Justice Earl Warren, remained about agents' late night out.

Chief counsel Lee Rankin asked Rowley to read aloud the Service's rules banning the detail from drinking on trips. Rowley agreed that the detail agents broke those rules that night. But, he said, he had decided not to punish them for it.

"To institute formal punishment or disciplinary action would inevitably lead the public to conclude these men were responsible for the assassination of President Kennedy," the chief said. "I did not think in the light of history that they should be stigmatized with something like that."

Justice Warren frowned and leaned forward. Like Rowley, the chief justice owed the late president a debt of gratitude. At a time when many were assailing his court's pro-civil-rights rulings, claiming they threatened the country's fiber, Kennedy publicly championed Warren.

"Chief, it seems to me that on an assignment of that kind, to be alert at all times is one of the necessities of the situation," Warren said. "Even a small amount of drinking" or reduced sleep could slow reflexes, he said.

"I don't condone this at all," Rowley explained. "But these men are young. They are of such an age that I think they responded in this instance adequately and sufficiently as anyone could under these circumstances."

This was not sufficient for Warren. He noted that people in the crowd—Arnold Rowland, for example—had seen a man with a rifle. "Now don't you think that if a man went to bed reasonably early, and hadn't been drinking the night before, would be more alert to see those things as a Secret Service agent, than if they stayed up until three, four, or five o'clock in the morning, going to beatnik joints and doing some drinking along the way?"

Rowley explained that Rowland, the witness who had seen a man with a rifle, never alerted police or the Service.

Warren cut Rowley off. "Now I say, wouldn't an alert Secret Service man in this motorcade, who is supposed to observe such things, be more likely to observe something if he was free from any of the results of liquor or lack of sleep than he would otherwise?" Warren asked.

"Well, yes," Rowley said. But he added that agents had often "in the past" gone to bed at 1:30 A.M. and gotten up at 4 A.M. for an early trip.

"I am not talking about the past," Warren snapped. "We are talking about nine men here who were out until rather unusual hours of the morning. . . . The next day they were supposed to be alert to anything that might occur along the line of the march. Don't you think that they would have been more alert, sharper, had they not been doing these things?"

Rowley paused. "Yes, sir," he said, crisply, without emotion. "But I don't know of anything they could have done that they did not do."

That wasn't entirely true. Rowley knew there were some things they could have done differently. Ten days later, the chief asked the commission staff if he could amend that statement. His final answer for the history books was this: "Yes, sir. But even so, I still do not believe this would or could have prevented the tragedy."

Agents across the Service, on the White House detail and in the faraway field offices, cheered for Rowley and how he had stood up for them under such a grilling. He had thrown his own body down for them. "He could have helped himself by blaming them. But he wanted to protect them—I thought that was wonderful," said Joe Paolella, a Kennedy detail agent. "He said he wanted to be sure they never would think for the rest of their lives that they were responsible for the president's death. He could have said, 'I'm firing these guys. They completely failed.' He never fired anyone. He could have taken the low road and he didn't. He protected the agents without lying."

BUT ROWLEY WOULD take far more abuse for his agency's losing Lancer.

Somehow, he didn't break under Johnson's almost weekly assaults—including angry phone calls, scolding demands, and threats. Instead he fell over himself to say "Yes, sir" and "I'll get right on it."

Rowley took refuge in the quiet pews of his church off Chevy Chase Circle, the Shrine of the Most Blessed Sacrament. He walked along wooded Brookville Road to late mass there with his youngest daughter, Donna, on Saturday afternoons. He tried not to miss that reflective time when he was home. For his forbearance, the chief got the final word on the Secret Service's next chapter.

On August 27, 1964, a month before the Warren Commission's report was to be released, Rowley completed his confidential "Planning Document." The twenty-seven-page plan called for hiring 205 new special agents—a 50 percent increase over the 415 agents now on the job ten months after the assassination. Rowley wanted most of the new hires, 145, to beef up field offices around the country, where they could help investigate threats and prepare for presidential visits while also chasing counterfeiters.

In Washington, the Rowley plan would add eighteen people to the White House detail and create the fourth shift he had always wanted. It would finally add twenty-five people for the vice president's detail—more than doubling what he called the "obviously not adequate" team of ten. It's exactly what he had proposed before Kennedy was killed.

Rowley's most substantial proposal was for a tenfold increase in manpower and money to investigate and track threats against the president. His plan sought $1 million just to design a computerized system for their files of suspicious people.

Rowley's plan also revealed the groundwork he had laid for a new agent training facility: twenty empty acres in rural Beltsville, Maryland, offered by the Agricultural Research Service. There, he proposed, agents could drill for specific attacks: if a sniper fired shots into an open street, if a spectator pulled a knife. The government's landlord, the General Services Administration, he said, planned to set aside funds to build a firing range, a track for simulated driving, and mock buildings and city blocks for attack drills.

To get his blueprint from paper to reality, Rowley found a crucial ally in someone who had been close friends with the Kennedys. Treasury Secretary C. Douglas Dillon had a wealthy patrician's quiet power. He could have been making ten times his salary at a family investment firm, but instead he chose to help the country. A Republican, he was admired by his party, by Democrats, and by the business elite. He may have been one of the few public servants that President Johnson couldn't easily pressure.

When he sat for his own Warren Commission interview on September 2, Dillon admitted he was driven in some measure by regret. Neither he nor Congress had seen just how desperately the Service was running on fumes before the assassination, when Rowley pleaded for more agents. Mr. Rowley tried to tell us, Dillon told the panel. "But he did not have a very good reception from the Appropriations Committees at that time."

Dillon then did something rather brazen, a break with Washington protocol. He gave the commission Rowley's plan, along with its suggestion of 205 new hires, before the president had agreed to it. "He hasn't approved this. He hasn't seen it," Dillon said. He called the plan simply "our report as to . . . what has to be done."

Dillon gave Justice Warren and Congress what they were both clamoring for: the comfort of a well-reasoned plan. Three weeks later, on September 27, the Warren Commission released the results of its $1.2 million, ten-month examination. As the president had hoped, the 888-page investigation found no evidence that Oswald was part of a broad conspiracy to kill Kennedy. The commission lashed the Secret Service, however, calling for "substantial improvement" to its "seriously deficient" protection methods. The panel cited systemic problems in the nearly hundred-year-old agency. It hadn't kept pace with its expanding workload or technology. It acquiesced too often to the White House on security matters. "If I were Chief Rowley, I'd just read this report and resign," a top deputy on the National Security Council told his boss.

The commission criticized the Service's failure to require agents to check buildings and other places gunmen could lurk along a motorcade route. The panel called for a complete overhaul of the agency's method of identifying people who might pose a danger to the president. Its report faulted the agency for a lack of routine agent training—and the lack of quick reaction in Dallas—which gave the assassin the advantage.

"All of the Secret Service men seemed to me to respond very slowly, with no more than a puzzled look," the report quoted Senator Ralph Yarborough, who rode in Vice President Johnson's car, as saying. "Knowing something of the training that combat infantrymen and Marines receive, I am amazed at the lack of instantaneous response by the Secret Service, when the rifle fire began."

"We were shorthanded," the report quoted Tom Kelley, the Service's investigator of the breakdown in Dallas, as explaining. "We did not have the number and kinds of people and training that this serious responsibility called for."

The panel made twelve different recommendations for shoring up the Service and said it assumed the agency would have to substantially increase its staff to accomplish these goals.

Johnson's blood boiled when he heard the early reports of those recommendations. "My problem is I'm afraid some of these fools'll get ahold of it and just go to recommendin' more Secret Service," the president told his national security adviser, McGeorge Bundy. "My own judgment is they endanger me more than they protect me now!"

But Dillon and Rowley kept pushing Congress over the winter and spring to endorse the plan, over Johnson's protests. On February 15, 1965, Dillon and Rowley met privately with the House Appropriations Committee. The president had formally requested $8.7 million to fund the Secret Service in his new year's budget, a modest 5 percent increase. Dillon and Rowley instead insisted they needed $12.6 million.

"I am aware that it is perhaps unprecedented, for a cabinet officer, especially a secretary of the Treasury, to ask for an appropriation in excess of that requested in the president's budget," Dillon told them. But he called it a "very special and indeed unique situation." The Service couldn't stop another assassination without the money, he said, but President Johnson wouldn't ask for it.

"Nothing can redress the tragedy of that day,"

Dillon said. "But we all bear an awesome responsibility both to the country and the entire free world to ensure that the protection now and hereafter provided our president, whoever he may be, is the most effective possible in our democratic society."

Almost everything the chief penned in his August 1964 plan came to fruition. Appropriators—fearful of another tragedy and eager to assuage voters still mourning a martyred president—backed Rowley's plan.

In the fall of 1965, the Service began an unprecedented wave of hiring that brought aboard more than 200 new agents. Several of these new hires, inspired to serve because of the assassination, would later save other presidents' lives and become legends in their own right.

However, some of the original Kennedy detail members, pained by the tragedy they couldn't stop, sighed at the reinforcements' late arrival.

"Look at that," said former Kennedy detail agent Larry Newman. "We got a new training center, we got new agents. Unfortunately, we had to lose a president for Congress to wake up and give us what we needed to protect him."

CHAPTER 5

ONE LAST DAY ON THE TRAIL

The governor's wife could tell something was wrong.

Cornelia Wallace had finished a quick breakfast downstairs and returned to her sunny silk-draped bedroom in the Governor's Mansion. She ran her hands over a wall of dresses in her closet. The pretty thirty-three-year-old First Lady of Alabama enjoyed this part of preparing for a big campaign day: picking her outfits. She chose a cream-yellow dress that would highlight her tanned skin. She hoped the lightweight fabric would be comfortable in the hot, humid weather forecast for Maryland that day.

It was Monday, May 15, 1972. In a little more than an hour, she and her husband, Governor George Wallace, were scheduled to fly from their home in Montgomery, Alabama, to Washington. Once there, the governor planned to spend the day—the last day before Maryland's primary election—campaigning for president in two suburban Maryland counties that hugged the Washington Beltway.

But that morning, Cornelia Wallace heard an unfamiliar sound of worry and anxiety in her husband's voice, coming from the other side of the room.

"I don't think I'm going to go, C'nelia," he said. "I just don't think I'm going to make this trip."

"One more day of campaigning is not going to make any difference," he added. "If I haven't won it now, I can't win it with one day of campaigning."

Strange, his wife thought. **George never sounds nervous.**

He abruptly shifted gears. He scolded his wife that she was taking too long with her makeup and was going to make them late for their flight to Maryland.

They headed to the airport in a state trooper's unmarked sedan. Just one last day of campaigning. Just one more day and Cornelia Wallace and her husband could both take a much-needed break from the mental roller coaster of the campaign.

Her husband normally relished the trail. This was his third run for the White House, and he was doing surprisingly well this time. He had won the Florida primary and finished a strong second in two more states. He hoped primary wins in Maryland and Michigan would help him seize the Democratic nomination for president.

Wallace was a controversial candidate. Most Americans knew him as a famous segregationist, after he stood in a University of Alabama doorway a decade earlier and blocked two Black students from registering for college. His infamous 1963 speech calling for "segregation now, segregation tomorrow, segregation forever" cemented Wallace in many people's eyes as the embodiment of persistent white bigotry.

In his 1972 campaign, the Alabama governor toned down his rhetoric on race and focused on federal meddling in local affairs in order to appeal to a wider audience. His campaign manager deployed Cornelia—the governor's pretty second wife, nearly twenty years his junior—as a sidekick who could rebrand Wallace as a softer, more modern leader.

Still, some voters recoiled, seeing only the George Wallace of the 1960s when he arrived in their town. At a stop earlier in May, nearly two hundred white and Black protesters forced the governor to leave Hagerstown, Maryland, in mid-speech. Days later, demonstrators threw rocks at his stage in nearby Frederick, Maryland, and one hit Wallace in the shoulder. The governor's fiery past stalked him.

SOMETHING ELSE SHADOWED George Wallace on the campaign trail: the deaths of his old foes. It had been nearly ten years since President Kennedy's assassination, but the visceral debate about race and equality that Wallace and Kennedy had waged over American values still roiled the country. Kennedy's progressive push to extend equal rights for Black and white had laid bare the country's deep disagreement on civil rights, and Wallace had carried the flame for those holding on to hate and discrimination. In 1968, five years after Kennedy's assassination, two more of Wallace's enemies had been murdered: civil rights leader Dr. Martin Luther King, Jr., and presidential candidate Robert F. Kennedy.

Their deaths had a personal impact on Wallace. The governor had sparred face-to-face with both men. Though they disagreed vehemently, they shared the same stage in a caustic cultural battle.

Kennedy, then serving as attorney general for his brother the president, had flown down to Montgomery in 1963 to try to persuade Wallace to admit Black students into his state schools. Wallace refused, leading to the standoff in the university doorway. Kennedy and Wallace were rivals again as candidates running for president in 1968.

Wallace and King had served as each other's bogeymen with their followers. Wallace's 1963 pledge to preserve a segregated world spurred King to give his famous "I Have a Dream" speech that summer. In the powerful ode to simple human dignity, the civil rights leader pinned his most poignant hopes on Wallace's home state. "I have a dream that one day, down in Alabama, with its vicious racists, with its governor having his lips dripping with the words of 'interposition' and 'nullification'—one day right there in Alabama little black boys and black girls will be able to join hands with little white boys and white girls as sisters and brothers," he said.

In March 1965, after leading a protest march from Selma to Montgomery, King again directly challenged Wallace in a speech in front of Alabama's state capitol. "Evil is choking to death in the dusty roads and streets of this state," King said. "I stand before you this afternoon with the conviction that segregation is on its deathbed in Alabama, and the only thing uncertain about it is how costly the segregationists and Wallace will make the funeral."

In April 1968, King was shot dead as he stood on his hotel balcony in Memphis. He had been visiting the city to help lead a protest march for Black garbage workers seeking fair pay and benefits. The minister preached civil disobedience and was the target of a nearly constant stream of death threats. In quiet conversations with his wife and closest friends, King had predicted his own violent end. His death had a link to Wallace: The man who later admitted to killing King had been enthused about Wallace's presidential bid and volunteered in his campaign office in the months before the shooting.

In June 1968, just two months later, the late president's brother, "Bobby" Kennedy, was assassinated in a Los Angeles hotel as he closed in on the

Democratic Party nomination for president. The man who assassinated him, Sirhan Sirhan, was of Palestinian descent and had plotted for weeks to kill Kennedy because of his public support for Israel.

Overnight, President Lyndon B. Johnson ordered Secret Service Director James Rowley to assign new Secret Service details to immediately shield all the well-known presidential candidates. Wallace had been one of the five who got instant Secret Service protection that summer of 1968.

Ken Iacovone, then a shift leader on President Johnson's detail, was assigned to lead the Wallace detail. He warned his new shift that Wallace's vitriolic opposition to racial integration put a target on his back and might stoke potential assassins. The detail had to stay alert to this constant threat, he reminded them. Iacovone himself didn't take a day or a night off for the next five months, from the time Director Rowley assigned him in June until the election in November.

"Poor guy," said former agent Bob DeProspero, a junior peer who had been put in charge of Governor Nelson Rockefeller's detail at the same time. "They literally had to put him in a hospital. He collapsed at the end of that time. He knew the threats against Wallace and he just felt the responsibility so intensely he could never bring himself to take a break."

Eerily, four years later, Wallace found himself walking in the shoes of King and Kennedy. He was campaigning again for president, shielded again by a team of Secret Service agents provided in response to Bobby Kennedy's death. And as King had done, Wallace was openly discussing his own chances of being killed.

"Somebody's going to get killed before this primary is over and I hope it's not me," Wallace told a friend that spring.

Weeks later, Wallace told a **Detroit News** reporter that he didn't fear the chanting young hippies who taunted him at his rallies. Rather, he said, he feared the quiet ones. "The ones that scare me are the ones you don't notice," Wallace said. "I just see a little guy out there that nobody's paying attention to. He reaches into his pocket and out comes the little gun, just like that Sirhan guy that got Kennedy."

THAT SAME MONDAY morning, young Arthur Bremer woke in the lumpy blue vinyl backseat of his 1967 Rebel Rambler coupe in a parking lot in Wheaton, Maryland. The unemployed twenty-one-year-old had driven more than six hundred miles from Kalamazoo the previous day with some urgency. Since March, he had been trailing the candidate with single-minded purpose. But now he had run through all but a few dollars of the money he had saved up for this mission. He had to sleep that night in his car.

Nevertheless, Bremer chose his outfit for the day carefully. He wore dark slacks, a red, white, and blue shirt, and a slightly crumpled blue suit jacket. On each lapel, he affixed two Wallace campaign buttons. It was the same general costume he had worn a half dozen times already at the governor's campaign events. The young man didn't signal any physical threat: He stood just five feet six inches, with an average to slight frame, close-cropped blond hair, and a clean-shaven face.

Bremer hoped to look the part of an exuberant, loyal Wallace supporter. But in truth, he was an awkward, angry loner nursing fantasies of murder. "I've decided Wallace would have the honor," Bremer wrote in a diary after failing numerous times to get close enough to shoot President Nixon. "Ask me why I did it & I'd say. . . . 'I have to kill somebody.'"

Bremer's childhood had been defined by a cold, abusive mother and a truck driver father who drank to cope with her erratic mood swings and their door-slamming fights. Bremer could not recall his mother ever hugging him or his three brothers. He remembered the beatings she gave him, however, when he played outside as a child and got dirt on his clothes. Bremer didn't speak until he was four.

Fellow students at Bremer's school in Milwaukee, Wisconsin, shunned their awkward classmate, and some nicknamed him Clown. In a journal, he described the pain of never fitting in: "No English or History test was ever as hard, no math final exam ever as difficult as waiting in the school lunch line alone, waiting to eat alone, while hundreds huddled & gossiped and roared, & laughed and stared at me. Dozens of times I saw individuals laugh and smile more in ten to fifteen minutes than I did in all my life up to then."

Bremer got a job after high school as a busboy in a Milwaukee athletic club, but he was demoted to dishwasher when customers complained that his humming and marching made them nervous.

In October 1971, he found a new job as a high school janitor. In this lowly post, he found his first girlfriend and his first chance at a connection. But the sixteen-year-old girl broke it off after just two months, deciding Bremer was too "goofy." During an early date, he told her he took medication to keep his enlarged penis from "rupturing." At a Blood, Sweat and Tears concert, she felt embarrassed by his awkward stomping and yelling. He ran up to a woman he didn't know waiting in line and kissed her.

Bremer pleaded for her to reconsider. He gave up only when the girl's mother threatened to call the police.

Bremer then set off on a new and macabre journey. He bought a .38 revolver at a gunshop called Casanova's and quit his janitor's job. He began a diary, and in its pages, he described his plans to shed his "pathetic life" and become famous overnight by killing an important politician. "Now I start my diary of my personal plot to kill by pistol either Richard Nixon or George Wallace," he wrote March 1, 1972. "I want to do SOMETHING BOLD AND DRAMATIC, FORCEFUL & DYNAMIC, A STATEMENT of my manhood for the world to see."

The years of rejection and failure had reshaped Bremer into a desperate man who was willing to die in exchange for fame. The kind of man the Secret Service feared most.

Bremer became a student of the Secret Service's granite-faced agents. In the first few weeks after embarking on this plot, Bremer tried to learn how the security worked up close. In March, he showed up at a Wallace rally near his home, at the Red Carpet Airport Inn in Milwaukee, hoping to get a closer look at Secret Service habits and campaign protocol.

Bremer wrote how easily he could have killed the Alabama governor as he stood on the stage: "I figured Wallace would be dead or dying by now if I wanted it so." But he held back because he preferred to kill President Nixon. He reasoned that murdering a president would make him more famous: "The editors will say—'Wallace dead? Who cares.' He won't get more than 3 minutes on network T.V. news."

In the second week of April, Bremer set off for Ottawa in a rented car, with a gun he shoved into the trunk. He hoped to kill Nixon during the president's scheduled two-day visit there with the Canadian prime minister and parliament. For a day before Nixon's arrival, Bremer drove around to get familiar with the roadway that Nixon would take from Canadian Forces Base Uplands north into Canada's capital city. He took note of the extensive preparations along his path: "Three men in reflective orange overalls & carrying flashlights (it wasn't really dark yet) searched the road the President would travel for bombs, wires, strange diggings nearby etc. I guess," he wrote.

> Had heard that snowbanks were watered down to nothing to destroy a hiding place for bombs. Saw some men with hoses, cleaning the street He would use. . . . All the homes & businesses along the route were questioned by Secret Service men & asked to be on the lookout for strange movements in the bushes, strange cars etc. I saw a trench coated guy, an obvious SS cop, leave a home along the route & go into his car, he looked at me as I passed him.

The afternoon on Thursday, April 13, Bremer drove up to the base entrance seeking to attend Nixon's reception on the tarmac. But the guard turned Bremer away; only base employees were allowed. A policeman later directed him to the empty lot of a nearby gas station where about ten or twelve other cars had parked to see the Nixon motorcade roll past.

Bremer felt he had laid a careful plan. He had dressed in a business suit and conservative overcoat to appear a respectable supporter. He made a mental note to keep his hands out of his pockets even in the subfreezing temperatures, realizing that police and Secret Service agents considered hidden hands suspicious. "Didn't want to keep them inside my pockets & get searched," he wrote.

He waited on the edge of the road in the cold drizzle for more than forty minutes with other spectators. He retreated to his car to warm up, then ran back out when he saw the crowd rush toward the road. In a few moments, Nixon's black Lincoln Continental sped by.

"All over," another spectator said to no one in particular. Bremer hadn't even had time to reach for his gun.

"He went by before I knew it," Bremer wrote of Nixon. "Like a snap of the fingers. A dark silhouette."

Bremer would try again the next day, but he was frustrated to hear on local radio reports that Nixon would have the heaviest security of any visiting U.S. president in history, due to a sizable group of anti-Nixon demonstrators. Many came to rally against the Vietnam War, and others were Canadian nationals who considered the president a symbol of American control over their country. Dozens of Canadian police and Secret Service agents worked together with barricades and paddy wagons to keep protesters several yards away from the president's route.

"All along the fucking Ottawa visit I cursed the damn 'demonstrators,'" he wrote. "Security was beefed up—overly beefed up—because of these stupid dirty rats."

That next day, a Friday, Bremer milled mostly around the parliament grounds, trying to get close to Nixon's public events there. But he often found himself surrounded by protesters chanting "Nixon go home" with a bullhorn. They were met by rows of barricades and lines of Canadian police.

"Too much noise," Bremer wrote in his diary. "Nixon would never come up to shake hands with such a crowd, the one thing I hoped he would do at sometime during the trip."

At one point, Bremer saw Secret Service agents on a rooftop with binoculars, looking down at him and the crowds awaiting Nixon. "I waved & looked directly at one of 'em to mock their whole security system," he wrote.

Bremer counted a total of six times in two days that he saw Nixon but wasn't quick or near enough to fire. "Can't kill Nixy-boy if you ain't close to him," he lamented.

He had judged the Secret Service effort "a neatly-run operation." Still he held out hope he would find a flaw. "I just need a little opening & a second of time," he wrote as he left Ottawa.

In his campaign travels, Bremer began to notice the sharp difference between the level of Secret Service protection for the president and for his campaign challengers such as George Wallace and George McGovern. He saw an opportunity: The agents let the public get much closer to the candidates.

Bremer decided to home in on Wallace, and in early May, he began to engage in a kind of cat-and-mouse game with Wallace's Secret Service agents. During a string of Wallace events in Michigan, Bremer stood feet away from them. He chuckled to himself that they couldn't spot the assassin in their midst, and studied their patterns to find his opportunity. "These SS men are a different crew than was in Dearborn. No suspicions," he wrote about a May 10 Wallace event in Cadillac, Michigan.

"Another security breakdown," he wrote when he saw no police to keep him from stepping behind Wallace's car.

Bremer wanted to shoot at Wallace as he walked past him during a May 13 rally in Kalamazoo, Michigan. He may have assumed that the glass viewing wall between him and the governor would ruin the shot. But he credited his decision not to fire to his natural compassion for a pair of excited fifteen-year-old girls who pushed in front of him to get closer to the governor.

"Their faces were one inch from the glass I would shatter with a blunt-nosed bullet. They were sure to be blinded and disfigured. I let Wallace go only to spare those two stupid, innocent delighted kids," Bremer wrote. "We pounded on the window together at the governor. There'd be other times."

AFTER THEIR BUMPY start at the Governor's Mansion on the morning of May 15, the Wallaces and their entourage landed just after the stroke of noon at Washington National Airport. Jimmy Taylor, the leader of Wallace's detail, and his team of agents led the couple out of the Page terminal and into a four-car motorcade that took the entire group seventeen miles north to Wheaton.

Wallace's first event of the day was a rally and speech in a parking lot of this suburb's open-air shopping mall. An angry group of protesters awaited him.

Walking up to the Wheaton stage, Secret Service agent Lawrence Dominguez, a muscular agent from El Paso, immediately sensed the hostile vibe. He spotted gooey smears and streaks from eggs that had been tossed at the stage platform before Wallace arrived. Several dozen demonstrators chanted anti-Wallace singsongs and waved protest signs that called out Wallace's segregationist legacy.

WALLACE FOR PRESIDENT, HITLER FOR VICE PRESIDENT, one read.

REMEMBER SELMA, said another.

When Wallace did take the stage, sometime after 1 P.M., he opened with his concern about federal government efforts to meddle with community decisions. College-age hecklers dressed in bell-bottoms and sporting long hair began chanting to drown out the candidate's voice. "Bullshit! Bullshit! Bullshit! Bullshit!" they shouted in unison.

"Your vocabulary is mighty limited if that's all you can say is nasty words like that," Wallace called back.

Soon a few protesters began tossing objects that they found nearby at the candidate—with varying degrees of accuracy. Dominguez, standing toward the right front side of the stage, in front of Wallace and facing the crowd, watched the first mini-missiles with concern. Then someone hurled an orange, which missed Wallace's midsection by a foot. Next came a tomato, sailing straight for the governor's head. Alabama State Trooper E. C. "Doc" Dothard, the forty-year-old head of the governor's security team in Alabama, who stood on the governor's left flank, leaned in front of Wallace to deflect the tomato with his hand.

"I imagine the coach of the Baltimore Orioles might need to come do some scouting here for pitchers," Wallace said to a few weak chuckles.

Wallace could take comfort in one thing. He was standing behind a three-sided bulletproof lectern that his agents brought to each stop. But several agents, including detail leader Taylor, had the same general thought: **We need to get the governor out of here.**

Wallace's segregationist venom had put his detail

on edge in 1968, and now his agents in 1972 were on edge again about the high emotions Wallace was stoking in a Wheaton, Maryland, shopping plaza.

But civil rights and racial politics had nothing to do with the grinning young man who attended so many rallies with an oversized Wallace button on his chest and a revolver in his pocket.

In his clownish flag-colored shirt, Arthur Bremer clapped more energetically than anyone else around him at the Wheaton rally. He laughed when no one else did. People standing near Bremer immediately tuned in to his odd and suspicious behavior. Local television producer Fred Farrar noticed Bremer's Joker grin and thought he looked both unhinged— and familiar. Had he seen him at other rallies? "This guy is weird," Farrar reported thinking, with "a smirk that was almost spine-tingling."

Farrar directed his cameraman to film him for a few moments, then heard Bremer speak. "Could you get George to come down and shake hands with me?" Bremer asked a police officer as he stood behind a rope the Service used to keep the crowd back from the stage. The officer shrugged. Bremer asked the same question of a Secret Service agent a few feet away. But the agent walked away without acknowledging Bremer. He didn't fit the Secret Service's profile of a troublemaking hippie.

Taylor, in his dark sunglasses and brown suit, stood on the stage behind Wallace's right shoulder and whispered to the governor to wrap it up so they could leave. Wallace cut about fifteen minutes off his standard stump speech. Taylor then guided Wallace and his wife in a beeline to his blue campaign station wagon, with agents in front and behind them. After the team slammed the car doors shut and the agent driver pulled onto the main road, Taylor turned around from the right front passenger seat.

"I think it's best we cancel the next stop, Governor," the detail leader told Wallace.

But Wallace said he wasn't that worried. They had traveled all this way, he said. He didn't want to disappoint his supporters. The caravan sped on to the campaign's next engagement: the Laurel Plaza Shopping Center on Route 1.

The Wallace entourage arrived in the colonial Maryland town of Laurel at 2:15—way ahead of schedule for the 3 P.M. event. That gave the governor and his wife time to eat a quiet lunch of hamburger steak and put their feet up in a room reserved for them at the Howard Johnson's motel just down the road from the shopping plaza.

Agents responsible for perimeter security and surveilling the crowd—along with a few who would take over the afternoon shift at 4 P.M.—met for a brief lunch at the Hot Shoppes restaurant on the shopping center plaza. There, advance agent Tom Stephens walked through the outlines of where Wallace would enter and exit and gave each agent their assignment. He added that everyone should keep their eyes out for hotheaded hippies who might re-create the tense scene in Wheaton. As a precaution, county police stationed a rifleman on the shopping center roof.

But the Wallace entourage spilled out of their cars to find a very different audience in Laurel. Smiling spectators. Parents with children. It could have been a Sunday church outing, except for the straw hats and buttons that said WALLACE FOR PRESIDENT.

"It was a very calm crowd, a very nice, congenial crowd," Cornelia Wallace recalled. "Everything just seemed really nice."

Wallace began his speech by railing against the high volume of "hypocrisy in Washington, D.C., and I mean among the politicians." The crowd cheered. He urged bringing the troops home from Vietnam. More cheers.

As the governor spoke, two agents on the protective intelligence squad each paired up with a local police officer and folded into the crowd. Their job was to scan for any suspicious activity or trouble brewing. One of the agents was twenty-eight-year-old Ralph Basham, who had been with the Service for only two years. He would later rise to become director of the agency.

As the governor continued to speak, one of the roving Secret Service agents walked up next to Prince George's County police officer John Davey, who was standing near the rope line to help control the crowd. "Keep an eye on that guy," the agent said quietly. He pointed to a young raven-haired man off to Davey's left, who was wearing a bright orange jersey, a green jacket, and Wallace buttons. The young man has been loudly shouting, "Yay Wallace!"

The man was Daniel Capizzi, a student at Prince George's County Community College and an ardent Wallace supporter.

Some spectators in the crowd, however, were growing more suspicious about the behavior of another man: a short, blond, almost albino fellow who happened to be standing next to Capizzi.

This was Arthur Bremer.

Capizzi felt uneasy when he suddenly saw the wild-eyed look and grin plastered on Bremer's face. Bremer kept bumping up against him, too, leading Capizzi to suspect the young man might be gay and trying to make a pass. Bremer spoke to him only once, gently elbowing him and ordering him to applaud the country band performing onstage.

Prince George's County Police corporal Mike Landrum also took notice of Bremer because of that unsettling grin. He thought it odd how the man rhythmically rocked back and forth as if in a trance. Landrum pointed Bremer out to one of the Secret Service agents standing near the rope line. He wasn't sure where the agent went next; he never saw the agent approach Bremer.

Wallace, nearing the end of his speech, criticized

the "senseless and asinine" federal busing that yanked children out of their neighborhood schools. "You can send them a message," Wallace said, using his campaign slogan as his standard closing. "Vote for George Wallace tomorrow!"

The crowd clapped and cheered. Wallace waved from his lectern, then came down the front steps of the temporary trailer stage, with a state trooper leading the way. Taylor and Dothard followed on Wallace's heels. The governor pecked campaign worker Dora Thompson on the cheek as he reached the bottom of the stage, then signed autographs for her and a few others.

As the point man, agent Bill Breen then stepped forward from the base of the stage, intending to meet Wallace when he descended the stairs and lead him to the right, toward his waiting car. Just as Wallace began to fall in line behind Breen, shouts came from the roped-in crowd to the left side of the stage. "Hey, George, over here. Shake hands, shake hands, shake hands," Bremer yelled loudly.

A few others in the crowd piggybacked on his request. "George, come here, over here," a woman's voice called out.

"I suppose I better shake hands," Wallace muttered to Taylor. He took off his blue suit jacket and handed it to aide Frank Daniel.

"Don't go, Governor," Taylor said.

"That's all right," Wallace replied.

The detail shifted to follow Wallace's lead. Taylor,

a lanky man nearly a foot taller than the governor, walked behind Wallace to the rope line, placing himself immediately alongside Wallace's right flank, as every detail leader had done a hundred times before. Trooper Dothard did the same on Wallace's left side. Other agents filled in along the line to the right and left, and some shielded Wallace's back.

But on this rope line in Laurel, Maryland, the standard Secret Service choreography got thrown off once more. And changing rote Secret Service protocol on the fly was never a good idea. On a normal rope line, Wallace would move continually to the left as he greeted each person in succession, shaking hands with his right hand. Agents on either side would move in lockstep with him. Agents on the far left would carefully scrutinize the people—especially their demeanor and their hands—before the governor reached them. On this day, Wallace took a few steps to the right instead, apparently to move in the general direction of his car and eventual exit.

But an obstacle blocked their path. Taylor realized it after he tried to move forward, taking a few steps to the right, and bumped into Agent Ralph Peppers ahead of him. Taylor asked for more room; Peppers stepped back from the rope line. Then Taylor saw that a large PA system was in their way. The governor and his team stalled there.

"Governor, this is as far as we can go," Taylor said.

In that hardly noticeable span of three or four

seconds, the five-foot-six-inch Bremer rushed up to the rope through rows of taller spectators and found a tiny opening in the detail's blind spot. Bremer thrust his left hand forward as if he planned to shake Wallace's hand.

Bremer fired his .38 caliber revolver once, paused, then fired four more times in rapid succession.

All but one of the shots struck the governor. Wallace fell backward onto the black macadam pavement, a bloody hole in his blue shirt below his sternum, his arms flung out at his sides. Trooper Dothard, whose right arm had been pressed against Wallace's left arm when the shots were fired, saw Wallace fall backward and then realized he, too, was falling. A bullet had passed through the flesh of his abdomen.

Agent Nick Zarvos spun backward to the left, not yet realizing what had happened. He clutched at his jaw and began spitting blood.

Taylor and Agent James Mitchell both saw the faceless hand with a gun and lunged for the body behind it. Mitchell landed on top of Bremer with his knees in his back, losing his shoe in the scuffle. Agent Peppers held Bremer's head, squished sideways, to the pavement. He and Mitchell ended up having to protect Bremer as some men in the crowd yelled, "Get him! Kill him! Kill him!"

Cornelia Wallace had been talking to campaign workers and rushed to her husband. She fell to her knees to cover his body, spreading herself over his frame.

"I thought they'd shoot him again. And so I jumped on top of him, trying to cover up his head and his heart and his vital organs, his lungs. And there just wasn't anybody around him. Well, the Alabama bodyguard had been shot and blown out and knocked down. The Secret Service agent that was—these two were supposed to protect his body—got shot in the jaw and was vomiting and vomiting blood," Cornelia Wallace recalled in a PBS documentary. "I kept saying, 'George, I'm going to take you home. I'm going to take you home. And we're going home now.'"

Wallace's campaign manager had once boasted that Cornelia's photogenic good looks and energetic personality were going to help take her husband all the way to the White House. He pledged he would make her "the Jackie Kennedy of the Rednecks," a nickname that tickled her. That hot Monday afternoon, on her knees in the Laurel parking lot and sprawled over her husband's body, the resemblance was darker.

Blood welled up in a puddle around the bullet hole in Wallace's stomach, and a wet maroon circle bloomed on his dress shirt. Smaller trickles of blood showed where bullets had hit his arm. Cornelia had grasped onto Wallace's frame in the seconds after his fall. When Secret Service agents and police officers lifted her to let a doctor tend to the governor, drops of her husband's blood dotted the hem of her yellow dress.

CHAPTER 6

THE PRESIDENT'S SPIES

A round 4:30 P.M. Monday, President Nixon was in the Oval Office after finishing a jam-packed afternoon of meetings on the budget. He had just started a meeting with his secretary of state and the chief executive of Pepsi to discuss his upcoming trip to Moscow. About fifteen minutes into their meeting, the president's chief of staff, Bob Haldeman, interrupted to ask for a moment. He pulled his boss into a side room adjoining the Oval Office. He had startling news.

"We just got word over the Secret Service wire that George Wallace was shot at a rally in Maryland," Haldeman said. Nixon's most trusted aide laid out the little he knew: Wallace was seriously injured but had been taken to nearby Holy Cross Hospital in Silver Spring, Maryland, where trauma room doctors were preparing to remove a bullet from Wallace's belly.

Incapable of restraining himself from strategizing, Nixon's mind immediately started calculating how this shooting might help him. Working late that evening and continuing to make calls past midnight, Nixon fixated on two goals. First, he wanted to use the violent attack on one political foe to justify shadowing another rival. Then, the president wanted to control the investigation of the shooter and find a way to quickly blame the left for the shooting. In both these endeavors, the president would try to use Secret Service agents as his minions.

Nixon knew he had to appear serious and concerned, especially since the victim was one of his Democratic opponents. He called his wife, Pat, to tell her about the shooting and let her know he could no longer attend a dinner reception she'd planned for a group of wealthy benefactors who'd come from across the country to celebrate the reopening of the Blue Room. It would look terrible to be photographed in tuxedo, smiling and sipping champagne, while Wallace lay in a hospital, he said.

Nixon next summoned Treasury Secretary John Connally, who oversaw the Secret Service, to the Oval Office. The Laurel shooting had changed everything, he said. Because of this attempt to kill a Democratic candidate, the president said, Connally needed to persuade the last living Kennedy brother to accept Secret Service protection immediately.

The president was on shaky ground legally, his

White House counsel warned. Senator Kennedy was not a candidate running for president, so he was not someone the Service was authorized to protect. But Nixon plowed ahead. The president stressed to Connally that Kennedy was a target because of his famous family name and because he was out campaigning as a surrogate for Nixon's reelection opponent, Democrat George McGovern.

The president neglected to mention to Connally that for the last two years he'd been obsessed with digging up dirt on the young senator, part of his long-running jealousy of the Kennedy family. He'd nursed both bitterness and admiration for America's political royalty ever since losing his White House bid to John Kennedy in 1960.

Though Ted Kennedy had ruled out a presidential run in 1972, he was considered a likely contender for 1976. Nixon hoped to tarnish the senator's political star by leaking some embarrassing information. "I'd really like to get Kennedy taped," Nixon had told Haldeman a year earlier, in April 1971.

Nixon's cabinet secretary called Ted Kennedy from the Oval Office while the president stood by listening. "Ted . . . the president asked me to come over here a minute ago. He said he doesn't really care what the hell the law provides for as far as our counsel is concerned," Connally told Kennedy. "He thinks out of all the people who are susceptible to some nut, you [are], probably more than anybody except George Wallace. And he would like this afternoon to offer you a full Secret Service protection, and I'm calling to tell you that, and it's available to you, and it'll be available as of tonight if you want it, Ted."

Though Ted Kennedy was privately tormented by his brother Bobby's death, he knew full well Nixon's disdain for his family's political dynasty. It was no surprise the president made Connolly the messenger. The former Texas governor served in the Nixon administration, but he shared a kinship of trauma with the Kennedys. Connally had been shot and injured while riding in the same open limousine with Ted's older brother, President John F. Kennedy, when he was assassinated in Dallas.

For a few seconds, the youngest Kennedy brother paused, silently pondering the offer. "John, maybe they could just start as a temporary type of thing now and then we can just see," Kennedy replied in his clipped Brahmin accent.

Connally pushed for a firm yes. "I think the president wants to g'awn and announce that it's done," he said in his Texas drawl. "We'll give you full coverage. I think Ted you ought to g'awn and take it. Hell, very frankly, I don't know that they can save you, but there's a damn good chance they could if some nut came up. I know you're not a candidate, but you're exposed. I've known that all along."

"Why don't we just do it as a temporary . . . Thank you very much," Kennedy said in a flat, quiet voice, sounding neither grateful nor enthused. "Then we can think about it."

Connally agreed. They would dispatch a team of

agents first thing in the morning. When the two men hung up, Nixon thanked Connally and they parted. The president had what he wanted.

The president had just moments earlier called Cornelia Wallace at Holy Cross Hospital, telling her that he was "terribly" worried about the governor and that he and his wife were praying for him. The governor's wife told Nixon she had not been worried at first, but hospital X-rays showed one bullet lodged against Wallace's spine. "He doesn't have much feeling and he's not able to move from his waist down," she told Nixon. "So that's concerning."

"You tell him to just keep his spirit," Nixon said. "Tell him that all of us people in politics have got to expect some dangers and that we, Mrs. Nixon and I, both send our very best wishes and you can be sure that we'll remember him in our thoughts and our prayers."

Before they said goodbye, Cornelia Wallace teasingly warned the president, with a modest laugh, "Well, he's liable to be out there running against you in November."

Nixon gave a flat laugh, said "All right," then quickly said goodbye. After these key calls, Nixon next went to the residence to change and then accompanied his wife to a reception in the East Room. He welcomed their guests, thanked them for the contributions, and then quickly excused himself. "I am sure you will understand that under the circumstances I will want to return to the office to see what the situation is with regard to Governor Wallace's condition," Nixon told them.

Later, when the president could speak unfiltered in his Executive Office Building office with his three closest aides, he blamed Wallace for the shooting. "You know, how long did it have to be said that somebody was going to shoot Wallace?" Nixon told Haldeman and special counsel Charles Colson. "Didn't he ask for it? He stirs up hate."

NIXON KEPT STRATEGIZING through the night with his deputies, fretting over his second goal. He insisted that the Secret Service and FBI share with the White House every shred of information about the shooter as soon as they learned it. He wanted them to clamp down on information and prevent early leaks to the press. "We damn well better know the details on this before the press does, Jim," Haldeman warned Director Rowley when demanding an update for the president in a phone call at about 7 P.M. "Get us a full run on it as soon as you can. . . . The key thing now is the identity of the assailant and all the particulars on it before they start reporting it in the press."

Nixon fumed about the lack of information the White House had received about the suspect. He ordered that the Secret Service not lead the investigation. "This son of a bitch Rowley is a dumb bastard, you know. He is dumb as hell," Nixon vented to Haldeman. "We've got to get somebody over there right away. Get Ehrlichman on him! Get Ehrlichman over there right away, Bob, to work on it. Don't you agree? Secret Service will fuck this up!"

Just after the Rowley call, Nixon called Deputy Attorney General Richard Kleindienst to order that the FBI take over the probe and quickly find out more about the shooter. "Get somebody over there . . . on our side who gets in and questions the son of the bitch before the left wing press and the rest gets in and does it," Nixon said. "Do you understand?"

Kleindienst, sounding puzzled by Nixon's concern, explained that the alleged shooter was securely locked up in jail, where no reporters would be able to interview him.

"Let me say the first news must not be in **The Washington Post**," the president continued. "Goddammit be sure the FBI gets there before they do."

Rowley and his top inspector correctly told the White House that Bremer was the shooter and they believed he acted alone. But within minutes of that call, a senior Justice official had given Nixon incorrect and outdated information. Kleindienst insisted that police had three teenage boys in custody as suspects, one who had been identified as the shooter and two accomplices.

Nixon kept banging his desk for the facts, but

what he really wanted were his "preferred facts." As the evening wore on, he told his aides to leak some fabricated "evidence" to friendly reporters. They should claim the investigation found Wallace's shooter had ties to the left wing and the McGovern campaign. "Put it on the left right away," Nixon told them. "Just say he was a supporter of McGovern and Kennedy. Now just put that out. Just say that you have it on unmistakable evidence."

Haldeman took note that Bremer had a previous arrest record, which would provide concrete clues about his mental health problems. "Screw the record," Nixon interrupted. "Just say he was a supporter of 'that' and 'that' and put it out. Just say we have an authenticated report."

The president was focused solely on his reelection. He worried aloud that if investigators found Bremer had ties to the right wing or a Nixon supporter, Nixon could lose the White House. Sitting with Colson later in his office in the Executive Office Building, Nixon sipped a cocktail, rare for him, and mused aloud about a way to solve the problem. "Oh, wouldn't it be great if they had left-wing propaganda in that apartment," Nixon said. "Too bad we couldn't get somebody there to plant it."

Colson, familiar with Nixon's practice of making requests in this indirect way, excused himself and called Howard Hunt, a former CIA operative. Hunt had several times worked off the books for the White House to dig up dirt on its enemies, including Ted Kennedy. Colson said he needed him to head to Milwaukee in the morning on a little mission.

But none of Nixon's plans worked out as he had hoped. In the wake of the shooting, Director Rowley was also determined to learn everything he could about Arthur Bremer that night. The Service needed to know whether this breach was part of a bigger plot. Rowley instructed an agent temporarily stationed in Milwaukee to go check out Bremer's apartment.

The building caretaker let the agent inside immediately. He searched the messy two-room flat and found several campaign news clippings, one with the headline MEET NIXON AT THE SHERATON-SCHROEDER, and pamphlets from the Black Panther Party and American Civil Liberties Union. A pornographic comic book featured, among other subjects, a pig named Arthur Herman who detailed his sexual plans for fellow pigs. The agent took one of Bremer's notepads for a writing sample the Service could analyze. Spiral notebooks were filled with his disjointed thoughts and unintelligible scribbling.

"Just call me canoe, my mother liked to paddle me [sic] lot."

"Nixon uses a night light."

"In America, here one [sic] lived a pig named Arthur Herman."

FBI agents, who planned to get a warrant the next morning, were interviewing neighbors and heard someone inside Bremer's place. They burst in, and a fistfight almost broke out over who was running the Bremer investigation. When the two sides agreed to move their jurisdictional quarrel away from Bremer's apartment, some local reporters saw an opening and asked the caretaker to let them inside. They took extensive photographs—and made an informal inventory of the suspect's belongings.

The plan to plant evidence died. Colson's secretary called Hunt to cancel his trip to Milwaukee. The president was furious at the Secret Service's interference and demanded that the FBI control all the evidence in the case.

Soon after, Kennedy parted ways with his protective Secret Service team. Though it wasn't widely known, Kennedy had been struggling with post-traumatic stress from his brother Bobby's violent end and had been drinking heavily to cope. The Wallace shooting in Laurel had sent new waves of shock through the whole Kennedy family, especially his mother, Rose, and the senator's young son Patrick.

Despite the fear of a family curse, Kennedy formally called off his security detail on June 5, about three weeks after Nixon ordered it. Kennedy told Rowley he no longer needed protection because he would be off the McGovern campaign trail and spending the summer with family on Cape Cod. Kennedy's aides also told the press that the stern-faced bodyguards unintentionally added to the family's stress, his aides said. "He doesn't like to have to explain to his children who those men with guns are hovering around everywhere," his press secretary, Dick Drayne, told reporters.

THE SECRET SERVICE struggled to recover and learn from what they deemed their collective failure in the Wallace shooting. Yes, Wallace had put himself in harm's way by ignoring Taylor's advice. Yes, Wallace had lived, although he was paralyzed for life. And yes, their security around Nixon had frustrated Bremer and caused him to abandon his plans to kill the president.

But still they believed their security system had failed. The incident revealed what agents already knew: Security for candidates had never been as choreographed and routinized as that for the president and vice president. Many agents rotated on and off the campaign trail with such frequency that they didn't typically work together as a cohesive unit. "Things were not as structured and the agents didn't work together a lot," said Joseph Petro, who protected the vice president then and later became head of President Reagan's detail. "They were constantly being rotated. It took that tragic event to get everybody's attention."

In the wake of the Wallace shooting, the Service conducted more frequent and intensive drills on how to handle different kinds of attackers on a rope line. Agents and officers practiced over and over, playing the roles of detail agents and spectators on either side of the line. The drill instructor warned the agents ahead of time that a person in the crowd would play the role of the shooter and approach the principal with a gun. The drill instructor even pointed out who that person was.

"The agents were told who had a weapon," said one former agent. "And the guys are working the rope line and they're constantly looking at this guy waiting for the moment when he's going to pull the gun. They know who it is."

Agents swiveled their heads back and forth from the spectators in front of them to the mock gunman in the crowd. They tried to anticipate his move and readied themselves for the fastest dive or lunge. No matter how many times they did the drill, the result was the same. "They never once stopped him before two shots," the former agent said.

THE PRESIDENT'S INSTANT reaction to Governor Wallace's shooting—to use it against his enemies—was just a tiny piece of a much larger stealth operation run by Nixon's top aides and allies. He and his political operatives had big plans in the works for how to tarnish the liberal left and ensure the president's reelection.

Just a month after the shooting, though, some of the president's henchmen got caught. On June 17, 1972, D.C. police arrested five men for breaking into the Democratic National Committee offices at the Watergate hotel complex at about 2:30 A.M. **The Washington Post** reported that one of the men caught with bugging devices during the break-in had previously worked for the CIA. That man, James McCord, also worked as a security consultant for Nixon's reelection campaign.

Most of the public and press soon forgot about the small, odd burglary. It would take a little more than two years, a team of FBI agents followed closely by two local **Washington Post** reporters, and a Senate investigation to eventually uncover the evidence that Nixon both knew about his top aides' role in the break-in and ordered a cover-up from the earliest days.

But inside the White House that summer, Nixon and his aides were apoplectic about FBI agents' tracing the burglary back to them. Though his government was then investigating the Watergate break-in, Nixon suggested bending more rules, breaking more laws.

The president obsessed over the loyalty of his senior officials. He persisted in his wish to use Secret Service agents as White House listening posts. Both topics—loyalty and spying—dominated a long conversation the president had with Haldeman that July at Camp David.

"I don't suppose there's any way we've got any line on the McGovern camp through their Secret Service?" Nixon asked.

"We sure ought to try but I don't know how to do it," Haldeman replied. "We got some potentials. . . . to my knowledge we're not using them, and I am not so sure we should. If we get caught at that . . ." The chief of staff didn't finish his sentence.

In their Camp David chat, Nixon ran through a list of top officials then working in government and rated their loyalty to the White House. At each name, the president and his top deputy debated who should be dropped in favor of a more faithful yes-man.

They talked first about acting FBI director Pat Gray, who was leading the investigation. Nixon felt he had to go.

Next, Nixon shifted to the director of the Secret Service. "Incidentally, that's one thing we're going to change," Nixon said. "Who the hell's that—Rowley—the head of it?"

"We can change that chapter," Nixon scoffed.

"Yeah, yeah, we should," Haldeman agreed. "The problem is we've not had an idea of who we wanted to put in."

The chief of staff said he had been monitoring the Secret Service's deputy director, California native Lilburn "Pat" Boggs, and been pleasantly encouraged. He said Boggs appeared obedient and might meet their loyalty standard. It was Boggs who had alerted Nixon chief domestic adviser John Ehrlichman on the night of the Watergate break-in to the arrest of a former CIA operative.

"We've run some tests and he's worked out awfully well," Haldeman said. "He is the one guy in all this investigative area we've been able to trust and who's done what we've told him to do."

"I want one who's our boy," Nixon said. "I'm not going to screw around on that score."

JUST AFTER LABOR Day, as the Nixon and McGovern campaigns heated up, Nixon again pushed to have the Secret Service tail Senator Kennedy.

In a September 7 sit-down, Nixon instructed Haldeman and his deputy Alexander Butterfield to have Bob Newbrand, a senior agent based in the Miami field office, reassigned to lead the new Kennedy detail. Nixon knew Newbrand from when he'd served on his vice presidential detail, and White House aides considered him highly loyal to Nixon.

The president said he wanted Newbrand's shift to help catch Kennedy in something politically embarrassing so they could leak it to the press. The junior senator was rumored to be having an affair with New York socialite Amanda Burden. Nixon had been fixated on the idea ever since his secretary of state, Henry Kissinger, had told Nixon some stories of seeing Kennedy proposition and stalk a different woman at a Manhattan society event.

"Rowley is not to make the assignment," Nixon told Butterfield. "Does he understand?"

"He's to assign Newbrand," Haldeman said.

"Does he understand that he's to do that?" Nixon asked.

"He's effectively already done it," Butterfield answered. "And we have a full force assigned, forty men."

"A big detail is correct," the president said. "One that can cover him around the clock, every place he goes."

Nixon and Haldeman laughed.

"And . . . Rowley doesn't bitch, now," Nixon said later to Haldeman.

"He won't bitch," Haldeman assured him.

"And you'll talk to Newbrand?" Nixon said.

"And I'll talk to Newbrand and tell him how to approach it, because Newbrand will do anything that I tell him to," Haldeman said. "He has come to me twice and absolutely, sincerely said, 'With what you've done for me and what the president's done for me, I just want you to know, if you want someone killed, if you want anything else done, anyway, any direction.'"

"We just might get lucky and catch this son of a bitch and ruin him for '76," Nixon said of Kennedy. "That's going to be fun."

HALDEMAN HAD TOLD Butterfield to call the Service about making Newbrand the detail leader, but Clint Hill resisted the change when the White

House staffer called. Hill, now the assistant director over protection, explained that the detail was already chosen and the men were ready to ship out. The two men hung up.

Assistant Treasury Secretary Gene Rossides then called Hill about Newbrand. Hill repeated that the Service had already selected a team. The Treasury appointee stopped him. "You apparently don't get the picture, Clint," Rossides said. "This is not a request, it is an order."

Hill knew that Newbrand, a loner who seemed to steer clear of agents, was close to Nixon staff and suspected something was fishy. Hill would always feel protective of the Kennedy family, but more than that, he was insulted at the idea of using agents for political purposes.

Hill shared his suspicion with Jim Burke, the deputy assistant director in charge of field offices, and Newbrand's boss. Burke called Newbrand at his field office to warn him there should be no political spying or funny business on the detail.

On September 8, the day the new detail was to start, Butterfield told Haldeman's secretary he needed to talk to the chief of staff urgently about Kennedy. It's unclear what Butterfield was so eager to tell Haldeman. But as they spoke, Haldeman wrote a terse note about the boss in charge of deploying Secret Service agents: "Hill knows will happen."

At 3:15 P.M., Haldeman called Newbrand in his

Miami office. It's unclear who won the tug-of-war for Newbrand's loyalties—the Secret Service's code of honor or Nixon's chief of staff. Newbrand's assignment leading the Kennedy detail ended in two months, when Nixon won reelection and beat McGovern by a landslide in the first week of November. No embarrassing pictures or startling stories about the young senator publicly surfaced.

Newbrand's career fared well afterward with Nixon's blessing. He became a Secret Service spokesman during Nixon's second term and was later promoted to head of the Miami field office.

NIXON'S INTENSE RESPONSE to the Wallace shooting highlighted a few of the president's personal flaws that would eventually lead to his resignation and ruin. Because he saw his political rivals as demons, he convinced himself he was the righteous victim, entitled to manipulate government for his own gain. Nixon grew inured to ordering his aides to skirt and break the law.

But the episode also highlighted the way a president's behavior can shape and taint the Secret Service. Under Nixon, the president and his aides displayed an arrogance toward the Service that hurt its morale and mission.

In 1969 and 1970, Nixon's lawyer and staff had pressured the Secret Service to approve and pay for pricey purchases and renovations at Nixon's private

San Clemente and Key Biscayne homes. By having
the Service label the expenses as necessary for security, Nixon was able to get taxpayers to buy new
den furniture and fabrics to freshen the décor of his
California estate. He also got them to pay for a new
sewer line and new heating system in his home in
Key Biscayne and to restore a crumbling gazebo his
wife enjoyed because it overlooked the ocean.
Nixon and his close friend Bebe Rebozo owned
homes near each other in Key Biscayne; Nixon
aides asked the Secret Service to pay for a helipad
and docking equipment for Rebozo's yacht, and a
"booster transformer" to help power a sauna bath
in the friend's home, according to work orders.

One of the president's legal assistants bragged at
her success in getting a new exhaust fan for the
house fireplace labeled a security expense when
Nixon complained it didn't draft properly. "Ken
Iacovone informed me that SS would pay for the
installation of the fireplace fan after I informed him
that it definitely was placed for security purposes
and how would he like it if you know who was
asphyxiated ever," she wrote.

DIRECTOR ROWLEY, CONCERNED about the expenses
added to his agency's tab, privately pleaded
with the chairman of the House Appropriations
Subcommittee responsible for overseeing the Secret
Service's budget to visit San Clemente with him,

but the chairman never found the time. "I think what he was trying to tell me is that the White House hot shots were trying to get him to take the rap for a whole lot of imprudent spending," Democratic representative Tom Steed of Oklahoma told Washington columnist Jack Anderson in July 1973. "They were trying to put the rat on poor old Rowley's back."

Nixon also tried to use the Service to help him stage political theater. More than once, he ordered agents to remove protesters from speeches.

The most dangerous example unfolded on a visit to San Jose on October 29, 1970. Nixon and his staff infuriated agents by trying to provoke demonstrators crowded outside the civic center, where Nixon was giving a speech in support of Republicans, including Governor Ronald Reagan, before the midterm elections.

The agents had learned in the days before the event that White House staff hoped to gin up unflattering photographs of an unruly mob in order to generate public sympathy for Nixon and the Republicans. Larry Newman, an agent working on the advance preparations, listened incredulously in the hotel bar as a White House aide described the plan to bring in "dummy" demonstrators to appear violent and damage property. "If you do that, you're going to get people hurt, and we're going to arrest you," Newman said. "Look, don't even try it."

When Nixon arrived for his 7 P.M. speech, a

crowd of more than a thousand had gathered outside. Most were San Jose State students who had migrated to the civic center after participating in a peaceful antiwar rally nearby. Mixed in were some others picketing the valley's high unemployment rate, as well as some militant activists. There was also a large overflow crowd of people who couldn't get tickets to attend the Nixon speech. This motley crew held signs, chanted, and generally waited for the president to emerge.

A police captain alerted a Secret Service agent coordinating security that he thought he saw Nixon volunteers trying to open doors to let demonstrators inside. The senior agent followed the captain to find White House spokesman Ron Ziegler.

"What the hell are you doing?" the agent said.

"We want a meaningful confrontation," Ziegler said.

"There ain't going to be no fucking meaningful confrontation," a local police captain replied.

The crowd outside remained peaceful but kept up a steady drumbeat. They chanted the standard antiwar slogan: "One, two, three, four, we don't want your fucking war."

After about forty minutes, Nixon exited the civic center with Reagan and a fellow Republican, Senator George Murphy, in tow. But the president didn't immediately leave in his motorcade as scheduled. Instead, his entourage paused for a while in a large rear parking lot that was hemmed in on two sides by demonstrators, mostly behind barricades.

But then, to the shock of the agents and police surrounding him, the president hopped up onto the hood of his limousine with the help of an aide. Nixon lifted both hands to wave a taunting "victory" sign at the crowd.

San Jose police chief Ray Blackmore opened his eyes wide "like he was watching a horror movie," one agent recalled. The chief had been sitting in the lead car, prepared to leave in a hurry. A lead detective coordinating security said he was "startled" by such a daring move, especially in the wake of recent assassinations.

Protesters were also shocked by the gesture. A young protester said he and several around him quickly looked down at the ground for a rock or anything to throw, but "rocks were hard to come by."

Still, police a few feet from Nixon reported some small stones whizzing past them. Nervous Secret Service agents rushed to stuff the president back into his limo, and within a minute the motorcade set off.

"They just hate to see that," Nixon chuckled to an aide as he took his seat.

The president had whipped up the crowd. His Secret Service detail then made a last-minute change in the exit strategy, according to an account that Chief Blackmore shared years later.

Blackmore, riding in the lead car, heard the

Secret Service agent next to him jump on the radio and order the motorcade's motorcycle escort to turn left onto Park Avenue. "No, right," Blackmore said. The plan had been to turn right, where his police officers were posted as a barrier between the avenue and the crowds. "All our strength is to the right."

"We know that," the agent said. "We want to feed the press to the wolves. We're not getting along with them during this trip." The agent told Blackmore that most of the front of the motorcade would have time to escape the protesters by quickly turning left, but the press buses bringing up the rear and left defenseless without a police barrier would be "clobbered."

Later, on the dark tarmac of the airport as they waited to fly to San Clemente, a young aide in a pin-striped shirt took out a sledgehammer and started pounding on the side of the president's limousine.

At least one agent was incredulous.

The aide explained, "We're just trying to show what kind of people these [folks] are."

The agent insisted he stop: "It's a government car. That's destruction of government property."

The young staffer finally stopped pounding.

Nixon leaped to "make some hay" of the event that night, telling Ziegler to issue a statement from his plane about having rocks thrown at his car. "The stoning at San Jose is an example of the viciousness of the lawless elements in our society," it read. "This was the action of an unruly mob that represents the worst in America."

A headline the next day in **The Sacramento Bee** boomed SAN JOSE PROTESTERS STONE NIXON PARTY. Another local headline read MILITANTS ATTACK NIXON MOTORCADE.

Both spectators and reporters at the event scratched their heads at what they considered the overblown reports of danger to the president. The police agreed that the rock throwing got started after Nixon's V-day taunt but built after Nixon's car was exiting. Rocks were of "minor consequence" to the president's car, Blackmore said, but they did pelt the later cars in the motorcade and traveling press bus that shielded the backside of the motorcade.

The White House had gotten what it wanted. "San Jose turned into the real blockbuster," Haldeman said in his recorded diary entry that night. "We wanted some confrontation and there were no hecklers in the hall, so we stalled the departure a little so they could zero in outside and they sure did."

BY THE FALL of 1973, Nixon's White House was imploding. His two most trusted aides, Haldeman and Ehrlichman, had resigned in late April at Nixon's request. Their resignations came after the

White House counsel told Nixon he was cooperating with federal prosecutors, and prosecutors notified the president that Haldeman, Ehrlichman, and other White House officials were implicated in the Watergate break-in and cover-up. The Senate and an independent counsel were making headway in their separate investigations into the White House's ties to the Watergate break-in. A former top aide alleged that Nixon had personally discussed how to cover up the White House's role. Butterfield had revealed a potential treasure trove of evidence that could prove it: a secret tape recording system set up in the Oval Office and West Wing offices, which recorded nearly all of Nixon's calls and conversations. Nixon's presidency hung on those tapes.

The Secret Service's reputation was on the line too. The public didn't yet know how much the White House had manipulated its protective team for its own political ends. But Rowley did, and that fall, the director could see it was about to spill out.

On September 6, **The Washington Post** reported that the Secret Service had agreed to eavesdrop on Nixon's brother, on the president's orders. The wiretap appeared to be illegal, the **Post**'s sources said. Nixon ostensibly wanted to prevent his financially troubled brother from embarrassing him. A day later, the Senate's Watergate Committee sent Rowley a formal request asking him to explain the wiretap and his legal justification for it.

There were other secrets that Rowley knew were

bound to come out as the investigations heated up. A pending lawsuit that named Rowley personally would uncover that Secret Service agents had removed anti-Nixon protesters from public events on White House orders. Internal memos would show how Nixon aides had forced the Secret Service to make taxpayers foot the bill for expensive renovations to his California and Florida homes by claiming that the work was done for "security reasons."

Weeks after the wiretap story, the battle over the White House tapes reached a climax. On the night of October 20, Nixon fired the independent counsel who demanded he comply with a new court order and turn over the White House recordings. The attorney general and deputy attorney general, who had refused to fire the counsel as Nixon ordered, resigned in protest. The papers called it the Saturday Night Massacre.

Two days later, Director Rowley notified colleagues that he was resigning too. He explained it was time; he'd served thirty-five years in the Service, twelve of them as director. Losing President Kennedy had felt like his worst career failure, but he'd been proud of his work with his fellow agents to make the Service stronger in the aftermath of that tragedy.

In private, Rowley acknowledged that he left with some deep regrets. He and some of his trusted deputies had resisted as best they could. But

Rowley's method had been to resist quietly, without raising a ruckus. He hadn't been able to fully stop Nixon from making the Secret Service his tool.

Still, the departing director knew he was leaving the ship in capable hands. Nixon had tapped Stuart Knight, one of his deputies, as the new director. The president knew Knight best as the brave detail agent who had likely saved his life by helping him escape a mob in Venezuela when Nixon was vice president. Rowley knew Knight as a bright and fiercely independent leader. "This appointment is different from the past Nixon track record; he's not a former Nixon advance man," one administration official told a reporter when asked about Knight's appointment. "He's his own man—and he doesn't owe anybody anything."

In Rowley's tenure, Nixon had deployed the Secret Service as if it were another arm of his political operation. He had tried to task Secret Service investigators with gathering facts about Wallace's shooter so the president could blame the assassination attempt on a murderous liberal activist. He had tried in three cases to get agents to spy on his political opponents Ted Kennedy and George McGovern to gather political dirt. Nixon ordered the Secret Service to follow his own brother to help him learn about and control potentially damaging activity that could be used by Nixon's enemies. He had sought to portray anti-Nixon protesters as violent mobs, and he succeeded in getting the

Secret Service to flout their own security rules so he could foment a riot. He had ordered that agents push his protesters off the White House fence line and out of his sight when it annoyed him, despite rules that prohibit agents from doing that. In perhaps his pettiest move, Nixon and his aides stretched the truth to get the Secret Service to pay for renovations at his personal home and claim they were necessary for his security.

Knight pledged to continue and expand Rowley's emphasis on training, and "to close the gap between the actual and the ideal" in the Secret Service. It was polite code for his new task: Clean up the Service's reputation, sullied by the way Nixon had tried to abuse it.

Nevertheless, Knight wouldn't be working for the Nixon White House for very long. Roughly nine months after choosing a new Secret Service director to replace the one he derided as a "dummy," Nixon would leave the White House in disgrace. Ironically, a step the Secret Service took on Nixon's orders early in his first term would play a central role in the president's fall.

AFTER A YEAR in office, Nixon had ordered the Secret Service to set up a unique voice-activated recording system in the White House, Camp David, and other key offices where he conducted business. Haldeman told Butterfield to make the arrangements.

In February 1971, Butterfield approached Al Wong, who headed the Service's technical security division. He knew Wong well because his team regularly swept for electronic bugs in the Oval Office, sensitive meeting rooms, and hotels where the president stayed. When Nixon left on February 12 for a weekend in Key Biscayne, Wong's team installed six inconspicuous microphones in the president's desk in the Oval and four more in lamps on the fireplace mantel in the Cabinet Room. The system recorded sensitive conversations on cassette tapes stored in a bricked-in compartment in the basement.

Wong warned Butterfield that the Service had created similar taping systems for Kennedy and Johnson, and "these things don't always work out as planned."

Nixon had one primary question when he returned that Tuesday and Butterfield briefed him on the taping system. "On this tapes thing," he asked, "who knows about that?"

At least four Secret Service agents and technicians had helped in the installation and knew about it, Butterfield told him.

"Goddamn it," Nixon snapped. "This cannot get out."

The secrecy surrounding the tapes began to unravel just after the July Fourth holiday in 1973, when Nixon's deputy chief of staff, Alexander Butterfield, was summoned to an interview with staff for the Senate Select Committee on Presidential Campaign Activities who were conducting some random pre-interviews with White House staff. Butterfield hoped they wouldn't know—or ask—too much. He thought all was well as the interview wound toward a close. But just when he thought he was going to be excused, the deputy Republican counsel, Donald Sanders, asked why the wording in a report they received was so exact. He noted to Butterfield that it had verbatim quotes from the president and senior aides, from a specific meeting.

"Were there ever any recording devices other than the Dictaphone system you mentioned?" Sanders asked.

Butterfield had decided before walking in the door that he wasn't going to lie to a direct question.

"Yes," he gulped.

In the room, the investigators buzzed with electricity. Butterfield felt panicky as he sensed their excitement. Here was the evidence the Senate investigators needed in order to prove the president's role in the burglary cover-up. One of Nixon's right-hand men had let out the secret the president most wanted to keep locked up tight.

For the next year, Nixon fought hard—all the way to the Supreme Court—to keep from releasing those tapes. Nixon's lawyers argued that these secretly recorded conversations were protected by executive privilege. But nearly a year after Butterfield revealed their existence, on July 24, 1974, the court voted 8–0 to compel the president to turn over the tapes.

Fifteen days later, Richard Nixon, the thirty-seventh president of the United States, resigned.

MEETING THE TEST

FORD TO CLINTON (1974–1999)

CHAPTER 7

A CASUAL WALK TO CHURCH

"Hi, Bobby. I think you better come on over. We're going to go to St. John's in about twenty minutes."

President Reagan's deputy chief of staff, Mike Deaver, was calling the ranking Secret Service supervisor on the White House compound that Sunday with an abrupt change of plans. The new president and his wife wanted to go to church across the square from the White House front gate. Both Reagans were eager to stretch their legs, breathe some fresh air. They wanted to walk.

It was just before 11 A.M. on March 29, 1981—and Bob DeProspero was in charge of the president's watch. Ronald Reagan had been inaugurated just two months earlier, and DeProspero had been named the second in command of his detail. Either DeProspero or the head of the detail, Jerry Parr, had to be on the White House grounds at all times in case the president wanted to leave the presidential cocoon.

DeProspero was surprised to hear this talk of a walk to church and wrinkled up his nose. The senior agent, better known as Bobby D, had earned a reputation as a rigid boss who didn't like shortcuts or surprises. A former wrestling coach, he demanded that his agents maintain a constant intensity in the face of exhaustion and boredom. "Never let up" was one of his favorite mantras.

Since Reagan's election, Bobby D had several times reviewed the ground rules with Deaver. The Service didn't take presidents on impromptu trips off the complex. The detail needed at least an hour's heads-up. Now DeProspero, sitting at his office in the Old Executive Office Building, exhaled deeply into the black telephone receiver.

"Mike, I thought we agreed you were going to give me tiiiime," DeProspero said in a mild Southern accent that stretched out the vowel sound.

"I know, I know, I can't help it. They just decided to go," Deaver said hurriedly, mild irritation in his voice. Deaver had served as one of Reagan's closest aides from his time as governor, and part of his job was burnishing Reagan's image.

"Let me get the cars up here at least," DeProspero said.

"No. We're going to walk," Deaver replied.

DeProspero paused before politely laying down the law.

"So, Miiiike," he said slowly, in a controlled, almost pedantic tone that brought out his Southern accent even more. "You can't **do** that."

Deaver cut him off and gave the final order instead.

"Bobby, I suggest you get over here," he said. "Because we're going to be leaving shortly."

With that, the White House deputy chief of staff hung up.

DeProspero had to dash. The president of the United States was about to walk across a public park and down Pennsylvania Avenue with absolutely no security plan in place. The detail supervisor put down the receiver, jumped up from his desk chair, and jogged down the hall toward the West Wing.

He talked into the radio microphone in his sleeve the whole way. He alerted his shift in W-16, a ready room under the Oval Office that agents used as a base, to get themselves and the limo motorcade ready. POTUS was on the move.

DeProspero still hoped he would arrive in time to undo Deaver's plan. He dashed through the Executive Office Building courtyard to a basement-level ramp that emptied onto West Executive Avenue, rapidly rolling around in his mind ways he could stop this jaunt. As he trotted through the West Wing lobby, he found the newly minted President Reagan and the First Lady outside the Oval Office in their coats, ready for their walk.

The Secret Service man saw them and felt stuck. They were going.

As their small entourage walked together out the Northwest Gate, DeProspero flanked the president on his right side, just behind his shoulder. He confirmed on the radio line through his sleeve that his agents would bring the limo and follow-up car to the church. No matter what Deaver said, Bobby D was putting the president behind bulletproof glass and armored doors for the return trip to the White House.

Eight agents from the shift had made the mad dash to gather their gear for the walk. They fell into formation and created an amoeba-shaped barrier around Rawhide and Rainbow—the Reagans' code names. Crossing Pennsylvania Avenue and then entering Lafayette Park, the Reagans beamed, delighted for any chance to be **outside** again. Nancy Reagan had been floored by her inability, since the election, to simply go for a walk or meet friends for dinner. Now she was inhaling the chill spring air and taking in the park's budding magnolia trees. The president waved with a wink when a few shocked pedestrians recognized the famous couple out for a stroll.

Deaver walked close behind the Reagans, too. For most of the six-minute walk, DeProspero and Deaver bickered in a low whisper. They resembled two married people who hadn't finished a spat before arriving at a party.

"Mike, you cannot do this," DeProspero said, trying to keep his tone calm but feeling the heat in his face. "Had I had time to talk with the president, I would have told him this was not okay."

Deaver, the man in charge of burnishing Reagan's public image, shot back that the Secret Service rules were overbearing, even ridiculous. The president wanted and needed to be seen out in public, he said.

"Mike, I'm telling you—" DeProspero started.

Deaver cut him off. And this time the White House adviser got loud.

"Bob, are you telling me the president of the United States can't walk down Pennsylvania Avenue?" Deaver asked. "Are you telling me he's not safe to even walk down a city street?"

The agent shot back just as loudly.

"That's **exactly** what I'm telling you, Mike!" DeProspero boomed.

At that, the aforementioned president of the United States swung his head around.

"What are you guys arguing about?" Reagan asked, frowning.

Deaver waved his hand to signal this was a trifling matter.

"Oh, it's okay, Mr. President," Deaver said. "It's nothing to worry about."

DeProspero fumed. He didn't care how unpopular he was with agents and White House staff. He knew his constant emphasis on risk made others see him as the agent who cried wolf. He knew he was right, but he wasn't going to rile the president. He bit his tongue for now. He would deal with this later.

In about twenty-four hours, this conversation would haunt both men. Deaver would cringe at his words and soon become DeProspero's biggest backer.

For now their bickering had been silenced. The Reagans walked into the church and took seats in the back.

At the same time, about ten city blocks away, a twenty-five-year-old drifter suffering from schizophrenic delusions stepped off the bus at the city's Greyhound terminal. His affluent parents, on the advice of a therapist, had told their son to leave their home and get his life together. He ordered a Whopper at the bus station's Burger King counter and studied his map of downtown Washington. He had come on a mission.

He knew he could win the heart of a famous young actress. All he had to do was shoot and kill the president of the United States.

IN THE SEVEN years between the end of Richard Nixon's reign and the start of Ronald Reagan's, the Secret Service experienced a much-needed season of rebound and recovery. It had suffered some bruising years with Nixon in the White House. But after Nixon resigned in August 1974, Secret Service director Stu Knight finally had the room to focus on what had been his goal since he took the job: professionalizing the Service.

No longer would the mission of the Service have to compete with the distraction of an embattled president who sought to make agents his political henchmen. A gentle and humble new president, Gerald Ford, eschewed the trappings of power and fame, stunning his detail agents by his family's down-to-earth life that resembled their own. He invited agents to share a drink or a sandwich with him, and he wanted little from the Secret Service except to understand their security instructions.

At the time that Ford replaced Nixon, however, a cauldron of tensions within the Service was about to boil over. The Nixon years had divided the ranks and emboldened Nixon detail agents to form a secretive ring about the president and adopt his model of distrust and arrogance with outsiders. Crossing paths on the job, the Presidential Protective Division agents had sniffed at their own brother agents as inferior interlopers who should be kept at bay. Nixon shift leaders treated the White House as their turf and demanded that other "lowly" agents explain what business had brought them to the complex, when the reason was obvious: They were doing their jobs on their own detail assignments, either protecting Vice President Ford or Secretary of State Henry Kissinger.

The evening that Nixon announced he was

resigning, Ford's agents stayed overnight with the vice president at his modest brick home on Quaker Lane in Alexandria—camped out in the basement while nearly ten thousand people paraded on nearby streets to celebrate Nixon's departure. In about twelve more hours, on August 9, Ford would become president and Ford's agents would lose their role protecting him. According to tradition, the experienced presidential detail agents who had shielded Nixon would take over, replacing most of the Ford detail agents that they had treated like dirt for years.

The morning of August 9, the presidential and vice presidential details both arrived to work at the White House, each staring the other down. There was no more acrimonious handoff in Secret Service history. "The next morning PPD shows up . . . and you could cut the tension with a knife," recalled Joseph Petro, a member of Vice President Ford's detail at the time. "They start bossing everybody around and being prima donnas."

Starting at about 9 A.M., Nixon gave a pained farewell speech to his aides, cabinet members, and staff gathered in the East Room. With his family standing behind him, Nixon thanked his staff for their "great heart" and sacrifice, tears welling in his eyes and his voice breaking at times. A few secretaries sniffled. He departed by helicopter from the South Lawn. A few minutes after noon, in the same room, Ford was sworn in as the thirty-eighth president.

Ford, a no-drama Midwesterner, spoke briefly in a televised address in which he acknowledged that the American public had not elected him to office and promised to put them above any political affiliation. "My fellow Americans," he declared, "our long national nightmare is over. . . . Our Constitution works; our great Republic is a government of laws and not of men. Here the people rule."

Dick Keiser, who had been the special agent in charge of presidential protection for Nixon for just a year and now would be the point man responsible for Ford, struggled to absorb and juggle all the emotions he felt. "My personal mood was very emotional," Keiser recalled. "It's amazing what happened that day. I felt what you were seeing was one man's life and career crashing, and another man's life and career changing completely, beyond perhaps what he even imagined. But for me, it's just—you've got to keep them safe."

After his speech, Ford headed to meet privately with his cabinet. But raw emotions and tensions were still rising among his protective agents. One floor down, under the Hall of States, the whip in charge of the new president's detail began barking orders at the outgoing Ford team, trying to show who was boss now. The other shift leader—who was relinquishing the duties of protecting Vice President Ford—shouted back. The two began spit-cursing in each other's faces. Agents standing nearby feared one of these top-ranked detail leaders would throw a punch, and a hockey-team-style brawl would ensue on this first day of Ford's presidency. But the crisis was averted. A few agents pulled them apart.

Trying to restore the Service's esprit de corps, President Ford himself stepped in a day later. He got wind of the tension and offered that any of his vice presidential detail agents who wanted to could join his new presidential detail. Only one agent took him up on the offer that day—the hatred between the two teams was that raw at the time. But the gesture set a new tone, and the tensions gradually subsided.

With Ford's emphasis on restoring the public's faith in government, Knight had a president who left the Secret Service alone to do its job. Ford's approach also helped Knight revive the Service's professional standing as an apolitical force that protected the democracy and not merely one man. This period also gave Knight the room to reassess whether the Service needed to rethink its methods of securing the president. In the wake of the Wallace shooting, Knight encouraged the agency to test new security formations and implement the best ones. He urged more focus on electronic intelligence gathering on threats, a powerful new tool that was in its infancy under Director Rowley. Knight also pushed to make the Service much more than a phalanx of interchangeable bodyguards. Energized by his own earlier experience at an executive training fellowship at Princeton University, Knight broke long-standing Secret Service tradition and hired agents who weren't exclusively former cops and servicemen, but also people with experience in private sector management and accounting. In the late 1970s, Knight surprised Secret Service veterans by taking the radical step of inviting an outsider to conduct in-depth, classified interviews with agents. He commissioned a noted psychologist, Frank Ochberg, to conduct a yearlong study to pinpoint the sources of agents' stress and examine whether their jobs increased alcohol abuse and divorce rates.

The years between Nixon and Reagan were also marked by a brief spate of incidents that set the Secret Service on edge. They experienced close calls that rekindled the nightmarish days after Jack Kennedy's last limo ride in Dallas. September 1975 brought the Secret Service two separate and harrowing attempts on President Ford's life—just three weeks apart.

On the morning of September 5, 1975, President Ford had woken in his suite at the Italianate Senator Hotel in Sacramento. He was scheduled to address the California state legislature that morning. The white-domed state capitol was steps away. His subject: curbing violent crime.

"So, we arrived the night before and stayed in a hotel right by the park in view of the capitol building," recalled Larry Buendorf, then a supervisor on Ford's detail. "That's why, when he got up and saw such a beautiful morning, he decided to walk instead of ride" in his motorcade.

Buendorf was walking immediately behind Ford as the president and his team headed for the hotel front door and the short walk in the city park along a sidewalk that led to the capitol. Buendorf, known to friends as Boonie, was a lanky man in his forties with a tousle of dirty-blond hair that curled around the corners of his hip silver-framed reflective sunglasses. He was admired on the detail for his ability to keep his sense of humor after a grueling day—and for his flawless skiing. His prowess enabled him to lead the president's "ski team." It meant he spent many hours at Christmastime and during the spring season skiing in Vail alongside Ford, who was an avid skier himself and had a vacation home in the Colorado resort town. Today would be far less glamorous than the slopes. He just had to make sure Ford got through the teeming, sweaty crowds without trouble.

But once they exited the hotel's front doors, Buendorf saw a chaotic scene. A throng of people had gathered on the park side of the street outside the hotel, along with local media camera crews craning for the right shot. Ford didn't wait; he immediately went for the outstretched arms of all those California voters. The lead agents in front of the president had rushed ahead to clear a path; they herded people to the edge of the walkway to the capitol so Ford could safely pass.

A sprite of a woman—115-pound, twenty-six-year-old, auburn-haired Lynette Fromme—was standing in the throng gathered outside. With a tiny voice to match her frame, she had been nicknamed Squeaky. One of the earliest and most devoted followers of Charles Manson's violent "family" cult, she had come that day for a different purpose than waving at the president. She stood on the park path outside the Senator Hotel with hopes of delivering a message to politicians who weren't stopping the pollution that was killing animals and plants. She wore a ruby-red cape with the hood over her head, and a .45 caliber pistol in a holster strapped to her ankle.

On this sunny, warm day in California, Buendorf saw the standard mass of smiling, eager faces jostling haphazardly on the edges of the concrete walk. He had to be alert for anything, though most of the time he just needed to be sure no one grabbed Ford's watch or held on to his hand too long. After walking for just a hundred feet with the president, though, the detail supervisor spotted something out of place: a hunk of metal in two hands, coming up from knee level, just three feet from Ford.

"So I'm looking down. Squeaky was back in the crowd, maybe one person back, and she had an ankle holster on with a forty-five," Buendorf recalled. "That's a big gun to have on your ankle. So, when it came up, it came up low and I happened to be looking in that direction. I see it coming and I step in front of him, not sure what it was other than that it was coming up pretty fast."

"Gun!" Buendorf yelled, knowing he had to give the detail the critical trigger word.

At the same moment he yelled, Buendorf put his hand on the barrel of the gun. On the other end was Fromme, a tiny woman with a red hood. Fromme was at that moment pulling back on the gun's slide to chamber the first round. Buendorf's finger blocked the slide, keeping her from being able to get a round in place.

At the word "gun," the president and Buendorf's fellow detail agents were gone. They had surrounded Ford and hustled him through the park, knocking into a few spectators in their hurry. That left Buendorf, a two-hundred-pound former naval officer, wrestling with a tiny young woman. Fromme was screaming, and so was the panicked crowd.

Buendorf's mind raced with thoughts, all compressed into seconds:

I don't have my vest on.

She's probably not alone.

Where is the next shot coming from?

Fromme was still screaming, and she wriggled to turn away from the agent. Buendorf pulled her arm behind her back and dropped her to the ground.

"It didn't go off!" she complained. "It didn't go off!"

Buendorf helped cuff Fromme, then handed her over to the police and took off running across the park. The detail was already short one member that day, so Buendorf quickly fell back into formation to help shield Ford on the rest of his visit.

Inside the capitol, Ford acted as though nothing had happened. He didn't even mention the scuffle when he met with Governor Jerry Brown just before addressing the legislature.

"Well, I really didn't think it'd be very polite to say someone tried to shoot me outside your capitol," Ford said when asked about it.

But later, after FBI agents finished interviewing Buendorf, Ford took the agent aside for a private moment to thank him. His bosses and the director praised him for his quick reaction.

"He was heroic," said Buendorf's friend Joseph Petro. "He grabbed the weapon from Squeaky Fromme. . . . Otherwise the gun would have gone off. I mean that's how fast these things are."

But the agent, whose only injury was a bloody finger, didn't think he had done anything special. Buendorf used his training to react quickly. He often mused about the what-ifs. If someone else had gotten his attention in that moment, he said, he and the president might both be dead. "If she'd had a round chambered, I couldn't have been there in time," he said. "It would've gone through me and the president.

"It's the right place at the right time," he said. "I mean, you go and look back at the Kennedy assassination, and is there guilt with a lot of those agents?

Yeah, I think so, because they weren't in the right place at the right time. They reacted after the fact."

Just seventeen days later, on September 22, it nearly happened again. Ford was visiting Northern California for a weekend of public events. On that Monday afternoon, he entered the downtown St. Francis Hotel to give a speech to the World Affairs Council. Outside, amid the crowd of onlookers, waited a forty-five-year-old mother of five who kept the books for a maintenance firm but was obsessed with Patty Hearst and the idea of being a figure in the radical underground. She had been an FBI informant, but the bureau cut off the relationship when she blew her own cover in a newspaper interview. Still, she offered local police tips for money.

Secret Service agents had interviewed Sara Jane Moore late the night before because San Francisco police alerted them they were worried she might be a risk. She told a police investigator that she was going to take a gun to a Stanford event Ford was attending and "test the system." Police took away her gun that night, and the agents who interviewed her concluded she was telling the truth when she said she was just mouthing off and had no intention of hurting Ford.

But Moore took the seizure of her gun as a police effort to control her life. Early Monday morning, she called the Secret Service office in San Francisco twice—hoping to talk to the agents who interviewed her—but there was no answer. Instead, she called a gun dealer she knew about buying a used .38, rushed over at about eleven o'clock, and paid with a $145 check. Then she headed to the St. Francis hotel and joined the crowd waiting to see Ford. As the president exited around 3:30 P.M., he wondered if he should go shake hands and paused a minute before stepping toward the door of his limousine. From forty feet away across the street, Moore pointed her pistol at him and fired.

Moore didn't know it, but the gun's sight was off, and her shot missed Ford's head by several inches.

A disabled Marine and Vietnam veteran, Oliver Sipple, was steps from Moore. He heard the shot and immediately grabbed for her gun. He pushed Moore's arm and stopped her from making a second attempt. Ford's detail agents had stood frozen for a few seconds while Ford ducked behind the car. One agent then flung open the limousine's rear door, and another pushed the president headfirst inside so they could speed away. A local police officer pulled the gun from Moore's hand while another Secret Service agent grabbed her.

In both cases, the special agent in charge of Ford's detail, Dick Keiser, had not accompanied the president on the trip. Some superstitious agents mused about the absence. Was the president taunting fate without the head of his detail by his side? "I felt very bad I was not there," Keiser recalled. "The Secret Service—nobody ever understood that—to this day. Why President Ford? He was the good guy, he was vanilla ice cream, an Eagle Scout, going to make us feel better about ourselves."

On Director Knight's orders, the Service tightened up its rules on presidential access. For most of the president's future trips, agents were supposed to keep large unscreened crowds at least fifty feet from the president. In studying tapes of the shooting outside the hotel in San Francisco, supervisors were disturbed at the delay in getting Ford to the safety of his car. From then on, agents were required to have the limo door open and waiting as the president approached.

Keiser remained detail leader when President Carter was elected just two years later. Carter's presidency was an awkward time for the Service. Agents lamented that Carter lacked the warm personality of Ford and was even dismissive of the Service. Uniformed officers and agents at the White House were instructed that Carter preferred that they keep at a distance and not speak to him unless necessary. When Ronald Reagan foiled Carter's reelection plans, Democrats mourned the country's decision to put a conservative movie star in charge of the White House. But many Secret Service agents openly acknowledged they had voted for Reagan and cheered the election of this new Boss as a welcome change.

Though the Service investigated hundreds of people who made threats against Carter, no one plot or attacker posed a critical danger to the president. The greatest risk of assassination Carter ever faced came in the form of an odd man no one noticed. He would remain unknown to the Secret Service until Carter had left office.

AFTER PRESIDENT REAGAN'S momentous walk to church on Sunday, the rest of the shift had been quiet. Early on Monday morning, Jerry Parr rose before daybreak and laced up for a quick two-mile jog in the cold drizzle around his leafy Montgomery County subdivision. The fifty-year-old special agent in charge of the president's detail didn't love running, but he did appreciate the way it cleared his head. Sure enough, a thought occurred to him while he ran: He needed to change his plans for the day, get out from behind his paperwork and spend some time alongside the new president.

Parr, a former power company lineman and Air Force veteran, had joined the Secret Service later in life than most, at age thirty-one. But his excitement about the career had been kindled at a very young age. As a kid growing up poor in Depression-era Miami, Parr got a special treat when his out-of-work dad took him to see the new B movie **Code of the Secret Service**. Parr was mesmerized by the central character, agent Brass Bancroft, a brave, dashing crime fighter who trotted the globe to chase down counterfeiters.

A young actor named Ronald Reagan played the agent. Now, four decades later, the oddest of career trajectories had brought them together. That actor was a seventy-year-old politician and the new president of the United States. Parr was the fifty-year-old special agent in charge of the president's security detail.

Parr had headed up President Carter's detail as Carter sought reelection in 1980. He assumed that same job when Reagan defeated the president. But in Reagan's first two months in office, Parr had spent most of his time at the Federal Executive Institute, a prestigious fellowship program for senior government leaders in Charlottesville. Parr was anxious about the time he'd missed and felt he needed to get up to speed. He wanted to learn the new Boss's rhythms and build a rapport.

Parr found Johnny Guy, one of the detail supervisors who worked for him, as he arrived at W-16 that Monday morning. Parr asked Guy if he could take his place alongside the president on the short hop to the Washington Hilton hotel. Reagan was giving a speech to a labor union that afternoon. Guy quickly agreed.

Parr saw the Hilton stop as pretty routine, and low risk. The Service had taken presidents and vice presidents to the Hilton nearly once a month for the last few years. Parr decided bullet-proof vests weren't necessary for the president or his detail. The weather was wet and muggy, so not having to wear another layer was a relief.

Routine as it was, Secret Service agent Bill Green had nevertheless spent five days mapping out a detailed security plan prior to the outing. Green, the advance agent for the visit, had made sure protective research agents ran background checks on everyone who would meet the president or come close to him. Green's team had inspected every part of the hotel, from the garbage bay to the basement, for hidden threats. They had mapped out every step Reagan would take: from the VIP entrance to the elevator to the holding room to the stage and back.

This "routine" visit would require the teamwork of sixty-seven agents. Together they would create rings of human, metal, and technological barriers to shield "the Man." More than two dozen more would stake out positions in the ballroom, rooftop, hallways, entrance, and perimeter. Many more would help search for explosives with bomb-sniffing dogs, run background checks on guests and hotel workers, monitor crowds outside, and help clear streets for the motorcade. Green had visited the site during all five days of planning and done a walk-through the morning of the visit.

The White House advance man, Rick Ahearn, hoped to have the traveling press at the front of the ballroom, but the union complained that the cameras would block their own members' view and asked to have them pushed back. Some enterprising cameramen from the three big local television stations, however, ended up finding a much closer spot to get a good close-up of the new president.

They staged themselves outside the Hilton, just fifteen feet from the back of Reagan's limousine, in a viewing area the public could reach without being screened by agents.

After the two attempts on President Ford's life in California, the Secret Service usually kept spectators at least fifty feet back from the president. But that rule was typically applied for out-of-town trips. Here at home, a handful of gawkers clustered behind the cameramen, eager for a closer look.

A blond-haired college dropout joined them as the photographers were setting up their gear, looking for a good camera angle. He nervously paced and fidgeted every now and again with his pants pocket.

"Coming out," agent Bill Green radioed at about 2:20 P.M. He was alerting the agents and motorcade outside to get ready for the president to emerge.

Reagan had finished a fairly uninspiring speech to a fairly unexcited audience. The Building Trades Union was deeply concerned about Reagan's pro-business policies, but nevertheless they offered polite applause as he ended his speech. Three minutes after Reagan waved goodbye, the president's detail shepherded him across the length of the expansive hotel into a holding room until the traveling press could get in position to film his departure. Then he rode in the VIP elevator to the ground-floor VIP exit along T Street.

As Reagan emerged onto the downward-sloping

hotel sidewalk, four agents formed the standard "diamond" around the president, a security formation that they had used for 360-degree protection with more regularity since the Wallace shooting in 1972. Barrel-chested agent Tim McCarthy took the point position in front. Parr and fellow supervisor Ray Shaddick stood less than two feet behind Reagan. With his right hand, Reagan waved to a crowd of spectators on the other side of T Street, opposite the hotel.

The president now stood just twenty-five steps from the open door of his limousine. Parr expected he'd have the Man safely back inside the West Wing within ten minutes.

"Mr. President, President Reagan," a woman called out in a singsong voice from the Hilton driveway area where some local cameramen, press, and random passersby had gathered.

The president paused for a second, turned his head toward the woman's voice, and good-naturedly smiled. The local cameramen from all three major news networks had their cameras running. They had waited patiently here for an hour in hopes of some good tape. Now Reagan was looking directly at them, just steps away.

Deaver walked briskly in front of the president to field any press questions. Reagan lifted his left hand to wave a polite goodbye to the woman's voice and the cameras. He was six feet from his armored car.

Then came a crackling sound that stung Parr's ears: **Pop! Pop!**

Crouched in a combat position next to one of the cameramen, the troubled drifter from the Greyhound station, John W. Hinckley, Jr., had pulled the trigger. There were two gunshots in quick succession. Reagan grimaced, turning left toward the jarring noise.

For nearly nineteen years, Parr had repeatedly rehearsed what to do the second he heard gunfire so that his response would be automatic. His training was partly a credit to Director Rowley, who wanted every agent after President Kennedy to be prepared for any threat. Agents of Parr's era practiced a series of drills known as AOP—attack on the principal—training them to respond in seconds to several kinds of danger.

Now, after all those years, the moment had finally arrived, and Parr's training immediately kicked in. Instinctively he knew he had to cover the president and evacuate. Those were the orders the Service had imprinted in the skull of every protective agent.

Parr didn't have any time to think, or even time to look up. He didn't actually see that the first two bullets had already dropped two men on the sidewalk. Spokesman Jim Brady was hit in the forehead; Metropolitan Police officer Thomas Delahanty was shot in the neck.

Parr simply sprang into action. He clamped his left hand down on the president's shoulder, bending his torso forward while shoving his entire body toward the limo's backseat. Under Parr's power, the two men sailed behind the protective shield of McCarthy's body and the limo door he had been holding open.

Reagan's chest slammed down onto the transmission riser on the limo's backseat floor, with Parr's 185 pounds landing on his back. Shaddick grabbed at the detail leader's feet, now hanging akimbo out the door, and folded them up into the car. He slammed the door closed behind both the president and his boss.

While Parr and Shaddick were instinctively shoving Reagan into his armored car, John Hinckley shot four more bullets in the president's direction. McCarthy had turned to face the sound of gunfire coming from the red velvet rope area to the rear of the limo. He extended his body and arms wide at the edge of the limo car door. The beefy redhead, wearing a new powder-blue suit, had been a walk-on for the University of Illinois' Fighting Illini football team. Now he struck a defensive pose rarely seen on a football field. He heaved himself up to make his body fill the largest space possible. McCarthy, trained from years of AOP drills, was blocking bullets meant for the president.

The third shot hit McCarthy in the right side of his midsection, just as Shaddick was slamming the limo door closed behind Parr and the president. The impact lifted McCarthy briefly off his feet and twirled his two-hundred-pound frame backward and counterclockwise, like a top.

Two more shots—the fourth and fifth—hit the limo, code-named Stagecoach. The last bullet, the sixth, sailed over the motorcade and hit the building across T Street.

Inside the limo, Reagan groaned on the floor. Parr yelled to Drew Unrue, the agent driver who had been waiting in the driver's seat, "Get **out** of here! Go, go go!"

Agent Unrue had his foot ready to hit the gas, but he had a gruesome feeling as he pulled out of the drive. Through the passenger window, he had watched his friend McCarthy spin and drop amid the gunfire. Unrue couldn't tell for sure if McCarthy's legs or arms were lying somewhere in the two-ton limo's getaway path out of the Hilton driveway.

God, don't let me run over Timmy, Unrue silently prayed. **I hope I don't run over Timmy.**

Dennis McCarthy, a senior agent in charge of surveilling the crowd that day, leaped over spectators to tackle the shooter. It took the agent just seconds to get to Hinckley. But it had taken the nervous amateur only two seconds to fire six shots.

"Motherfucker!" McCarthy's junior partner, Danny Spriggs, yelled. With his gun drawn, Spriggs bolted over to help McCarthy restrain the shooter.

"Get him out!" Spriggs yelled at the spectators and staff, trying desperately to get the crowd to clear a path for the limo. "Get him out, get him out of here!"

As Stagecoach sped off, Parr pulled himself off the floor and saw a golf-ball-sized cluster of feathery cracks in the glass of the limo's passenger window. A bullet—the fourth one Hinckley fired—had been stopped by the bulletproof glass. Parr helped Reagan up onto the backseat of the limousine. He checked his shirt. No blood. He ran his hands inside his coat, feeling for an injury or moisture. Nothing.

Parr, realizing his radio had fallen off his belt, grabbed Unrue's radio from the front dashboard of the car. "Rawhide is okay, Follow-up," he told Shaddick, who was riding in the car immediately behind the limo. "Rawhide is okay."

"You wanna go to the hospital or back to the White House?" Shaddick radioed back.

"We're going to Crown," Parr said, using the code name for the White House.

But as soon as he turned back to his seatmate, Reagan grumbled in pain. He was pale and told Parr his chest had been really hurting ever since Parr landed on his back.

"I think you broke my rib," Reagan said, his voice rough and wheezy. "I'm having trouble breathing."

"Is it your heart?" Parr asked.

Reagan shook his head, coughing. He retrieved a white Hilton paper napkin from his pocket and dabbed at his lips. When the president pulled the napkin away, Reagan looked down to see spots of bright pink blood.

Parr had taken a "ten-minute medicine" training, which was modeled on military courses to diagnose injuries in the battlefield. The frothy bright color suggested to Parr that the blood was full of oxygen, fresh from the lung.

Parr's mind raced. Reagan was hurt. But how?

"MR. D, YOU gotta get down here," a rattled young agent said on the phone. "There were shots fired at the Hilton."

Just before 2:30 on Monday afternoon, DeProspero had been sitting in his first-floor office checking some of his advance agents' security plans for the president's upcoming events. But he was interrupted by the anxious duty agent calling from W-16.

DeProspero again jogged through the EOB to the West Wing, his jacket flapping behind him. It was the second time he'd done that in two days. As he entered W-16, he heard Shaddick's voice announcing over the radio that the president was departing the Hilton.

"Back to the White House. Back to the White House. Rawhide is okay," Shaddick said over the detail's frequency.

DeProspero radioed Shaddick, looking for more information. Agents were reporting the

White House military aide, Lt. Col. Louis Muratti, who was supposed to be at the president's side at all times in case of a nuclear threat, had somehow gotten separated from Reagan amid the confusion.

"Halfback, Crown," DeProspero said. "We have Muratti requesting a status report on Rawhide."

"Tell him to stay off the air for now," Shaddick said quickly. "Rawhide's all right."

"Thank you very much," the ever-polite DeProspero replied.

But Parr's deputy, DeProspero, did not feel reassured. He heard Shaddick's rush of words saying everything was all right, but his clipped tone suggested the opposite. DeProspero locked eyes with George Opfer, Mrs. Reagan's detail agent. He had stood up from his chair to listen to the jittery radio traffic. DeProspero told him to quickly find the First Lady in the residence, and without frightening her, explain there had been a shooting at the Hilton. Opfer bounded out the door.

A minute later, a radio call from the agent driving the president's limousine confirmed DeProspero's suspicion. "We want to go to the emergency room of George Washington," Unrue said over the radio, then paused.

"Go to George Washington fast."

DeProspero could hear his boss Jerry Parr's voice next.

"Get an ambulance, I mean get the, um, stretcher

out there," the detail leader added from the backseat of the limousine. "Let's hustle."

President Reagan has surely been shot, DeProspero thought. He wasn't going to wait for confirmation, though, or take time to get his car from the Ellipse. He exited through the Northwest Gate, turned west on Pennsylvania Avenue, and walked briskly toward George Washington University Hospital six blocks away.

WHEN OPFER ARRIVED at the quiet Solarium on the third floor of the First Family's residence, he gulped and told the First Lady a little white lie. He hoped it would work for a little while.

The lanky blond New Yorker was trying to keep from sounding breathless, since he had dashed from the command post up four flights of stairs to get there. On the way, he heard in his earpiece that Parr was changing course and taking Reagan to the hospital. Not a good sign. Opfer found the First Lady as she chatted with her decorator and the White House usher in the casual sunroom.

Opfer was fairly sure the president had been shot, but he didn't want to alarm Mrs. Reagan without concrete information. He motioned to her to come over to him. She was immediately on guard. Agents rarely entered the residence.

Forcing himself to speak slowly, Opfer told her that there had been a shooting at the Hilton as the president left after his speech. "Some people were wounded, but your husband wasn't hit," he said. "Everybody's at the hospital."

"It's best if you stay here. It's a madhouse over there," he added.

"Why would they be taking him to the hospital if he wasn't injured?" she asked, her eyebrows arching.

"Maybe he's insisting on seeing the condition of the other people who were wounded," Opfer offered.

Mrs. Reagan wasn't buying that. She walked past Opfer straight to the elevator. He urged her to stay. She threatened to walk to the hospital herself if her detail leader didn't take her there immediately. Opfer folded. On the ride over in their two-sedan motorcade, they hit traffic a block or so from the hospital. The First Lady reached over Opfer's seat-back and gripped his shoulders. "George, if this traffic doesn't open up, I'm going to run the rest of the way," she told him.

"No, no, you can't do that," Opfer said. He was glad he had thought to automatically lock the rear doors before they left.

While Mrs. Reagan was en route to the hospital, Parr and DeProspero worked to make sure agents set up a secure perimeter around the building. They weren't sure whether the Hilton shooting was part of a larger plot, and whether more attacks might be coming. They also needed to keep onlookers and random hospital personnel at a distance, not hanging out in the halls to catch a glimpse of the new celebrity patient.

In Trauma Room 5, several doctors rushed in to assess the president, who had collapsed into agents' arms after walking in the emergency room entrance. They thought he might have had a heart attack. Parr felt sick when he heard one nurse say she couldn't get a pulse reading. The unconscious patient's blood pressure was dangerously low. A thought flashed through his mind: **This must be how JFK's agents felt at Parkland Memorial.**

Then nurses cut Reagan's blue suit from his frame with big utility shears. George Washington's trauma surgeon, Joseph Giordano, scanned the president's chest. Aided by a surgical intern who had seen plenty of bullet wounds in Vietnam, they found the bullet's well-concealed entry point under Reagan's left arm. It was a tiny slit. They couldn't see the bullet yet, but they could tell it had been flattened. It must have ricocheted off something hard. They were lucky they figured it out as soon as they did.

STANDING IN THE trauma bay, Deputy Chief of Staff Mike Deaver helped relay the early, chaotic reports from GW to the White House. He had absorbed a painful lesson: Two seconds of gunfire could ring out on any downtown Washington street and wreak havoc.

Within minutes of his arrival, Deaver had called Chief of Staff Jim Baker and deputy Ed Meese to report what had happened at the Hilton. He told them White House spokesman Jim Brady and a Secret Service agent had been hit by the shooter's gunfire. Luckily, he said, the president sustained only a bruised rib.

But then one of Reagan's doctors emerged into the trauma bay with news. In five minutes, Deaver got back on the open White House line with a far grimmer report. "It looks like the president has been nicked," he said. Reagan was also losing blood rather rapidly, he added.

As Deaver held the receiver, a team wheeled through the trauma bay with a stretcher carrying Jim Brady. He sighed a bit seeing his grossly swollen head. "He's in very bad shape," Deaver explained.

Deaver urged Baker and Meese to go find Mrs. Reagan in the residence and persuade her not to come to the hospital. Too much blood, Deaver said, too much chaos. They agreed and sent someone to the residence. They didn't realize that the First Lady had already left.

Less than ten minutes later, Deaver was shocked to see Mrs. Reagan, in her red raincoat, bursting into the trauma bay. Special Agent Opfer trailed behind.

"He's been hit," Deaver told Mrs. Reagan.

"But they told me he **wasn't** hit," she said.

"Well, he was. But they say it's not serious," he said.

"Where?" she demanded. "Where was he hit?"

"They don't know. They're looking for the bullet now."

Mrs. Reagan had heard enough. "I've got to see him!" she said.

Deaver was afraid of precisely what she might see. The First Lady didn't know it, but her husband had lost consciousness and was losing blood quickly, and doctors weren't entirely sure how to stop it.

Deaver told her he needed to check with the doctors first. He needed a place to park her for a few minutes. The deputy found a small hospital office and a familiar, fatherly face that he knew could provide her some comfort: John Simpson of the Secret Service.

JOHN SIMPSON, ONE of the two Secret Service agents with the closest bonds to President Reagan, had arrived at the hospital with a high-speed police escort. Simpson was the assistant director over all protective operations, and he had been getting a physical that day at Bethesda Naval Hospital. He didn't hear about the shooting, because the radio in his car wasn't working. The Secret Service sent out an alert to local police asking them to track down Simpson's car using his license plate numbers, stat. A trooper with flashing lights pulled him over on Rockville Pike.

"Sir, they need you right away," he said. "The

president's been shot." With that, they hightailed it to George Washington University Hospital.

Reagan wasn't just any protective assignment to Simpson. The Boston native had forged a special bond with the First Couple, dating back to when Reagan had first campaigned for the White House in 1968 and Simpson headed his detail. Simpson was short, with a compact, athletic build. His feathery white hair added to his general aura of gravitas. He had mentored many of the agents in the Service, who looked up to him for modeling quiet strength and personal integrity. He wasn't a puritan, but he frowned on agents who drank heavily and chased women. Simpson was the former head of President Carter's detail and had hand-picked many of the agents leading the protection team for the Reagans, including DeProspero and Opfer.

When he arrived at the hospital, Simpson first tracked down Parr to learn more about what happened at the Hilton. He worried that Parr looked a little wide-eyed, but Parr insisted he was fine. Simpson met with DeProspero in an empty hospital office that had become a small command post. They went over the ring of security he had set up around the hospital with the help of extra Metropolitan Police officers. DeProspero gave a status report on agents' efforts to locate and secure some key people under their protective wing—the Reagan children, the Bush family. They had to consider the possibility that this could be part of a broader attack on the country.

Now in a small empty office with the First Lady, Simpson reminded Mrs. Reagan how hale and hearty her husband was. The president was going to be fine, he told her.

"I just knew he was an extremely strong individual. His faith, physically," Simpson later recalled. "If anybody is going to make it, it will be him."

The surgeons, however, were just now discovering that a flattened Devastator slug—a bullet designed to shatter upon impact in order to cause maximum damage—had punctured Reagan's lung. This one hadn't shattered, however, and they had to operate to get that bullet out and find the source of his steady bleeding. They wheeled him into surgery at roughly 3 P.M.

SIMPSON PULLED ON green scrubs and joined Parr toward the back of a large operating suite. The two sentries stood watch for the next three hours. Two things struck the Secret Service men. First, they were in awe of the two surgeons, a middle-aged man and a younger female resident, who refused to give up the hunt for the flattened slug and the source of the bleeding. And they noticed the bags of blood hanging next to the operating table that the nurses kept replacing. The president had lost nearly half the blood in his body before the surgeons found a nick in a slender artery under his lung and stitched it shut.

"I prayed all the prayers I knew from being Catholic," Simpson recalled of that day. "The Lord's Prayer. Hail Mary. You name 'em, I did 'em."

THE PRESIDENT SURVIVED his surgery. Despite the doctors' and nurses' nagging fears that Reagan had been close to dying when he was on the operating table, Reagan's surgeon concluded the next morning that he would make a full recovery. The lives of so many people who had been helping protect him that day would be forever changed, though. The bullet that struck James Brady would leave him permanently disabled. Parts of his mind still worked fine, but the wiring connecting them had been severed. He laughed at sad news and cried on happy occasions. He remembered that he "answered questions for a living" but didn't know for whom. But Brady had lived, thanks to the fierce insistence of White House advance man Rick Ahearn. He demanded that the ambulance driver change course from a trauma hospital and take Brady to the closest one, GW.

McCarthy would fare the best. Doctors removed the bullet from his chest, and he was able to visit and talk with his family a few hours later.

At Washington Hospital Center across town, doctors initially chose to leave the bullet in Officer

Delahanty's neck to reduce risk of more damage. But three days later the FBI lab alerted the medical team that it was a Devastator bullet and could explode at any time. They consulted with Delahanty, who agreed to another surgery to remove it. He suffered nerve damage and retired early.

Jerry Parr's wife, Carolyn, survived the shock of her life that day. She worked as a lawyer in the building across from the Hilton. At her husband's suggestion, she had come out onto T Street to see the president leave. As the shots rang out and the limo sped away, one woman's shrieks could be heard above all the male agents barking instructions. Carolyn Parr ran across the street, straight toward the bloodied sidewalk and an agent brandishing an Uzi. "My husband! My husband!" she wailed, thinking hers was one of the men on the ground. "My husband is Jerry Parr."

The agent who had grabbed the Uzi in case of more attacks realized who she was. "He's in the car!" he yelled over the noise, pointing in the direction the limo had headed. "He's with the Man!"

Back in her office, Carolyn Parr called the command post at W-16 to check on him. Jerry Parr had gone straight into surgery with Reagan and never had time to call her. The agents told her they thought Jerry was okay. She hurried that afternoon to reach their three daughters before they heard any news of Secret Service agents being shot. Their father was fine, she said. The two older ones broke down on the phone, having already heard about the shooting at the Hilton. Their mother kept her voice steady. She didn't want to reveal just how badly the scene outside the hotel had shaken her.

A worried co-worker drove Carolyn Parr home. As she crossed through the laundry room to enter their house, the agent's wife stopped in her tracks and broke down in tears. Her husband's bulletproof vest hung on a hook in front of her.

"ARE YOU OKAY, Jerry?" the assistant director asked Parr.

John Simpson could sense the adrenaline still pumping through the detail leader. They had left the operating room after the lead surgeon told them the president was no longer losing blood. While Reagan wasn't out of the woods yet, his condition had stabilized. The two men now stepped into the Secret Service's makeshift command center in an office of the hospital's intensive care unit. It was the first time Parr had a chance to sit down. The shooting had occurred nearly four hours ago.

"What happens now?" Parr asked.

Simpson sketched out the basics: The FBI would investigate the attempt on Reagan's life. The Service would do its own internal review to see whether any of its security plans had unknown gaps or had failed. Parr would be placed on a brief administrative leave to be evaluated for physical and psychological shock. Simpson felt Parr had performed impeccably, but he was glad at that moment for a reason to make Parr take a break.

Parr had one more thing to do before heading home. He walked back to W-16 to write his statement, a first-person account of everything that had happened that day, while it was still fresh in his mind. When he finished typing up several pages of notes—from assigning the advance security plan five days before to carrying a collapsed president through the emergency room doors—it was after nine o'clock. It finally dawned on Parr that he hadn't eaten anything since breakfast. He trudged to the White House mess. There he found Ed Hickey, a former agent who had been on Reagan's detail in 1968. He had resigned to run Governor Reagan's security team and become one of Reagan's lifelong friends. Now he worked as a White House aide.

"Why don't we have a drink?" Hickey suggested. Parr drank two glasses of vodka as if they were water. He felt nothing.

"I think you saved the president's life," Hickey told the agent.

Parr was surprised. He had agonized in little fitful moments in the hospital about what he might have done wrong. He hadn't stopped to think about all he had done right.

CHAPTER 8

BATTENING DOWN THE HATCHES

While the surgeons were still working to save Ronald Reagan's life on Monday, March 30, the Secret Service inspectors had already begun the deep inward look at the strength of its force field around the president. Director Stuart Knight and his assistants scanned the news cameramen's film clips from every angle, freezing each frame for a closer look.

President Reagan had come closer to dying that afternoon than anyone in the White House or the Secret Service wanted to share publicly. But the agents' snap reflexes and judgment had saved the president. McCarthy had literally taken a bullet for him. The agents had proved the wisdom of the agency's focus on routinized training after Kennedy's death. They had cheated an assassin.

Knight took immense pride in their collective

performance. The Secret Service, and the administration, rightly applauded them as heroes. "After viewing the video tapes, we believe the presidential protection was as effective as it could possibly be," spokesman Jack Warner told reporters the next morning. "These guys were competing with a bullet."

The world, watching the same newsreels, wholeheartedly agreed.

"The Secret Service did an absolutely marvelous job," Paul Laxalt, the Republican senator from Nevada, said in an interview the next day on NBC's **Today** show. "Those close to the situation believe the Secret Service handled itself in exceptional fashion."

But inside the Secret Service family, agents knew the shooting also revealed a serious weakness in their procedures for taking the president to events. A man with a gun had been able to walk within fifteen feet of the most heavily guarded person in the country and open fire. The Secret Service's screening for the union members attending the speech inside the Hilton had been far more rigorous.

The First Lady gave Deaver his marching orders the next morning. "Give the Secret Service whatever they need," she said. "This will never happen again—you see to it."

"Ronnie could have died!" she reminded Deaver.

In the Secret Service hierarchy, Deaver was closest to John Simpson, the assistant director over protection, whom Deaver had gotten to be friendly with when Simpson ran the detail protecting Reagan in his 1968 campaign for the presidency. Both were hearing directly from the First Lady that she wanted to see the security rules tightened. She didn't know how they should do it—she just wanted it done. When they were alone, Deaver and Simpson strategized about the next steps they should take to put her—and themselves—at ease. Simpson had in mind a man who had been itching for years to ramp up security at the White House and around the president: Bobby DeProspero. Simpson had mentored him. DeProspero proudly acknowledged his reputation for "overkill" when it came to reducing risk. Bobby D treated protection as a kind of religion.

Jerry Parr, Tim McCarthy, Ray Shaddick, and others had just saved President Reagan's life. Simpson figured Bob DeProspero could help the Secret Service stop the next bullet from getting so close.

DEPROSPERO, A SON of Italian immigrants who had settled in West Virginia coal country, had grown up wrestling, playing football, and dreaming of being an Air Force pilot. He married his high school sweetheart, Pat, and headed to Travis Air Force Base for training, but an officer erroneously turned him down for flight school because he was missing two molars. DeProspero took a job as a high school biology teacher and wrestling coach in Vienna, Virginia. He was driving home from wrestling practice one afternoon when he heard on the radio that the president had been shot and killed in Dallas. DeProspero's emotions surprised him. He pulled the car to the shoulder to focus. He felt tears on his cheeks.

One thought kept going through his mind on the roadside: **I wonder how the man in charge of his security feels right now.**

At the time, DeProspero was coaching the sons of two senior Secret Service agents, including Lem Johns, the head of the president's detail. They encouraged him to apply for the Service. He got hired in the summer of 1965, one of the two hundred new agents Director Rowley had fought so tirelessly to add to his force. When the twenty-six-year-old had been on the job only nine months, Johns brought DeProspero over to President Johnson's detail. No rookie had ever joined the elite president's team that fast. Many of the veterans on the detail looked askance at the rapid promotion of this new favored son.

He couldn't win the acceptance of most of them, but DeProspero got to study the strange art of security under the man who would become his most important mentor, John Simpson. He watched Simpson sweat over every doorway, highway ramp, and storefront in an advance plan.

With just three years under his belt, DeProspero

got a call from headquarters at 4 A.M. one night. It was a history-making assignment. An hour after presidential candidate Bobby Kennedy had been shot in a Los Angeles hotel, President Johnson had summoned Director Rowley to the West Wing. Overnight, the president had ordered that teams of agents begin shadowing all presidential candidates. Roy Kellerman, who had been the detail leader with President Kennedy in Dallas when he was killed and now oversaw operations, called DeProspero, waking him from his sleep with gruff instructions. "Pack your bags. Pack a lot," Kellerman told DeProspero. "Don't know where you're going. Don't know when you'll be back."

DeProspero walked out of his Northern Virginia home in the early light that June morning and didn't return to his wife, Pat, and two kids until after the November election. In the first six weeks, DeProspero single-handedly crafted the advance security plans for eleven cities where Rockefeller campaigned. It was a record-setting pace for one agent—the equivalent of choreographing a modest-sized high-security wedding every four days.

After Rockefeller dropped out of the race in late July, DeProspero didn't get sent home. Instead, the Service flew him to Chicago to shield Democratic nominee George McGovern from rock-throwing antiwar protesters gathered for the party's convention. Pat barely recognized him when he showed up at their front door five months later. Her muscly weightlifter had lost twenty-five pounds.

When Richard Nixon won the election, DeProspero joined Vice President–elect Spiro Agnew's detail. Each day he drove from north Virginia to Annapolis at dawn and returned home late at night. "I believe I drove many times in an unsafe condition," he said of his career. "I would have to pinch myself, do whatever to keep myself awake. There are times I would tell Pat, 'I don't remember the last part of my trip home.'"

As he rose to supervisory jobs, DeProspero earned a reputation as a tough, no-exceptions kind of boss. He didn't ask more of his team than he did of himself. He would counsel his shift agents on problems they'd overlooked on a rope line or in their advance plan—but he did it privately, so as not to embarrass them in front of their peers. He would go to bat for his advance agents when White House staffers resisted their hard-and-fast rules. He had a formal style, often calling people Mister. He avoided becoming chummy with agents. He wanted to judge them on their work and not be clouded by friendship.

Bobby D tried to be candid in assessing his own weaknesses, too. "I am not overly intelligent," DeProspero once said. "I am certainly not the most suave person. I don't have the greatest personality. But I think I have the ability to lead men."

By the time he joined President-elect Reagan's detail as the number two in command of his safety, he had spent the vast majority of his sixteen-year career in the grueling work of protection details. It was more than any other agent at the time, and likely since.

Simpson had heard DeProspero agitating for a more rigid circle of flesh around the president whenever he left the White House. He visibly bristled whenever the White House political staff resisted his demand for proximity. They argued it would look unfriendly to the public, or ruin a photograph the news media would use of the event. White House staff had dubbed DeProspero Dr. No or Agent No behind his back. He was one of the few detail leaders who told their protectees they couldn't do something.

On one of Nelson Rockefeller's first days as Ford's vice president, he walked out of his second-floor office in the Old Executive Office Building as if he were touring the grounds of his Tarrytown mansion. He announced casually to DeProspero, his detail leader, that he wanted to walk over to visit staff in the new executive office building. Door to door, the distance might have been two blocks across Lafayette Square.

"I'll get the limo ready," DeProspero said.

"Oh, I'll walk over," the vice president said, not wanting to make a fuss.

"No, sir," DeProspero said calmly. "We'll get the car."

The vice president shrugged, a little surprised.

"Okay, Bobby."

Tom Quinn, one of the shift agents on duty, blinked in amazement. He had told the vice president no!

"We'd never heard a supervisor say that to a principal," Quinn recalled.

DeProspero was about to get a lot of opportunities to say no—to the president of the United States.

ON THAT ANXIOUS Monday night after the Hilton shooting and Reagan's surgery, nurses wheeled the president to a large trauma recovery bay around 6:30 P.M. Agents had set up impromptu screens to separate him from other patients. DeProspero took over the watch, relieving Parr after his tumultuous day. The deputy stood guard four feet behind Reagan's right shoulder as he lay in his hospital bed, until about nine o'clock the next morning.

DeProspero watched the president regain consciousness that evening, full of questions. His doctors explained to the president that he had been shot, a bullet had been removed, and now he was doing fine. Because Reagan couldn't talk through his oxygen tube, a nurse brought Reagan a pencil and a pink scratch pad to scribble notes. Every now and again that night and in the wee hours of the morning, the president would tilt his head back toward DeProspero to signal that he had written a new message.

More often than not, the president of the United

States wanted to share a joke: "Can we take that scene over?" Reagan wrote. "Does Nancy know about us?" he wrote to a nurse who came in during the night to check his vital signs.

He also jotted down a question DeProspero couldn't bear to answer: "Was anyone else hurt?" the president wrote.

"You need to get some rest, Mr. President," the agent said. "Let's not talk about that now." Later that day, tears would run down Reagan's cheeks as he learned of Brady's permanent brain damage. He quietly cursed, "Oh damn. Oh damn."

Around 3 P.M., a medical team moved the president to a bare room in the intensive care unit. DeProspero took up the same position, looking over Reagan's shoulder and facing the door. When morning came and his unique midnight shift ended, DeProspero had been awake for twenty-eight hours. The president had to have either Parr or DeProspero with him at all times now that he was away from the White House. But Parr had been temporarily relieved of duty in the immediate aftermath of the shooting, so DeProspero felt compelled to stay. Finally, he let another agent spell him. Despite his weary bones, he headed home to his wife and children with a sense of relief. Doctors checking the patient that morning gave Reagan a thumbs-up. The president was going to make it.

For the rest of Reagan's twelve-day convalescence at GW, DeProspero took regular turns at Reagan's bedside. One day, Reagan awoke fuzzy-eyed from the sedation of painkillers. He struggled to orient himself, then saw the familiar serious, line-creased face at the foot of his bed.

The president's first words surprised the agent. DeProspero had weeks earlier advocated that the president wear a bulletproof vest. Reagan had preferred not to unless there was some special reason, a clear danger.

"Bobby, I'll wear that vest whenever you tell me to," he said quietly.

PRESIDENT REAGAN RETURNED to the White House on April 11, a rainy Sunday. Vice President and Barbara Bush, along with a crowd of 250 friends and staff, stood under umbrellas on the South Lawn to welcome him back. Reagan lifted his left arm to wave. Deaver glanced at him and felt a chill up his back. It was the same pose the president had struck just before he was shot.

The president and the First Lady never faulted the Secret Service for the shooting. Mrs. Reagan thanked Parr repeatedly for "giving me my life back," by which she meant saving her Ronnie. But his brush with death transformed her. She instantly became a fierce, anxious voice in the ears of Michael Deaver and the Secret Service detail leaders.

"He's seventy," she told them repeatedly. "He can't survive this happening again."

Deaver had two dueling fears as Reagan returned to the White House: First, he had to get the president back out in public, to show he was in the saddle again and ably running the country. Second, he had to deliver on his promise to Mrs. Reagan that no harm would come the president's way.

In the wake of the shooting, he saw DeProspero as a new and critical ally. The two men—who had bickered only the day before the shooting over the danger the president faced on a city street—became partners in the same project.

Deaver called a meeting in the West Wing for the Tuesday after Reagan's return. He wanted top Secret Service leaders, White House staff, and military officials to brainstorm on their new top priority: tightening up security around the president. DeProspero brought a typed, three-page, single-spaced list of thirty-four new security measures he wanted the White House team to consider. Truth be told, he wanted them all adopted on the spot, but he didn't say that.

That day, DeProspero proposed steps that would be taken for granted and viewed as obvious in another decade. But at that point, they weren't standard procedure at all.

The shooting at the Hilton had left the president exposed on a city street for too long. From now on, DeProspero said, the president should arrive and depart from buildings under the cover of a tent whenever possible. This would obscure and shield him from possible shooters in buildings nearby. If that was not possible, his limo should deliver him to a building's garage or loading dock.

DeProspero wanted the armored limo or some other defensive shelter to be near the president at all events—a place agents could whisk him to in case of attack. He wanted the president to stand behind an armored podium at every speech in public. He wanted two agents within arm's reach of the president at all times, and he said he didn't care if staff wanted agents out of camera range for the all-important photo. The bodyguards had to be close enough to move him within a few seconds. Hinckley had shot at the president six times in 1.7 seconds. "Don't have 20 seconds," DeProspero wrote of how little time the president could be out in the open at first sign of a threat. "Have less than 2."

DeProspero's top priority, though, centered on stopping the guns from getting close in the first place. He wanted to add a security tool that had been around for years, and that agents had been talking about using for some time. The White House had always resisted it as too radical and unfriendly. But Hinckley's success made it necessary, the agent explained.

DeProspero wanted to screen all guests at presidential events for weapons by having them walk through metal detectors. "We've talked about it," DeProspero told the group. "Now we need to do it."

Several White House advance staff were aghast.

Metal detectors would ruin the warm feeling that was the very point of having the president gather with the public. The White House didn't want guests and voters to feel like criminal suspects. Nor did they want to make the president's big-dollar donors and VIP allies wait in long lines.

The argument grew more urgent and heated in a countdown meeting May 11—the week before Reagan would make his first public appearance outside the White House since the shooting. The White House was secretly arranging for Reagan to give a commencement speech at Notre Dame on May 17. His appearance would reassure the public and score sentimental points, too. Reagan had portrayed "the Gipper"—Notre Dame football player George Gipp—in a movie about the university's legendary coach Knute Rockne.

"I understand you have some problem with this trip, Bobby," Chief of Staff Jim Baker said at the top of the May 11 meeting.

DeProspero reiterated his concern about hidden guns. The Service had gotten some intelligence from the British government about people sneaking guns into events that were supposed to be screened and secure, he said.

"What do you want to do about it?" Baker asked.

"I think it's time we used magnetometers when the president is away from the White House," he said. "It's just too dangerous for him to make this trip unless we do more thorough screening."

Baker went around the room, letting Deaver, the White House advance staff, the military aide, and the White House physician offer their opinions. Then it was time to hear from Joe Canzeri, the president's director of scheduling and senior advance man. Canzeri jokingly called himself the highest-paid bellhop in America, but he enjoyed the president's trust. He didn't hold back.

"That's absolutely ridiculous!" Canzeri said. "People are going to think the president is afraid. People are going to be quite frankly insulted we're questioning their integrity. It's going to cause big time delays. We can't have people waiting outside to go through a magnetometer."

DeProspero said the Service could find ways to reduce the time waiting in lines.

Canzeri said the delays would be inevitable. An estimated fifteen thousand graduates, family members, university teachers, staff, and friends were expected at the Notre Dame commencement ceremony.

DeProspero said the risks of a gun slipping through were too great.

"Well, if it's that bad, maybe the president shouldn't go to Notre Dame," Canzeri boomed.

"Yes!" DeProspero said, raising his voice. "If we can't have magnetometers, maybe he **shouldn't** go!"

Baker tried to cool down the dispute. "Hold it, guys," he said. "We're not making this trip right away, we still have time. Let's table this until a later date."

Two days later, fate helped make the Secret Service agent's case. On Wednesday, May 13, an escaped Turkish convict shot Pope John Paul II four times. The gunman approached the pontiff during his weekly general audience as he passed through St. Peter's Square in an open car. He began shooting his semiautomatic pistol in the pope's direction. The bullets ripped into Pope John Paul's left hand and abdomen, causing severe blood loss. The pope was rushed to the hospital and eventually recovered. Authorities later found evidence that the shooter was part of a larger KGB plot.

The day after the assassination attempt, staff met in Baker's office as scheduled to discuss security at the Notre Dame trip. The room was quiet as they took their seats. Before Baker had time to say a word, Canzeri turned to face DeProspero and raised his hands in surrender.

"I give. You win!" he cried. "We'll use magnetometers!"

The Secret Service's best methods, agents often say, are developed in the wake of a crisis, a teachable moment that exposes a weakness. Every assassination attempt or attack reshaped the agency's tactics and shored up its defenses against a threat the Service had previously failed to foresee or address.

After Kennedy was shot and killed, agents adopted a raft of changes. They focused on every potential line of sight to the president, and on creating barriers that blocked anyone from having a clear shot at him. They began checking the security of buildings along motorcade routes to prevent sniper fire. Though President Johnson carped about it, agents also pushed presidents to give up riding in open-top convertibles. The Service moved for the first time into the computer age, using technology to keep track of thousands of suspicious and mentally ill people who could pose a threat to the president. Congress doubled the agency's budget and let the Service hire two hundred new agents.

After Wallace was shot, the Service imposed new routines for rope lines. They practiced over and over how to move the president quickly from one end of a line to the other without confusion. Agents stepped up their studying of crowds of people, like a lifeguard surveying a pool for signs of trouble. For the Service, it might be a raised arm, a quick movement, or a strange look in the eyes. "I taught my agents to pick certain sectors, to keep their eyes open, trust nobody," Parr wrote in a 1981 report. "You look for eyes that glitter with hatred—that set of eyes that's hostile, angry. Most people are curious, expectant, happy. But every once in a while you catch a pair of eyes."

After Reagan was shot, the Service added or tweaked more than two dozen other security measures. The most important was the addition of magnetometers for all events the president attended.

"The Secret Service methodology is born of blood," said Jonathan Wackrow, a former agent on

President Obama's protection detail. "You can only protect for what you know. Every time the Service is tested, it gets better."

Rick Ahearn, who was Reagan's White House advance staffer at the Hilton, had watched the Service react and adapt to attacks for two decades before that fateful day in 1981. He began working presidential advance in 1968 after Bobby Kennedy's assassination, had watched three men standing next to him drop to the ground outside the Hilton, and would later advise advance teams working the chaotic campaign rallies for Donald Trump. "The Secret Service changed policies and protocols after every shooting incident," Ahearn said. "After Kennedy's assassination, we don't have any open-top limousines anymore. After the George Wallace shooting, when he just waded into a crowd . . . that led to the use of more [uniform] rope lines to control the crowd. And after March 1981, you couldn't get within handgun range of the president without being magged."

IN ADDITION TO adding magnetometers after Reagan's brush with death, the Service also shifted to adopting other ideas DeProspero had pushed. That included the new tactic of "covered arrivals," having the president's limo enter a concealed garage or loading dock. These hotel and convention center loading areas were low on glamor, but great for concealing the Man from gunmen or attackers. "We spent those years really advancing security to a new level," said Joe Petro, who succeeded DeProspero as special agent in charge of Reagan's detail in 1985.

One day, Petro opened the limo door for President Reagan so he could step out into a hotel loading dock and give a speech inside. Reagan joked that he noticed this particular security enhancement the most.

"I would think I was in the wrong place if I didn't smell garbage," the president quipped.

CHAPTER 9

NIGHT OF THE LONG KNIVES

The director of the Secret Service, Stu Knight, had many reasons to feel proud of his work and secure in his position. The nation had suffered a shock in the attempted assassination of Reagan, but everyone from Tip O'Neill, Speaker of the House, to Sam Donaldson, ABC News anchor, cheered the Secret Service for averting a national tragedy. Knight could take some comfort in knowing that his investment in agent training had helped save the president's life.

Unbeknownst to many in Congress and the public, however, the arrival of Reagan and his political staff had put Knight's job in danger. The Secret Service's senior leadership had split into two dueling camps. In the aftermath of a frightening close call, the two sides escalated their battle for control of the Secret Service.

One camp backed Director Knight, a deep thinker and apolitical manager credited with helping wipe away the ethical stain President Nixon had left on the Service. Knight had emphasized professionalizing the Service for its many missions, including protection. But he didn't believe the Secret Service could shield the president with brawn and bravery alone. He wanted to mine intelligence to intercept potential assassins. He encouraged agents to develop investigative, financial, and management expertise as well.

The other camp supported Knight's chief rival— Bob Powis, a Vietnam vet who inspired followers with his clear directions and commanding presence. He had a macho swagger but was also respected for his keen investigative instincts. The ambitious supervisor had earlier headed up the sizable Los Angeles field office. He became known as "the West Coast director" because of his power base of loyal agents and independence from Knight. He had also been a driving force behind the Service's early creation of the Counter Assault Team, a heavily armed group of marksmen who were supposed to swarm and suppress any attack on the president.

Before Reagan's inauguration and the drama of the shooting, Knight had been examining ways to modernize the way the Service protected the nation's leaders. A Michigan State graduate and beneficiary of a Princeton fellowship, he had a bit of a cerebral bent, and he turned to behavioral science in his search. Knight felt strongly that the Service needed to bolster its knowledge of the typical profile of would-be assassins and find them before they could strike. Knight had been sounding an alarm for years within the administration about the Secret Service's dwindling intelligence on lurking killers. Because of rules adopted in the 1970s to bar the FBI from improperly spying on Americans, the Service in 1981 was receiving half as many leads as a decade before on people who made threats against the president.

Knight also tapped behavioral science to help him measure something he feared was dwindling in his overworked agency: employee morale. This concern made him an outlier in the history of the stoic Secret Service. He was the first director ever to commission an in-depth behavioral study of his workforce. Knight worried that agents drank to medicate themselves after stressful back-to-back shifts. He feared the job's toll might also be straining marriages and families. He asked National Institute of Mental Health psychiatrist Frank Ochberg to spend a full year studying twelve hundred agents and interviewing many of them and their wives.

Ochberg saw the agents on the whole as "an admirably dedicated and mature group of people." But the nation couldn't expect them to be robots, he said.

Ochberg was impressed by the professionalism and devotion to duty that many agents shared. He arranged to interview one agent on a protective shift and was surprised to find he had a 105-degree fever and a rapid pulse.

"What are you doing here?" the psychiatrist asked.

"This is what we do," the agent said flatly. "You never call in sick."

Ochberg talked with agents who interviewed mentally ill people who had threatened the president. He felt many were more adept at building rapport with a stranger and gathering information than were professionals in his own field.

Ochberg's unique ethnography of the Service was never made public. Ultimately, it concluded that alcohol abuse and marital strain plagued some agents but were not rampant. The study did, however, root out a surprising source of agents' stress. The highest stress levels resulted not from any particular activity in the line of duty, but rather from the Service's rigid, authoritarian management style.

An old guard of supervisors silenced discussion of the Service's orders from on high and ignored younger agents' questions about methods and procedures. The older agents of Kennedy's era proudly shared stories of how many family Christmases and Thanksgivings they had missed. The younger agents, whose wives were less interested in marrying the Secret Service, felt the opposite. They considered it a sign of professional disrespect when bosses refused to give them flexibility to attend important family events.

"The attitude was, 'Yours is not to wonder why. Yours is just to do or die,'" Ochberg said. "The newer agents were insulted at being treated like children."

Armed with Ochberg's research, Knight orchestrated the early retirement of several field office bosses who behaved more like tyrants than leaders. He also ended the hated cost-saving requirement that agents double-bunk in hotel rooms. That change was by far the most popular decision in Service history. Now agents could have some small privacy on the road, and sleep without waking to another man's farts and snores.

While still in the midst of all these changes, Knight was aware he had a serious rival in Powis. In the late 1970s, the director had tried to exert some control over Powis by forcing him to return to Washington to be assistant director of investigations. On the surface, it appeared to be a promotion, but Powis didn't want to be under Knight's watchful eye and preferred to continue running his own fiefdom in California.

After he reluctantly accepted the headquarters job, Powis didn't disguise his contempt for Knight, often calling him "that asshole" in front of subordinates. He also ignored Knight's explicit directives and privately lobbied lawmakers to let the agency expand its powers into FBI turf to investigate bank fraud. Knight was furious: He wasn't trying to start a turf battle with the FBI. As their battle grew more tense, a headquarters audit found that Powis

misused confidential informant funds in Los
Angeles to buy thank-you meals for agents working
double shifts. It was a violation of the rules that
made him a hero with some of the working stiffs.
Knight didn't think it was a major scandal, but felt
it was a poor model for a high-ranking official to
set. In the aftermath, Knight demoted Powis several
levels down, sending him to work in the Washington
field office. Powis agreed to retire in 1980, on the
condition that Knight let him head up the office in
his final year.

But when Ronald Reagan won the White House
in November 1979, Powis and his allies ended up
having a direct link to the throne. In Los Angeles,
Powis had developed a friendly relationship with
Governor Reagan's team as he campaigned for
president. Powis was especially close to two men
Reagan considered confidants and friends: White
House aide Ed Hickey and senior counsel Ed
Meese.

As Reagan recovered from the shooting, Meese
and Hickey quietly pushed to make Powis Knight's
boss, as an assistant deputy secretary of the Treasury
overseeing the Secret Service. Knight and his
camp pushed back, arguing it would unfairly
politicize the office. But Knight's camp lost. The
White House chose Powis to take over in June at
the Treasury position overseeing Knight.

In November, Knight publicly announced he
was retiring at year's end. He insisted that it had

nothing to do with Powis's rise. "Absolutely not true," he told a reporter. "I realize that is the popular perception and from some perspectives even a logical or reasonable assessment. But it's absolutely not true."

Very few in the Service believed him. Knight had privately lobbied the White House, complaining to his deputies that he could never bow to Powis. Before Powis's promotion, Knight had planned for his deputy, Myron "Mike" Weinstein, to inherit his job. He saw that that plan was now doomed. He chose to exit without raising a public ruckus.

The next week, the White House announced that John Simpson—one of Reagan's very first bodyguards and a Powis ally—would be the new director of the Secret Service. He was sworn in Friday, December 4, in a small ceremony attended by Baker, Deaver, and Meese. All three men had been granted Secret Service protection in the wake of the shooting.

Soon the Reagans would celebrate their first Christmas season in the White House. They hosted an endless series of holiday parties at the mansion for donors, friends, volunteers, staff, agents, and even reporters. The Secret Service family normally looked forward to December, too, as a homecoming of sorts. Former directors and senior detail leaders returned for a Christmas luncheon and informal visits with their old friends.

This holiday season, however, the Service was implementing a headquarters purge. In a dramatic late-night meeting the week before New Year's Eve, top aides to Powis and Simpson gathered to select preferred agents for key supervisory assignments. Agents dubbed the secretive session the Night of the Long Knives.

A handful of agents on duty that night at headquarters at 1800 G Street spotted an ominous list of names on the desk of Powis's right-hand man, the deputy in charge of the Office of Investigations. On a yellow legal pad, the names of agents favored by Powis and Simpson were written on one side. Those considered loyal to Knight were on the other.

Starting that night, an estimated sixty agents were transferred into or out of plum headquarters jobs. "For the rank and file watching this, it had quite an impact," one midlevel supervisor from that time recalled. "It was really kind of nineteenth-century management."

Joe Petro, another rising young supervisor, had previously worked as a Treasury Department liaison for former director Knight and for his deposed heir, Deputy Director Weinstein. Though Petro had not actively rooted for either side, the agent assumed he was doomed. **My career is over,** he thought. **I got the wrong game jersey on**.

But Petro, a Vietnam combat officer, had also caught the eye of Powis because of his natural leadership skills. Powis had earlier asked Petro to temporarily help oversee training for the fledgling Counter Assault Team. While enjoying the holidays at his mother's, Petro got a call from a deputy of the Powis-Simpson team. Did Petro want to join the new director's staff as an agency spokesman? It was a position of trust. **I guess my career's not over!** Petro thought.

Many others, though, learned they were out of favor. Agents and managers had banded together in power clusters with hopes of putting their own stamp on the Secret Service. The small close-knit family that agents had enjoyed under President Kennedy was a quaint memory. Small cliques had formed before, but now a civil war of rival bands had cut the Service in two.

Rank-and-file agents generally respected both Knight and Powis and many of their senior lieutenants. Several senior managers who picked sides in the epic 1981 battle for the directorship acknowledged the strengths of the other. "I can see the value in both of them," said one former assistant director who backed Knight and fell out of favor afterward. "There was a great tension between the two of them. But they both had a vision of . . . a better Secret Service in different ways."

In their battle for power, Powis had the advantage of a friendly, long-standing connection to both President Reagan and his closest aides dating back to Reagan's time as governor in California— a connection that Knight sorely lacked. Powis's ally

John Simpson boasted an even stronger personal tie. He had led Reagan's detail when he ran for president in 1968, and he was the person Mrs. Reagan wanted at her side in the hospital after the shooting in 1981. Reagan overturned the Secret Service director's demotion of Powis and made him a top Treasury official. Not long after, Reagan named Simpson his new director of the Secret Service.

Every president has the right to choose his Secret Service director. But in the agency's short history of protecting presidents, the White House had generally respected the Secret Service's tradition of building its own internal, professional line of succession and had chosen directors from that cadre of contenders. Even in the wake of Kennedy's assassination, a paranoid President Johnson had several times considered changing directors and not actually done it. The most startling disruption to the tradition of succession had taken place in 1948, when President Truman replaced a Secret Service director after Truman's surprise reelection victory. The director at the time, James J. Maloney, had irked the president by dispatching many of his Secret Service detail agents to New York to begin shielding New York governor Thomas Dewey. The director had presumed, as had many election watchers, that Dewey would beat Truman. He sought to favor the man he believed would be his new boss, and lost his job when he guessed wrong.

President Reagan had bucked Secret Service

tradition in a way that left some scars. His decisions on promoting Powis and Simpson had elevated one rival faction in the Secret Service over another. Reagan believed he was simply choosing the comfort of trusted lieutenants, and Simpson went on to be one of the Service's most revered directors. But Simpson's ascension sent a message throughout the agency, from the aspiring shift leader hoping to rise farther all the way down to the youngest, newest recruit: Pleasing a president had its rewards.

REAGAN'S BRUSH WITH death led the entire White House political team to defer far more often to the Secret Service, at least for a while. Political aides, normally eager to get Reagan as close as possible to the public, now agreed to keep him several yards away.

But the natural tug-of-war between the White House and the Secret Service arose again from time to time. As the shooting receded in the rearview mirror, the White House angled for Reagan to have more closeup contact with voters. DeProspero said he went to work every week "knowing I had to be willing to get fired for requiring tight security . . . and angering senior staff."

Though DeProspero stood just five feet seven, he could cow White House staff and his own agents with his wide shoulders and furrowed brow. He followed a rigid diet and weight-lifting routine throughout his career. As detail leader, he could bench-press twice the president's body weight. "He was intimidating," said Petro, who added he felt lucky to have him as a boss. "He's not a big guy. But boy, I'll tell you. He was like eight feet tall to me."

DeProspero stared down the White House staff when Reagan visited the Midwest during campaign season. DeProspero said the Service was then receiving intelligence about terror groups trying to detonate truck bombs to kill world leaders. He warned Deaver that the Service would place tractor trailers at key intersections that Reagan passed on his Midwest trip. He said staff could not publicize the motorcade route, as they often did to bring out crowds.

"You know people like to see the president," Deaver objected.

"Yes, Mike, but this is not the time," he said.

But the night before they left, DeProspero's advance agent called to warn him he suspected the White House was going to leak the route to the local press. DeProspero told him if that happened, they would use the alternate route. Sure enough, reporters had learned the path by the next morning. DeProspero notified his advance agent that they would use the alternate one.

"Who the hell do you think you are, changing the route like that?" Mike Deaver shouted at DeProspero when they reached the auditorium where Reagan would speak. "You had no right to do that."

DeProspero repeated his concern about truck

bombs and the risk of an explosion. As he spoke, he thought, **I may have just blown it. This is what is going to cost me my SAIC position.** DeProspero headed off to join the president. Reagan's aides never broached the topic again.

DeProspero held briefings for new White House aides, hoping to make clear to them the life-and-death choices they might be pressuring a Secret Service agent to make just by asking them to relax a small rule. The responsibility for a president's life, and the nation's stability, hung over agents like a lead weight. "And I'm not attempting to have you share that responsibility," he told the political staff. "But I want you to feel it."

He reminded them of the advance staff in Dallas with Kennedy, in Laurel with Wallace; of Rick Ahearn, the White House advance staffer with Reagan at the Hilton. He described Ahearn calling out for a handkerchief to stanch the blood oozing from press spokesman Jim Brady's forehead. The Secret Service and Ahearn had followed the standard security plans that day—but still had been devastated by the result.

"Because I can assure you the gentleman who headed up the advance at the Hilton Hotel still feels it!" DeProspero concluded.

DeProspero also liked to describe meeting the head of the South Korean president's security detail just weeks after a tragic assassination attempt on his own president. He had met the security official in November 1983 while planning Reagan's visit to

Seoul to show support for the country's fight against Communism.

South Korea's president had been scheduled to lay a ceremonial wreath that October at a mausoleum in Rangoon in honor of an attack there on his citizens. His security team had trusted Burmese officials to check the safety of the site rather than insisting on sweeping the area themselves. President Chun Doo Hwan was running a few minutes late, but senior members of his government took their places on the risers. Just minutes before the president's limo arrived, a bomb in the roof exploded. North Korean plotters had detonated it early by mistake. It killed fourteen senior South Korean officials, including four cabinet members and two of the president's security agents. "I wish we had done what you do," the South Korean security leader told DeProspero.

Speaking later to White House staff, DeProspero said, "I don't want to minimize your job, but should you screw up royally, the consequence may be that you have bad press." He added, "Should we, on the other hand, allow something like what happened in Rangoon to occur, it would definitely affect the entire world."

AN ALREADY PETITE Nancy Reagan dropped ten pounds and two dress sizes fretting about her husband after the shooting. And despite being a size 2, the First Lady kept a tight grip on her husband's hulking security team. After March 1981, she became the most demanding voice in the detail leaders' ears, but also the Service's most dogged champion.

Mrs. Reagan worried after the shooting that she'd never shake the panic she felt each time her husband left the White House's fenced compound. Visions of her husband being shot again tormented Mrs. Reagan on and off throughout the couple's two terms in the White House. Like a passenger in a plane tossed by turbulence, she thought she could ensure a safe landing with concentration.

She developed a minor obsession with astrology to help her gauge risk. Working with an astrologer named Joan Quigley, the First Lady would scrutinize good and bad omens on days her husband had a public outing or a major trip scheduled. She feared for him when he traveled without her, because she had not been with him at the Hilton. And though she knew it was irrational, given that he was shot in Washington, the First Lady also grew especially jittery when he went out of town. Mrs. Reagan would summon Deaver after talking with her astrology adviser and suggest pushing the departure back a day or two or rescheduling an event. Deaver then alerted the president's scheduler and the detail leader to the last-minute change in plans, often without any explanation.

"Very few people can understand what it's really like to have your husband shot at and almost die, and then have him exposed all the time to enormous crowds, tens of thousands of people, any one of whom might be a lunatic with a gun," Nancy Reagan wrote in her memoir. "I have been criticized and ridiculed for turning to astrology, but after a while I reached a point where I didn't care. I was doing everything I could think of to protect my husband and keep him alive. Living without Ronnie was unthinkable: I was willing to do anything I could to possibly keep him safe. . . . Astrology helped me cope and no one has ever shown that it caused any harm to Ronnie or to the country."

At first, Mrs. Reagan hid her astrology crutch from her husband. He didn't know she and Deaver were secretly adjusting his schedule. One day, President Reagan heard his wife on the phone with Quigley and asked what that was all about. Mrs. Reagan told him.

"If it makes you feel better, go ahead and do it," he said. "But be careful. It might look a little odd if it ever came out."

Mrs. Reagan often asked Deaver, as well as the detail leaders Bob DeProspero and Joe Petro, whether they "felt sure" about security for a trip. She frequently asked whether they planned to have Reagan wear his bulletproof vest. Reagan detested the extra heat and bulk of the vest. But he complied when agents asked him to wear it—just as he had promised in his recovery room. Once, while helicoptering on Marine One to a church for Easter services, Petro saw the First Lady giving him the signal when her husband wasn't looking. She patted her breastbone with her right hand. "She was traumatized by the assassination attempt. You can imagine," Petro said. "She was very engaged in his protection. And in my experience, she was often right about things."

In 1983, spurred by Nancy Reagan's push for the funding, the Secret Service opened a training facility on five hundred acres of federal land in Beltsville, Maryland. There agents trained for bombings and shootouts on a life-sized replica of a city street with nearby buildings. They conducted simulation exercises for moving the president quickly in and out of a building entrance, evacuating in a medical emergency, scrambling to cover him during a sniper attack, and swerving his limousine through roadblocks to escape danger. The service named the center the James Rowley Training Center, in honor of the work the former director had begun.

OF ALL THE people who lived through the Hilton shooting, Reagan seemed the least fazed by the attack. McCarthy, the agent who had taken a bullet in the gut, remained amazed at Reagan's ability during his recovery to forgive John Hinckley. Several in his detail were also struck that he never questioned the Service's efforts to ensure his safety. Reagan was respectful of his detail's concerns, but also eager to make light of his risk. "I never saw fear or concern in the president as a result of the assassination attempt. Never," said Petro, who succeeded DeProspero as head of the President's Protective Detail.

In the summer of 1986, Petro grew quite worried that Reagan could be vulnerable to an assassination attempt at the upcoming United Nations General Assembly. The White House wanted the president to sit with the American delegation during a full meeting of the United Nations. Two problems: The U.N. building wasn't screened, and Reagan would be sitting directly in front of the Libyan delegation. A few months before, Reagan had ordered a missile strike on Libya in retaliation for an attack on American citizens in Berlin. The April bombing had destroyed part of Gen. Muammar al-Qaddafi's compound and killed his daughter. Petro strongly urged Reagan's chief of staff, Don Regan, to keep the president from attending this wide-open forum.

"No, this is what we want to do. This is important. There are diplomatic reasons why we have to do this. Just make it work," Regan told the detail leader.

"Don, I'm not comfortable with this. And I want to talk to the president," Petro said.

"Be my guest!" Regan snorted.

And with that the two men marched to the Oval Office. Reagan was finishing up a scheduled lunch with Vice President Bush. He invited Bush and a chief of advance to stay while they sorted out what his aides called an urgent security matter.

Petro and Regan gave their competing arguments, each growing heated at times. Petro explained that Qaddafi was hard to predict and it was easy to sneak a weapon into the United Nations building. Regan said the White House had to hold its head high on the international stage. There had to be ways to control the risks.

Reagan interrupted: "Well, I think I agree with Joe. I don't think I should do this," the president said. He paused, crinkling his brow.

"But maybe this is something George could do," he added.

Everyone, including the vice president, broke down laughing.

"Yeah, sure, paint a bull's-eye on my back!" Bush said.

Reagan roared. The president had managed to get his whole team bent over laughing at a possible assassination attempt.

CHAPTER 10

A HAPPY SERVICE,
A RISING THREAT

To hear agents and officers tell it, the Secret Service enjoyed some of its happiest days when George H. W. Bush occupied the White House.

Bush came from a patrician lineage that stretched back to Queen Elizabeth I. His father, who became a U.S. senator, had instilled in his son the creed of well-off WASPs: "Of those to whom much is given, much is expected."

George H. W. Bush stepped into his first turn at public service on his eighteenth birthday. As a senior at Phillips Academy, Bush postponed leaving for college at Yale to instead enlist in the Navy after the attack on Pearl Harbor in 1941. He set a record at the time as one of the youngest naval aviators serving in World War II. Starting with a family stake, he then made his own millions in an oil and gas company in Texas. In the 1960s, Bush entered

Republican politics and began serving his country in a string of lofty roles: congressman, chief liaison with China, CIA director, and vice president.

Despite his life of wealth and privilege, Bush forged a genuine kinship with fellow public servants on far lower rungs. The Secret Service agents assigned to surround him and his family both won his respect and tugged at his heart. Bush, as eager as any president to get closer to the public, politely held his tongue and accepted his agents' restraining security recommendations. As vice president in 1981, Bush had lived through the shock of President Reagan's near death after the shooting at the Hilton. He credited Reagan's Secret Service team and their instincts with saving his life.

Bush and his wife, Barbara, treated the Secret Service agents who protected them and their large brood like part of the extended family—not like "the help." The Bushes drew the agents closer into their unscripted lives than most First Families allowed. The warm feelings were mutual. Agents had seen the president try to calmly counsel a fuming grandchild and watched him cry recalling the death of his three-year-old daughter from leukemia. The president and First Lady often asked about the agents' children and families. Bush and his children frequently pulled the agents into the family's legendary sporting battles—as a fourth in a doubles match or as helpful ringers in a family football game. Barbara Bush was forever pushing extra sandwiches and appetizers left over from ceremonial events into agents' hands and urging that aides take coffee to agents standing outside. Barbara Bush didn't think twice about mothering—and bossing—the agents.

"Can you get the phone, dear?" she hollered to one through the family home at Kennebunkport during a summer break. And one winter, she scolded an agent to put on one of her husband's knit caps that she held out in her hand—or else.

"You better do what Bar says," President Bush warned.

One of the detail agents assigned to the Bush family, Marc Connolly, ended up becoming part of that extended family in a whole new way. He married the nanny who worked for the Bushes' daughter Doro.

The Bushes demonstrated their gratitude to their security team with gestures large and small. President Bush made a habit of thanking his agents by name when he ended his workday and returned to the executive residence for the night. When the Bushes knew they'd be staying for several weeks in the summer at Kennebunkport, the First Couple invited the agents' families over for big barbecues and swimming at Walker's Point.

George H. W. Bush had been aghast as vice president to learn that the agents historically postponed their Christmas celebrations with their own families in order to be with the president at his family home. As vice president, Bush chose to delay leaving for Houston until Christmas Day so agents could enjoy some of the holiday with their own family. As president, the Bushes began spending Christmas Eve at Camp David for the same reason. The Maryland retreat is guarded year-round by military service members, which allowed more detail agents to take that day off. "That's unbelievable, that the most powerful man in the world would think enough of other people to delay his vacation by twenty-four or forty-eight hours just so other people could be with their families," Rich Miller, the former head of Bush's detail, said. "That's why people would do anything for the president and Mrs. Bush."

Bush and his detail had a mutual respect and affection hard to match in another White House administration. The affection had its downsides, though. The Secret Service's eagerness to please one of their favorite presidents ended up delivering him to danger's door.

IN APRIL 1989, just three months after President Bush's inauguration, his White House aides and the Secret Service were working together to help the new president score some political points. They wanted him to get some credit for the United States' steady stream of victories over Communist regimes in Eastern Europe, a key reason for President Reagan's popularity at home. They scurried to put Bush on the perfect political stage to highlight a similar "win" in Poland. But their effort gave Bush's secret stalker—a man named John Spencer Daughetee, who was entirely unknown to them at the time—an opportunity to shoot at the president.

Daughetee had been lurking around Bush without the Secret Service's noticing, starting when Bush was a vice president and GOP nominee campaigning for the White House in the fall of 1988.

That spring, his aides wanted to showcase Bush's role in helping Polish workers shake off their government effort to ban their Solidarity Party. The White House advance team proposed that Bush travel to one of the most predominantly Polish towns in America: an enclave near Detroit. He would use this stage to announce hundreds of millions in aid to the country just as Poland's government was moving to recognize its popular, reform-minded workers' party. They chose Hamtramck, a two-square-mile Michigan town of tightly packed brick homes and apartments, as the best symbolic stage for this news. Poles had emigrated to Hamtramck for a century, drawn to the familiar foods and the common language of this Polish community—and the steady work of the nearby auto manufacturing plants. The president was going to proclaim his financial support to Poland's popular union leader Lech Walesa, just as Poland's high court was expected to legalize Walesa's banned labor party.

What better place to find cheering supporters for Bush's announcement than a town full of Polish Americans rooting for Walesa?

But at Secret Service headquarters, agents and supervisors heatedly disagreed about the wisdom of taking the president to Hamtramck. Agents in headquarters and the Detroit field office recommended against it, arguing that the cramped physical layout of the town made it hard to shield the president from an ambush.

This working-class hamlet had narrow streets that often required cars to slow down to pass one another. Hamtramck's downtown was cut off from highways, and the main street consisted of a tight corridor of squat brick buildings jammed against each other, providing no escape route if agents had to quickly whisk the resident away from danger. "There was no real freeway and no hospital nearby," said a former agent who traveled to Hamtramck for Bush's trip. "Really nowhere to land a helicopter. It was just a really crowded place . . . hard to get the president in or out quickly. . . . Sometimes you have to say, 'This is a terrible place. We can't do this here.'"

But this was the stage the White House wanted. An advance agent on Bush's detail took a trip to Hamtramck and reported back that he felt the Service could make it work. That pleased the president's political advance team, which was rushing to place the president in the bosom of a Polish

American community for his speech in time for the Polish court's vote.

To beef up the president's security, Secret Service advance agents landing in Detroit commandeered a string of school buses and lined them up bumper to bumper to create a walled-in corridor on either side of the Hamtramck City Hall where the Secret Service would erect a stage for the president. About four thousand residents and other spectators gathered to see the president on April 17, and the Service corralled them into a grassy park facing City Hall.

"We brought in all of these school buses and we just parked them in two parallel lines and literally cleared everyone into this park," the former agent said. "We had to fight with the White House people because the optics were terrible."

Nevertheless, between those buses poked the head of a stringy-haired Army veteran who believed it was his duty to kill President Bush.

Daughetee, a failed medical student, was then thirty-three and living with his mother in tiny Flora, Indiana. He had read about Bush's much-publicized visit in the local paper and made the four-hour drive the day before. He thought this might be his golden opportunity to assassinate the president.

He dressed in a dark blue suit and white shirt and shoved into his waistband a .38 caliber handgun he had bought ten days earlier. He hoped his outfit would help him pass for a Secret Service agent so he could slip unnoticed past their security lines and closer to the stage. A day before Bush's scheduled arrival, Daughetee had cased the Hamtramck park and chosen a piece of ground off to the left of the stage from which he thought he could get a clean shot at Bush.

For the past several years, Daughetee's mind had been playing tricks on him—and egging him on to kill. Daughetee had graduated from the University of Wyoming with a degree in zoology and then spent two years on the U.S. Army's enormous base in Korea. He had enrolled in medical school but quit after the second year. He struggled to keep up friendships and to keep a job. He kept hearing voices telling him to kill the president. If he couldn't kill the president, the voices said, he should try to kill a group of school children.

The Secret Service had met Daughetee before. In 1987, while living in Indiana, he had blurted out to a friend that he wanted to kill President Reagan. Secret Service agents interviewed him at the time but concluded that he suffered from mental illness and was just confused. There was no evidence that Daughetee had crafted a credible plot to hurt the president, they decided, and so no grounds to charge him with the crime of threatening the president's life. The agents in Indiana decided not to list him in the Secret Service's computer database as "a person of protective interest." That meant the Service didn't think he was enough of a threat to check on his movements periodically. So the Secret Service didn't know that, several months after his threat in Indiana, Daughetee had to be hospitalized twice at the Veterans Administration hospital in Indianapolis. He told his doctors that voices in his head kept telling him to kill.

The next year, in 1988, Vice President Bush was campaigning for president and Daughetee noticed news stories about his upcoming visits to battleground states and the big cities near his home: Detroit, Indianapolis, and Chicago.

In the frantic final weeks of the presidential campaign, in late October 1988, Daughetee stood outside Heritage High School in Saginaw, Michigan, hoping to catch sight of Bush at a late afternoon rally there. Later, just weeks after Bush was elected, Daughetee saved enough money to drive to Washington. He stood for hours outside a downtown Washington building—much as John Hinckley had—waiting for Bush to emerge from a public event inside.

Daughetee never took a shot at Vice President Bush—not in Saginaw or in Washington. He was frustrated that he couldn't get close enough to him. Agents never noticed him. So he decided to keep trying.

That chilly April afternoon he stood on the edge of Hamtramck's downtown park, looking over the heads of strangers toward the building where Bush would give his speech. It was nearly time for

Bush to arrive onstage—11:45 A.M., according to the precise schedule—and Daughetee felt trapped. Local police were directing him and other spectators toward a bank of magnetometers so they could enter the front portion of the park. Daughetee feared he couldn't reach his chosen spot without police finding the gun in his waistband. He looked for another way but found no opening. He tried jogging to other high spots in the park, behind the magnetometers, but by the time he found a clear shot, Bush had finished his speech and was leaving the stage. Daughetee stood there, dejected.

The Secret Service agents later took the president off the stage, unaware how close Daughetee had gotten to the president. Oddly, a different threat did show itself that day. When Bush's speech was over, the motorcade sped the president back to Selfridge Air National Guard Base north of Detroit to board Air Force One for the return trip to Washington. Along the way, agents in the follow-up car saw something fly across the motorcade's path. They thought it was a bolt from a crossbow. The president never noticed anything. But because of the possibility that this was a real attack, motorcade agents alerted their colleagues back at the site. A team of Secret Service agents from the Detroit field office and Michigan police officers were dispatched to the nearby woods. They searched the area along the road for days for traces of the possible attacker. They found nothing. "They tramped through the woods with the state police for days trying to find out what the heck happened," one former headquarters agent said. "But there was somebody out there."

The agents never figured out the source of the projectile they thought they saw. But four months later, the Secret Service learned Daughetee had been plotting to kill Bush in Hamtramck—and the discovery was entirely by accident. That August of 1989, police in Oakland, California, chased Daughetee from a Bay Area bank after he tried to hold up a teller. They found him hiding in a nearby elementary school park with a gun.

Daughetee explained to detectives that he was trying to raise enough money to finance a quest. The voices in his head had been telling him to kill the president. The man they had interviewed years earlier for threatening President Reagan's life readily confessed that he was still trying to kill a president. He had been plotting ways to kill Bush for nearly a year.

What he shared next stunned the local detectives.

"I almost killed President Bush when he was in Detroit, but I couldn't get through the security," he said.

Four decades later, an agent who helped plan the Hamtramck visit said the Daughetee case still bothers him. He believes that even after this incident, and even after all the years that have passed since that near-disaster, the Secret Service still fails to focus enough of its investigative power on the delusional, mentally ill people who are most likely to kill.

These assassins in the making start with random and even silly-sounding threats. Their co-workers or family might initially brush off these threats as one-time outbursts. But over time, they refine their plots and their targets. Psychologists who have studied assassins for the Secret Service said this category of would-be killer believes they are fulfilling their destiny by pulling off a high-profile murder. Shooting a large group of people at a public gathering is one fixation. Assassinating a president is another. The fixation rarely has anything to do with politics but everything to do with fame. So it doesn't matter if the president is named Carter or Reagan—as was the case with John Hinckley. And for Daughetee, it didn't matter if the president was named Reagan or Bush, either—his target just needed to be the president.

Daughetee kept honing his plans to kill for four years before he was caught. And the Secret Service's ability to spot and stop a person who had fantasies of killing a president could help prevent other mass shootings.

The Service had commissioned a massive psychological study to help pinpoint the types of people who were likely to try to assassinate a president. The Exceptional Case Study Project examined the paths of eighty-three people who had attacked or come close to attacking a prominent American public figure from 1949 to 1996. The findings were clear: Most would-be assassins were seeking notoriety and cared little about the politics of the person they tried to kill. They were often well educated but isolated. Many had made some disturbing reference to their plan to a neighbor, a relative, or a co-worker. Nearly every one had stalked their target and even switched targets if they faced obstacles.

TONY BALL, A hulking, muscular agent with a bald head and a quick smile, resembled a cross between former NFL lineman Terry Crews and the actor Morris Chestnut. The former Houston police officer had been thrilled to join the Secret Service in his early twenties in the Houston field office. The job had lots of perks: He'd met Queen Elizabeth and Margaret Thatcher, and he'd experienced intimate concerts by Barbra Streisand, Diana Ross, and Stevie Wonder as they entertained the president and his guests. But like many agents, he prided himself on not getting too worked up about all the famous celebrities and VIPs he brushed up against. "You have a job to do, and you can't get too excited," he said. "The first time I saw George H. W. Bush, I said, 'Okay, now I'm cured. I just saw the president.'"

But Ball had one VIP assignment that overlapped with a dangerous turning point in the country's history. Late one night in September 1990, as Ball left his job at the Houston field office, a supervisor told him he would be temporarily assigned to help protect the visiting leader of Kuwait. At the time, President George H. W. Bush was wrestling with whether to take the United States to war in the Middle East. The emir of Kuwait, Sheikh Jaber al-Ahmad al-Sabah, had recently gone into exile in neighboring Saudi Arabia. He had fled under threat of assassination when Iraqi troops had invaded his tiny, oil-rich country on the afternoon of August 2, 1990. Now, seven weeks later, the emir was flying in a private jet to the White House seeking a personal audience with President Bush to urge him to deploy U.S. troops and drive Saddam Hussein's forces out of his country. Ball's only job for the next seven days was simply to make sure the emir, who was marked for death, remained safe while he was on American soil. "You're thinking all I've got to do is make sure he stays alive from touchdown until he's gone," Ball said. "That's it."

The man had a target on his back. U.S. intelligence sources believed the Iraqis had originally hoped to kidnap or assassinate the emir when they invaded his country a month earlier. By keeping the emir close, the matter-of-fact agent was unknowingly part of sealing a quiet deal that would rock the Middle East and cast a long shadow over the United States for decades after.

The emir didn't have to work hard to persuade

President Bush to take on Saddam Hussein. Bush already strongly agreed with Prime Minister Thatcher and his defense secretary Dick Cheney that allowing Iraq to invade Kuwait without consequences would set a dangerous precedent. More powerful states considering hostile takeovers of smaller neighbors might feel emboldened. But more than that, his administration feared that Saddam now held in his grip a country that was a loyal exporter of oil to America and that controlled 20 percent of the world's oil reserves. Iraq could be emboldened to invade neighboring Saudi Arabia next. If that happened, Hussein would seize 45 percent of the world's oil supply. Starting in August, Bush ordered a massive influx of U.S. troops to bases in and near Saudi Arabia. In short order, there was a buildup of up to 250,000 troops in the area.

In November 1990, at the urging of the White House, the United Nations Security Council voted to sanction Iraq for its invasion of Kuwait. The council ordered that Saddam withdraw his forces from the tiny country by January 15, 1991—or else. Bush announced that the United States would send as many as 200,000 troops to the border, amping up the pressure.

The Iraqi leader refused to back down. The day after the deadline, on January 16 at 11:30 P.M. in Baghdad, a U.S.-led coalition unleashed Operation Desert Storm. The unprecedented air bombing campaign dropped more than 88,000 tons of bombs in a hundred thousand separate sorties on Iraqi military strongholds, weapon arsenals, air bases, and communication systems. It continued for forty-three days, sapping the Iraqi military's morale while also knocking out much of the country's defense and power grid.

IN DESERT STORM, U.S. television viewers for the first time got to marvel at their military's technological might from the comfort of their living room couches and gym treadmills. Live satellite images showcased the pounding explosion of Tomahawk cruise missiles and new Nighthawk Stealth fighters dropping scores of bombs undetected by radar. CNN broadcast video of a bomb slicing into the ventilator shaft of the Baghdad headquarters of the Revolutionary Guard. The images of the target in the neon-green crosshairs from the cameras on board the fighter jets became so frequent on the nightly news, the media gave Desert Storm a new name: the Video Game War.

Just four days after the air campaign, the war was over. The vast majority of Iraqi forces had either surrendered or retreated. The Americans had won a decisive victory and lost only 147 soldiers in battle. The government of Kuwait, a major exporter of oil to the United States, was liberated. The royal kingdom and the princes of nearby Saudi Arabia breathed a sigh of relief.

The American-led pummeling on the Arabian
Peninsula produced one of the most lopsided battles
in history. But the buildup of more than 450,000
U.S. troops on Saudi Arabian soil stirred a new and
dangerous threat—which was coiling up to strike.
The Gulf War had showcased the U.S. military at
its zenith, and yet the traditional American war-
fighting machine couldn't detect this new enemy.

OSAMA BIN LADEN was the millionaire son of a
Saudi construction magnate whose family had long
enjoyed close ties to the royal House of Saud. A
strategic thinker and introvert, bin Laden had
returned to his homeland a war hero a year before
the Gulf War began. Saudi citizens cheered his triumph in helping finance and train the mujahideen
fighters who successfully repelled the Soviet invasion of Afghanistan. From the army he had helped
build in the ten-year war in Afghanistan, bin Laden
and a co-founder had created a ready network of
fighters and knew they could be summoned as
needed for future jihad in hot spots around the
globe. They called it al-Qaeda, or "the Base."

Bin Laden opposed the pending arrival of U.S.
forces on Saudi's holy lands and criticized the Saudi
princes for allowing it. He called the sight of U.S.
military cargo planes inbound to Riyadh "the most
shocking moment of my life." Bin Laden embarrassed the Saudi king by accusing him in public

speeches and writings of encouraging an "occupation" by American "crusader forcers" in Muslim
holy lands. Bin Laden cited the teachings of the
Prophet Muhammad in his campaign, warning
that two religions could never exist on Saudi soil
and infidels should never live and work on the same
holy lands as Mecca and Medina. The six-foot-five-
inch Islamic extremist also espoused the writing of
an Egyptian rebel who urged good Muslims to take
up arms against nonbelievers in order to preserve
Islam.

For bin Laden, the Saudi welcome of American
troops didn't just affront his religious views. There
was a personal aspect, too. After Saddam's invasion
of Kuwait in late 1990, bin Laden had offered the
royal House of Saud his services. He said he could
call up his trained army of Muslim fighters to beat
back the Iraqis. But the Saudis turned bin Laden
down in favor of President Bush and American
troops. And then, because he took his dispute public, the royal family put bin Laden under house
arrest. In 1991, he was expelled from the country,
whereupon he moved his headquarters to Sudan.

After the Gulf War, U.S. soldiers remained in
Saudi Arabian bases, further infuriating bin Laden.
"They can't let the American army stay in the Gulf
area, taking our oil, taking our money," he told his
followers at their new headquarters. "We have to
do something to take them out. We have to fight
them."

———

IN THE EARLY 1990s, the security protocols used to shield President Bush hadn't kept up with the massive technological advances that were revolutionizing everything from mobile phones to electronic surveillance. His protection appeared quaint compared to the massive arsenal of high-tech playthings the U.S. military deployed in the first Gulf War. Supervisors coordinating trips still made a rush of phone calls to put together teams of agents. They used computers sparingly. The newest technological toys were the magnetometers the Service had begun requiring to screen guests at presidential events after Reagan's shooting in 1981. As it had since Kennedy, the Service still overwhelmingly relied on the sheer will and determination of its people. Sweat and muscle were the Service's standard solution for most security problems. "It's always, 'Let's throw bodies at the problem,'" explained a former senior agent. "No strategy. Just reaction."

Bush's Secret Service detail leader, a square-jawed and crusty Midwesterner named John Magaw, embodied that traditional "sheer will and determination" approach. He was a former Ohio state trooper who became a special agent a few years after Kennedy's assassination.

Magaw was known as a stickler for very specific standards he held dear. Bush aide Joe Hagin had great respect for Magaw. But he once blamed Magaw's exacting personality—a sense that he was "too perfect"—for his not rising more quickly in the Secret Service. Another top Bush adviser translated this as Magaw's being "too serious, too straight, too well-combed to be one of the guys."

As a detail leader, Magaw didn't get close to agents. He was known to tinker with a security plan up until the last minute, moving by a few inches or feet the location where agents were supposed to stand if he thought their placement created a hole. Once, according to agents who overheard the story, he ordered an agent to move in close between President Bush and a bomb-sniffing dog who was passing. The agent asked why. "If that dog bites anyone, I want him to bite you and not the president," Magaw explained.

Magaw was known to wake in the middle of the night with a concern about a vulnerability in a security plan, and then phone in suggested changes. He also demanded a dress code and grooming standards that harked back to the 1950s. He wanted clean-shaven agents with close-cropped hair. He insisted that all agents wear laced shoes. No loafers, ever. If they had to run in a crisis, he said, their shoes might fall off.

He was a traditionalist in his approach to security. He focused on the threat he knew posed the highest risk to a president's life: a lone shooter. He drilled his detail agents in how to eye a crowd and spot suspicious moves, especially from a deranged gunman trying to become famous.

President Bush and Magaw had become close friends on the road, a relationship built on mutual respect and some shared characteristics. They both had a dry, cut-to-the-chase manner, and both took pride in their public service. In February 1992, as Bush entered the final year of his term in office, the president rewarded his family's loyal protector and public servant by naming Magaw the next director of the Secret Service.

That same month, from his exile in Sudan, Osama bin Laden made a declaration to his Islamic warriors across the globe. Few in the Secret Service knew the Saudi upstart's name or his cause. But bin Laden, tossed out of his own country by the Saudi royal family, had declared war against his chosen enemy: U.S. forces abroad. He and fellow leaders of al-Qaeda issued a fatwa calling for jihad against Western "occupation" of Muslim lands and American troops in particular. "We have to cut the head off the snake and stop them," bin Laden told his followers in a series of lectures. "The snake is America."

With the close of the Gulf War, bin Laden set out to expand the network of Islamic fighters that he had helped train and unite in the hills of Afghanistan. He and his old band of brothers were united in their shared hatred of the West. In his Sudan exile, bin Laden relied on an estimated

$25 million inheritance and money from other wealthy donors to finance this new quest.

Within a year of the U.S. victory in the Gulf War, bin Laden had drafted the first of several plots. He had grand plans to kill Americans, starting by bombing U.S. soldiers whom President Bush had sent to Somalia for a famine relief effort there in December 1992.

Soon he would add U.S. presidents to his kill list.

CHAPTER 11
A ROCK STAR PRESIDENT

As 1992 opened, a new presidential campaign season was moving into full swing, and a little-known governor from Arkansas had just pulled off the unthinkable. While Bill Clinton was battling a half dozen fellow Democratic candidates just to get noticed, a gossipy grocery store tabloid pelted him with accusations that he had carried on an adulterous affair with a pretty former television reporter and cabaret singer. The claim threatened to torpedo the young politician's fledgling run amid the all-important New Hampshire primary. But just days later, Clinton somehow managed to emerge not only unscathed but also, however unlikely, as far more famous and likable. He was now the leading candidate for the nation's highest office.

The **Star**'s January 23 edition splashed a picture of a pretty blonde named Gennifer Flowers across the cover under the screaming headline MY 12-YEAR AFFAIR WITH BILL CLINTON. In the article, Flowers recounted how she and Clinton first met and began a sexual relationship in 1977, just two years after Bill Clinton had married Hillary Rodham. She described their efforts to keep the affair a secret, especially after he became governor. At Clinton's urging, Flowers moved into a high-rise in Little Rock where some of Clinton's aides also lived. He said visiting her there would draw less suspicion. Flowers, who was reportedly paid $100,000 for her interview, later provided somewhat garbled tapes in which Clinton could be heard explaining that there's no story if two people deny having an affair. "They can't run a story like this unless somebody said, 'Yeah, I did it with him,'" he said.

Bill and Hillary Clinton knew the Flowers story could spell the end of his campaign. They both wanted to punch back at this accusation. The couple agreed to give a joint interview three days later on CBS's highly watched **60 Minutes** program, broadcast immediately after the Super Bowl. Clinton told interviewer Steve Kroft that he knew Flowers as a friendly acquaintance and state employee but "she changed her story" when the tabloid offered to pay for her account. In phrases that sounded straightforward but had actually been carefully parsed, Governor Clinton and his wife said Flowers's claims were false, suggesting without actually stating that they were denying all of them outright. The governor did signal that he had transgressed in some unspecified way, saying he and his wife had worked through some marital problems.

"Are you prepared tonight to say that you've never had an extramarital affair?" Steve Kroft asked.

"I'm not prepared tonight to say that any married couple should ever discuss that with anyone but themselves," the governor replied. "I have acknowledged causing pain in my marriage."

Flowers, who was telling the truth about her affair with Clinton, told reporters she was "disgusted." "I saw a side of Bill that I have never seen before," she said. "He is absolutely lying."

But though Clinton was indeed lying, he nevertheless came across as likable and genuine without being defensive. He also had a powerful counter against Flowers, which gave pause to reporters, many of whom were already squeamish about pursuing a story about a past affair. The state clerk and sometime nightclub singer had been paid handsomely for her story, which Bill Clinton dubbed "cash for trash."

The couple's **60 Minutes** interview set records for viewership. With its airing, the Arkansas governor became the leading Democratic candidate in the race overnight. Over the next two months, Clinton won several more states in primary after primary. Secret Service leadership agreed now it was time for them to "pick up" Clinton. In protection agency parlance, that meant the Service had

concluded that the Arkansas governor was no longer a long shot, but a front-runner who by law was
entitled to full-time protection on the campaign
trail. Providing Secret Service protection for leading candidates had become the law after Democratic
nominee Robert F. Kennedy was gunned down
while campaigning in Los Angeles in June 1968.

Within several weeks, his new shift agents
quickly learned what the public didn't know: That
grocery store tabloid had been on to something
about Bill Clinton and his extracurricular activities.
A small handful of agents on the new Clinton detail
were uncomfortable when they slowly discovered
that part of their job was to discreetly look the other
way while the governor traveled to romantic assig-
nations.

Starting in February, headquarters began notify-
ing more than two dozen agents spread across
the country that they had been chosen to create the
fledgling Clinton detail, which would launch in
March. Presidential candidate protection was a
temporary gig that drained the Service of field office
agents every four years, but it was a routine that the
drafted agents expected and understood. They
would be required to serve on rotating shifts—
working three weeks alongside Clinton wherever
he traveled on the campaign, then returning for
three weeks at home at their normal field office or
headquarters jobs.

The three shift leaders for the detail, temporarily

based out of Little Rock, briefed their new team on Clinton's routine when he was at home and not campaigning on the road. One key feature: He liked to jog many mornings from the governor's mansion to the downtown YMCA, a historic tan brick building with a gym, pool, and offices on South Broadway.

Depending on his route, Clinton and two agents in tow usually ran a little less than two miles north, at something between a nine- and ten-minute-mile pace. They took the quieter side streets off the downtown's main boulevard to get to the Y, where Clinton said he planned to have a short workout or swim. Inside, he would dress and shower in a private room. When he emerged, the team would shadow him one more block on foot—to the nearby McDonald's at Seventh and Broadway. There the governor would grab a decaffeinated coffee and maybe an Egg McMuffin, and they would drive him back to the mansion.

But several agents noticed a security deviation in Clinton's YMCA visits. In the Service's peerless security standards, protocol required someone to be steps away from the principal at all times. But no agents went inside the YMCA to stand within reach or eyesight of Clinton during his workout. During some of the governor's visits, detail agents were standing post just outside the Y and just inside the entry door. None shadowed him inside to intervene in case a problem developed inside a public facility full of unscreened strangers. A handful of newly arrived agents, flummoxed by this gym routine, discussed it among themselves, figuring this must be a mistake. A few of them felt compelled to ask: What the hell?

"Why don't we have anybody inside with him?" one shift agent asked a higher-ranking agent.

"It's not a problem," replied the supervisory agent.

"But . . ." the new shift agent began.

"Let it go," the elder agent replied.

The shift was mostly made up of junior field agents tossed together randomly, but they had been trained in the same mold. No agent told another to "let it go" when they raised a security concern. One critical strength of the detail culture was that agents looked out for one another's flank, and they were expected to flag any vulnerability they spotted. The Secret Service lived the motto "See something, say something" long before it was a post-9/11 catchphrase.

The younger agent approached the supervisor.

"They're working out in there," the younger agent said. "He could get hurt. There could be a wacko. We need to go inside. Something could happen in there."

The elder sighed, shook his head.

"There's a woman in there waiting for him," the senior agent said. "They're having sex."

The junior agent let that information sink in.

The detail was now in the business of aiding and abetting a ruse, helping the candidate pretend he was exercising a few times a week when in fact he was just meeting women for trysts. After a pause, Governor Clinton's new protector asked what Kennedy's detail agents had asked decades earlier: "How do you know she isn't going to hurt him?"

To better protect Clinton, a Secret Service agent responsible for securing the site had already helped check out the private room where Clinton and one of his presumed girlfriends would rendezvous. They had concluded that this precaution resulted in an acceptable level of risk, agents said. A Clinton spokesman said it was completely implausible and "flies in the face" of basic security protocol that a presidential nominee would be allowed to enter a large, highly trafficked building unaccompanied by anyone from his elite security team. "There's simply no truth behind this," spokesman Angel Urena said.

Some agents considered Clinton's morning routine in 1992—heading to the YMCA and sometimes meeting women for trysts there—a crafty accommodation to his new high profile as a presidential candidate. When he was just the governor of Arkansas, Clinton had used his early morning jogs as an excuse to dash out of the mansion and secretly meet his regular girlfriends. The women would pick him up in their cars somewhere along his route and drive off for some privacy. Clinton's state troopers would later pick him up in his Lincoln Town Car at the downtown McDonald's. They would sometimes teasingly ask Clinton about his unruffled appearance after his jog. He didn't have any sweat on his face or clothes, even in the height of summer.

"He'd say he just ran five miles," former state trooper Roger Perry said. "And I'd say, 'Governor, you better see a doctor. There's something wrong with your sweat glands.'"

They said Clinton once replied, "I can't fool you guys, can I?"

After such morning outings, Clinton would stop in the troopers' guardhouse bathroom to splash water on his face and shirt, which gave the appearance that he had been sweating.

Interestingly, some women remembered Clinton inviting them to work out at the Y when he was campaigning in 1992. A notorious flirt, Clinton was described as striking up saucy conversations with the pretty young stewardesses who were part of the Dallas-based crew on the private Express One plane his campaign rented.

Christy Zercher, then twenty-seven, was one of six women—all young, all blondes—who were hired to hostess on Clinton's plane, dubbed Longhorn One. She had grown up a farm girl in rural east Texas and worked briefly as a topless dancer in a high-priced Dallas strip club before getting the hostess job with Express One. The very first time she flew on the plane with Clinton, just weeks after the Flowers affair story broke, Clinton tried to hit on her, she told former **Washington Post** reporter Michael Isikoff. The candidate, she said, walked back to the galley, looked at Zercher appreciatively, and said, "Oh, those blue eyes. Let's just blow the campaign and go to Bermuda."

Clinton kept up his suggestive banter with the women on Longhorn One throughout the campaign. On future flights, he asked Zercher about the quality of the sex in her previous marriages, complimented her figure, and rested his head on her shoulder. He made come-hither comments to the stewardesses, once remarking, "You don't know what that outfit is doing to me."

Zercher said she generally laughed off the candidate's doggish advances. But one thing stood out as odd. He repeatedly asked her and some of her fellow stewardesses to join him for a workout at the YMCA when they landed in Little Rock. The women often had layovers in town because of the frequent campaign flights.

Bruce Lindsey, Clinton's campaign aide, just as frequently stepped in to rescind his boss's invitation. "It would not be a good idea," a nervous Lindsey told the women.

Lindsey also repeatedly reminded the stewardesses to do him a favor when they landed. Could they please wait and not exit the plane with Clinton? Lindsey didn't want the press photographing the candidate with a bevy of pretty young blondes in tow.

Clinton had loyal staffers who worked overtime to help him create a public image of a loving dad and husband, a hardworking public servant focused on his voters' needs. And he truly possessed most of those noble traits. Though he and his wife appeared to be mostly political partners, he did dote on his daughter and work into the wee hours of the night negotiating legislation he believed would help the people of Arkansas. But also, as governor, he had commandeered a few trusted state troopers to help him feed his sexual appetite, duck out to various getaways with women, and hide his dalliances from his wife and the public. From his very first days under the protection of the Secret Service, Clinton had asked his new federal security guards to do the same.

Clinton zoomed to the front of the very large pack of Democratic candidates in what pollsters described as an opportune moment in history. Candidates historically faced stiff odds when they challenged an incumbent president. But not so in 1992. Half of American voters disapproved of President George H. W. Bush's handling of the country's economic slowdown, a poll in early February 1992 found. They believed a Democrat could do a better job. At the same time, the governor of Arkansas was surprising the pundit class and sewing up more than twice as many Democratic Party delegates as any of the five other candidates. He soon became the party's nominee for November.

Clinton would triumph over Bush and become America's forty-second president. He had enjoyed the luck of great timing, campaigning as a fresh-faced outsider during an economic downturn that soured the public on its current leadership. The charming governor had doused a sizzling scandal, overcoming it with political mastery and a generous helping of luck.

THE CLINTONS' RELATIONSHIP with the Secret Service didn't start off on the best footing. In fact, it began with palpable distrust.

The new president and First Lady were wary of the agency at the start of their tenure and particularly suspicious of those ensconced in senior positions on the presidential detail and at headquarters. The Clintons, after living day to day for nine months with a small group of agents, had picked up their own intelligence about the culture of the Service. They quickly detected the strong loyalty many on the presidential detail and Secret Service leadership felt for the former president. They saw the RE-ELECT BUSH bumper stickers on the cars parked behind the White House. As tradition dictated, Clinton would inherit the most seasoned detail agents when he became president—Bush's detail.

An early sign of the Clintons' suspicion flared just days before his election—in the final sprint of the presidential campaign. With a group of agents listening intently, Clinton and his aides let their guard down outside a high school near Detroit where the candidate was scheduled to kick off a campaign rally.

On that Sunday—October 25, 1992—the dueling campaign planes carrying President Bush and Democratic challenger Bill Clinton both flew in to the Detroit airport for separate events. Bush's team flew in that morning, and the president received a standing ovation at the Detroit convention center when introduced for a speech to the International Association of Chiefs of Police. Bush's plane then departed Detroit's airport, carrying the president and his campaign team onward to stops in South Dakota and Montana. Clinton's plane touched down within a few minutes at the same airport so the Democratic challenger could speak at a rally at a high school in nearby Utica, Michigan.

John Magaw, the director of the Secret Service, had flown to Detroit with Bush on Air Force One, but he did something unusual. He stayed behind to catch up with Clinton's team. The silver-haired director, a stiff man of few words who had helped lead Bush's protective detail since Bush first campaigned for the White House back in the late 1970s, wasn't welcome in the Clintons' circle.

"What is **he** doing here?" one of Clinton's senior aides snorted to Clinton as their sedan reached the high school. Clinton looked over to see Magaw, the former Ohio state trooper and Secret Service lifer, dressed in his trademark trench coat and standing with a smaller cluster of agents near the entrance to the school football field. Clinton and his campaign aides didn't see a future senior adviser and chief protector; they saw a spy for the other team. They knew of Magaw's long history and close bond with President Bush. The president had named Magaw to the director's job that February, just a few months earlier. Clinton's closest aides fumed. This was the first time they had seen Magaw's face at a Clinton event. And without really knowing, Clinton aides presumed they knew why. The winds had shifted, and the latest polls showed that Magaw's rabbi was likely on his way out of the White House. Pollsters announced that week that Clinton had a strong lead going into the final two weeks of the race, and the Bush campaign acknowledged it would be hard for them to overcome. Was Magaw playing the modern version of the Secret Service director who famously rushed to challenger Thomas Dewey's campaign headquarters on election night, seeing reports that Dewey would beat President Truman?

"Now he decides to come?" another Clinton aide sniffed.

Agents working the site and shadowing Clinton could hear the disdain in their voices as George Stephanopoulos, James Carville, and Bruce Lindsey bemoaned Magaw's arrival. The agents overhearing this saw the writing on the wall: Magaw was going to be out of a job if the polls were right. If Clinton won the election, Magaw would end up in the Secret Service annals as its briefest-serving director. "The body language was clear," said one agent who witnessed the discussion. "He was a dead man walking."

Once Clinton won the election and prepared to move into the White House, both he and his wife immediately felt tension with the Secret Service. Clinton, now carrying the Secret Service code name Eagle, feared he was losing control over his favorite activity: hanging out with people. He chafed at his detail supervisors' increasing the constraints on his movements now that he was president-elect, trying to discourage him from running on city streets. He insisted they allow him to continue, and to stop and say hello to people. Clinton was the king of the drop-in, still wanting to stop by the local diner and surprise the locals.

"It's no secret that the governor loves to have that one-on-one contact with the people" and the Secret Service must adjust to that, Max Parker, a spokesman for Clinton's transition team, told reporters. "Each time there is a new president, there is a little bit of a 'getting-used-to-each-other' period."

Retired agent Dennis McCarthy, who had helped tackle President Reagan's shooter in 1981, told a reporter, "He's got to be driving the agents crazy."

After the inauguration, the couple also feared the loss of their privacy. In his first week on the job,

Bill Clinton was flabbergasted that he couldn't pick up the phone and make a call by himself. He insisted that the White House change the phone system. He wanted to be sure no one was listening in on his private calls.

The president bristled at the agents stationed on the staircase landing near his bedroom hallway when he woke up. He liked to go jogging in the morning but hated having to plan it the night before. The detail relented, and each morning they had one group of agents dressed in running shorts and another wearing business suits, so he could decide on the spot whether he wanted to go for a run. He cursed one evening when his shift leader explained that he couldn't go to a friend's book party on the spur of the moment: There wasn't time to secure the location of the party.

Since Reagan's presidency, agents had tradition-ally been stationed on the second floor—the heart of the president's private residence—for quick reaction in case of an emergency. One stood at a staircase landing, next to the president's elevator. Another agent was positioned at the top of the Grand Staircase across from the Treaty Room. Mrs. Clinton ordered that agents would no longer stand on the second floor, so the family could have privacy.

"It saves a few seconds if there is trouble," said one former Clinton detail agent. Agents positioned on the second floor can more quickly evacuate the president or First Lady. "But during the Clinton years, they didn't want to see us." Hillary Clinton had her staff spread the word: She also didn't want to see agents or officers when she came through the White House. They should stand back and not say a word.

The First Lady's actions may have seemed cold. But a warning from a trusted friend had caused her to be on guard with her guards. After the inauguration, friends Harry and Linda Thomason had been living at the White House part time. Harry Thomason returned one night from a party with a group of reporters and relayed some bad news to the First Lady: He'd heard that agents on Clinton's detail were leaking information to reporters about the First Couple's private moments in the White House.

Hillary Clinton went to her confidant Vince Foster, the president's deputy counsel, to propose they replace the entire detail and perhaps bring back agents from the campaign detail. Foster urged against it, warning that such a drastic change would leak to the press and could make the Clintons look guilty when they'd done nothing wrong.

Then, on February 19, 1993, a column ran in the **Chicago Sun-Times** that infuriated the Clintons but also vindicated their suspicions about the agents. The item claimed the First Lady had a wicked temper and had thrown a lamp at her husband in the residence during an argument, according to an anonymous "White House source." The couple convened a group of aides, including Foster, special assistant David Watkins, and others, to discuss replacing the entire detail. "They were both really hot about the way the Secret Service had handled the news reports about the lamp throwing," Watkins said. "They wanted the agents in question trans-ferred out of the White House at once."

A few days later, Foster and Watkins visited Magaw at his office to privately discuss the Clintons' grievances. When they walked back the few blocks from Secret Service headquarters, oddly, they were body-searched at the White House gate by a Secret Service officer using an electronic monitor. Both men were wearing their White House passes and IDs, but this was the first time either of them had been searched in this way. "It occurred to us at the time that Magaw must have thought that we were wired," Watkins said. "We just couldn't believe it; we were incredulous."

After that incident, Foster grew paranoid, and the Clintons' angst about the Service rose. There was one thing the president could change without being questioned: the director. "The Clintons couldn't wait to get rid of Magaw," said a former protection super-visor who worked with both of their details.

It was normal for a president, after about a year or more of getting to know the Secret Service staff, to choose a new director of his own, typically from among the senior assistant directors. "They want their own man in there guarding the family door," said one retired senior leader who supervised details during Clinton's era. But new presidents didn't typically rush to change horses right away. They focused first on firming up their cabinet and key political appointees, learning the job and chalking up some priority accomplishments they'd promised voters in the campaign. The Clintons, however, felt they'd never be able to trust the Secret Service with Magaw at the helm.

An opportunity for change presented itself in late summer of Clinton's first year. The Treasury Department was close to finishing its internal investigation of the Bureau of Alcohol, Tobacco and Firearms' tragically botched raid on the Branch Davidians' religious compound in Waco, Texas. Considered one of the worst law enforcement failures in history, the raid was supposed to be a surprise seizure of a stockpile of illegal weapons. Instead, it led to a fifty-one-day standoff and ended in a deadly fire, set by the compound's leader. The death toll was staggering. Four law enforcement agents and five residents died in the raid, and seventy-five compound residents, including twenty-five children, perished in the fire. Ron Noble, the assistant Treasury secretary who led the investigation, warned the White House that he'd found that ATF supervisors botched the planning, then lied to cover up their errors, and that the ATF director was reflexively defending his team. The White House would have to do some housecleaning at the ATF.

Noble, who also oversaw the Secret Service, suggested Magaw could leave the Secret Service to be the ATF's new director. The Clintons jumped at the idea. "Ron Noble helped them figure out a way to unceremoniously dump him without looking uncharitable," the retired senior supervisor said. Clinton then picked a director he felt some rapport with, Eljay Bowron. Then the assistant director for protection, the hulking former Michigan State football player was only forty-two—close in age to Clinton. Though he had grown up in Detroit, Bowron had a touch of the South in him. He had formerly headed up the Service's Atlanta office.

The Secret Service culture is steeped in deference and discretion when it comes to the First Family. But many agents had a very negative reaction to the Clintons and didn't work to conceal it from friends and co-workers. Politically, most Secret Service agents leaned Republican and law-and-order, so they didn't see eye to eye with Clinton on his Democratic social agenda. Most of the agents had also served Republicans for the last twelve years, two presidents they very much admired. Still, despite some of Clinton's early testiness about Secret Service protocol, most of Clinton's political opposites on the detail came to enjoy, even admire, his personality. He could be warm and genuine, talking about his own life and asking agents about theirs. He had a knack for storytelling. He sometimes cursed at a mishap and then apologized later for his outburst. He didn't hide his elevated station, but he put on no airs. One detail agent remembered Clinton drawing him into a lengthy policy debate on a longer-than-usual car ride to an event in the rural Corn Belt. The agent and the president heatedly went back and forth on the pros and cons of Clinton's support for aid programs for impoverished families. Clinton said the support would grow more productive taxpayers. The agent said the results of welfare programs so far weren't encouraging and they had created an enormous deficit for taxpayers.

"Don't you care 'bout the chil'run?" Clinton teased the agent, trying to deescalate the argument by exaggerating his Southern drawl.

The agent had to chuckle. Clinton could charm anyone if he chose to. A retired supervisor on the presidential detail said Clinton was genuine with his agents—"not buddy-buddy" but respectful. He asked agents about themselves, thanked them at the end of a hard day. "He was just a guy who wanted to have a good time."

The vast majority of the Secret Service, however, detested the First Lady. Some smarted at the difference between Mrs. Clinton and Mrs. Bush. The former First Lady had treated her agents like extended family, inviting their wives and children to the family's home for barbecues and swimming. Barbara Bush ran her family with a fierceness, but she was also grandmotherly to agents and was always sending out food and coffee to agents standing on post at the family compound or outside in the cold. The new First Lady chided and cursed her husband in private, and snorted at the idea of baking cookies when she was forging public policy. The way she rejected the traditional role of a wife rankled the conservative-leaning agents who were used to a warmer, more feminine mother figure in the White House. The dismissive way she treated agents made them quietly seethe. Several agents on Mrs. Clinton's detail complained among themselves that she barely said a word to them after months and months of their being with her nearly every day—greeting her when she exited the residence each morning, helping her into her limousine, keeping a watchful eye on her back at every rope line. But it was hard to know who bore more responsibility for this chilly relationship and its rocky start. Had the agents' early signals of loyalty to the Bushes, and their information leaks, made her understandably distrustful and standoffish? Or were her silent treatment and brusque manner just part of her dismissive manner with low-level staff? Whatever the answer, Mrs. Clinton became the Secret Service's least popular First Lady on record.

A retired detail supervisor who helped protect Bill and Hillary Clinton said Mrs. Clinton ran roughshod over people when she sensed they were afraid of her. She was quick to dismiss or chew out the house stewards, career employees, and junior agents who couldn't stand up to her. The few agents who had the temerity to disagree with her, however, she seemed to respect.

"Hillary is a mean person," said one retired supervisor. "I get angry at people who disrespect the folks who clean your room. Guys who mistreat the people who can't do anything for [them]. She was like that. She was the person in that crew who would cut a person's heart out."

Young agents arriving to the Hillary Clinton detail remember one of the detail supervisors, Faron Paramore, warning them about the First Lady's sensitivities: "Whatever you do, just don't touch her," Paramore said. But good lead detail agents knew they sometimes had to grab the person they were protecting, to push them into a car quickly or to hold onto their belt in a rope line to be sure they didn't get swept into a rowdy crowd. "She hates us, right?" one detail agent said. "But if she didn't feel the agent right behind her on the rope line, taking care of her, she would look over her shoulder for him."

Riding around with Mrs. Clinton, agents were shocked by her foul mouth and dual personality. Some of her assigned protectors found her not only unpleasant in private but also fake in public. One agent remembered Hillary Clinton bitterly complaining with her close aide in the back of a limousine about how she couldn't stand a young female fundraiser they were moments away from meeting. She ridiculed the woman's ignorance up until the moment the car came to a stop. When an agent opened the limo door and Mrs. Clinton stepped out, she greeted the object of her critique brightly. "Oh, Julie, it's so wonderful to see you," she said.

Word spread like wildfire through the White House and the Service in the early months of the administration about an awkward exchange between the Clintons' thirteen-year-old daughter, Chelsea, and a member of her detail. The agent had walked up to the second floor of the residence and was waiting in a common hall for Chelsea, who was on the phone. It was time for the agent to take her to her high school, Sidwell Friends, a few miles away.

"I've got to go," Chelsea said to her friend on the phone. "The pigs are here."

The agent stood shocked for a moment. "Ms. Clinton, I want to tell you something," he said. "My job is to stand between you, your family, and a bullet. Do you understand?"

"Well, that's what my mother and father call you," Chelsea said.

Many agents blamed the First Lady. They developed a new code name for Chelsea: Eagle Droppings.

Cheryl Montgomery, one of the tiny group of Black female agents in the Secret Service at the time, watched the macho agents who worked protection take an instant dislike to Mrs. Clinton before they knew much about her. She represented a major culture clash for the Service. Montgomery saw the First Lady as a sharp thinker who spoke to her husband as an equal and "was just trying to help him." Other agents saw a ballbuster and a harpy who lacked personal warmth. Unlike Barbara Bush, this new First Lady wasn't doting on her husband—or the agents.

"I don't think she ever had a chance with them," Montgomery said. "She wasn't bringing them cake and leftover food. After a party, Barbara Bush would always bring them food or tell them, 'Please have this.' She treated them kind of like a mom. Who doesn't like being treated that way? Hillary didn't do that."

But Montgomery found Mrs. Clinton to be a surprisingly forgiving person. In the middle of the 1992 campaign, Montgomery had been assigned to help on the Clinton detail. On one of her first days on the shift—a trip the governor took to Tampa, Florida—Montgomery made what she later realized was an inexcusable faux pas on a rope line where Clinton greeted a crowd of supporters. She had been responsible for clearing the path on the right side of Governor Clinton as he moved down the line, so there would be nothing blocking his way. But as Montgomery kept moving to the right, she found she kept bumping into the same woman.

The first time this random woman got in her path, Montgomery figured it had to be a staffer and told her to please move out of the way. The second time, she said it more forcefully: "Lady, you're going to need to move." The third time, Montgomery was about to physically pick the woman up and remove her from the agent's path, but a state trooper who worked with the Clintons looked at Montgomery with a horrified, mouth-wide expression. So instead, the agent took both hands and placed the staffer next to Clinton. Of course, the "staffer" Montgomery had been manhandling was in fact the governor's wife, Hillary Rodham Clinton.

The next morning, Montgomery was back in Little Rock, sitting in a Secret Service car outside the governor's mansion, waiting for the shift's workday to begin. The First Lady of Arkansas came down the side steps from the house, walked over to the agents gathered outside on the drive, looking for Montgomery.

"Good morning," Montgomery said anxiously, rolling down her window.

"Hi," Clinton said, smiling. "I think we met in Tampa yesterday. I'm Hillary Clinton."

"Hello," the agent replied. "I'm . . . Cheryl Montgomery."

"I wanted you to know I'll be traveling with my husband from now on," Clinton said.

The agent thanked her. Clinton smiled wide and the agent smiled back. They said goodbye.

"She did this very cool thing," Montgomery recalled. "She could have complained and gotten me thrown off the detail," but she didn't. "When she got her own detail, the word was she asked for an all-female detail. They turned her down." The Secret Service leadership said that that wouldn't be possible. Montgomery was disappointed but not surprised that the macho all-male bosses felt that way. A vice presidential detail leader once compared the Secret Service to the National Football League when rejecting a female agent who applied for his shift, saying, "Women don't play in the NFL."

Hillary Clinton's close friends and trusted aides said her rocky relationship with the Secret Service was unfortunate but doomed early on. She had ample reason to be suspicious in those early days. The Secret Service's love affair with the Bushes was well known, and there was evidence that they were telling tales about her private life. She eventually developed close bonds with specific detail leaders and agents, especially the late Donnie Flynn. But she was wary of this bastion of Republican cops. Could they be trusted to keep the Clintons' most sensitive secrets?

CLINTON'S VORACIOUS APPETITE for contact with the public was a shock to the Secret Service's system in the 1990s in the same way that Kennedy had floored the detail agents of the early 1960s. Both were young, vigorous men in their forties when they stepped into the White House. Both "Lancer" and "Eagle" had the energy to travel from early morning to late at night, and a drive to make public appearances nearly every day of the week. Both enjoyed throwing themselves headlong into crowds. Like Kennedy, Clinton did more than embrace the retail politics of chatting with the grinning towns- people waiting for them at airports and fairgrounds. He was addicted to it. And the crowds were addicted to him.

"I've never met anyone with the natural talent that Bill Clinton had," said his former deputy chief of staff Harold Ickes. "He could look into your eyes—man or woman—and make you feel, for however many minutes, that you were the only thing he cared about, that what you had to say was the most important thing to him."

Pete Dowling, a supervisor who had been one of Clinton's first agents on the presidential campaign and built a close rapport with him, was promoted to become the Secret Service's assistant director of protective operations after Clinton's election. He said Clinton's desire to mingle drastically turned up the pace for his detail.

"It was a challenge," Dowling said. "President Clinton was younger and more active than Presidents Reagan and Bush. They liked to spend quiet time at Camp David. He rarely went there. He liked getting out. I can remember once at Martha's Vineyard we had to plead with him not to go out to get ice cream one Saturday night because it would have brought the town to a halt. One of the other guys went out and got the ice cream for him."

Agents also quickly took note of Clinton's wandering gaze and frisky winks to pretty women on nearly every rope line. Detail agents learned to spot his pattern of walking toward knockouts. Their job was to keep him from lingering too long with any one woman. "There was this blonde, jiggling everywhere, wearing a skimpy dress, big bust," a former detail agent recalled about a later trip that exemplified his habit. "Oh, President Clinton. He's going to her in a beeline. He thinks Hillary has gone to the car."

Many agents who worked on Clinton's detail and Secret Service officers who kept watch at the White House said they never directly witnessed Clinton having sex. But they also insisted they weren't fools and they could tell the purpose of his secret meetings behind the doors they secured. Who couldn't recognize the obvious signs of a man ducking off to be left alone undisturbed with a series of comely twentysomethings? Secret Service agents and officers were at the door when Clinton ushered pretty young female staffers into his office for extended periods of time, and they saw the disheveled women leaving thirty minutes or an hour later with blouses loosened, hair mussed. They got the alert over the radio when Clinton told his detail late at night that he wanted to be taken alone to another random, unknown address in the nearby Virginia suburbs or a private Georgetown row house.

"I don't know how many times President Clinton

would say, 'I want to make an off-the-record movement tonight,'" said one retired senior agent who
worked protection during the Clinton years. "He'd
go visit so-and-so. We all knew why."

Were detail agents so sure Clinton was sneaking
off to have sex?

"Absolutely. No doubt," the retired supervisor
said. "POTUS would go into his private study late
at night. . . . You'd see women go in there. They
aren't going in to take dictation. He'd go visit certain people late at night. Eleven and twelve o' clock
at night. You're not going to watch a movie."

Few of the detail agents judged Clinton harshly
for his extramarital activities; scores of married
agents had their own history of dalliances on the
road. Handsome and fit, Secret Service men had a
reputation for drawing the admiring attention of
women in whatever hotel bar they landed in after
their shift ended. Some had multiple girlfriends in
different cities. "The agents back then even had a
rule: It's not an affair—it's not a real violation—
if it's four hundred miles out from home," said one
longtime protection agent who worked on Clinton's
detail. "There are so many agents who have had
affairs on the road. They cover for each other. It
wasn't my business. But I saw it all the time."

But Clinton's bad-boy behavior with women—
both from his past and some bubbling rumors of
new misbehavior—created a major distraction inside
the White House. In his first year in office, Clinton

faced a daunting set of domestic and international fires that tested his leadership abilities. Clinton's top political lieutenants, George Stephanopoulos, James Carville, and Bruce Lindsey, were often juggling the business of governing and safeguarding the country with the challenge of saving Clinton's political hide. Not long after the inauguration, they were flung into episodic bursts of panic and damage control as new accusations arose about Clinton's sexual activities and misconduct. During the campaign, Clinton campaign aide Betsey Wright had called these moments "bimbo eruptions," a phrase intended to dismiss the accusers' credibility. Once he reached the White House, Clinton blamed reports of past sexual dalliances on a right-wing cabal manufacturing stories to hurt a popular Democratic president. But some were fresh new scandals of Clinton's own making.

THE DISTRACTION WAS obvious in the summer of Clinton's first year. While his political aides rebutted rumors of Clinton's past affairs, the president's military and intelligence agencies were piecing together what they would later identify as a dangerous global threat: Islamist terrorism. Clinton's presidency coincided with a rapid rise in little-known radicalized Muslim groups plotting to kill Americans. The plotters were rarely connected to one another, but they shared a desire to strike U.S.

troops abroad or, more boldly, to target citizens on American soil.

Almost exactly one month after Clinton's swearing-in, on February 26, 1993, one such plot paralyzed and terrified Lower Manhattan. A thirteen-hundred-pound truck bomb driven into the parking garage under the North Tower of the World Trade Center exploded. The mastermind, Ramzi Yousef, hoped the detonation would so damage the North Tower that it would fall and knock over the South Tower, killing tens of thousands of people. Instead, the explosion's damage was largely limited to the underground area of the building. The bombing killed six people, injured more than a thousand with falling debris and smoke inhalation, and caused a panicked evacuation. But though Yousef's bomb failed to kill on a grand scale, it was the first terror attack by Islamists on U.S. soil. The boldness of the attack caught the attention of Osama bin Laden, who knew of Yousef's uncle, Khalid Sheikh Mohammed, from fighting with him in the mujahideen army in Afghanistan.

As Clinton spent 1993 learning the ropes of the presidency, bin Laden was busy trying to find ways to strike the head of the snake, the troops of the United States. He found a possible target later that year. President Bush had committed U.S. troops to help with the United Nation's transport of food supplies amid a famine in Somalia the previous year, in 1992. But the situation only grew more violent as the months passed, until a growing rebel Somali military force attacked and killed humanitarian aid workers. The new president, Clinton, then sent in troops in the summer of 1993 to capture the rebels' commander and strike his stronghold. But after more U.S. troops were killed by rebel bombs, Clinton authorized a special forces mission to seize the rebels' top deputies in the city of Mogadishu.

The extraction team set off the night of October 3 for a mission they estimated would take an hour. Instead, Somali rebels supported and trained by bin Laden's fighters used rocket-propelled grenade launchers to shoot down the two Blackhawk helicopters. In a bloody firefight lasting through the night, they trapped like cornered prey the special ops soldiers who had been riding through the streets in Humvees. The next morning, the rebels triumphantly dragged U.S. soldiers' bodies through Mogadishu's streets on live television. Nobody in the Clinton White House knew then that bin Laden was a backstage player in the battle.

Back in Washington, the president and his confidants were simultaneously trying to investigate and prevent another "bimbo eruption." Arkansas officials close to the Clintons alerted the president's political aides that reporters were in the state sniffing around, meeting with state troopers and asking them about claims the troopers had helped sneak Clinton around to meet women for sex. Chief of Staff Mack McLarty dispatched Clinton's trusted aide Betsey Wright to find out what the troopers were saying.

Bill Rempel, an investigative reporter at the **Los Angeles Times,** and David Brock, working for the conservative **American Spectator** magazine, got the same tip about four troopers with firsthand knowledge. They set out that August to interview them. But after Brock finished his first sit-down interview, three of the four troopers got unsolicited phone calls from the former head of Governor Clinton's security detail, Captain Buddy Young. The previous month, Young had been named by Clinton to a federal emergency management post, overseeing Texas operations. Young scolded Roger Perry, then a sixteen-year veteran of the state police and president of the Arkansas State Police Association, for talking to the press. Perry told friends that Young made himself clear: "I represent the president of the United States. Why do you want to destroy him over this? You don't know anything anyway. This is not a threat, but I wanted you to know that your own actions could bring about dire consequences."

Young later acknowledged calling the troopers, but he disputed claims that he had done so in coordination with the White House. "I called Roger as a friend, and I told him I thought this was wrong, it was unethical, and it was a disgrace to security people," he said. "But I never said I spoke for the president, because I don't."

Another trooper, Danny Ferguson, told friends

that Clinton personally called him twice about his interview with the reporter. Perry said Clinton had offered Ferguson help with jobs and had peppered the trooper to "tell me what stories [the troopers] are telling" so Clinton could try to "clean it up."

On Sunday, December 19, 1993, the scandal known as Troopergate broke wide open. That night, CNN broadcast interviews of two Arkansas state troopers who served on Clinton's security detail and recounted years of facilitating and covering up the governor's liaisons. Roger Perry and Larry Patterson's tell-alls had been coordinated to air just before the **American Spectator** released its monthslong investigation of the same subject. The article published that Monday told all the tawdry details a group of troopers had seen: Clinton getting oral sex in a car from a department store cosmetics clerk; his long-running affairs with an office staffer, a local judge, the wife of a judge, and a reporter; Clinton directing troopers to seek out attractive women and bring them to an office or hotel suite to meet him.

Two troopers signed sworn affidavits that their accounts were truthful, and two more provided supporting information but asked not to be named. On Tuesday, the **Los Angeles Times** reporters who'd been chasing the same claims published their own extensive report. The security agents said they were coming forward because they were tired of covering up for Clinton, and in some cases they felt he had misled them with promises of jobs. "We lied for him and helped him cheat on his wife, and he treated us like dogs," state trooper Larry Patterson told a reporter for the **American Spectator**.

The troopers described in detail their supporting roles in a lengthy series of cover-ups for a compulsive womanizer, suggesting that the forty-second president had lied to voters during the campaign about many things, including his long affair with Gennifer Flowers. The law enforcement officers also provided probable cause to launch an investigation into misuse of government resources. The **American Spectator** noted:

> They were instructed by Clinton on a regular basis to approach women and to solicit their telephone numbers for the governor; to drive him in state vehicles to rendezvous points and guard him during sexual encounters; to secure hotel rooms and other meeting places for sex; to lend Clinton their state cars so he could slip away and visit women unnoticed; to deliver gifts from Clinton to various women (some of whom, like Flowers, also had state jobs); and to help Clinton cover up his activities by keeping tabs on Hillary's whereabouts and lying to Hillary about her husband's whereabouts.

When the story first broke on Sunday night, Clinton's team was panicked. Bruce Lindsey issued a bold-sounding statement dismissing the claims as "ridiculous." "Similar allegations were made, investigated and responded to during the campaign, and there is nothing here that would dignify a further response," he said.

Lindsey confirmed that Clinton had called one trooper before the stories ran, but there was "nothing improper" about that because the president had a right to question false stories about him. "Any suggestion that the president offered anyone a job in return for silence is a lie," Lindsey said.

Behind the scenes at the West Wing, senior aides knew that these specific, precise stories, backed by multiple law enforcement officers, could not all be false. They also intuited the truth of the claims by reading the First Couple's body language. In the wake of the report, Bill Clinton was contrite and shamefaced around his wife, a reaction that David Gergen compared to "a bouncy golden retriever who has pooped on the living room rug" and gotten caught.

Hillary Clinton appeared humiliated and downcast with close friends, but she didn't reveal her personal pain publicly. With aides, she fumed at the political cost. She was then negotiating with Congress on massive health care reform, and she told McLarty, "It's going to distort everything that we do."

The Troopergate stories upset a few of the younger aides working in the White House, raising doubts in their minds about whether President Clinton had lied to his wife, to the voters, and to them. Clinton's closer confidants—Lindsey and Stephanopoulos—scoffed at the idea. Clinton was a victim of a political hit job, they said. An avowed Clinton foe, Cliff Jackson, had coordinated the troopers' stories. The troopers were lured in by the prospect of a profitable book deal. And if all these affairs had taken place, some aides asked, why had not one woman come forward to confirm any of it? Actually, Flowers had come forward, but Team Clinton didn't dwell on that. Dee Dee Myers pleaded with reporters to see reason. "It's just not true," she said. Joe Klein, a **Newsweek** columnist who had covered the Clinton campaign, echoed the White House line in a piece he wrote titled "Citizens of Bimboland": "Where are the women?"

Within a week or two, the dust kicked up from the Troopergate tremor began to settle. But there was an earthquake yet to come.

On May 6, 1994, Paula Corbin Jones stepped forward in a federal court to say that she was one of the women in the Troopergate stories. That day, she sued Bill Clinton, accusing him of luring her to a hotel room and pressuring her for oral sex when she was a $6.35-an-hour state clerk. Jones, a bubbly woman with dark brown hair, had tried to convince reporters earlier that year that Clinton had sexually harassed her in a Little Rock hotel in 1991. But she'd refused to give specific details, so mainstream newspapers and national networks had been wary of her claim.

Now she and her lawyers spelled it out in a seventy-nine-point civil complaint, seeking $700,000 in damages. She said she had come forward because the Troopergate stories had gotten a key detail wrong. Yes, state troopers approached her when she was working at a governor's conference at the Excelsior Hotel in Little Rock, saying Governor Clinton would like to meet her in one of the hotel rooms they set aside for him for private meetings. She went thinking it might lead to a better job. The troopers then escorted her to the room.

But, Jones insisted, despite what the troopers said in their stories, she was in fact not a happy or willing participant. She said that when she and the governor were alone, she pulled away once he tried to pull her close and kiss her. But he followed her to her seat on a couch and dropped his pants, exposing his erect penis.

"Kiss it," he said.

Jones said she jumped up to leave.

"I'm not that kind of girl," she said. "Look, I've got to go."

White House aides continued to tell reporters that Jones's claims were fabrications. But in private, they and Clinton's lawyers discussed the serious threat that Jones's civil lawsuit presented. If the suit proceeded, Clinton would become the first sitting president to have to sit for a deposition under oath and face trial while in the Oval Office.

Hillary Clinton had foreseen this threat months earlier when Jones first aired her claims that Clinton had sexually harassed her. She'd turned to Wright, pleading with her longtime aide-de-bimbo-eruptions to go down to Arkansas and investigate this woman. "Please," Clinton had said. "Put a stop to it."

The Clintons' newly hired lawyer Bob Bennett instinctively felt it wise to settle the case. But when he met one-on-one with Hillary and then Bill, it was clear that Hillary didn't want to settle and that the president wasn't sure what to do. Clinton seemed focused on convincing people, including his wife, that he hadn't whipped out his penis with a random woman he'd lured to a hotel room.

"I swear to God, it didn't happen," Clinton told Bennett.

ON SEPTEMBER 12, 1994, a very different kind of threat came at the president—in the form of a stolen red-and-white propeller plane. At about 1:45 A.M., the small two-seater Cessna flew low over the office buildings along Seventeenth Street in downtown Washington, made a U-turn when it reached the Washington Monument, and then headed straight for the South Lawn of the White House. The pilot shut off the Cessna's power as he set a glide path, but then tried to pull the nose up slightly when he spotted a sea of metal bleachers set up on the grass for an event planned for later that afternoon.

The plane clipped a massive magnolia tree, planted when Andrew Jackson was president, and then skidded fifty feet to a stop within inches of the White House's sandstone wall, just outside the State Dining Room. The crumpled wreckage smoldered with the dead pilot inside, just two floors below the Clintons' bedroom. Fortunately, that night, the Clintons happened to be sleeping in the nearby Blair House while their residence's ventilation system was being repaired.

Neither the Secret Service nor anyone else did anything to protect Crown—largely because they had no idea the plane was coming. Some officers stationed on the South Portico noticed a low-flying plane over the Mall, but they had only seconds to scramble out of the way when it turned back toward the White House. After the fact, fire trucks swarmed the South Lawn to douse the area. Bomb detection teams carefully picked through the wreckage to see if any explosives were aboard the plane. Secret Service Deputy Guy Caputo woke up senior agency leaders at home to alert them to the close call. A detail agent woke Clinton to inform him of the crash, and the president then went back to bed.

Frank Corder, a depressed truck driver feeling hopeless after the breakup of his third marriage and the death of his father, had stolen the plane from an airport in Harford County, Maryland, sometime around midnight. A friend claimed Corder had once threatened to kill himself by crashing into the White House.

But Corder's amateurish plan revealed that the Secret Service had crafted no strategy to foil an attack from the skies. Agents insisted to White House officials and reporters the next morning that the president was never in danger and that there was no sign Corder wanted to kill the president. The Service claimed that it had a plan for incoming planes—to rapidly move the president to safety— and didn't strategize about how to stop the aircraft.

President Clinton's White House aides and Treasury Secretary Lloyd Bentsen, who then over-saw the Secret Service, weren't comforted by the Service's assurances early that Monday morning. Though it was illegal for planes to fly in the restricted airspace around the White House, known as P-56, the Service had not formulated a plan to deal with planes that ignored the rules. The FAA didn't have an automatic protocol for alerting the Service to looming threats in the skies. And Corder's small, low-flying plane appeared to have ducked under FAA radar when he was downtown. The Service had scrutinized every way to enhance the physical barrier around the president—but they hadn't taken steps to defend against this somewhat unusual threat.

Beginning at 2 A.M. and continuing throughout that long Monday morning, there was a tense push and pull over who would control the investigation of this near-catastrophic miss: the Secret Service or the White House. The Secret Service, reflexively resistant to having anyone peer into their business, wanted to investigate this breach like all the others in the past—entirely on their own. The White House insisted on coordinating the show, and after a series of teleconferences with Director Bowron, who had been up most of the night, and Bentsen, who was flying back to Washington to deal with the crash, they presented their compromise.

Under a rare presidential order, Bentsen tasked his undersecretary Ron Noble to lead an external investigation to determine the security gaps at the complex and to figure out how to patch them. The Secret Service would act as a partner in the investigation. At a news conference at roughly 2:45 P.M. that Monday, Noble and Special Agent Carl Meyer fielded a barrage of questions from a room of reporters, who seemed to be shocked that this kind of attack had so easily breached the White House perimeter. Many in Washington assumed the Secret Service and U.S. military had some early detection system for incoming planes, and even perhaps anti-aircraft missiles installed in the White House roof.

"Mr. Noble, can you tell us to the best of your knowledge . . . how something like this could happen?" a reporter asked.

"That's precisely the sort of question I can't answer," Noble replied, a grim look on his face.

Noble and Meyer both tried to sidestep detailed questions about whether the Secret Service had had any warning of Corder's plane or had taken any action to try to deflect or stop the threat.

After officers noticed the plane, reporters asked, was there enough time for agents to "get off a shot"? Noble said he didn't know.

"Was the plane fired upon by your agents?" a reporter then asked Meyer.

"A little too early to get into that," Meyer said.

"You would know," the reporter replied. "It's a yes or no answer, sir—yes or no answer."

Another reporter called out: "And how would that hurt the security of the president by letting us know whether or not . . ."

"The answer is no," Meyer said finally.

To help coordinate the fact-finding mission, Noble enlisted a team of lawyers, while the White House named an impressive panel of senior leaders, including former CIA and FBI director William Webster, to oversee the probe. But just as they began their work, a new scare shook the White House.

ON A PLEASANT Saturday afternoon in October, Francisco Duran stood on Pennsylvania Avenue outside the White House. He pulled a Chinese-made semiautomatic assault rifle from under his tan trench coat, pointed the barrel through the bars of the iron perimeter fence, and opened fire on the White House. Duran, a convicted felon who despised the government and Clinton, shot twenty-nine rounds at the North Facade of the White House, striking it eleven times and shattering a window in the press briefing room before three civilians on the street tackled him.

Duran's shots never endangered President Clinton, who was in a south-facing room in the Executive Mansion at the time. But the incident shook the White House staff. Leon Panetta, Clinton's chief of staff, asked Noble's team to include Duran's shooting in their review.

The eight-month investigation that followed was one of the most comprehensive in Secret Service history, second only to the Warren Commission's examination of the Kennedy assassination. They reviewed every element of White House security, interviewing former presidents Bush, Carter, and Ford to get their perspective. The investigative staff sought advice from a series of technical experts in radar and X-ray detection, aviation, explosives, counterterrorism, and more.

In one of the investigation's more secretive steps, the Secret Service dispatched a pair of trusted senior supervisors to visit the Delta Force commander at Fort Bragg to discuss a novel way to test the White House's vulnerability. The Secret Service wanted Delta to try some exercises to see if they could succeed in getting past the Secret Service officers, and perhaps inside the mansion.

At the meeting to discuss the operation, the burly commanding officer of the U.S. Army's Delta Force greeted his Secret Service guests in a conference room, then ushered in about a half dozen of his operators, introducing them to the special agents from the president's protection squad in Washington. "They want to task you guys with attacking the White House," the commander said, pausing to let the idea sink in. "Under different circumstances, we would be arresting you right now," he deadpanned.

The special operators didn't succeed in breaching the White House. But in mock exercises, they warned that if a helicopter or light aircraft were to land on the White House grounds with six to eight attackers aboard, there was a strong likelihood that in the confusion, at least one assassin would make it inside the White House.

Noble's investigative team was close to finalizing their draft report in April 1995—and was leaning toward a highly controversial step. They wanted to close Pennsylvania Avenue in front of the White House to create a wider barrier around Crown, but the street was a critical artery through downtown Washington. Before the final draft was made public, a moment of terror gave urgency to their recommendation. On April 19, two Army veterans used a truck loaded with explosives to blow up a federal building in Oklahoma City, killing 168 people, including six Secret Service agents and staff. A few weeks later, President Clinton reluctantly agreed to the Secret Service's proposal and announced the closure of Pennsylvania Avenue.

Perhaps the most significant new protection adopted after the 1994 review was a new classified program called Tigerwall. It allowed the Secret Service to monitor the FAA's real-time radar when planes got suspiciously close to downtown Washington's restricted airspace. It would provide the Service with critical early warning if an errant plane ever headed over the White House again. Agents hoped they would never need it.

CHAPTER 12

THE INTERN

Have you seen a young congressional staffer?"

President Clinton poked his head outside the cracked-open door of the Oval Office to speak to his protectors stationed outside the door. In the small vestibule office, Lewis Fox, a silver-haired Secret Service officer, had been sitting in a chair near an agent on the president's detail. Unusually heavy snow had been falling all weekend, but inside the West Wing it was an unremarkable Sunday afternoon. A football game, which they'd been glancing at from time to time, played at a low volume on a television in the corner. To Fox, it had been a fairly humdrum weekend shift at E-6, the Secret Service's code name for this position outside the Oval Office.

"No, sir," Fox said.

"I'm expecting one," Clinton said. He asked if

the officer would let him know when the staffer showed up.

"Yes, sir," Fox said, nodding.

After Clinton shut the door, Fox told the agent he had a good idea who the president was expecting a visit from alone on a weekend afternoon.

"I'll bet it's Monica," Fox said.

Less than ten minutes later, just as Fox had predicted, up the hall came Monica Lewinsky, with a mane of shiny nearly-black hair and a big lip-glossy smile. The bubbly twenty-one-year-old had joined the White House as a new intern just that summer but got an unusually quick promotion after working in Chief of Staff Leon Panetta's office that fall and had been hired several weeks earlier as a permanent staffer in the East Wing's congressional affairs office. She greeted Fox with a warm "Hi" and then explained the reason for her visit: She had some letters for the president.

It had gotten to the point that winter that Secret Service guards were starting to set their watches to this subtle weekend dance. The president would come down from his private residence on a Saturday or Sunday afternoon and stride into the Oval Office without any aides in tow. In roughly ten to thirty minutes, Lewinsky would show up in the hallway saying she had something to deliver to the president.

This Sunday afternoon, Fox knocked on the Oval Office door. He heard Clinton say "Yes," and the curved white door opened. The president nodded to Lewinsky and ushered her into the Oval. He turned back to Fox, signaling to him to close the door. "She'll be here a while," Clinton said.

Fox, an officer with twenty-five years on the job, more than half of it watching the comings and goings of presidents in the White House, sensed something more than official business was going on with Eagle and the intern. Fox had developed an informal friendship with Lewinsky from her first days in the White House. The previous fall, Fox met Lewinsky while he'd been posted at a security checkpoint in the West Wing basement. He let her linger there, long enough so she could run into Clinton when he was going to pass through to the Executive Office Building and get her picture taken with him. Fox didn't know it then, but Lewinsky had been aggressively flirting with the president since getting her intern position in the chief of staff's office in July. She routinely tried to position herself in places she knew the president was going to pass. A week after the basement meeting, Lewinsky found Fox on duty and gave him a box of Godiva chocolates to thank him for helping her get the picture. Fellow officers had started teasing Fox by calling Lewinsky "your girl," though there was nothing between them.

However, after the picture and the chocolates that fall, fellow officers kept updating Fox on Lewinsky's frequent visits to the West Wing—especially on quiet weekends. "Your girl was here again yesterday," one said. Fox saw Lewinsky in the Oval two times while he was working the weekend shift: once in January with the papers and another time when Fox saw Lewinsky quickly leave the president's office through a side exit. In April 1996, another Secret Service officer, Gary Byrne, took Fox aside to warn him: "There's something you may want to know." Byrne said he'd complained to a junior White House staffer that Lewinsky was making an unusual number of trips to the hall outside the Oval Office, as if she were loitering to stay close to the action. He got an urgent call soon afterward at home from Evelyn Lieberman, the White House's chief enforcer, the deputy chief of staff for operations. She wanted to talk to Byrne in person immediately, and he agreed to come see her before his shift the next day. Byrne relayed what he had seen.

Lieberman had already scolded Lewinsky once before, finding her lingering outside the Oval in late November and reminding her interns weren't supposed to "hang about" near the president's office. Lewinsky surprised Lieberman, telling her she was now a permanent staffer, prompting Lieberman to apologize for her mistake. But now this young staffer's behavior was causing hallway gossip among the Secret Service officers. **I have to get rid of her,** she thought.

She told Chief of Staff Leon Panetta that she wanted to transfer Lewinsky to another agency.

She dubbed Lewinsky a "clutch" who spent too much energy trying to get face time with the president. "The appearance it was creating" wasn't good for Clinton, she said. Panetta, a longtime government hand, trusted his aide's instincts for heading off trouble and approved the plan.

A few days later, Fox was working his morning shift in the West Wing. He saw Lewinsky in the hallway crying and asked what was wrong.

"I don't work here anymore," she said in a high voice, wiping her eyes. "I'm going to the Pentagon."

LEWINSKY HAD BEEN promoted from intern to permanent staffer and then ejected from the White House as a threat to the president's reputation, all in just ten months' time. Indeed, it wasn't long after Lewinsky started working in the West Wing that Jennifer Palmieri, one of Panetta's top aides, and others were already "worried that an affair between the president and Lewinsky had begun." They'd noticed how "clutchy" Lewinsky was with the president and that she seemed "giddy" in his presence. Likewise, Clinton loitered by her tiny cubicle outside Chief of Staff Panetta's office on so many afternoons that fall of 1995 that senior aides began to take notice, dryly joking that the president had never visited his chief of staff's office this much before.

"You sure are getting a lot of face time with the president," one Panetta aide told Lewinsky.

Lewinsky batted her eyelashes at Clinton, giggled at his jokes, and finally, when they were alone late one evening in the West Wing, they both confessed their attraction. On November 15, the White House was working with a small portion of its normal staff due to a government shutdown that began the day before. Unpaid interns were a critical part of keeping the White House running during this period. Clinton ushered Lewinsky into a windowless hallway between his dining room and study around 8 P.M. The intern playfully lifted the back of her jacket to flash him the strap of her thong bikini above her pants. They kissed, then parted. A few hours later, Clinton brought her again to the study, where he unhooked her bra to fondle and kiss her breasts. She began performing oral sex on the president. Midway through, Clinton had to take a phone call from a member of Congress.

Secret Service agents and officers, who monitored the president's comings and goings, didn't see the racy stuff happening behind closed doors—the heavy petting in the president's private bathroom, Lewinsky performing oral sex under the desk. But several of them, including Officer Fox, had a gut instinct that something was up.

Indeed he was right: Those "papers for the president" Lewinsky told Officer Fox she had that day in January 1996 were just a pretext Clinton and Lewinsky devised so they could make their weekend rendezvous look like official business. She would pass by the office with some papers. Clinton would keep the office door open when she was supposed to arrive, and then he would invite her in.

He had called her at her Watergate apartment earlier that January day to alert her he was going to his office soon.

"Oh, do you want some company?" Lewinsky asked him playfully.

"That would be great," the president replied.

When Fox closed the door behind them, they talked on the sofas in the Oval for a few minutes and eventually Clinton led her into the bathroom, where no one could see them. They began kissing, and things got hot quickly. The president suggested he'd like to go down on Lewinsky, but she stopped him. She was having her period, she explained. Lewinsky instead performed oral sex on Clinton.

After about twenty minutes in the bathroom, they returned to the Oval Office, where Clinton picked up a cigar and started chewing on the end. He took the cigar into his hand and stared at it with a lascivious look.

"We can do that, too, some time," Lewinsky said. Then Lewinsky let herself out, thinking no one was the wiser.

All that winter, as he appeared well positioned to win a second term, the president felt safe and even a little cocky. Nobody would be able to say with any certainty what he and Monica had been doing in their weekend interludes. He had told no one, and she seemed to like the secret they were keeping. They had fooled around only in a window-less hallway or closed rooms that not even the Secret Service could see into. They, along with some staff working in the White House, might suspect, but that was all.

BY DECEMBER 1997, however, President Clinton had new reasons to fear that his private sexual romps with other women might not remain private. He had won reelection handily and was serving the first year of his second term. But he now had ample reason to fear that chatty agents could sink his presidency. He was currently under severe scrutiny by Independent Counsel Kenneth Starr, whose evolving investigation was deep into its third year and now sniffing around into his interactions with women.

At the same time, two eras of Secret Service agents collided in a high-stress standoff. An older generation of agents who had protected President Kennedy came forward with memories of their service, unburdening themselves of a secret they'd kept for more than three decades. But they made their contribution to history at the same time the current president was struggling with his very own "Kennedy problem."

Clinton was also being forced to answer uncom-fortable questions about his sex life as part of a sexual harassment lawsuit filed by Jones, the Arkansas state employee that Clinton met in a hotel room. The president's lawyers had argued all the way to the Supreme Court that the suit should be delayed until after Clinton left office— but lost their final appeal in May 1997. The White House had also just been stung by an August 1997 **Newsweek** article, which reported on allegations that Clinton had groped the breast of a White House volunteer, Kathleen Willey. She told friends the president forcibly kissed her and pushed her hand onto his genitals when they were alone in his private study next to the Oval Office.

As the president's team battled on several fronts, on December 4, 1997, ABC News aired a two-hour history special about President Kennedy's "Camelot." The prime time broadcast featured a handful of well-respected agents describing the reckless philandering they had witnessed while protecting JFK. They told anchor Peter Jennings of their conflicted feelings about shielding the leader of the free world so he could swim naked in the White House swimming pool with his young secretaries and sneak around to one-night stands with women whose names they rarely knew. The agents, four somber men in their retirement years, spoke with the authority of having served their country twice— in the military and in the president's guard.

Larry Newman, a former Kennedy detail agent, told Jennings he admired many qualities of the president, and he choked up when he described watching Kennedy stop in a Boston hospital unit to take time to write encouraging notes to burned children during what was easily the worst hour of Kennedy's own life. The president's newborn son was near death in an adjoining ward, and he passed away later that day. But Newman was nevertheless unsettled by Kennedy's recklessness in pursuing an endless string of sexual conquests. "You were on the most elite assignment in the Secret Service, and you were there watching an elevator or a door because the president was inside with two hookers," Newman said. Tony Sherman, a fellow agent, said the president's disregard for his office and the stream of random women ushered into his bedroom eventually angered him.

At the time, reporters did not catch on to the panic this sex-tinged history program caused in the Clinton White House. If agents who had shadowed the late President Kennedy were now coming clean about his voracious philandering, Clinton and his aides wondered, what stories might the Secret Service staff shadowing President Clinton tell? The president later confided in Lewinsky that he feared the Secret Service officers who manned the White House complex were gossiping outside the White House family.

Lew Merletti, whom Clinton had recently named the director of the Secret Service, was charged with protecting the president's physical safety. But his reaction that December to the ABC program on Kennedy was regarded as a move to shield Clinton from political peril. In one of his first high-profile acts as director, Merletti urged all agents to keep their mouths shut about what they had seen and heard at the president's shoulder. Without their silence, he warned, they would be endangering the life of the current president and all future ones.

Merletti, a tightly wound, wiry agent with dark hair and an intense gaze, had been mentored by some of the best, including Bob DeProspero, and earned high marks when he served in lower-level positions on President Reagan's and President Bush's security details. In the summer of 1995, he realized the dream of any agent, becoming the special agent in charge of the president's detail. He could not have known, but his timing was ill-fated. He took over the detail a few weeks before Clinton began his sexual relationship with Lewinsky.

In his December 5 letter circulated to all current agents and the alumni network of former agents, Merletti called the ABC statements "very troubling and counterproductive to the mission of the Secret Service." Merletti asked the entire Secret Service corps "to refrain" from "providing any information to any source regarding any aspect of the personal lives of our protectees."

Merletti said the Service had to keep a president's trust, even during his most private moments. If not, presidents would keep agents at a distance and the Service would be unable to safeguard them properly. Merletti insisted he wasn't doing this for Clinton's personal benefit. "I'm not a Clinton man. I'm not a Bush man. I'm not a Reagan man," Merletti said in an interview when asked about his stern warning. "This is about the office of the presidency."

The Kennedy agents, however, found Merletti's letter insulting.

"The director of the Secret Service, a taxpayer-funded agency, has sent out a letter that suppresses and attacks my right of free speech," Sherman told **The New York Times.** "He implies that perhaps the four of us are not worthy of trust and confidence. This is a slap at us. What we said, I think, contributed to the history of the United States.

"I liked JFK," Sherman added. "He was one of the nicest guys I ever met. But he was reckless, morally. And for thirty-five years I kept my mouth shut."

Seymour Hersh speculated that something more must be motivating Merletti. "Is he condoning cover-up?" he asked. "Why would the Clinton White House care what happened thirty-five years ago? Two and two is always four and there are certain things that are obvious." Sherman and fellow agent Tim McIntyre later asked Merletti for a public apology and called his comments defamatory. They asked that he retract his claims that they had endangered future presidents.

Merletti stood firm. In fact, he was about to double down.

The same day that Merletti scolded agents for talking out of school, two storms swirling over Clinton's head began to converge. At about 5:40 P.M. that Friday, December 5, attorneys for Paula Jones faxed to Clinton's lawyer a list of witnesses they planned to depose in their lawsuit against Clinton. The two sides had been battling for weeks in court over whether Clinton would have to answer whether he had sexual contact with other women. A new name now showed up on Jones's witness list: Monica Lewinsky. Clinton's lawyer Bob Bennett did not know who that was.

The next morning, on Saturday, December 6, Lewinsky showed up at the Northwest Gate of the White House at 10 A.M. and ended her visit by blowing up in anger in front of the Secret Service officers manning the guardhouse. It had nothing to do with her being called as a witness—Lewinsky and the president hadn't yet learned about the list sent to the lawyer. Instead, Lewinsky came over that Saturday to drop off some gifts and a personal letter for Clinton, as a final gesture now that the secret duo had officially broken up. But the president told his secretary, Betty Currie, to tell Lewinsky he'd be too busy meeting with his lawyers to see her that day, though she could drop the items off. When officers at the gate reached Currie by phone to get approval to let Lewinsky in, Currie told them to keep Lewinsky at the gate for forty minutes until she could come out personally to meet her. Currie let slip to the officers that she was a little busy that moment because the president had a guest. As Lewinsky waited and chatted with the Secret Service officers, one officer mentioned that Eleanor Mondale was visiting the president. Lewinsky stormed off, jealously fuming, certain Clinton was now dating the pretty blonde. She later called Currie from a pay phone, yelling that she didn't appreciate being lied to about who the president was really seeing. Currie then came to see the officers, with her hands shaking and her voice about to break into tears.

"The president is so upset he wants somebody fired over this," Currie told Secret Service captain Jeff Purdie, the watch commander at the White House that day. Currie urged him and a fellow officer to find out which officers had been so indiscreet and caused this ruckus. The secretary came back outside later, explaining there was a way to keep heads from rolling. If officers did not "tell a lot of people" about Lewinsky's dramatic meltdown at the gate, she said, then nothing would happen.

The president summoned Purdie to his office, too. "I hope you use your discretion," Clinton told him.

Captain Purdie returned with a warning to his officers: Don't mention anything to anyone. He told his deputy not to generate any paperwork about Lewinsky's visit. "I was just in the Oval Office with the president and he wants somebody's ass out here," Purdie explained. "As far as you're concerned . . . this never happened."

Clinton found out more bad news that evening. In a meeting, his lawyers told him that Jones's lawyers had listed Lewinsky as a possible witness. How did she get connected to this, the president demanded to know. Clinton grew increasingly anxious that Secret Service officers were gossiping.

On January 19, 1998, the secret that Clinton feared would come out did come out, launching a media frenzy that engulfed the White House and soon caused his closest aides to fear he would have to resign his office. A new conservative website run by Matt Drudge indirectly landed a blockbuster scoop. He reported that **Newsweek** was holding back on a story alleging that Clinton had been having a sexual relationship with a White House intern named Monica Lewinsky. The startling news came not from Secret Service agents or officers, but from Lucianne Goldberg, a literary agent who represented Linda Tripp and urged her to secretly record her conversations with her friend Lewinsky. Goldberg had been talking to the **Newsweek** reporter and was disappointed that his magazine had cold feet about running the story.

All the big media outlets jumped in, scurrying to confirm the details, and wrote dueling stories about the alleged affair over the next forty-eight hours. Clinton summoned some of his former top political aides to return to the White House in his time of crisis. The president swore it was a lie—in private meetings with his cabinet and on live television a few days later at a White House event to tout quality afterschool care for children.

"I want to say one thing to the American people. I want you to listen to me. . . . I did not have sexual relations with that woman, Miss Lewinsky," Clinton said at the January 26 event, with his wife standing by his side. The story continued to dominate every newspaper and television channel.

That same week, 350 miles away in Waynesburg, Pennsylvania, Lew Fox, a fifty-four-year-old enjoying the first few months of his retirement from the Secret Service, was having breakfast with a small group of friends at a restaurant near his home. His pals were agog at the news from Washington and asked Fox if he'd ever heard of this intern named Monica when he was at the White House. "Sure," Fox said. "I know her." He shared a few more details about the friendship they had struck up and how often she seemed to put herself in the president's path.

He wasn't sure how, but not long after his meal, Fox got a call from a television reporter with WPXI in nearby Pittsburgh who asked to interview him on the biggest story in the country. Fox agreed and said what he had told his friends: He knew Lewinsky and had seen her a lot in the West Wing. He didn't say much, but the broadcast set off a chain reaction down in the nation's capital—excitement in Ken Starr's office and panic in the West Wing. A Secret Service agent working in public affairs called Fox at home, asking him gruffly whether he planned on doing any more interviews. Fox joked with the agent, but he got the hint. He said no, he wasn't planning to.

"You're probably going to get a subpoena" because of the interview, the Secret Service spokesman warned.

"I've got nothing to hide," Fox replied.

The professional association of former Secret Service agents, a powerful alumni organization that was often dispatched to defend the agency, called Fox at home. A member of the group discouraged the officer from revealing anything more about what he had seen while standing outside the Oval Office.

Meanwhile, Starr's office got busy. They subpoenaed the television station for a copy of Fox's interview. FBI agents went to Fox's home and quietly interviewed him there on February 6. They had many questions about when he'd seen Lewinsky with the president. He described ushering her into the Oval Office at the president's request one weekend when he appeared to be working alone. She stayed inside for about forty minutes. Fox thought it was late in 1995.

Fox didn't know it then, but he was a fact witness who appeared to contradict the sworn testimony of President Clinton. Just a few weeks earlier—in fact just two days before the Lewinsky allegations broke—the president had testified in a closed-door deposition in the Jones case that he had never been alone with Lewinsky. The retired Secret Service officer, who days later shared his story with **The Washington Post**, was the first person to suggest otherwise.

DIRECTOR MERLETTI WRESTLED with his own personal and professional concern about the Lewinsky news. He was driving to work at 1800 G Street and racking his brain when he heard an interview on NPR about allegations that the president had carried on a fling with a White House intern. As the head of the Secret Service, he hoped none of this news was coming from agent or officer gossip. But he had a more personal connection to the events, too. If these stories were true, one of the biggest presidential scandals had unfolded directly under Merletti's nose. He had been in charge of Clinton's personal detail precisely when Clinton and Lewinsky were accused of secretly rendezvousing in the cramped quarters of the West Wing, starting in the fall of 1995. Merletti would tell others he couldn't remember meeting her or hearing about her from his detail agents. He later learned Lewinsky had written him a congratulatory note on his work protecting the "Big Guy," but Merletti didn't remember that either.

Days after the Drudge bombshell, stories began to surface about other unnamed eyewitnesses from the White House. ABC News reported that a White House source claimed to have seen Clinton and Lewinsky engaged in a sex act. **The Dallas Morning News** posted a story on its website saying a Secret Service agent was talking to Starr and was prepared to testify that he had seen the president and Lewinsky in a "compromising situation." The paper later retracted the "compromising" part. On January 22, Starr's office subpoenaed Secret Service logs and records. The Secret Service's general counsel, John Kelleher, came to Merletti's office to alert him that Starr was preparing to subpoena active duty Secret Service agents and officers. Merletti told Kelleher they had to meet with Starr immediately and show him the danger this would unleash. The director was determined to not let the Service be used in a political fishing expedition.

A few days later, Merletti brought what he thought was a sobering and strong case against turning agents into witnesses to the Pennsylvania Avenue offices of the independent counsel. In a conference room with Starr and his deputy, Robert J. Bittman, Merletti used his slide show to describe the attempts on presidents' lives going all the way back to Lincoln's assassination. He told them that in each case, the protectors' proximity to the president had made the difference between life and death.

President Lincoln? Dead, because his protector had left the president's box at the theater to get a drink across the street. President McKinley? Dead, because his agent was asked to move back to make room for another official. President Reagan? Alive, because Agent Jerry Parr had been standing directly behind the president and pushed him into a waiting car within seconds of John Hinckley's firing the first shot.

Merletti played a cut of the old Zapruder film and black-and-white stills from the day JFK was shot in his open-top limousine. The director pointed out that his agents had hopped off the rear steps of Kennedy's limousine because the president had asked them to: He didn't like to appear to need protection from the public. It cost him and the country dearly, Merletti said. When the first shot rang out from behind the motorcade, agents were in a follow-up car behind the limo, too far away to help Kennedy. Merletti ran the heartbreaking clip of Mike Wallace's **60 Minutes** interview with Jackie Kennedy detail agent Clint Hill. The agent, a hero to many in the Service, broke down while describing his feelings of guilt at being unable to reach the president in time to take the third bullet that killed him. Recounting the assassination twelve years later, Hill said he would've much preferred to have died that day. Though he sprinted a car length to Kennedy's limousine in seconds, he still agonized over whether he could have gone faster.

"But you couldn't, Clint," Wallace said, incredulous. "You got there in less than two seconds. You surely don't have any sense of guilt about that."

"I certainly do. It's my fault," Hill said. "If I had reacted just a little bit quicker . . ." His voice broke off, trembling. "And I'll live with that 'til my grave."

In the quiet after the presentation ended, Merletti tried to put the prosecutors in the shoes of an agent. "The sound of a gunshot is what every Secret Service agent prepares for his whole life," he said. "That takes place in a second."

He told Starr and Bitman that presidents would inevitably push agents away if they could be forced later on to act as witnesses testifying about a president's private moments. That would render agents effectively useless. "Secret Service history has proven that **confidentiality** affords us the proximity that is critical to the success of our mission," Merletti told them. "If our protectees cannot trust us, if they believe that they will be called to testify before a grand jury to reveal confidences, the president will not allow us that critical proximity."

But Merletti sensed that Starr was indifferent and even chilly to his presentation. "It's as if he couldn't have cared less," Merletti reported thinking. "He's not listening." He left more agitated than when he arrived.

Starr appreciated the Service's zero-fail mission, but he saw this as a legal matter. The law clearly required that all law enforcement agents, including those in the Secret Service, provide testimony when it was necessary for a criminal investigation.

Days later, Treasury Secretary Rubin and Merletti agreed their agency lawyers would seek to pursue a novel privilege, which they dubbed the "executive protection privilege." They wanted to use it in court to shield agents from Starr's subpoenas so they'd never have to testify before a grand jury about anything they had seen or heard the president do. There was no legal precedent for this argument, and legal scholars snorted at the idea that security guards had a special privileged relationship with their client akin to that of a lawyer or a psychologist. A few veteran Justice Department lawyers shook their head, sure it would get laughed out of court. But Merletti's team pursued it anyway, arguing the lives of presidents hung in the balance.

Starr had reasons to doubt Merletti's motives. Starr's deputy got a phone call from a veteran Washington journalist around New Year's Eve. The reporter had been contacted by a man very close to the senior leadership of the Secret Service. The man was afraid to come forward for fear of retribution, but he had said that Secret Service leaders told him that Clinton had pulled Merletti into his office in December when Paula Jones's lawyers were seeking to ask Clinton and other possible witnesses about his relationships with women other than his wife. The attorneys in that case also wanted to question Secret Service agents about Clinton's activities.

According to the Secret Service deputies, Clinton told Merletti, in effect, "I want you to find ways to keep your guys from talking in the Paula Jones case. Look into it."

Merletti, when later questioned by an FBI agent about the idea that he had been conspiring with Clinton in a cover-up, told the agent it was pop-pycock. The idea to assert the privilege was his.

Many agents solemnly agreed with Merletti that lack of proximity to the president would risk more assassinations. Merletti put out an all-hands-on-deck call to retired agents who had witnessed assassination attempts, including Hill and Parr, and they gave gripping testimonials in support of shielding agents from testifying. Tim McCarthy, who had taken a bullet meant for President Reagan, said Reagan could have died if he'd been asked to hang back even a few feet. But the former presidents themselves were split on the debate. President Bush sided with Merletti. Presidents Ford and Carter said that investigators' search for truth in a criminal probe outweighed the possible risks.

Louis Freeh, then the FBI director, whose agents were helping the Starr investigation, said the Clinton administration had repeatedly sought to use various legal defenses to block investigators from getting access to witnesses and records, claiming the president should be allowed the privilege of seeking his senior advisers' counsel in confidence. But he said the dubious claim that there was some sort of Secret Service privilege represented the moment the Clinton administration hit "rock bottom." The privilege was based on a flimsy logic, which Freeh said amounted to this: A president could increase the risk to his life by keeping his agents farther away because "a president might not want to have the Secret Service around when he's committing a crime."

"The argument was pure craziness," Freeh later wrote. "A dozen comedy writers couldn't invent anything more ludicrous, but of course the Secret Service had to lend its support and the president's lawyers had to do their bit for it, and the court had to waste its own time considering the matter before it did the obvious, which was to throw the 'executive protection privilege' out the door."

That legal battle went on for six months, with the privilege claim resoundingly rejected by every judge who reviewed it, from the federal district judge who first got the case to the entire appeals courts in Washington. Finally, in mid-July 1998, the Supreme Court's chief justice, William Rehnquist, effectively declared the privilege dead. Rehnquist issued a two-page opinion refusing to block the agents from testifying and saying the previous court's rejection of the privilege claim was "cogent and correct." He said he felt sure his fellow justices would unanimously agree. The Justice Department decided to fight no more. In public statements, President Clinton continued to stress that the Secret Service had chosen to fight this subpoena battle but complained the court's decision "could 'have a chilling effect' on the way presidents work."

MERLETTI'S LOSS WAS Starr's victory, clearing the way that same day for the independent counsel to interview Secret Service staff. Before the questioning began, he and his deputies assured the Service that his team wouldn't ask questions that could jeopardize sensitive security secrets. The rest of that afternoon, Secret Service officers Gary Byrne and John Muskett and retired agent Bob Ferguson filed into the witness stand in the grand jury room in Washington's federal courthouse. There, taking questions from Starr's chief deputy, they described the multiple occasions when they'd seen Lewinsky enter the Oval Office to visit the president alone.

Next up in the grand jury was Larry Cockell, then the special agent in charge of the president's detail. Starr's team believed Cockell might unlock the greatest secrets about Clinton. His testimony, they hoped, would reveal whether the president sought to obstruct the probe and conceal his lies. They were sorely disappointed.

Cockell, a deeply serious professional, had little time for politics or spin. He was the first Black agent to lead a presidential detail in an agent corps that was 80 percent white. Though he more than earned his promotions, some white agents resented his rise. There were also some Black agents who were disappointed in him, believing he had not fought hard enough against a promotion system that still favored whites. Regardless, Cockell was used to being tough, and he wasn't going to gild the truth for anyone.

In fact, Cockell didn't even know who Monica Lewinsky was, and he had far less information to share about Lewinsky than many of his colleagues. He hadn't been stationed in the White House for most of the time period Starr was investigating. Indeed, the first time Cockell had heard Lewinsky's name was in January 1998—two days before the Lewinsky story broke. He had sat beside Clinton when the president was deposed in Clinton's lawyer's office in the Jones lawsuit, and one of Paula Jones's lawyers had asked Clinton about his relationship with an intern named Monica.

Cockell told Starr's prosecutor, "Although there were a number of rumors regarding these situations, I think I would be the last person that agents would come to and bring these rumors because I specifically discouraged that, because there so many erroneous reports going around that it was counterproductive for us to focus on what the rumors said and agents were specifically discouraged not to be purveyors of rumors."

Cockell drew a clear line between a manager's best practices and an agent's legal duty. As a manager, he urged his agents to let the private details of the president's conversations and visitors roll over them, and to shut down the gossip and chatter. But as an agent, he discounted the idea that he or his colleagues had sworn an oath to keep a president's secrets for eternity.

"I took an oath to uphold the laws of the United States and, in the capacity of an agent, to protect the life of the president and all those persons that the Secret Service is authorized to protect," Cockell said.

"Did you take an oath, or as part of that oath you just described, did you pledge confidentiality of any type?" the prosecutor asked.

"No, sir," Cockell said.

The Starr team learned something from Cockell in the end, but it was a far cry from what they had expected, and most Americans never got to hear it. In the grand jury room, he gave the clearest explanation yet for why the Secret Service didn't care if the president got blow jobs from interns in his private study.

A Starr investigator asked Cockell whether, in hindsight, the Secret Service should have done something to limit Clinton's ability to spend so many hours with a young woman in private nooks, entirely unseen by his protectors. Cockell pointed to the fact that the White House was an office, and Lewinsky had been cleared to enter. "Sir, my focus is the safety and security of the president," Cockell said. "And if it does not threaten his safety and security . . . then my responsibility ends."

Though Cockell's testimony wasn't the bomb-shell Starr had hoped for, Cockell did lead Starr to another witness, who ultimately helped Starr build his case that the president had lied under oath. Cockell said one agent, Nelson Garabito, had confided in him after the story broke that he, too, had seen Lewinsky enter the Oval Office when the president was alone there.

Four months later, after Clinton admitted having a sexual relationship with Lewinsky, after Starr issued a report detailing Clinton's lies, and after the House began an impeachment inquiry against the president, Director Merletti shocked the Secret Service by saying goodbye. On November 12, 1998, Merletti announced he was retiring after only seventeen months as director. He had lined up a job as a top security executive for the Cleveland Browns, a football team owned by Al Lerner. Merletti was following a longtime Secret Service ally who had recently left to become worldwide corporate security chief for Lerner's credit card giant, MBNA bank. Agents that Merletti had mentored were stunned. Merletti had been in the middle of a national tour of field offices, telling agents about his long-term plans for the agency, and cut the tour short, announcing he was out. Some were suspicious at the timing. Merletti insisted it was just too good a job to turn down. The next day, Clinton settled his lawsuit with Paula Jones, agreeing to pay her $850,000 to drop her case.

Now Clinton had to choose a new director, and

the top two contenders were both former leaders of his detail: Larry Cockell and Brian Stafford. Both had proven their ability to lead. Treasury Secretary Rubin recommended that the president pick Cockell. Rubin felt that Cockell was a strategic thinker, and that his ethical standards were beyond reproach. In Stafford's favor, he was a pushy advocate for the Service's budget, and he had an intensely loyal following too. There were pros and cons with both men. Stafford, a married father, was known in the Clinton White House to have had at least one romantic indiscretion that might prove compromising. Clinton's aides also fretted that choosing Cockell could trigger bad press and cause some to speculate he was rewarding the agent for not divulging anything embarrassing about the president to Starr. They tossed around the options, but the decision was ultimately the president's. He chose Stafford, who in May 1999 was sworn in as the next director. Stafford would oversee a major expansion of Secret Service duties, including the Service's new role studying school shootings in the wake of Columbine and protecting major events like Super Bowls and the Winter Olympic Games in Salt Lake City.

Just a year after Stafford became director, a group of Black Secret Service agents would take the gutsy move of suing their agency and accusing the Service of a systemic racism that enabled Stafford's own rise and that of his white deputies.

TERROR AND POLITICS

THE BUSH YEARS (2000–2007)

CHAPTER 13

SCRAMBLING ON 9/11

The White House and the press pool considered the president's trip to Sarasota that fall a relatively low-key visit. He and his entourage would land in the evening on Monday, September 10, and spend the night in a luxury resort on Longboat Key, a barrier island just off the coast in the Gulf of Mexico. They'd visit a local elementary school first thing the next morning. Bush's brief stop at the school was part of a weeklong series of events to promote literacy and, more important, to showcase an education reform bill that Bush was pushing Congress to pass called No Child Left Behind. Total time on the ground in the Tampa Bay area: under eighteen hours. The president's traveling circus was scheduled to be back at the White House by lunchtime on Tuesday, September 11.

Reporters in the White House press corps

dubbed Bush's visit a "scrub trip." That meant they didn't expect the president to make major news. The networks and other media organizations could send their lower-level staff on Air Force One to give the veteran White House reporters a break from the road. They just needed a warm body to cover their bases in case something unexpected happened.

Bush's most senior aides, including White House chief of staff Andy Card and adviser Karl Rove, had tagged along in large part for a secondary political purpose. They planned to join the president and his brother Jeb, the governor of Florida, for a private dinner that night at the resort with major GOP fundraisers.

The president enjoyed the steak and tortilla soup, the easy jokes with familiar friends, and headed back to his suite a good bit after his normal 10 P.M. bedtime. Still, he rose at 6:30 the next morning for a run. A lanky reporter who was part of the small group traveling with Bush that day and whom Bush liked had joined him for four fast miles around the resort's golf course while a member of his Secret Service detail followed in a golf cart. The agents tried to ignore a noxious smell wafting over the island: the odor of dead fish that had washed ashore thanks to a toxic "red tide" that plagued the Gulf Coast that month.

Card visited Bush—now showered and dressed—in his suite just before 8 A.M. for his Daily Intelligence

Briefing. Mike Morell, his high-level CIA briefer that day, gave a pretty routine report. Some violent skirmishes between Palestinian fighters and Israeli soldiers, but no crisis that demanded U.S. action. The chief of staff ran through the schedule for the school visit as the detail shepherded Bush to his limo for the ten-minute ride to Emma E. Booker Elementary.

"This should be an easy day," Card told the president.

The Secret Service likewise rated the Sarasota trip a comparatively minor in-and-out. Weeks ahead of time, they had planned every step Bush would take in the sleepy Tampa Bay area town. They'd placed snipers and surface-to-air missiles on the rooftop of the Colony Resort. Coast Guard boats patrolled just offshore. The head of the president's detail, Carl Truscott, had opted to skip the trip entirely and stay back home in Washington. Eddie Marinzel, a seasoned lieutenant, would be the lead agent protecting Trailblazer.

There's a strain of superstition in the Secret Service culture that dates back to an eerie confluence of events on the day of President John F. Kennedy's assassination. Kennedy's detail leader and constant shadow, Jerry Behn, had decided to skip the trip to Dallas in November 1963 to take a short vacation, his first in three years. Now Truscott, the head of Bush's detail, was back in Washington for the September 11 visit.

"Nobody in the Service can forget that," a retired agent said of the day Kennedy was shot.

BUSH WAS IN a good mood as he sprang out of his limousine, nicknamed the Beast, in front of Emma E. Booker Elementary School in Sarasota at about 8:50 A.M. Marinzel walked a step behind him on his right as the president strutted confidently toward his welcoming party on the school entry sidewalk. The agent was about Bush's height and weight, and he followed closely as Bush began shaking hands with the assembled local politicians and school leaders.

Bush's senior adviser, Karl Rove, was several feet away on his cellphone with his assistant, who had called from the West Wing with news. Rove hung up and leaned over to quietly alert Bush. "A plane has hit the World Trade Center," he said. "Maybe a prop plane, we don't know."

Bush arched his brows, then said, "Get more details."

Marinzel, a half step from the president's back, overheard. Like nearly everyone in official Washington and across the country first learning this news from CNN, he assumed it was a tragic accident, so he kept moving. He had no reason to connect a prop plane in Manhattan to the president's safety in southwest Florida, only to eyeball every hand or shape that got close to POTUS as they walked into the school. As the leader of the detail, his training was to solely focus on protecting "the package" in front of his face, not to look at a television screen. If there was something worth worrying about, he would get an alert from headquarters. He stayed on the president's heels as Bush walked inside with the school principal, and then to the library where Bush would join a group of second-graders for their reading lesson at 9 A.M.

BACK IN WASHINGTON, Nelson Garabito arrived a few minutes early for the daily 9 A.M. meeting on White House security. The standing meeting was held in the Emergency Operations Center, on one of the higher floors of the Old Executive Office Building, next door to the White House. A few of the agents gathering for the meeting were already speculating about the plane that had crashed in downtown Manhattan just minutes earlier. Was it a small private plane or something bigger? Had the pilot had a seizure?

Garabito was particularly concerned. He was the Secret Service's liaison to the Federal Aviation Administration, a supervisor on the president's detail who worked with the FAA to coordinate safe air travel for the president and monitor the airspace around the White House. From an overhead television monitor on one wall, the assembled group could see CNN's live broadcast of the fire and smoke billowing from about ninety stories up on the North Tower. The audio was turned down to avoid interrupting the meeting.

"It's an awfully big fire," one agent remarked.

But just a few minutes after the meeting got under way, another agent's voice blurted out: "What the hell?"

The images on the live broadcast seemed to have changed, with far more smoke and flames rising from the World Trade Center's North Tower. With no audio, Garabito and co-workers at first thought they were looking at new images of the first crash. But then CNN flashed a new angle of the two towers, and a fresh new horror came into focus. A second passenger jet had swooped across the Manhattan skyline and torn a hole in the backside of the South Tower. They knew in unison: Terrorist attack.

Those in the meeting bolted to their own offices and to check on their teams. Garabito stayed put and immediately reached for the phone in front of him to call his contact at FAA headquarters, Terry Van Steenbergen, a twenty-year veteran air traffic controller. Ever since a stolen plane had crashed on the White House's South Lawn in 1994, the Secret Service and FAA had worked out an information-sharing relationship. A classified FAA radar system, known as Tigerwall, gave the Service the ability to see in real time any planes coming into the airspace of the nation's capital and getting dangerously close to the White House. That morning, Garabito wanted to learn whatever he could about this unprecedented terror attack in New York using planes.

"Terry, this is Nelson. What do you got?" Garabito asked.

Steenbergen told Garabito he had been trying to reach him at his office, to warn him of something that the Secret Service couldn't yet see on Tigerwall.

"We have four aircraft compromised," Steenbergen began. "Two have hit the towers. Two are headed in the direction of Washington."

The FAA suspected that these two incommunicado planes veering off course had been hijacked too.

"One is over Cleveland, forty-five minutes out," Steenbergen said. "Another is over Pittsburgh, thirty minutes out."

"What should we do?" Garabito asked him.

"We need to turn all the planes away from Washington," Steenbergen said.

Garabito, a tall, lean agent with more than ten years on the job, sat upright. The longtime member of the presidential detail would later tell the 9/11 Commission that he'd told a subordinate officer at a nearby desk to "notify upstairs" about the two errant planes. "Upstairs" was the brain and communications center for White House security, the Joint Operations Center on the top floor of the Old Executive Office Building. The JOC could monitor plane movements on the Tigerwall radar and also issue urgent alerts and warnings to the protective details and to officers throughout the White House complex. But something misfired. The officer ran upstairs, but the supervisory agent running the JOC sounded no alarm. For reasons that remain a mystery, Van Steenbergen's early warning about two more suspicious planes as little as thirty minutes out from Washington wasn't shared with Secret Service supervisors.

The result was that no one in the Secret Service leadership or the director's command center knew that downtown Washington was already a likely next target. Nobody told the protective agents safeguarding Vice President Cheney, the next in line for the presidency, that he could be a sitting duck in his West Wing office.

But all over the D.C. area, Secret Service agents instinctively knew that things had just broken bad. Off-duty Secret Service agents saw the news, hopped into their cars from as far away as Annapolis and Ashburn, and sped toward the White House to help. Agents from the Washington field office made a beeline to Crown, the White House. Uniformed Division officers hightailed it to intersections around the complex to harden the security perimeter.

IN SARASOTA, LEAD detail agent Marinzel shepherded Bush into a classroom of seven- and eight-year-olds one minute after 9 A.M. Their teacher introduced the president, and he took a seat next to her. He grinned as the children took turns calling out answers, then reading aloud from a book about a girl's voracious pet goat. Artists on the White House staff had created the colorful art projects taped to the wall behind Bush, all part of the stagecraft to improve the photo op for this presidential visit touting the No Child Left Behind bill.

Standing point behind the children and keeping his eye on the president, Marinzel knew little about what was happening in the staff holding room behind him. The rest of the detail would normally wait quietly in this room until it was time to move the president back to the motorcade and then Air Force One. But upon entering the school, Marinzel and his deputy Dave Wilkinson had gotten the vague report from headquarters. "There's an incident in New York." Now the detail scrambled to learn more.

A Secret Service agent called the Intelligence Division, the arm of the Secret Service responsible for assessing threats to the president. "Is there any direction of interest towards the president?" the agent asked. "Or is this just an attack on New York?"

The question hung there. The Intelligence Division didn't know.

A few agents, along with the local sheriff, Karl Rove, and White House military aide Paul Montanus, meanwhile scrounged around for a television. They finally found one in the school office and turned it on in time to see a nightmare unfolding. News stations were replaying tape of Flight 175 hitting the South Tower at 9:03 A.M.

CNN cut away to an ABC broadcast, which at that very moment had been interviewing an eye-witness about the North Tower crash when the dark silhouette of a plane soared across the right side of the screen. The CNN signal flashed momentarily, as if there was a technical glitch, and then another fireball rose from the South Tower.

"Oh my God! There's more explosions right now, hold on!" the eyewitness shouted.

Montanus, the Marine Corps officer, processed what he was seeing and then turned to the local sheriff. His officers helped clear the roads for the president's motorcade.

"We gotta get out of here!" Montanus said. "Can you get everyone ready?"

Wilkinson and other agents began coordinating with the JOC, planning the president's rapid evacu-ation, along with requesting extra police cars to block every intersection on the way to Air Force One. There was good reason to be on alert for a larger plot to incapacitate the government and kill Bush. The Tampa event had been publicized for more than a week. Another plane could be inbound to torpedo the school at that very moment. The tension in the staff holding room rose as Bush political aides and Secret Service agents disagreed about what to do next. The political team, led by Card, didn't want to abruptly stop the reading and scare the children—or the viewers watching on live television. They wanted to let the president finish the classroom event and then go to another location nearby so the president could make a statement about the attack—and hopefully calm the nation. "You can't do it in front of second-graders," one staffer said.

But the Secret Service was thinking in terms of seconds. On the slightest chance that some unseen enemy had drawn a bull's-eye on the president, the detail wanted POTUS on the move right away. And preferably on his way to a plane specifically designed to jam enemy radar and foil incoming missiles—not pausing at yet another vulnerable spot on the ground. "We need to get him secure," a Secret Service agent said.

The Secret Service and the White House were fighting their age-old battle: whether the president's ability to speak to his public or the president's security was more important.

Meanwhile, Card knew he had to tell the president, who was still on camera, reading with the class. Rove saw the chief of staff linger in the threshold collecting his thoughts. Card was trying to figure out how to discreetly deliver such dire news. "I have to say something so that the president won't feel compelled to ask a question," Card thought.

It was about 9:07 A.M. Card leaned down and whispered in Bush's right ear: "A second plane has flown into the World Trade Center. America is under attack."

Bush's face froze into a tense expression. As Card retreated from the camera frame and whispered the same news to Marinzel, the president stayed in place for seven more minutes, listening as the children continued to read. At one point, Bush noticed the reporters in the back of the room putting their phones to their ears for incoming calls. They were getting the same alert Bush had received.

Ari Fleischer, Bush's press secretary, held up a piece of paper from the side of the room. On it was written, in big block letters: DON'T SAY ANYTHING YET.

When the reading program ended and Marinzel whisked Bush into a staff holding room adjacent to the classroom at 9:15 A.M., he and senior aides saw that the affable, relaxed man they knew had vanished.

"We're at war," Bush said. "Get me the vice president and the director of the FBI."

In the holding room, Bush reached Cheney to discuss the best intel on the attacks and the FAA's order to ground all planes. With Fleischer and Card offering their ideas, Bush then scribbled on a legal pad the statement he wanted to make to the nation.

Marinzel, however, was itching to leave. He feared the attackers could be planning to fly a plane into the school. Any half-organized enemy plotting an assassination attempt could have learned the president's location, which had been posted on a public website for the last three days. "We need to get you to Air Force One and get you airborne," Marinzel told the president.

Card proposed a compromise. More than a hundred parents, teachers, and students were waiting at that moment in the school library, where Bush was scheduled to talk about literacy, Card said. They could use this opportunity for Bush to speak about the recent attacks and reassure the public. Then they would bolt. Marinzel reluctantly agreed. There was no evidence of an imminent attack on POTUS. But this delay went against any agent's training.

THE INSTANT AFTER the second plane struck, Truscott called an emergency meeting to discuss how to harden security around the White House, one of his overall responsibilities as the head of the Presidential Protective Division. He paged three top lieutenants and told them to come to his office ASAP to discuss adding snipers and emergency response teams to the complex. He knew nothing about suspicious planes heading toward Washington. By the time they gathered at 9:18 A.M. in room 10 of the Old Executive Office Building, the danger to the complex was headed in their direction, about thirty miles out.

At the same time, air traffic controllers in Cleveland were trying to find a plane they presumed had crashed: American Airlines Flight 77. It had vanished from their radar thirty minutes earlier. At about 9:27 A.M., Danielle O'Brien, a controller at Dulles International Airport in northern Virginia, spotted a green blip in the southwest corner of her radar screen. She could tell this plane had all the signs of trouble: the jet, then twelve miles out from Washington, had turned off its transponder and shut off radio contact. It was moving due east toward D.C. at full throttle—roughly 500 miles an hour. O'Brien didn't know it was the same plane Cleveland had lost. But she could see that this aircraft had charted a course straight for Area P-56. That was the code name for the restricted airspace around the White House. She flagged her co-worker and supervisor, who contacted the Secret Service headquarters to warn them. It was about 9:30 A.M.

At around the same time, Danny Spriggs had walked into the Director's Crisis Center, a ninth-floor battle station. With terrorists attacking New York, he had one goal at the top of his mind: making sure all nineteen people the Secret Service protected, including the First Family, were holed up somewhere safe. Spriggs had been a young agent who helped establish control outside the Washington Hilton when President Reagan was shot. Two decades later, he had risen to become a trusted confidant of the director and an assistant director over protective operations.

The crisis center was outfitted with a series of live camera feeds and monitors, a First Family locator board, and desks for intelligence gathering teams to process minute-by-minute reports. From this room in the Secret Service's new headquarters on G Street in Chinatown, the director was supposed to be able to manage any emergency. But this crisis was quickly overwhelming Director Stafford's new center. The Intelligence Division agents were fielding a barrage of reports and burning a lot of time responding to reports that turned out to be bogus. Many could have been easily checked and discounted. They dispatched a team to deal with a car bomb that had detonated in front of the State Department. There was no bomb. They scurried to track down more details on a plane that had crashed near Camp David. Also false. On top of that, Spriggs found many of the phones in the crisis center weren't working. Spriggs had been trying to reach Becky Ediger, the deputy agent in charge of the Presidential Protective Division, who he thought was stationed at the Joint Operations Center, to discuss plans for quickly securing all the First Family members and shoring up the perimeter around the White House. A JOC officer told him she was at an emergency meeting with Truscott, so Spriggs rang Truscott's line.

But just as Spriggs had begun his phone call with Truscott, the deputy director of the Secret Service, Larry Cockell, rushed over to Spriggs to share urgent news from local air traffic controllers. The FAA was warning headquarters that an inbound plane was rapidly approaching downtown Washington. It was an update on the warning Garabito had received just after 9:05 A.M. and said he had passed to the JOC.

As Truscott heard Spriggs's report and repeated it aloud, Ediger was on an extra phone line and staring at Truscott in disbelief. Garabito, who had just called Truscott's office to alert him to the two inbound planes, was giving Ediger a similar report. Key phrases rang in her ears: "Two more outstanding aircraft . . . not responding to the Tower . . . considered suspect . . . at least one headed toward D.C."

All the top bosses in the Secret Service were learning this same scary news at the same time—and far too late. It was twenty to thirty minutes after the FAA had first warned the Secret Service about the two rogue planes coming in the general direction of Washington. Truscott thanked Spriggs and hung up. He checked with his team in the White House to help implement an emergency evacuation.

Some White House employees had earlier decided to leave the building on their own after the second plane struck. They calmly streamed out to their cars in different directions—toward the Ellipse, the Metro, or their children's daycare centers. But with the FAA's warning now reaching senior managers, Secret Service officers and agents ran from room to room, sometimes with assault rifles at their side. At a series of doorways, agents paused and bellowed: "Get out of the building. Everyone needs to leave. Get out now!"

Staffers described a chaotic exodus. Some were told to go north to Lafayette Park, because the plane was reportedly approaching from the south.

But others were shooed out the closest door and exited onto the South Lawn. In the East Wing, agents found clusters of well-dressed young women in high heels, who worked for First Lady Laura Bush. They grew wide-eyed at the barking agents' approach.

"Take off your shoes," one agent commanded. "Run!"

As aides fled, some officers and agents ran past them in the Cross Hall and through the stairways with long guns, running in the opposite direction of the exits. A small cluster of agents bounded up the White House stairs two risers at a time. Their bosses had told them to get up on the roof.

"What the hell are we supposed to do up there?" one of them asked. They'd never be able to shoot a plane out of the sky with rifles. If the jet stayed on its current collision course, they'd all just accepted their last assignment.

WATCHING THE PLANE from the Dulles radar, O'Brien could feel her heart pounding in her chest as she, her seatmate, and her supervisor counted down the distance. Eleven miles out. Ten miles. Nine. She kept hoping the plane would change course or respond.

At eight miles out, her whole body clenched. Traveling at this speed, the jet plane could hit the White House in sixty more seconds. A tower supervisor at Reagan National Airport, just across the river from downtown, was watching too and called the Secret Service hotline in the JOC. It was 9:33 A.M. Secret Service officer Gregory LaDow answered the line.

"We have an aircraft, moving very fast," the supervisor said. "Coming at you and not talking with us."

This was a very grim update on the warning the FAA headquarters had shared with Garabito nearly a half hour earlier. LaDow prepared to push the emergency alert button to broadcast the news to the whole complex, but suddenly the Reagan National tower supervisor reported a change in course. "The plane is turning," he said. "Looks like it's coming back to the airport."

The green blip that had been on a collision course for the White House had turned south in a semicircle, as if looping back to Reagan National Airport. In the Dulles control tower, O'Brien sat back in her chair and took her first deep breath in what felt like an hour.

Oh, thank God, the controller thought, assuming it had to be a fighter that had scrambled to protect the city. **It's one of our jets. It's one of ours.**

As agents cleared staff out of the White House, Truscott told his lieutenants gathered in his office that they should all head to the White House's underground shelter. Built for President Truman with reinforced concrete in the early 1950s, the subterranean structure was designed to withstand a nuclear blast. The vice president, cabinet members, and national security team would be rushed there for their own protection. For the foreseeable future, they would have to run the country from inside the PEOC, the underground Presidential Emergency Operations Center.

But Becky Ediger, a Kansas native who spoke plainly, shook her head. "No," she told Truscott. "I need to go back upstairs."

"There's no time," Truscott warned.

Ediger, who had returned to her old field office in Oklahoma in the wake of the bombing there to help recover the bodies of her co-workers, was a trailblazer for women because of her senior role as deputy in charge of presidential protection. She was now effectively proposing to place herself in the path of an incoming plane. The plane heading toward the White House would likely have to crash through the top of the JOC in order to crash into the stately white mansion. Truscott outranked her, but he acquiesced. They both knew Truscott needed to be in the bunker to help relay communications to Marinzel, who was traveling with POTUS, while she needed to be up in the JOC, located on one of the top floors of the Old Executive Office Building, to help coordinate with all the Secret Service teams protecting other officials and family members aboveground.

"I'll catch up to you guys later," she called as she

ran up the five flights of stairs to the rafters of the OEOB.

When she reached the Emergency Operations Center, Ediger found that the office deadbolt had been left open. She saw Garabito standing in the central conference room, holding down a noisy but understaffed fort. He had a phone receiver tucked against one ear and four more open phone lines set on speaker. On one open phone line was the director's crisis center. On another was the Reagan tower.

As Ediger arrived, a technician on an open conference call line with the FAA warned that one plane suspected of being hijacked was about five minutes out, and the FAA alerted the Secret Service. It was American Airlines Flight 77, flying low and fast. It had departed Dulles early that morning but had made a U-turn near Cleveland back toward D.C. At 500 miles per hour, the plane was covering a mile every seven seconds. Ediger took a breath, then turned to a specialist on duty and dictated a text message to send to Truscott several stories belowground. "Don't wait on me," it said. "I'm staying upstairs with the guys."

When the incoming plane was three minutes out, an officer helping with the White House evacuation asked if she wanted to evacuate the JOC. Ediger told the crew that anyone who wanted to leave could. There would be no judgment, she said. The White House now had a bull's-eye on it.

Everyone stayed.

The FAA supervisor relayed a new alert: The plane had dropped off their radar, signaling it was heading to the ground. Ediger and Garabito looked at each other. They braced for what they expected next: impact.

WHEN THAT HORRIBLE morning started and the first plane rammed into the side of Lower Manhattan's iconic North Tower at 8:46 A.M., the vice president had no idea what was going on. He was closeted in his office. But a senior budget aide who arrived for a meeting with Cheney just before 9 A.M. urged the vice president to turn on his office television to see what was happening in New York.

"How the hell could a plane hit the World Trade Center?" Cheney later reported thinking.

Outside the closed door, an agent on the vice president's detail sat biding his time and chatting with John McConnell, Cheney's chief speechwriter. McConnell was waiting there too, hoping to speak to the veep after his budget meeting about an upcoming event. After Cheney's meeting began, the agent got a call from the Intelligence Division alerting him that the plane that had crashed into the tower that morning had been a jumbo jet. The agent frowned and told McConnell. The speechwriter got a sick feeling in his stomach. **A passenger aircraft is not going to crash into the World Trade Center,** McConnell thought. The agent and the speechwriter wondered aloud about the odds. Something was not right.

James Scott, the whip for Cheney's detail that day, heard about the second crash shortly after 9:05 A.M., while he was in the Old Executive Office Building. Scott alerted the shift to the news by radio. He consulted with his supervisor on the Cheney detail about what they should do. With the second crash, they knew that some mystery terror group or foreign power had attacked New York. Scott then walked over to the West Wing sometime before nine-thirty and briefed each of the shift agents outside Cheney's office. He ran through the contingency plans they might put in place if any danger came to Washington. Scott had no way of knowing, but danger was rapidly coming their way.

In the JOC in the Old Executive Office Building, Officer Greg LaDow thought they had just averted Armageddon in the nation's capital. The white Boeing 757 approaching downtown at such a rapid speed hadn't dived straight into the White House, but had instead turned south. But after a few moments, controller O'Brien in Dulles and her counterpart in the Reagan tower winced as the plane continued its loop. LaDow heard the Reagan tower supervisor narrate the path: The plane was heading back in the direction of the White House.

This time, a JOC officer hit the emergency alert button. It was 9:33 A.M. The broadcast traveled over the Charlie and Tango frequencies, used for the White House and the vice president:

"Unidentified aircraft coming toward the White House!"

As they stood talking outside Cheney's office, a familiar crackling sound came over their radios. The agents instinctively fell silent. Scott didn't miss a beat. He had to evacuate the vice president. He flung open the door to Cheney's office, and four fellow detail agents rushed in behind him. The surprised vice president was monitoring the news coverage on a TV next to his desk.

"Sir, we have to leave immediately," Scott said, looming in front of his desk.

Cheney began to ask a question, but Scott didn't wait for him to finish. He slammed his open palm on Cheney's desk and bellowed: "Now!"

Scott then put his left hand on the back of Cheney's shoulder and the right hand on the back of Cheney's belt and partially lifted the vice president a few steps toward the door. Cheney got the point. He and Scott then began jogging together, down a narrow West Wing corridor to what Scott hoped would be safety.

But Scott's forceful character made up for a major hole in the Secret Service's emergency planning. Neither Scott nor other key members of the vice president's detail were fully briefed and empowered to get into the military-controlled shelter below the White House. An agent standing at a post usually manned by an officer—near the West Wing's front desk—shouted out directions to make sure agents knew how to get to the stairs and tunnel leading to the shelter under the East Wing. Odd as it sounds, no one had envisioned the kind of attack that kept the president away from home and required safeguarding the vice president at the White House.

When Scott and Cheney reached the bottom of the stairs in a tunnel leading to the bunker, called the Presidential Emergency Operations Center, Scott still had one major problem. He couldn't enter the shelter on his own authority. The military tightly guarded access to the PEOC, and unlike top presidential detail agents, many vice presidential agents hadn't been given the S-keys to get inside.

The Secret Service would later tell the world that Cheney and his detail had reached safety underground, a "secure location," just a minute or so before the Pentagon crash. They reported that he got to safety by 9:37 A.M.

But the truth of what happened was kept a closely held secret for years. The suspicious hijacked plane crashed into the west side of the Pentagon at 9:38 A.M. At that moment, Cheney was standing at the base of the stairs outside the bunker, powerless and far more exposed if there had been a crash. Cheney had to wait a few more moments for someone to open the door and let him inside. If American 77 had kept heading toward the White

House that morning, Vice President Cheney and his detail would more likely have been added to the long list of victims of the 9/11 attacks.

AT ROUGHLY 9:30 A.M., President Bush spoke to the nation from the podium at the Emma E. Booker Elementary library. A group of students, their parents, and teachers had gathered to hear him talk about education reform. Some of the teachers' mouths dropped open and a few children looked confused as he uttered the first sentences.

"Today, we've had a national tragedy," he said. "Two airplanes have crashed into the World Trade Center in an apparent terrorist attack on our country." He assured the audience he had directed all the nation's resources to help the victims and catch the enemy. "Terrorism against our nation will not stand," he said.

The president had no idea that as he spoke, the White House was being evacuated and a hijacked plane was flying fast and low toward downtown Washington. His speech lasted one minute and seventeen seconds. When he finished, the president and his entourage vanished.

"Poof, he was gone," Principal Gwendolyn Tosé-Rigell recalled.

After Bush stepped back into the Beast, his fourteen-car motorcade sped away, doing 80 miles an hour, nearly double its normal speed. As they flew down an empty highway, Bush noticed a stream of police cars riding alongside. The Service had asked that they be placed there in case the enemy tried to launch a rocket-propelled grenade into the side of the limo.

In the quick eight-minute ride to the Sarasota airport, at about 9:40 A.M., the president took a call in the limousine from National Security Adviser Condoleezza Rice. Marinzel, riding in the right front seat, and Rove, riding in the back, could hear only one side of the conversation.

"Oh, no," Bush said, sounding alarmed. There was a pause, then he asked, "Is Rumsfeld alive?"

Bush's fellow passengers learned the grim news when the president hung up. A hijacked plane had hit the Pentagon at 9:37 A.M. and a massive fire had engulfed the west side. Massive casualties were expected. It was almost too much to absorb. On this day, nobody knew exactly where or when the next plane would drop out of the sky.

IN THE COURSE of fifty-one minutes, three commercial passenger planes had been used as missiles to attack symbols of U.S. power. After the U.S. government had first learned it was under attack, the Secret Service's presidential detail allowed the president of the United States to remain in a fixed location for thirty minutes. His advisers and agents had broadcast his location to the world by allowing him to spend some of that time sitting in a chair or standing at a lectern on live television. The vice president, too, had been a vulnerable target without his or his detail's knowing it, despite a warning thirty minutes before his evacuation about suspicious planes heading to Washington. Because no one had planned for this kind of attack, Cheney did not reach the safety of a bombproof bunker and control room before a third plane crashed a half mile from the White House.

The 9/11 attacks had caught federal agencies flat-footed. So many individuals acted with heroism and sound instincts, and yet the attacks revealed gaping holes in the ability of the government to spot risks and respond to crises. The Service's role was protecting the stability of the democracy, and on this day, they'd been lucky not to lose the head of that government. In the wake of the attacks, the Service quietly shredded and rewrote its emergency action plans. In the case of a terror attack or incident, the Service's first command would be to evacuate the president to a secure and unknown location. No political staffer could overrule them.

The Joint Operations Center and Emergency Operations Center—which had been co-located on the top floor of the Executive Office Building, next to terrorists' top target, the White House—would have to be moved. The Secret Service leaders realized a plane crash at the White House that day could have paralyzed the Secret Service's command center for all communications and decision making.

"There is a line of demarcation in the Service: before and after 9/11," said former presidential detail agent Jonathan Wackrow. Before 9/11, "we talked about an attack like Squeaky Fromme. No one ever thought of the option of this type of attack, including the military. The military considered a nuclear attack. The Secret Service worried, what if the president is shot at? But this type of attack was completely unknown."

AFTER 9/11, DETAIL agents drilled over and over how to respond to a terrorist attack similar to those of that day, with multiple bombings or chemical releases scattered around the country. "The goal is getting the president airborne within minutes. It's not even a debate anymore," Wackrow said. "Internally, we spent a lot of time criticizing the decisions on those days. But nobody thought about relocation before. Relocation from where? They'd never had to make that kind of decision before.

"It comes back to the fact that the policies and procedures of the Secret Service are born out of blood," he said. "The Service will get better once it's tested. Every time it is tested, it gets better. As the global threat environment constantly changes, the Service has to change in response."

———

JUST BEFORE MIDNIGHT on this horrendous day, an agent working the midnight shift and standing at post F8 got a radio call with a chilling warning—and an equally daunting assignment. The Air National Guard's combat air patrol had spotted a plane nearing downtown Washington and not communicating with the tower.

"You have to wake up the president and the First Lady right now," the supervisor explained. "Go get them and take them to the basement."

The agent knew this was important, and dreadful.

"I'm telling you, he didn't like to have to go into that bedroom," a fellow agent recalled.

The president didn't like it either. His detail leader, Truscott, had earlier tried to persuade Bush and his wife to sleep in the underground bunker for the night. But Bush had seen that dusty room with a pullout bed and refused. Still, despite the comforts of his own bed upstairs, Bush had struggled to fall asleep that night. Suddenly he realized someone was at the door, breathing heavily as if they had been running. "Mr. President," the agent said. "You've got to come now. The White House is under attack!"

The president put on running shorts, the First Lady got her robe. Together they grabbed their cat, Ms. Kitty, and Scottish terrier, Barney, and called for their springer spaniel Spot to follow. Two agents, one in front and one behind, ran toward the basement with the First Couple and their pets, carrying automatic rifles at their hips.

Down in the 1940s-style bunker, the Bushes were met by Condoleezza Rice, who had been staying at the White House for safety reasons. An Air Force military aide was there as well.

"What the hell is going on?" Bush asked.

The airman explained the inconvenience. The military had spotted a suspicious plane that wasn't communicating flying just south of the Capitol. The suspicious plane turned out to be an F16 that had switched on the wrong transponder code while returning to Andrews Air Force Base.

"Don't worry, Mr. President, it's one of ours," he said.

The president snorted. His day had started in Florida with a jog at dawn, then a wave of shocking, bloody attacks. It ended eighteen hours later, with a bogus threat, and his protectors walking him and his wife back upstairs in their bedclothes to get some rest.

CHAPTER 14

"YOU DON'T BELONG HERE"

September 11 shook the moorings of the country, and the public's faith in the nation's security shield. The startling success of the terrorists revealed a "failure of imagination"—a failure to see and fend off a gathering threat in al-Qaeda. The attacks also made clear some basic weaknesses in the nation's ability to respond to a crisis, including the Secret Service's preparation for an attempt to decapitate the government.

"Nineteen men armed with knives, box cutters, Mace and pepper spray penetrated the defenses of the most powerful nation in the world. They inflicted unbearable trauma on our people," Thomas Kean, the chairman of the 9/11 Commission, said when releasing his panel's extensive report. "On that September day we were unprepared."

The Secret Service thought it had prepared for

an attack by air, in the wake of the 1994 aircraft crash at the White House's South Grounds. But the FAA Tigerwall system hadn't helped much on 9/11. Any antiaircraft weaponry the Service had was viewed as either insufficient or unwise to use because of the carnage it could cause to bring down a plane in downtown Washington. Agents were flabbergasted as their bosses told them to go up to the roof with their rifles. Years before 9/11, Richard Clarke, a top national counterterrorism adviser, had raised his concern that the Secret Service's solution was inadequate. In 1998, he led a tabletop exercise with the Secret Service, the FAA, and the Defense Department to game out what they could do if terrorists flew a hijacked Learjet loaded with explosives toward a target in downtown Washington.

The catastrophic losses of 9/11 strengthened the country's resolve to prevent anything like it from catching our government off guard again. In the days and weeks after the World Trade Center towers fell, the White House and Congress were consumed with how to ramp up the nation's defenses. At the Secret Service, Director Stafford instructed his staff to prepare a plan for hardening the White House's borders on all four sides. After conferring with Chief of Staff Andy Card, the Service decided against closing Fifteenth and Seventeenth streets— two major downtown arteries to the east and west of the White House complex. But at 1:30 A.M. on the Monday after 9/11, crews finished installing the

Jersey barriers that would indefinitely close E Street to cars and dramatically expand the White House's southern flank. That was window dressing compared to the much bigger changes that were coming to the Secret Service.

On September 20, nine days after the attacks that killed nearly three thousand people in two of America's largest cities, President Bush made a rare address to a joint session of a somber Congress. "Night fell on a different world" after the attacks on New York and Washington, the president said to the still chamber. "Tonight, we are a country awakened to danger and called to defend freedom."

He said the military would be called to action soon, a foreshadowing of the bombing and invasion of Afghanistan, al-Qaeda's headquarters. But the nation had to also forge a new coordinated plan to shield the homeland, he said. "Our nation has been put on notice, we're not immune from attack. We will take defensive measures against terrorism to protect Americans. Terror unanswered can not only bring down buildings, it can threaten the stability of legitimate governments. And you know what? We're not going to allow it."

Bush announced he had asked Tom Ridge, a Vietnam combat veteran and the governor of Pennsylvania, to join the White House staff as his point man on protecting the homeland.

Senator Joe Lieberman of Connecticut clapped wanly from the Democratic side of the chamber.

LIEBERMAN WOULD HAVE been vice president then—if the Supreme Court had ruled differently almost a year earlier in the bitter **Bush v. Gore** 2000 election recount decision. He was not persuaded that simply adding a new czar for homeland security would fix the problem. Before September 11, some of his Democratic peers had pushed for a wholesale reorganization of the government's many splintered agencies that dealt with security. Lieberman believed September 11 had further proved the need for their plan. Thousands of border control, air travel, investigative, and intelligence agents who were scattered across separate departments and reported to different cabinet secretaries needed to work in concert.

In early October, Lieberman pitched this plan to President Bush in a private meeting with a small group of lawmakers at the White House. A security czar needed the power that came with a new department, the senator said, with his own budget and troops. But the president politely waved him off. Just as Vice President Cheney had done before the attacks, Bush warned that creating a new bureaucracy was a knee-jerk response.

"It's just more big government, Joe," he said.

But Lieberman left the White House meeting with the same resolve. In the early weeks of 2002, Lieberman had whipped up so much support among his colleagues for a new Department of Homeland Security that Congress was close to passing a bill to create what the president had rejected. The White House Legislative Affairs Office started to count the votes. Lieberman's Homeland Security bill had enough. That was bad news for the White House and the GOP leadership. Neither wanted to cede a powerful national security win to the Democrats. "That was driving decisions," one senior Ridge aide told **The Washington Post**.

PUBLICLY, THE WHITE House maintained a veneer of mild opposition. "Creating a cabinet office doesn't solve the problem," Bush spokesman Ari Fleischer told reporters in March. But secretly, in a basement conference room in the White House, a stealth team of White House aides chosen by Chief of Staff Andy Card began meeting in April to create just such a new department. Their task: Build a new civil defense agency and choose which parts of forty different agencies should join it. They worked on a blueprint, which would reassign tens of thousands of employees and likely piss off half of them, for six difficult weeks without one leak.

A devastating revelation in mid-May intensified the pressure for Bush to take concrete action. CBS News, citing anonymous sources, reported that the president had been vaguely warned about a possible Osama bin Laden plot in the weeks before

September 11. Bush's Daily Intelligence Briefing in early August mentioned specifically some chatter that the attack could involve the hijacking of planes.

On June 6, Bush sprang the new department on his cabinet secretaries, the day before he planned to announce it to the public. Ridge, who had been battered with endless kvetching from cabinet members when he proposed a similar reorganization plan, had to stifle a chuckle as each one politely lied to Bush: "Seems like a good idea, Mr. President," they said.

In truth, nearly every one of them hated it. Some, like Health and Human Services Secretary Tommy Thompson, weren't even out of the cabinet room before they started calling their aides on the phone, working ferociously to reclaim parts of their turf the new department would swallow.

There was one cabinet member, however, who didn't put up a fight. Treasury Secretary Paul O'Neill viewed the president's centralization of security agencies as ill-conceived and unlikely to make the country safer. But he readily relinquished the Treasury law enforcement divisions that Card's "basement team" had tentatively chosen to put in the new larger Homeland Security Department. One of them was the United States Secret Service. Without a tear, O'Neill said so long to a three-thousand-employee agency that had been a part of the Treasury Department since 1865.

O'Neill had himself many times tried to eliminate his own Secret Service detail, and each time his staff had talked him out of it. The protective team had been provided to every Treasury secretary since the Service's first days, but O'Neill felt it was wasteful and annoying. "His view was they just help you get through intersections," said one of O'Neill's senior aides.

O'Neill's belief that the Secret Service wasn't that essential—either to his safety or to his Treasury Department—increased that spring. The White House was sending signals that Treasury would also lose the U.S. Customs Service to the formation of a consolidated border agency. With the exodus of Customs, it became clear that the secretary simply didn't care about the rest of the assorted law enforcement agencies within Treasury. What connection, he asked, did the Bureau of Alcohol, Tobacco and Firearms, the Federal Law Enforcement Training Center, or the Secret Service have to Treasury's central mission of setting national economic policy? "I think it was O'Neill himself who said, 'Why do we even have these other law enforcement entities?'" said Richard Bonner, who was then the customs commissioner. "My impression was he said, 'Let's get rid of them.'"

The president's blueprint rattled many in the tradition-bound Secret Service. Some insisted they stay in their original birthplace, but Stafford deputy Paul Irving argued that Treasury had long ignored the Service and DHS might be their ticket to larger budgets. Stafford hadn't reached a decision on what was best, but ultimately he didn't feel he had much choice, as Card notified him the day before the president's meeting that it was a done deal. The Secret Service would join the new department. "The Secret Service could have argued to stay," Bonner said. "It had enough juice to stay in Treasury if it wanted, in my opinion. They thought they would be better off getting out of Treasury, since law enforcement was such an afterthought there."

On June 6, Bush announced his reorganization plan in a televised address to the nation, taking Lieberman's name out of the bill and calling it simply the Homeland Security Act. He told the audience this new Department of Homeland Security would be called upon to defend the country in a "titanic struggle," and that it would comprise 169,000 employees and a budget of $37 billion. Only the Defense Department would be larger.

"Tonight, I ask the Congress to join me in creating a single permanent department with an overriding and urgent mission—securing the American homeland and protecting the American people," Bush said. "Thousands of trained killers are plotting to attack us. Employees of this new agency will come to work every morning knowing that their most important job is to protect their fellow citizens."

Many Secret Service agents, but especially the powerful and defensive alumni club of former agents, worried about the future. Creatures steeped in tradition, they eyed the change warily, and some second-guessed Director Stafford's choice to go along with the idea. But five days later, the grousing and fretting became an afterthought as the Secret Service's reputation took a swift kick in the gut.

ON JUNE 11, 2002, **U.S. News & World Report** published the results of a monthslong investigation documenting a trail of horrendous behavior the Secret Service had tolerated in its highest ranks. At the time, members of Congress called it the most embarrassing moment in the agency's history. The bombshell investigation painted a picture of the Secret Service as a team of arrogant louts, with senior leaders engaged in covering up for other lawbreakers and incompetents in their chain of command, or tarnished by misconduct themselves. The article reported on a senior agent, later promoted, who took a female informant back to his apartment for drinks and sex. She ended up dead in his bathroom from a drug-related brain hemorrhage. In one reported incident, a Los Angeles agent was caught having sex with a friend's sixteen-year-old daughter at night and giving her methamphetamines to stay awake in her classes at high school. The report also cited several instances of agents caught stealing federal funds for personal use. In another case, agents left behind a highly sensitive and detailed security plan for protecting Vice President Cheney at a snowboard store after shopping during the Olympics in Salt Lake City.

All this gave Andy Card, President Bush's chief of staff, a case of heartburn. Card might have been able to understand if this was a few bad apples. But the allegations of misconduct at the very top demanded action. The investigation cited sources and sworn statements from Secret Service personnel who said that Director Stafford, former director Lewis Merletti, and A. T. Smith, a top supervisor who used to lead Hillary Clinton's detail, had all had well-known adulterous affairs with staffers and aides in the Clinton White House. Smith and Stafford declined to comment at the time and would repeatedly decline to discuss the allegations. In a letter to the magazine, Merletti denied an improper relationship but suggested that these rumors of affairs had been investigated and debunked by the Independent Counsel. But Starr's office insisted they had investigated no such thing.

Extramarital affairs were viewed as a black mark on an agent's security clearance because the secret made them vulnerable to blackmail. Agency protocol urged against close personal relationships with protectees or their staff. Several anonymous agents signed sworn affidavits attesting to widespread belief within the agency of Merletti's and Stafford's affairs. Agents had taken particular note of Stafford's romantic relationship with a pretty blond White House political staffer who had handled advance planning for Mrs. Clinton.

Not since a Washington columnist had questioned whether agents were sluggish and hungover the morning Kennedy was shot had the agency faced such a public tarring. It was a particularly painful smack at Stafford, whose son was then in the Secret Service training academy preparing to join the agency. It also raised questions about previous directors' tolerance for bad behavior. The investigative piece cited internal agency sources who said previous directors had repeatedly promoted Stafford despite widespread knowledge of his affair among senior leadership. Stafford privately blamed Moore's group of Black agents who brought the discrimination suit against the Service, arguing that they tried to hurt him by exaggerating claims to the magazine.

Stafford, a handsome and athletic man, was jokingly nicknamed Elvis inside the Service. Like the heartthrob rock-'n'-roll singer, he had a husky voice and a Southern accent and wavy brown hair. In addition to being six foot four and broad-shouldered, he was a natty dresser. He frequently wore cufflinks and custom shirts. He sported a hipster's black turtleneck on more casual outings.

Stafford had a very good reputation as a dedicated agent, an image cemented when he headed up President Clinton's detail in his second term. He had been a fierce advocate for Secret Service budgets, at times going around his Treasury secretary to press for more money so he could add staff and ease the load on overworked agents and officers.

Stafford also had acquired a reputation for enjoying the company of a woman who was not his wife.

Card made up his mind quickly. The director of the Secret Service simply had to be above reproach. Card alerted key White House deputies a few weeks after the article appeared that the president planned to make a change at the Secret Service, and he told Secretary O'Neill to direct Stafford to submit his retirement papers. Stafford asked Card why he was being pushed out and whether it had anything to do with the **U.S. News** piece. Card denied that, vaguely indicating that it boiled down to several things. "We just want to go in another direction," Card said. But one senior Bush adviser said Card was in fact disturbed by the allegations in the magazine piece. "It's such a sensitive position," the adviser said. "That kind of conduct deserved immediate action. It speaks to arrogance beyond belief."

Stafford's days as director had been numbered anyway. Every incoming president had eventually made his own selection of director. But because of the article, the clock sped up a bit and Stafford's departure was less graceful. Card quietly sought names for his replacement.

The negative publicity came at a bad time for the Service. The National Public Radio program **All Things Considered** interviewed one of the article's chief reporters, Chitra Ragavan, about her findings just as Congress was discussing the formation of the new Department of Homeland Security. The

reporter warned that the Service's lack of accountability and morale problems would likely get far
worse if it was moved inside this larger bureaucracy.
"You're going to have a brand-new agency which is
going to have very little time—initially at least—to
correct any problem," she told the NPR host. "Our
analysis is that any agency that inherits the Secret
Service is going to inherit these problems. So you
can imagine that these problems will go unresolved
and may fester in this new agency."

On July 9, "Elvis" showed up to testify about
the new department and reorganization plan before the House Judiciary Committee. Stafford
explained to the committee that he fully endorsed
the plan to move his Service of four thousand agents
into the new Homeland Security Department of
169,000.

But as the hearing progressed, a friendly member
of the committee asked Stafford to speak about the
U.S. News & World Report allegations. It was a
softball question, meant to give the director a chance
to rebut the claims, but still it stung.

"Director Stafford, recently one of the major
national news magazines did an investigative report
on the Secret Service that skewered the agency
pretty severely," said Republican congressman Bob
Goodlatte of Virginia. He continued,

It cited literally dozens of various types of problems in the agency. Everything from security

lapses to embezzlement or theft, sex scandals, barroom brawls, morale problems. Now I don't want to turn the hearing into a review of all the allegations that are made in that story. I do want to give you an opportunity to tell us how the agency is responding to that, whether you're addressing any of the concerns in the article, and most importantly, how you think this transfer of the Secret Service from the Treasury Department to the Department of Homeland Security will affect any efforts you are undertaking to reform the agency.

Stafford looked up, stone-faced and grim. By all appearances, he was angered by this subject. "Um, that article was yellow journalism," he said. "I think anytime you go back in any agency's history over thirty years, which is what they did . . ."

He started again.

"It wasn't an investigative report on the part of that magazine," he said. "It was taken directly from a twenty-eight-page document that was submitted anonymously, I might add, by people who may have been fired by the Secret Service, by people who may be suing the Secret Service, by people who are sinister and have motives of revenge. That article took some truths, again going back over thirty years, [and] mixed with some distortions and a number of untruths. I can't explain why they did that."

Agents watching the director knew that his

words carried some measure of spin for the cameras and the lawmakers, yet they saw that he didn't specifically reject anything in the story as inaccurate. Many of the incidents described in the **U.S. News & World Report** article were buttressed by witnesses, lawsuits, police reports, and the Service's own internal inspection reports. Agents on the president's and First Lady's details also knew that the part about Stafford's extramarital affair was true. The woman he had been seeing had made no secret of the relationship in conversations with a small circle of co-workers.

One agent hearing Stafford's claims remembered being a newbie on the Clinton detail, waiting in a helicopter while the team's liftoff for Andrews Air Force Base was delayed. Mrs. Clinton's staffer was late to meet them as they headed out for a trip. "Sorry. We're not allowed to leave without the SAIC's girlfriend," a more senior agent told the new one.

IN NOVEMBER, STAFFORD publicly announced he would retire at the end of the year. As all his predecessors had done, the outgoing director offered a list of names for potential replacements. They were all active-duty senior supervisors who worked for him.

But the White House wasn't interested in Stafford's suggestions. As December arrived, none of Stafford's crew had gotten any calls for interviews. Bush's chief of staff instead had focused primarily on a string of retired Secret Service executives that the Bush family knew well, and after final interviews during the week of December 10, he had narrowed the field to two. One leading candidate was Ralph Basham, who had retired from the Secret Service six years earlier as an assistant director and was a trusted member of the extended Bush "family" after serving on Papa Bush's detail. Another was William Pickle, a former assistant director who had led vice president Al Gore's detail and had retired in 2000.

This cannot happen, Stafford told his mentors and longtime allies in the Secret Service family. In Stafford's view, the Bush White House was politicizing the agency by reaching outside the current management team and looking for a friendly crony in the rearview mirror. That would make the new director beholden to a president and break a sacred tradition of succession at the Secret Service.

The country had been hit by the most traumatic attack since Pearl Harbor and needed a forward-looking, independent leader to bring the president's security to a new level. Stafford argued that Basham and other retired agents had been out of the game too long and weren't up to this challenge. Stafford had worked alongside both—as an assistant director with Basham and as Pickle's peer and boss. Basham had been turned down for the job once before. In 1997, Basham interviewed for the director's position, but Clinton chose Lew Merletti, the former head of his detail, as the next director.

"I have seven people ready to replace me," Stafford complained to colleagues. "Basham was an assistant director who got passed over. He couldn't make it as director when he was here. He doesn't deserve it now." But Stafford was also smarting over more than the qualifications of Card's candidates. He was personally insulted that Card didn't think enough of his recommendations to interview any of them.

Stafford turned for help to the alumni club of SAICs—special agents in charge, the former heads of the presidential and vice presidential details, many of whom he knew well. Twelve were scheduled to come to the White House for the annual Christmas festivities in mid-December as well as a luncheon and small information briefings arranged just for them. Typically, in honor of their service to previous White Houses, the former Special Agents in Charge received a private audience with the current director, the president's chief of staff, and the vice president to hear about the White House and the current state of security.

On the day of their visit, Card popped in to the Old Executive Office Building to welcome the old guard as they gathered in a conference room drinking coffee and telling war stories of presidential trips past. But after the introductions and pleasantries, a number of the former SAICs turned the holiday greeting into a chance to air a grievance. A few spoke up, saying they feared Card was tossing out the Secret Service tradition of picking a director from within the institution. John Magaw, then sixty-seven, had served as director for Papa Bush's last year in office and had reason to believe his voice carried some clout with the Bush family and the younger Bush's White House. Magaw, a purist about traditions, had mentored and promoted Stafford on the president's detail, and now he and others echoed some of the director's complaints. Plucking a former agent out of retirement would end the traditional selection for the director, he said; it would be "a mistake."

Card had listened quietly, but he was growing angry. He said he understood the former leaders of the Secret Service had strong opinions about who should be the next director. He told them he completely disagreed with their assessment and had heard there weren't very strong leaders in Stafford's executive suite. "Neither the president nor I am asking for your opinion, gentlemen," he said.

With that, the White House chief of staff wished all the former detail leaders a happy holiday, excused himself, and walked out.

"YOU KNOW YOU don't belong here," Stafford said gruffly.

The director, six feet three inches tall and broad-shouldered, stood to address Ralph Basham, the man who was the top contender to replace him.

Stafford made little effort to control the frown hardening over his face at Basham's visit to head-quarters. A beefy former football player, Stafford remained in tip-top shape at age fifty-four. Without trying, he loomed large.

"I'm asking you not to accept the position," he said. "This will become a political position if you take it."

Stafford was frankly used to getting his way, yet it appeared quite likely he was going to lose the battle over his replacement. Thanks to the White House, his days were numbered and his opinion on the matter was being dismissed.

Basham looked at the outgoing director, pon-dering for a moment how best to respond. He chose to adhere to the Bush family creed: civility first. "I understand you're not happy," Basham told Stafford. "But I didn't ask for this job. I'm here because the president asked me."

At five feet ten inches, with gray hair and wire-rimmed glasses, Basham cut a far less imposing figure than Stafford, looking more like a folksy col-lege dean than a security agent. The sixty-year-old retired administrator had considerable advantages in the Bush White House, though. More than a decade ago, Basham had forged a close bond with the first President Bush, George H. W. Bush, while serving on the vice president's detail in the late 1980s. He was even Bush's occasional partner on the tennis court. Over the years, Basham rose to management posts at other federal law enforcement agencies, including assistant director of the Service. One of Basham's closest friends from the days on the road with the vice president was 41's former "body man," Joe Hagin. Now Hagin had risen to become 43's deputy chief of staff. The president would decide on the new director but would seek Hagin's recommendation.

To those watching the drama from outside the Service, Basham's selection didn't seem so strange. He was an agent the president and his aides knew well, just as Clinton had known Stafford well. "I can see why they chose him: calm, steady, model of rectitude," said a former senior Bush appointee. "He was head of [George H. W. Bush's] detail at some point. That's the route to becoming director. Maybe that's not the best way to choose the director. But that's how the White House gets to know the agents."

Both Basham and Pickle had been clued in by friends to Stafford's behind-the-scenes complaint about considering former agents, and the complaints raised at the former SAICs Christmas luncheon. They'd also both heard from friends that Stafford went so far as to dispatch senior agents to lobby key lawmakers against their selection.

In his standoff that day in January, Stafford told Basham: "You know this is wrong."

Basham smiled with gritted teeth. He knew something the current director didn't. He'd already accepted Stafford's job.

CHAPTER 15

"HE PREDICTED ALL OF IT"

In the late summer of 2005, Secret Service officer Charles J. Baserap stood at his post at Fifteenth and E streets and watched two supervisors approach. Known by officers as South Park 15, the post straddled an eastern drive into the compound and faced the grassy plaza between historic Hotel Washington and the Department of Commerce. The men seemed relaxed, friendly. They said they'd like Baserap's thoughts on something.

The supervisors asked Baserap, a college graduate and brand-new Secret Service officer who'd been on the job less than a year, whether he had any ideas about improving security at the White House complex. He was part of the Service's Uniformed Division, a twelve-hundred-officer unit that was primarily responsible for guarding the White House but also provided security at the vice president's residence, foreign embassies, and important events. Most people thought of agents with earpieces when they heard the words "Secret Service." But officers like Baserap were the guards and sentries who played a critical role in the protection of the White House and the president. The supervisors told him they were putting together a security awareness team and were conducting this informal survey of officers to collect suggestions for a stronger defense of Crown.

They had walked up to the right guy. Baserap beamed at hearing his bosses ask for some ideas. He had quite a few. After eight months on the job, Baserap had reached the sad conclusion that terrorists could easily pierce the White House complex if they wanted to. The newly minted graduate of Fordham University had been in his parents' home in the Bronx when the towers fell on September 11, and he feared the country was gradually growing complacent about the risk of more attacks. While standing midnights, early mornings, and afternoons on the White House's lonely southern flank, and on other perimeter posts that ring the complex, Baserap mentally cataloged a series of holes in the safety net around the president's house.

For one, the Secret Service officers who guarded the White House relied on handguns that couldn't compete if organized attackers showed up with a rifle or shotgun. White House posts were frequently left unmanned when staff was short. Officers at some posts couldn't reliably communicate with other parts of the complex in a crisis because radios were often broken or got spotty reception. Officers didn't regularly check administration staffers for weapons or explosives when they entered the complex on foot. And for reasons Baserap couldn't figure, his bosses assigned the most junior, inexperienced officers to the most remote perimeter entry points, the first line of defense if plotters wanted to infiltrate the complex. The most senior posts were the ones closest to the house.

Officer Baserap also saw that the sinking morale among the officers of the Uniformed Division was fraying the security net. Agents, with higher pay and profiles, occupied all the senior positions in the agency and controlled the Service. Their jobs were more coveted and required a college degree and a more rigorous screening by senior agents. They commanded respect. But the less-noticed part of the Secret Service were people like him, the lower-ranking officers, who were feeling taken for granted, tired, and beaten down. They had the typical guard roles, manning security posts at the White House, the vice president's residence, and presidential events. The Service leadership took away officers' vacation days on a whim and regularly forced them into grueling "short change" shifts. On top of the bad hours, officers were often treated dismissively, with agents issuing curt orders and calling them "box trolls" after the boxlike sheds in which they stood watch on the White House grounds.

In their draining hamster wheel of schedules, officers would routinely work a full eight-hour afternoon shift from 2:30 until 10:30 P.M., drive an hour to the faraway suburbs where they could afford to live, catch four or five hours' sleep, and then be required to report for duty at 6:30 the next morning. Their next shift could easily be the midnight shift that started later that same day. Such a schedule required an officer to stay alert for twenty-four out of forty hours. The result was predictable. Officers felt mistreated, as if they were faceless factory workers on an assembly line.

IN THE SUMMER and fall of 2005, officers were resigning faster than new ones could be hired and trained. In the worst month, thirty officers left—an average of one resignation a day. It amped up the exhaustion of those left on the job and further reduced the average experience level on each shift. Now Baserap felt a rush of hope. He offered to write up a few thoughts for his higher-ups, and the next day he began crafting a memo. Several friends and even his closer supervisors privately warned him not to put his thoughts in writing. **And absolutely do not attach your name,** they said. Your memo could make it all the way to the eighth floor—the director's floor at Secret Service headquarters. "You don't want to get a reputation as a troublemaker," Capt. Bill Vucci told Baserap.

"Everybody's tried to tell them. For years," one older officer warned, chuckling at Baserap's naïveté. "It goes nowhere."

But other officers were sick of being silent. Agents and supervisors at the time had just given a tongue-lashing to a fellow officer. His only crime was having the temerity to walk up to Director Ralph Basham at a social function and share his concerns about staff morale.

Baserap kept scribbling down his thoughts whenever he had free time. He was wary, but also excited at the chance to contribute to the Service and help fix the problems he saw after so many mindless hours at his post.

In early December, Baserap received what he considered an open invitation from the Secret Service equivalent of a four-star general. Joseph Clancy, the new number two in charge of President George W. Bush's detail, visited the officers' roll call in the East Wing. As the Deputy Special Agent in Charge of the detail, Clancy not only helped run the Service's most important protective detail, he also had overall responsibility for security at the White House complex. The chief of the officers reported to him.

Clancy got his nickname, Father Joe, because he'd studied to be a priest before joining the Service, but the name stuck because he was known for delivering his counsel and advice gently. That day at roll call, Clancy told the group his door was open to their concerns. "Even though there are agents and officers, we're all part of the same team with the same goal," Clancy explained. "If any of you have concerns or issues, feel free to ask me. You can always come to me or Nick Trotta."

Baserap took Clancy at his word. A few days later, on December 12, he finished typing up an email to Clancy and Trotta. In it he listed an inventory of security concerns he had been jotting down. He also revealed his fears: "I want a chance to do my job well . . . but I fear being a marked man if I openly criticize" leadership, he wrote.

A few days later Clancy called Baserap on his cellphone and asked him to come to his office in the Old Executive Office Building on December 22 at 5 P.M. Baserap showed up promptly at Clancy's office in room 60. Clancy asked Baserap what precisely he was putting in his list of security concerns. Later, Clancy asked who else had seen his list. Baserap told the DSAIC he had shared his concerns with a few officers to get feedback, but he explained he would never discuss it outside the Service. Clancy asked if he could have a copy of whatever the officer had drafted. Baserap had a copy in his jacket and happily handed it over to Father Joe. "Here's what I have," he said. "It's not really complete. But I'll give you a real copy when it's finished."

The meeting ended cordially. In fact, for Baserap, the last seventy minutes were a rush. **He really**

seemed interested in my ideas, Baserap thought as he shut the door and headed for home.

The compound was quiet over the Christmas holiday week; the Bush family was at Camp David for Christmas Eve and then decamped to their Crawford ranch until after New Year's.

But on Monday, January 3, 2006, Baserap got a call from another top Service leader. He was surprised that Julia Pierson, the deputy director for protective operations, was calling him at home on his day off. Pierson, then one of the highest-ranking women in the agency, suggested they talk "off campus" and asked him to meet her at a favorite Secret Service stop: the Starbucks on G Street near headquarters. But outside the Starbucks, Pierson's driver waved Baserap into a black Secret Service Tahoe outside. He talked with Pierson while the driver silently steered the car to a nearby parking lot.

"I thought it would be more comfortable for us to meet on neutral ground," Pierson explained. "I received word that you have some security concerns about the White House complex, and also some concerns about your career."

Baserap gave her the broad outline of what he had told Clancy: He had noticed White House security weaknesses and had been informally compiling them after two supervisors asked what he would improve.

"What are you hoping to do with this memo?" Pierson asked. "Where are you going with this?"

Terrorists want to get into the White House complex, Baserap said, and he believed it could be much more secure. He talked through the list that was now imprinted in his head: overworked officers, inexperienced staff placed on the hardest posts, posts that were left unmanned, failing radios, inadequate firepower, failure to wand pass holders entering the building. On the last one—the failure to wand pass holders—he shared his fear about how easily a disgruntled staffer or contractor could smuggle in a weapon or a bomb. "There is no reason why they shouldn't be doing that," Baserap complained. "It could be put into place in twenty-four hours."

After thirty minutes together, Pierson thanked Baserap for his candor and dropped him off at the Chinatown Metro stop. Despite the somewhat odd circumstances, Baserap climbed down from the deputy assistant director's truck feeling good about the exchange. "She was really receptive," he later told his friends.

When he returned to work, Baserap soon saw a sign that Pierson had listened to his concerns. For the first time in his career, he watched a vehicle inspection team run a hand wand over the body of a person entering on Fifteenth Street. The teams had always swept trucks and cars entering the complex but hadn't ever checked the drivers or passengers. At roll call that morning, a sergeant told officers the vehicle inspection team must always hand-wand people entering at South Park 15.

The next week, the morning of January 9, a sergeant called Baserap at his post next to the Treasury building. Clancy wanted him to come to his office at 11:30 A.M. It was important enough that the sergeant was sending another officer to relieve Baserap. Baserap cut directly across the complex and walked quickly past the posts he knew like the back of his hand: Baker 14, Alpha 1, Charlie 3, Charlie 6, Delta 10, and then to the Old Executive Office Building. **This is such an honor,** Baserap thought, hoping he might impress his superiors or at least win them over on some of his points.

But in room 60, Baserap found quite a different Clancy. The deputy chief of the Uniformed Division, Kevin Simpson, sat opposite Clancy's desk, his face a deep frown as Baserap entered. On Clancy's instructions, Baserap took a seat, then switched off his radio, turned off his cellphone, and removed his earpiece.

"Officer, is there a tape recorder or microphone in your bag?" Simpson asked. Baserap, taken aback, said no. Simpson asked him again. "Because I heard a click," the chief said.

The only things in Baserap's gear bag were a gas mask, a set of keys, and a bottle of Pepto-Bismol. "Would you feel more comfortable if I removed my bag?" Baserap asked. Clancy and Simpson both nodded. Baserap hung his bag and jacket on a hook on the wall outside the room and returned to his seat.

"Officer, when we met in December, I gave you a considerable amount of my time," Clancy said.

"Since then, I have had a chance to read your report about the security vulnerabilities at the complex, and I have to tell you, it is **completely** inaccurate. Many of the things you say are simply not true." Clancy believed Baserap was well-spoken and genuinely well-intentioned, but also very junior and a bit presumptuous to survey his fellow officers and bypass the chain of command to resolve his concerns. Clancy insisted that White House employees were always properly wanded, there was no need for two officers at posts where they now have one, and officers did not need to be swaggering around with long guns.

"This is not the Green Zone, Officer Baserap," Clancy said. "You think you have these great ideas. But you haven't been here long enough to know what you don't know. You don't have the big picture."

Clancy continued, "You seem to believe that since you are from New York you have a higher interest in preventing another terrorist attack. Well, you don't."

Baserap stammered at first, explaining that many of his fellow officers shared his concerns about the complex's security holes. Baserap searched his mind for someone whose opinion Clancy would value. He mentioned a Seal Team Six trainer who worked on drills with the Service and had recommended long guns as a critical deterrent on the perimeter.

"Long guns would cause the public to panic," Clancy interrupted. "And we don't do things by polls and surveys around here, Officer Baserap."

Clancy had one key question for Baserap: Who else had he told about his concerns? Who else had seen his draft report? "Did you make additional copies of this and share it outside of the Secret Service?" Clancy asked.

"No, sir, I did not," Baserap said. Clancy asked him two more times.

"Did you **ever** share this with anyone outside the Service?" Clancy says.

"Sir, I'm not sure what's happening here," Baserap stammered. "My intention was to share this only with my chain of command." Baserap could not believe the turnaround. Clancy was accusing him of trying to publicize the very security flaws that Baserap was trying to flag for remediation. Clancy seemed to believe that writing down concerns constituted a threat to leak them to the public.

"Officer, you are very close to crossing the line of the disclosure clause," Clancy warned. "And that could be grounds for dismissal. By putting your opinions on paper you have done a great disservice to the organization. If you keep pushing this and this material winds up getting out, it could be detrimental to White House security . . . and to you."

With that, the meeting was over. "You may return to your post," the DSAIC announced.

Baserap left the meeting shocked and dismayed. Over the next few days, he confided in a handful of co-workers. Some officers cursed the leadership. Others reminded Baserap they'd told him what would happen. "We've been trying for years," a senior officer said. "They don't want to hear it."

Baserap later noticed that a tiny handful of security tweaks he had recommended—all of which had been dismissed by Clancy—were implemented almost overnight at the White House. He'd warned about unreliable communications at the South Park 17 booth. Days later he discovered a cellphone placed in the booth as backup.

The excitement Baserap once felt at playing a leading role in improving White House security turned to anger. "I got mad," he said. "I had been treated like a common criminal and I had done nothing wrong. I was hoping to communicate the list of security risks and the culture of fear that people are afraid to speak up. . . . They acted like I was going to go out to Pebble Beach and start handing out copies to the press."

So on his night off, after the March 21 midnight shift's roll call at 10:30 P.M., Baserap set off on a bold and mutinous course. He walked into the officers' down room in the Old Executive Office Building to a secure Secret Service computer. He made a precise number of copies of a fifteen-page memo—enough for each member of his chain of command all the way up to the chief—and placed one in each of their work mailboxes. The memo documented not only the security risks he'd flagged, but the way he'd been unfairly accused and ridiculed by his superiors. Word spread quickly.

Early the next morning, a fellow officer called Baserap on his cellphone. "Dude, we read what you wrote in this memo," his friend said. "This is amazing. It's being circulated on all the posts"—the designated positions around the White House complex where officers were assigned to stand guard.

Baserap learned his memorandum had been copied dozens of times and shared with almost everyone on the force. Officers he'd never met were celebrating that someone had finally spoken up for the redheaded stepchildren, the officers of the Uniformed Division. Officers even gave his memo a name: the Uniformed Division Officer's Manifesto.

When he next reported for work, officers greeted Baserap with pats on the back and high-fives for his chutzpah. A former academy classmate found Baserap at his post near the Treasury building and confided that he was disgusted with how he had been treated. "I've seen you do some dumb things before," the classmate said. "But one thing I've never seen you do is lie. This memo is spot-on." He told Baserap he was proud of him, but afraid too. Baserap was now a marked man.

Baserap had an obsession with what he considered the Service's failure to plan for a serious, coordinated attack. But any officer or agent questioning the way things were done was deeply suspect and unsettling to headquarters. None of the leaders wanted staff debating security methods or putting concerns in writing. That, they believed, would only be used to lay blame for some mistake down the road. Behind the scenes, the eighth floor and the chief spread the word that Baserap was a troublemaker who might need to go. "Officer Baserap has repeatedly said he does not plan on going public with this but I recommend keeping an eye on him anyway," Clancy wrote in a memo to senior leadership.

A new director, Mark Sullivan, began leading the Service in the summer of 2006. He attended a diversity training seminar for officers, and while he was taking questions at the end, one officer mentioned that many of his peers in the Uniformed Division feared retaliation if they ever raised security concerns.

"I'm surprised to hear that," Sullivan said. "If anyone has any specific examples, I'd be glad to hear them."

One of the men pointed across the room to Baserap. "You may want to talk to this officer," he said. Sullivan looked at Baserap and told him he was welcome to share his concerns with him by sending them through his chain of command. He then excused himself for another appointment.

Baserap decided he was going to document the distress and frustration within the White House guard in a scientific way. He had become the Don Quixote of the Secret Service officer corps. On his own time, he launched a massive survey of 136 White House officers for their thoughts on the complex's security protocols and weaknesses.

"Are you sure you want to do this after what happened last time?" Captain Vucci asked him. Baserap nodded.

"Absolutely," he said. "It has to be done."

In January 2007, on the day that President Bush delivered his State of the Union address, Baserap turned in his completed forty-two-page survey to his superiors, copying everyone up the chain to the director. He titled it "The Secret Service State of the Union."

Baserap's survey found overwhelming agreement that the White House security net was vulnerable to attack. Nine out of ten interviewed agreed that the complex lacked the staff and training needed to foil simultaneous attacks on the complex. Officers overwhelmingly agreed that they didn't have adequate weapons to stop a lethal threat to the president and his family on the complex, and that political desires to appease the White House were regularly trumping reasonable security decisions. Nine out of ten officers also agreed that Secret Service leadership jeopardized the safety of the president in his own home by failing to address chronic problems. Those woes included routine staffing shortages, burned-out officers, and junior officers regularly deployed to the most isolated entry points. Finally, the survey concluded that officers complained of being routinely treated with disrespect by their supervisors and their "brother" agents.

This report landed like a stink bomb in the

supervisors' offices. Later that week, a sergeant took Baserap aside to share what he had heard in the chief's office. "They are circling the wagons trying to figure out what to do with you," he said.

Clancy summoned Baserap for another meeting. "I don't agree with [your] conclusions, but you wrote this in a very respectful way," Clancy said. "You're not going to get a response from the director. He has received it. We can't confirm he has read it. It has gone through the chain of command."

Things then settled down for a while. A few months later, in September 2007, Baserap was transferred to the Foreign Missions Branch, a standard rotation, where he would help protect embassies and visiting heads of state.

December would mark a critical milestone in Baserap's career. After three years and 120 days in the Service, he would reach career status. After that he couldn't be fired without cause. But on the day before he hit that milestone, a Secret Service inspector called Baserap at home and asked him to come to headquarters. There had been a problem, he said. They found he had violated sick leave policy by failing to get properly documented permission for some leave after he had oral surgery.

For the first time, Baserap gave up. He could see he was going to lose. The Service said they were not going to renew his contract.

After he left, the Service continued to try to punish Baserap. When he was offered a defense contractor job, he learned he lost the offer because the Secret Service told his prospective employer he had been dismissed for some type of misconduct. That wasn't true or legally correct. After an eighteen-month legal battle, the Service settled the case, paid him a modest amount that would cover attorneys' fees, and amended his personnel file to accurately reflect that his contract had expired. Baserap and his wife felt beaten, but they kept plowing ahead, trying to provide for their growing young family.

Back at the White House, dozens of officers and agents kept their dog-eared copies of the Officer's Manifesto, and they copied the pages again and again to show new co-workers whom they heard complaining about illogical flaws in the security rules for the complex. They wanted them to know someone else had tried to raise these concerns before. For many people on the job, the wiry, fast-talking Officer Baserap was a hero. A contemporary of Baserap's, who was not a close friend, said the stand he made is still legendary. The former officer, who resigned not long after Baserap left, asked to remain anonymous to protect his career in government. Baserap's experience proved just how far the Service leadership would go to punish its critics.

"The people who have the biggest heart for that get pushed aside in this agency," he said. "You just aren't allowed to speak up, and he did. That was my opinion at the time—he's just trying to do his job. We all saw the gaps in security at the White House. Nothing that has happened—the Salahis, the vehicle getting in, the intruder—none of it has surprised me. After all, Baserap predicted it."

THE WHEELS COME OFF

THE OBAMA YEARS (2008–2015)

CHAPTER 16

"HE'LL BE SHOT SURE AS HELL"

Barack Obama walked onto the Boston stage to deliver the keynote address at the 2004 Democratic National Convention a state senator from Illinois, a political nobody. At the previous convention four years earlier in Los Angeles, Obama hadn't even had enough clout to score a floor pass. He dejectedly watched speeches from one of the jumbotrons scattered around the Staples Center. By 2004, he represented just six hundred thousand people in a central Illinois district, but he had caught the eye of party nominee John Kerry and been offered a plum convention role.

Obama's seventeen-minute speech on this July night transfixed the crowd and the press corps. As he shared his personal story, he stirred a warm, patriotic longing for an America at its best. He was the child of a determined single mother and an absent African father. Raised in a home of modest means and Midwestern values, he shared his parents' commitment to hard work and their "abiding faith in the possibilities of this nation." "I stand here knowing that my story is part of the larger American story," he declared, "and that in no other country on earth is my story even possible."

Democratic activists quickly moved to harness the power of this electrifying voice throughout the campaign season. Obama won his own ambitious election that November, leapfrogging from state senator to powerful U.S. senator. And within a few short years, a tiny group of Democratic kingmakers were secretly grooming him to become president.

Harry Reid, the ever-calculating leader of the Senate, was one of Obama's secret weapons. The sixty-six-year-old Democratic lion had been impressed by Obama's oratory when he joined the Senate in 2005 and took note. He feared his party's expected top choice for president in 2008, Hillary Clinton, was more vulnerable and unpopular than she wanted to admit. Reid took Obama under his wing, giving him high-profile chances to shine. In 2005, he had Obama take the lead in a lobbying and ethics reform campaign, and he watched Obama translate complex law into smooth sound bites. The Senate leader summoned the younger senator to his office in July 2006. Obama thought he was in trouble.

"I know that you don't like it, doing what you're

doing," Reid told Obama. The young senator looked confused, so Reid explained. "If you wanted to be president, you could be president now," he said.

BEFORE THE THANKSGIVING weekend of 2006, Obama and Senator Dick Durbin, a friend and mentor, chatted at the tail end of a political fundraiser at the Union League Club in Chicago. Durbin asked Obama if he'd thought any more about running. Obama said his Black friends were discouraging him. They feared for his safety. His wife had the same fears—on top of not liking how a national campaign would shake up their cherished family life. Durbin could tell that Obama wanted to do it anyway.

"You need to talk to Michelle," Obama told Durbin with a wink. So Durbin and his wife, Loretta, invited the Obamas out to dinner. At a Chicago restaurant in early December, the foursome chatted about their respective holiday plans. Then, in the middle of the main course, Durbin shifted the subject to the 2008 race. **Now is the time,** he told both Obamas. He locked eyes with Michelle as he spoke.

She had teased Durbin in the past about egging Barack on: "What are you trying to do to us?" But this time, the elder senator was serious. They had a rare opportunity to do something great for the country, he told them. What was holding them back?

———

THE OBAMA FAMILY headed to Hawaii for the 2006 Christmas holiday to visit Barack's family, including his aging grandmother, who had helped raise him. Madelyn Dunham got time to fuss over her two great-granddaughters, just five and eight, while Michelle and Barack took long walks together on the beach, tossing over the pros and cons of running. Michelle shared her fears in blunt terms. He would rarely see the girls, she warned. Their family might not be steely enough for the attacks that came with a presidential campaign. And, she said, he could be killed.

Just six months earlier, Michelle had met Dr. Martin Luther King, Jr.'s widow at a glitzy luncheon hosted by Oprah Winfrey. At a garden-side table at Winfrey's Santa Barbara estate, Coretta Scott King told Michelle not to let fear seize her as she and her husband stepped into public life. God would be watching over them, she said, and she promised to keep the couple in her prayers. Michelle felt humbled thinking of the physical danger this icon had endured.

Their brief talk would stay with her, reminding her of the risk to her husband but also giving her strength. That December, at the end of their beach talks, Michelle agreed that they would go for it. But she had some demands of her husband. He had to promise to quit smoking. She had to be allowed to keep her career, since if Barack were killed, she would need to support the family. And he had to get professional protection soon, she said.

Michelle and Barack Obama couldn't know it then, but this forty-five-year-old former community organizer would go on to become the most endangered president in history. And the Secret Service to which the Obamas would entrust their lives was in a weakening state, about to buckle. As Michelle Obama had feared, the notion of a serious Black contender for the presidency would soon inflame the raw, vicious strain of racism still festering in this country.

ON A FREEZING February morning in Springfield, Illinois, Barack Obama formally announced his campaign on the steps of the state capitol where, almost 150 years earlier, Abraham Lincoln had launched his own political career. Michelle Obama put on a good face while cheering for him, but she didn't dodge the reality that America's racism put her husband at risk.

"I don't lose sleep over it, because the realities are that, you know, as a black man, you know, Barack can get shot going to the gas station," she said in her first television interview after he entered the race. "So you know, you can't . . . you know, you can't make decisions based on fear and the possibility of what might happen."

Left unsaid were the precautions the couple had already taken. At Michelle Obama's urging, her husband's campaign had hired a private security firm run by a former Clinton detail agent, Joe Funk. But Funk didn't block traffic, sweep buildings. His team didn't camp at night outside his home or the hotels where he stayed. Michelle wanted her husband to seek full-time Secret Service protection as soon as possible. She was afraid, not so much for herself as for her husband and daughters. Any major presidential candidate could request Secret Service protection, but no one had ever asked for protection this early—two years before the election. Obama's campaign team feared such a request would backfire politically. They didn't want him to start his fledgling campaign by calling out America's lingering racism.

"In our campaign narrative, we were saying America is ready to elect an African American, a new kind of leader," said Chris Lu, Obama's friend and Senate aide. "The last thing you want to say is, 'Oh. There is this whole segment of America that is not ready.' The idea that some people want to do harm to Barack Obama, that cuts against our narrative."

Obama didn't qualify for Secret Service protection under the agency's technical criteria. Candidates had to raise at least $2 million and win a modest percentage of the vote in two consecutive caucuses before requesting a detail from a special congressional panel, which could then recommend that the secretary of homeland security authorize protection. But states wouldn't begin to hold caucuses for nearly another year, in January 2008.

It didn't take long, however, for the Obama team to spot trouble in the senator's in-box. In February, Lu began collecting some of the more threatening emails sent to the Senate office and campaign. Lu also did his own Internet research, sniffing around on KKK and neo-Nazi websites. "Our world will become unbearable with him as president," one contributor wrote on a white power chat site. "Maybe there will be someone who would take [a] chance and do a Lincoln on him?"

Other anonymous writers claimed they knew where the Obamas lived, and mentioned his daughters. The emails shook both Obamas. "These people were saying: 'We're going to get you and your family in Chicago,'" one longtime Senate leadership staffer said. "They took it very personally as a family. I think it scared the crap out of them."

In public, however, Barack Obama never betrayed his fear. He continued to downplay his risks and his race. "I face the same security issues as anybody," he said in a late February interview. "We're comfortable with the steps we have taken." Reporters asked Obama if he had received any death threats. The candidate declined to answer.

In private, Obama's Senate advocates Reid and

Durbin were pushing hard to get him Secret Service protection. In the second week of March, Reid called a private session of a low-profile congressional panel he controlled, which made recommendations each election season about when to provide protection to the major presidential candidates for each party. He wanted the group to consider recommending full-time protection for Obama. In April, Reid's panel endorsed his wish and urged the Bush administration to give Obama a security detail due to "general concern" for this prominent Black candidate.

By the first week of May, Michael Chertoff, the Homeland Security secretary, signed off on a detail, at the cost of roughly $30,000 a day. The decision to give Obama protection so early would nearly break the Secret Service's bank. The costs for candidate protection zoomed up from $74 million in 2004 to $112 million in 2008. Obama began traveling with a twenty-four-hour detail more than a year before his party's nominating convention, and eighteen months before the election, the earliest any candidate had ever received security in Secret Service history.

On the night of Thursday, May 3, campaign reporters sniffed out the change as Obama attended a fundraiser in New York. Instead of greeting fans on West Forty-fourth Street outside the Harvard Club, Obama was whisked out the back door by men in dark suits. The next day, reporters asked why. Durbin explained that he had seen racial threats against Obama. He stressed that he—not Obama— had pushed for this coverage. "Unfortunately, some of the information that we found was racially moti- vated," he said. "And it is a sad reality in this day and age that Mr. Obama's African American heritage is a cause for very violent and hate[ful] reactions from some people."

After a security team began circling him twenty- four hours a day, Obama ended up with a bigger footprint and profile. When he arrived at a new city to give a speech or visit a factory, more people saw the SUVs with the flashing lights on the hood. More national television cameras spotted Obama and tracked the candidate's movements. On **Good Morning America** and on the front pages of **The Washington Post** and **The New York Times**, experts highlighted the historic nature of Obama's candidacy and the dangers he faced as a leading Black contender.

It didn't take long for extremist groups to notice too. In a rare interview two weeks after Obama first started traveling with a security detail, the Grand Wizard of the National Knights of the Ku Klux Klan agreed to meet a Fox News reporter from Chicago at an undisclosed hotel in Indiana for an interview. The topic: Barack Obama's run for the highest office.

Wizard Railton Loy, a tall man with wire-rimmed glasses and a handlebar mustache, appeared in his purple satin wizard robes and conical hat for the on-camera interview. Loy explained matter-of-factly that Obama would never reach the White House. "I'm not going to have to worry about him, because somebody else down south is going to take him out," said Loy. "If that man is elected president, he'll be shot sure as hell."

As Obama outperformed expectations in his campaign in the spring of 2008, the chatter on white supremacist websites rose sharply. Obama's staff was taken aback by a few threats that junior aides flagged.

On February 15, 2008, an anonymous poster on a white power blog wrote, "The KKK or some-one WILL assassinate Obama! If we get a NIGGER President all you NIGGERs [sic] will think you've won and that the WHITE people will have to bow to you. FUCK THAT. Obama will die, KKK forever."

On April 22, while Clinton and Obama were still duking it out for the nomination, one anonymous writer promised his online friends that "IF OBAMA BECOMES PRESEDANT [sic] I WILL KILL HIM MYSELF MAKE NO MISTAKE ABOUT IT."

These sparks of racist hatred toward Obama flared with alarming frequency, but they also mir-rored a long-simmering racism inside the Secret Service, one that was starting to spill out into the public eye. The guards who would protect the most threatened candidate in history had their own hidden history of mistreating and ridiculing Black people in their midst. The Service might have a national, elite profile, but just like a small-town police department, it employed rank-and-file agents and senior leaders who felt they could make racist jokes—or worse.

In April 2008, a Black Secret Service officer found a noose hanging in the Service's training facility in Beltsville in a room used by one of the center's Black instructors. The Black officer didn't call his boss, for fear the incident would be covered up. Instead he alerted a high-ranking Black supervisor at headquarters. Investigators found the white agent, who disputed that it was a noose. But when the news leaked to the press, Mark Sullivan, the director of the Secret Service, insisted that the agent be put on leave pending an investigation. Whether the noose was intentional or not, the Service chalked it up to one bad apple, not to the existence of a larger problem.

But on May 10, 2008, **The New York Times** published a story that made Sullivan and the rest of his leadership team gathered in their offices on the eighth floor of Secret Service headquarters cringe. It described how twenty supervisors, some of them at headquarters, had traded racially insensitive jokes and racist commentary in internal emails. One joke mentioned the good that would come from Jesse Jackson being killed by a missile hitting the plane in which he was traveling. Another was titled "Harlem Spelling Bee," ridiculing Black students as having poor English. A few of the sample spelling bee words were mockingly defined as follows:

"**Income:** I just got in bed wif da ho and income my wife."

"**Undermine:** There's a fine lookin hoe in the apartment undermine."

This seamy culture at the top of the Secret Service was revealed thanks to an eight-year-old racial discrimination lawsuit filed by Black agents back in 2000, one that the Secret Service had been trying to quash since it was filed. Led by presidential detail agent Ray Moore, the Black agents had claimed a racist culture had blocked and stalled their ability to rise in the organization. The senior leadership of the Service made promotion decisions informally and kept no official files documenting them. Moore couldn't take another year of being passed over for white agents who rated below him and others he had trained. He and his colleagues risked career suicide when they filed suit, seeking to find out whether race played a role in supervisors' pattern of elevating whites so much more frequently. In 2004, a judge had ordered the Service to provide supervisors' internal emails. But by late 2007, the Service was still dragging its heels, claiming it would take years more for the overburdened agency to gather the material.

In a three-day court hearing on the case in late

2007, federal magistrate Deborah Robinson said she was out of patience and rebuked the Service for its stonewalling. She gave them a do-or-die deadline and the threat of daily fines afterward: Turn over all electronic messages among supervisors within three months, or else. The Service hired PricewaterhouseCoopers to review 20 million electronic records on promotions and race, and ended up discovering more warts than it bargained for. In their private chats on email, some of the Service's highest supervisors had traded racist jokes about Black men's genitalia, the illiteracy of Black adults, and the sexual prowess of different races. With the agency already being questioned about the noose found at the training center, Sullivan decided the Service had to turn over the records mentioning race to the plaintiffs.

Two weeks later, a small slice of those emails leaked out in **The New York Times**. The centerpiece was the email about the "Harlem Spelling Bee" that then assistant director Thomas Grupski had shared with some other agents. The morning the story ran, aides to Homeland Security Secretary Michael Chertoff called Sullivan to ask him what he was doing to handle this mess. Sullivan decided he would put Grupski on administrative leave. "We are deeply disappointed by any communication or action on the part of our employees that exhibits racial or other insensitivity," Secret Service spokesman Eric Zahren told the **Times**.

But when another batch of emails surfaced in the news five days later, this time involving some of Sullivan's favored lieutenants, the Service reacted with anger rather than remorse. Two high-ranking leaders were implicated, including the Hispanic agent Victor Erevia, one of three detail leaders for Barack Obama. He had shared a single joke with two colleagues about how to cajole a woman into sex that stereotyped the sexual traits of Jewish, Southern, and Native American men. David O'Connor, a top supervisor overseeing all protection details and a close ally of Sullivan's, was also implicated. He had received a string of racist jokes and rants from his brother, a retired agent, about Al Sharpton and how favoritism toward Black people was "ruining virtually every aspect of American life." O'Connor replied that he would like to pass the joke along to a retired agent who was "worthy of trust and confidence." In a public statement, Zahren said these emails should be read in context, simply as jokes. He said the disclosure of email traffic was a "deliberate attempt to embarrass the agency" during "an unprecedented presidential campaign."

Receiving a racist joke in an email proved little about the receiver. Sending one, though, created a public relations problem. The Service temporarily transferred Erevia, who would later help lead the first major Black candidate's campaign detail, and promoted him to a senior position over the agency's technical security division. It isn't clear whether Obama ever asked Erevia to explain.

Meanwhile, in June 2008, Hillary Clinton officially ended her campaign, leaving Obama as the Democratic nominee. Almost immediately, the racist reaction to an African American contender advanced from Internet vitriol to real plots with real guns. Four times before he was even sworn into office, white supremacists, militiamen, and mentally unhinged loners hatched plots to kill Obama—a steady stream of venom the Secret Service had never seen for a nominee.

One of the most worrisome schemes unfolded at the Democratic National Convention in Denver in late August 2008. Obama chose to accept his party's nomination at Invesco Field, home of the Denver Broncos. An advance team worked in Denver for months to orchestrate a security plan for the convention, and that weekend, phalanxes of agents and officers poured into Denver to begin putting that plan into action. The four-day convention would begin Monday, August 25.

Late that Saturday night, three men and their girlfriends were smoking meth in a Hyatt Regency south of downtown. High on a mixture of methamphetamines and booze, they partied and talked about how to kill Obama, according to an informant. "No nigger should ever live in the White House," said the group's unofficial leader, Shawn R. Adolf.

Adolf, his cousin Tharin Gartrell, and his friend Nathan Johnson had traveled from neighboring towns into Denver on the eve of the convention.

They mistakenly believed Obama was staying in their hotel. Perhaps they could find him and shoot him there, they mused aloud. Adolf's girlfriend suggested one idea: They could put a gun inside a camera and shoot him while appearing to take pictures. Adolf suggested they kill Obama with a high-powered rifle from an elevated location, like the "shooting on a grassy knoll" that killed Kennedy.

Adolf, who claimed to be a member of the white nationalist group Sons of Silence, said he had less to lose because he was facing several felony warrants for robberies and gun charges. "I might as well kill him," Adolf told them.

After midnight, Gartrell wanted to get some cigarettes. Adolf handed him the keys to his rented blue Dodge truck. An Aurora police officer noticed Gartrell swerving down the road and pulled him over. In the back of the truck he found a shocking arsenal: a loaded Ruger bolt-action rifle with a scope and bipod, a Remington bolt-action rifle with a scope, boxes of ammunition, two wigs, a bulletproof vest, and walkie-talkies. Three backpacks contained a mobile drug lab: the chemicals and glass vessels needed to cook a good quantity of meth. FBI and Secret Service agents had been monitoring white supremacist agitators coming into Denver and their chatter about hurting Obama. This had the look of the heavily armed plot the agents had feared.

Gartrell's arrest led FBI and Secret Service agents to extensively question all three. Johnson admitted that he believed Adolf and Gartrell had come to Denver to kill Obama. He reaffirmed those plans in a jailhouse interview with a news reporter the next day. "Yeah, they were here to do that, to assassinate him," Johnson said. "He don't belong in political office. Blacks don't belong in political office. He ought to be shot."

A day after FBI agents told a federal judge they had unearthed a serious plot to kill a presidential candidate, U.S. Attorney Troy Eid in Denver pulled back from that claim. In a news conference, he dismissed the trio's chatter in a hotel as "more aspirational, perhaps, than operational." Eid said that the men would face charges for drug and gun possession, but that agents lacked evidence the men had done anything more than talk about hurting Obama. "A bunch of meth heads get together, we don't know why they do what they do," Eid said. "If you're talking about a true threat, there has to be some evidence they're not just talking about it or thinking about it, especially in a drug-induced state."

Nick Trotta, the Secret Service's head of protective operations, downplayed the white supremacist threat, despite the fact that the FBI did have hard proof that another set of white supremacist agitators had traveled to Denver with the goal of making trouble. "I think that it's something that, at times, the media tried to make more of," Trotta said in an interview. "We've always watched them, as we watch all the other groups."

The top prosecutor and Secret Service's agreement not to charge the armed men surprised other prosecutors around the country and former Secret Service agents. Throughout modern history, people who had gotten close to hurting the president rarely had the best-laid plans or clearest thinking. Obsession could sometimes make up for lack of precision. But Eid noted that the three men didn't even know the hotel where Obama was staying.

The Secret Service was slightly more worried that October when they were alerted to a strange killing spree that two skinheads had been planning. Daniel Cowart of Tennessee and Paul Schlesselman of Arkansas shared a disgust at the idea of a Black president. They met online through a mutual friend and soon got together to craft an action plan. First, they would behead fourteen Black children and shoot eighty-eight others, starting at a local Black school. Then, wearing white tuxedos and top hats, they would assassinate Senator Obama by driving into his motorcade with guns blazing.

The numerology meant something in the skinhead underworld. The number 88 represented the letters HH, standing for "Heil, Hitler." A fourteen-word credo guided white power groups: "We must secure the existence of our people and a future for white children."

A county sheriff's deputy arrested the pair, largely by luck. The men had fired some practice rounds at a Black evangelical church a few miles from Cowart's home. No one was injured, but it made the news, and they later bragged about their efforts to a friend. The friend's mother reported them to the police. While they were being questioned, the two skinheads confessed to their grander plan.

According to an agent's interview, "Both individuals stated they knew they would and were willing to die in the attempt."

ON NOVEMBER 4, 2008, at just after 11 P.M., CNN called the presidential election for Barack Obama. The Obamas watched the returns with extended family at a hotel room near Chicago's Grant Park, the scene of a quickly growing Obama campaign rally. The densely packed crowds gathered there broke into cheers and dancing when news broadcasters announced his win.

The elated throng was twice the size expected for the rally—roughly 240,000 people—when Obama finally took the stage at one in the morning. Few could know the lengths to which the Secret Service had gone to protect the president-elect for that memorable twenty-five-minute speech. The Service had installed two van-sized sheets of bulletproof glass—ten feet high and fifteen feet wide—on the right and left sides of Obama's lectern. Television viewers couldn't see the glass, but in person they were as obvious as a two-ton block of ice. The two-inch-thick plates were intended to shield Obama from the risk of snipers in the high-rises above the park. Agents tested the placement of the glass by taking up positions in apartments above and "firing" red laser beams at agents standing in for Obama. The airspace around the park had also been made a no-fly zone for the night. The supervisor overseeing protection for the event thanked the Obama campaign for instantly agreeing to a raft of extra precautions.

"They never blinked when we told them we had to do the glass," the supervisor said. "They understood."

That night, a large part of the country celebrated. But for Obama, the danger had ratcheted up exponentially, literally overnight. The Intelligence Division, which assessed threats to the president, immediately felt itself struggling to triage and assess a skyrocketing number of threats. Agents estimated that in the months immediately before and for several months after he took office, Obama received four times as many death threats as his predecessors—as many as thirty a day.

The weekend after the election, at a Maine convenience store, a sign invited customers to join a betting pool on when Obama would be assassinated. "Let's hope we have a winner," the sign read. In Vay, Idaho, police found a sign on a tree offering a "free public hanging" of Obama. At North Carolina State University in Raleigh, anonymous artists had spray-painted KILL THAT NIGGER and

SHOOT OBAMA in a tunnel that students used to cross the campus.

Other incitements to violence were less immediately visible. Just as Obama had tapped social media to reach voters and boost his campaign, so his enemies used this vast forum to propose harming him. The ubiquity of Internet chat groups made it far easier in 2008 for people to tap out threats on a keyboard. More than two thousand people joined Stormfront, the oldest and largest white supremacist site on the Internet, in one day—November 5, 2008—the day after Obama won the presidency. The site temporarily crashed due to overwhelming traffic.

"I want the SOB laid out in a box to see how 'messiahs' come to rest," one Stormfront poster wrote in a conversation section a day after Obama's election. "God has abandoned us, this country is doomed."

The Secret Service's well-worn playbook called for sending a field office agent out to interview every single person who made a threat on the president's life. But the Intelligence Division had no realistic chance of tracking down every person who promised to do harm to Obama on Facebook or in a virtual chat room. Which threats were the careless rantings of a drunk or puffed-up braggart? Which came from mentally unhinged sociopaths who represented a true danger?

CHAPTER 17
SULLIVAN'S CREW

Agency directors—like generals—must master two things to succeed: They need to choose strong lieutenants to execute their plan on the ground, and they must fiercely advocate for the money and equipment their team needs to do the job.

The new Secret Service director, Mark Sullivan, was a tall, handsome man with deep-set eyes and silver hair. He was the father of three girls, an avid athlete, and a former college hockey player who continued to play hard in his fifties. He projected vitality as well as gravitas. He had twenty years of experience in protection and was skilled at charming the powerful. On the surface, Sullivan seemed destined to succeed.

And yet, throughout his seven years as director, Sullivan repeatedly struggled to build an effective team and marshal the necessary resources. Though he was deeply loyal to the Secret Service, Sullivan ultimately left it weaker than he found it.

MARK SULLIVAN GREW up in the white middle-class Boston suburb of Arlington, Massachusetts, the oldest son in a large Catholic family. He applied to the Secret Service not long after college but was rejected the first time he applied. He regrouped, logged a few years as an investigator for the federal housing department's Office of Inspector General to improve his résumé, and got hired in 1983 as a baby agent in the Detroit field office. He quickly impressed his bosses with his ability to master complex fraud investigations. Senior agents also considered him a natural at protection, first as a new agent on the Clinton family detail and later as a top deputy in charge of Vice President Cheney's detail.

It was also clear to Sullivan's peers that he had big career plans for himself. He was always focused on the next promotion, and he continually angled for face time with the VIPs the Service pro-tected. As a rookie agent with the Clinton family, he complained to his supervisors about being relegated to the Chelsea detail, and he lobbied to replace other agents who had lots of shifts with Mrs. Clinton.

After George W. Bush's inauguration, it was Sullivan's turn to take over as a detail leader. But Stafford infuriated Sullivan by moving him to the

Vice Presidential Protective Division, or VPPD. It was an important assignment, but second fiddle to the president's detail. Some senior leaders felt threatened by Sullivan's ambition.

Fellow agents said Sullivan felt double-crossed and nursed a small grudge about never making it to "the show." One agent on Vice President Cheney's detail noted, "I didn't know him that well when he arrived, but a friend warned me about Mark and it turned out to be right: 'That guy will act like your friend to your face, but behind your back, he'll be talking about you so he can help himself.'"

Sullivan had risen quickly beyond the vice president's detail after a contentious Secret Service leadership shake-up in 2003. President George W. Bush had named Ralph Basham as the new director despite heated, vocal opposition from the previous director, Brian Stafford. Sullivan became Basham's right-hand man. Three years later, in June 2006, as Basham agreed to take the helm of an even larger federal agency, U.S. Customs and Border Protection, he successfully lobbied the Bush White House to name Sullivan the new Secret Service director.

In May 2008, when Obama became the presumptive Democratic nominee, Director Sullivan faced a cluster of retirements in his senior leadership ranks. He now had a significant opportunity to shape his own leadership team. His choices would guide the Service through a post-9/11 world and a historic presidency. Some of those choices, however, would prove to be disastrous. "He didn't build a strong bench," said one former assistant director.

Sullivan followed the lead of previous directors, picking some deputies based on their seniority and personal loyalty to him and selecting others to appease various Secret Service factions. Democratic representative Bennie Thompson of Mississippi, chairman of the House Homeland Security Committee, which oversaw the Secret Service, had been pushing Sullivan for higher visibility for Black agents, especially with the prospect of Obama's winning the White House. After the noose incident, Thompson made clear to Sullivan that it was time to demonstrate his commitment to racial diversity at the top. The next month, Sullivan chose Keith Prewitt, a seasoned Black supervisor, as his deputy director.

But Sullivan also selected a few leaders who—in some workplaces—might have been disqualified because of recent misconduct. In May 2008, auditors reviewing the emails turned over in the Black agents' racial discrimination lawsuit discovered that six high-ranking supervisors had been downloading or sharing pornographic or sexually explicit images and messages with peers and subordinates. Dubbed Porngate by some agents, this tawdry discovery was kept hush-hush and never made it into the press. The highest-ranking person involved was George Luczko, a deputy assistant director who'd viewed and sent graphic sexual material to another senior executive. A second top supervisor, Mike Merritt, had forwarded far less serious but also sexually suggestive content in emails to lower-ranking staff.

Just a few months after getting a confidential briefing about what Luczko and Merritt had done, Sullivan promoted them both to the second-highest rank in the agency. In August 2008, Sullivan promoted Luczko to assistant director over the Office of Professional Responsibility, the agency's internal affairs unit. He would be in charge of over-seeing all investigations of employee misbehavior and misconduct. He promoted Merritt to assistant director over the Office of Investigations, one of the two most important offices in the Service. Merritt would oversee a little less than half the agency's budget and all the field offices tasked with investigating financial crimes.

Luczko secured his job by promising complete and total loyalty to the director, he later told friends. He counseled Sullivan that he badly needed people who would have his back, and swore he would unfailingly support Sullivan if he gave him the promotion.

Many agents admired Merritt's operational skills, and some even saw him as an ideal future director. Merritt had been groomed by former di-rector Brian Stafford, and by promoting Merritt, Sullivan would get a respected leader but also pacify

Merritt's considerable backers and fans. "Mark was making peace offerings," the former assistant director said. Sullivan would later say the two men were the most qualified candidates. Whether it was Sullivan's intent or not, a subtle message had been sent: Loyalty and connections were key to rising in the Service.

Sullivan then sidelined his assistant director overseeing human resources and training, Julia Pierson. She had started as an agent in Miami, worked on the protective details of three presidents, and now reached the executive suite. Just months earlier, he'd asked Pierson, the highest-ranking female in the agency, to review Luczko's and Merritt's misconduct and recommend punishment for their actions in Porngate. Each of them ended up with a letter of reprimand in his file. Now, just weeks later, Sullivan promoted them and effectively demoted her. He created a new position for her, chief of staff, but everyone on the eighth floor, including Pierson, knew Sullivan was pushing her aside.

Pierson had irritated several of Sullivan's assistant directors in her role overseeing hiring and training, and in her previous job as a senior chief of administration. In one memorable case, she had objected to plans to promote a former detail agent who had been accused of statutory rape. The supervisors argued that the agent had admitted the conduct but had never been convicted—the father of the girl having withdrawn his criminal complaint. Pierson had also annoyed the bosses of major field offices by noticing they were leasing larger offices than they needed, and by pestering field offices about turning in the guns and computers of retiring agents so they could be reused. "She never knew how to just stay in her own lane," said another former assistant director.

Sullivan's trusted inner circle was made up mostly of white men in their late forties and early fifties whom he had worked alongside on protection details. They had proven themselves to be hardworking, dogged agents. That didn't always make them good managers. Many lacked specialized expertise their changing agency needed in technology, terrorism, and financial management.

Sullivan had an agency to run, and he relied on others to track the agency's finances. But this was and had always been the Service's Achilles' heel: failing to advocate strongly enough for the money and staff it needed to do the job. Agents heard that some directors didn't like to make big requests because it could give the impression the president was unsafe. Despite the Service's image as a James Bond operation, the Service was sputtering along on ancient technologies, storing some of its most important information in 1980s-era computers. The Service tracked its enormous team based on a nearly untraceable mix of telephone calls, emails, and paper logs. It lacked any automated way of monitoring its spending in real time. It operated in react mode, recovering from one big event and whipping out the agency credit card to hurriedly fly swarms of agents to handle the next one. In other words, the Service desperately needed to invest in technology, but instead it wasted its limited dollars on basics.

For years, the Service had bumped along without making very well supported arguments for seeking extra money. The financial team simply looked at last year's budget and factored in some inflation and extra events or projects it knew it had to pay for. The arguments that Sullivan's team made got a very poor reception from the White House and Congress. In 2008, Sullivan's team finalized its strategic blueprint for spending over the next six years. The plan oddly listed investigating financial crimes as the Service's top priority—ahead of protecting the president. Sullivan's lieutenants wanted to protect lucrative turf. With the Service's creation of several electronic crime task forces in the late 1990s, a steady stream of veteran agents had begun landing high-six-figure jobs on Wall Street.

But the Service's new boss, the Department of Homeland Security, viewed its central mission as foiling terrorist attacks. The White House and Congress were eager to spend money on keeping terrorists off planes and securing U.S. borders. Every other mission would struggle to get dollars.

Sullivan's choices of lieutenants and failure to demand money the agency badly needed hadn't yet caused a crisis. But these factors would drag this elite protection agency down during his tenure, and for several years after he was gone.

AFTER THE DIRECTOR, the most powerful embodiment of the Secret Service is the special agent in charge of the president's detail. The person who would eventually assume that role alongside President Obama came to the job kicking and cursing.

In early 2007, Vic Erevia was coasting into the third and final phase of his twenty-three-year Secret Service career. Then forty-eight, he worked as an assistant special agent in charge in the Atlanta field office, a cushy, low-stress position. Soon he'd retire, collect his pension, and likely double his income with a private corporate security job.

Erevia told friends he was delighted to have escaped the headaches and palace intrigue of headquarters. He had safely entered his "pre-retirement" years. Then he got a call from David O'Connor, who was overseeing the already crowded 2008 presidential campaign. He needed Erevia to saddle up as one of three supervisors on a detail they were creating quite early for a freshman senator named Barack Obama.

Erevia could be straight with O'Connor, and he politely declined this request. But O'Connor wasn't really asking. Erevia reported for duty.

Erevia didn't fit the stereotype of a presidential

detail leader: the buttoned-down, clean-cut hard-body. Most detail agents on the job looked like Marines trying to hide in Men's Wearhouse suits. Erevia, often wearing his workaday trench coat, more closely resembled the eponymous detective in the television series **Columbo,** but with a scruffy goatee. Still, the rumpled, irascible detail leader and the tall, trim, reserved Senator Obama hit it off famously.

Erevia and Obama became joking buddies, a teasing relationship that gave Obama a respite from the stress of the day. Obama, a closet smoker, teased Erevia about the cheap Swisher Sweet cigars he smoked. The senator still liked to smoke cigarettes, and though he told his wife he was quitting, he still sneaked them here and there. Erevia could spin a pretty good yarn, and they bonded while comparing the challenges they both faced as minorities who rose to higher-profile roles. Erevia also worked to lengthen Obama's leash by arranging more "off-the-record" movements—times he could have lighter security and no press entourage. Erevia also grasped the nuances in the Obamas' marriage. Michelle was anxious about threats to her husband, but Barack preferred to downplay those dangers, in part because he didn't enjoy being hemmed in and guarded all the time. Erevia provided Obama with safe breaks from his bubble.

An agent's career can rocket skyward when he happens to bond with the right candidate. If his wannabe president makes it all the way to the White House, that agent will likely find himself becoming the leader on the president's detail, the second most prized job in the Secret Service. He could even become the director. Several agents have traveled this path to the top in Secret Service history. But there's always been a fundamental flaw in this traditional route: Presidents are judging what amounts to a popularity contest. They aren't considering management skills, or the ability to craft a strategic vision. Instead, they all inevitably ask themselves the same question: **Who makes me most comfortable?**

Erevia made Obama comfortable.

MOST FIRST LADIES have enjoyed a special kind of connection with the American public. With few exceptions, they have served as the gentler, humanizing counterparts to their political spouses. Unlike their husbands, they have often enjoyed the public's warm bipartisan embrace.

Thus, for most of the twentieth century, the Secret Service considered the First Lady a less likely target for harm. They assigned her a modest number of detail agents to match the assessed risk. Jackie Kennedy began her life in the White House with just one agent. By the time Hillary Clinton and Laura Bush took up residence, First Ladies played a far more frequent role at political events, but still they were given less than a fourth of the number of guards that surrounded their husbands.

For agents, the FLOTUS detail signaled a lower stature in the Secret Service's status-obsessed pecking order. Clint Hill, Jackie Kennedy's first agent, felt his career had stalled out when he got the assignment. Yet agents dutifully shadowed the president's spouse, doing the circuit of good-cause luncheons and publicity events as well as personal trips to the hairdresser and the children's school. Agents had their own parody nickname for the First Lady's detail, code-named FLD: the Fine Living and Dining crew.

The prestige of working the First Lady's detail rose markedly after 9/11. For the first time, Laura Bush's protective agents were expected to apply some of the same standards for advance planning as they used with the president. That made the FLD detail a more rigorous training ground and increased agents' chances for promotion. But the biggest change for the Fine Living and Dining crew came when Michelle Obama, code name Renaissance, arrived at the White House.

Preston "Jay" Fairlamb III, the special agent in charge of Renaissance's detail, knew immediately that Michelle Obama wasn't your grandmother's First Lady. Fairlamb, a tall, ultrafit agent in his late thirties, saw the special connection she had with a country excited by a young, history-making First Family. Not since Jackie Kennedy had a First Lady drawn the tidal wave of fans that equaled—and even rivaled—her husband's.

Michelle Obama's appeal came in some ways from being the opposite of Jackie. She was a straight-talking girl from Chicago's South Side, an approachable Everymom comfortable in J. Crew sweaters or workout tights. She owed her success to hard work, not family wealth. Young people and African Americans for the first time saw someone like them in the White House, and they swarmed to catch a glimpse of her or listen to her life story. She didn't sugarcoat her opinions. Young people needed to eat better and exercise, she counseled. She told them to stick to their studies so they could make their own good luck. She hadn't reached the lecture halls of Harvard Law School on "magic or fairy dust."

Fairlamb, the son of a New Jersey state trooper, soon realized the Service would have to upgrade its security playbook to make sure she stayed safe. Uniformed Division officers added magnetometer screening when she attended public events. Mrs. Obama was also the first First Lady to have a Counter Assault Team regularly riding in her motorcade. CAT's sole purpose was to engage in a firefight with any attacker so detail agents could quickly evacuate their charge to safety.

Some older supervisors stationed in headquarters and in field offices were shocked to hear that Michelle Obama had a CAT truck on many of her trips. Many questioned whether it was necessary or wise. Those in the headquarters' Office of Protective Operations, who felt responsible for managing the costs of each visit, feared going broke if they routinely provided presidential-level resources for Michelle. Quietly, the Secret Service bickered among themselves over just how much security the new First Lady should get.

It all came to a head in the middle of the night during a mother-daughter trip to Disneyland.

Michelle had embarked on a fun getaway in the middle of June 2010 with eleven-year-old Malia and nine-year-old Sasha to kick off summer break. They visited a Hollywood movie set, toured a closed section of Disneyland, strolled the Santa Monica Pier, and attended a Lakers game. Tired after a jam-packed day, the family headed back to the Beverly Hilton Hotel with the evening shift of the detail. The midnight shift was waiting to relieve the agents who had been working since 2 P.M. The First Lady and her children were escorted to the Presidential Suite, an 1,870-square-foot penthouse on the eighth floor. Mom and kids turned in for the night.

At around 4:30 A.M., all the supervisors working the L.A. trip awoke to buzzing phones on their hotel room nightstands. There was trouble on the penthouse floor. "Please report to the security room," a duty agent said. "There's a problem."

A disoriented homeless man had wandered off nearby Wilshire Boulevard and into the hotel's side entrance. Somehow he'd walked through an interior staircase, gotten onto the freight elevator, and ridden it up to the penthouse floor of the hotel. He then walked down the hall and straight to the door of the First Lady's suite.

One lone Secret Service agent on the midnight shift, Vince Stofa, stood between a mentally unbalanced stranger and the sleeping Michelle Obama.

Stofa, a former CAT agent, had plenty of training in crisis tactics, so his instincts kicked in. He barked for the man to stop and asked what he was doing there. Stofa had a submachine gun leaning against the wall in case of trouble. The intruder didn't respond, but Stofa soon got him facedown on the floor while calling out for reinforcements.

Agents outside who came running to Stofa's aid were shocked. Why hadn't the homeless man been stopped at the ground floor or in a lower stairway?

"Where are all the other guys?" one of the supervisors demanded.

"Sorry, boss, the guys were cut in the stairwell," the agent said, referring to an earlier decision to eliminate the agents assigned to the stairwell at night.

The elimination of those men represented a major change to the advance security plan, which a member of Mrs. Obama's detail had choreographed in excruciating detail. The advance agent had prescribed that agents borrowed from the area field office would stand in the stairwells to secure the First Lady's suite at all times. But Paul Le, the Los Angeles field office supervisor, whose team was loaning several agents for this plan, had not blessed adding the field agents who were scheduled for the midnight shift in the stairwell. The Secret Service manual for First Ladies' protection said that high-level security was simply not necessary all night long. The Service expected field offices and the protective operations office to look over advance plans and make sure the plans weren't wasteful. The next morning, Le got to share his point of view in a tense dispute in the parking lot of the swanky Beverly Hilton.

Fairlamb, the detail leader for Mrs. Obama, stood six foot four, Paul Le five foot eight. Fairlamb leaned over Le, and at various points, agents watching saw a heated exchange. "Preston's life was dedicated to making sure that nothing happened to that lady," said one of his colleagues. "Anything that ever challenged that, he was a pit bull."

Nevertheless, Fairlamb and Le had equal rank. They were both GS-14s. So neither man held back, either on their strongly-held opinions or on expletives. Fairlamb insisted that cutting bodies at the last minute was wrong. It ignored the expertise the advance agent had put into the security plan. Le argued that the manual was on his side: It did not call for staff to stand on guard on the midnight shift. Le reminded Fairlamb that he was responsible for minding the financial resources of his field office. Though this was a First Family visit, overtime for that midnight shift for every day of the visit would cost his office dearly.

"I really wanted to punch that guy," Fairlamb later told friends. Through an agency spokesperson, Fairlamb and Le declined to discuss the incident but said they do not recall having a major argument.

Fairlamb shared his anger with the special agent in charge of President Obama's detail, Vic Erevia. Erevia immediately agreed with Fairlamb. He couldn't believe the L.A. office would change an advance security plan at the last minute. He called the special agent in charge of the field office to complain.

"He asked him, straight up, 'What the fuck?'" a colleague of Fairlamb's said. "[Erevia] didn't go to the mat on many topics, and on this one he did."

CHAPTER 18

THE NIGHT BULLETS HIT THE WHITE HOUSE

The gunman parked his black Honda directly south of the White House, on a closed lane off Constitution Avenue. It was about ten minutes to nine on the evening of November 11, 2011. He pointed a semiautomatic rifle out the passenger window, aimed directly at the home of the president of the United States, and pulled the trigger. Then again, and again.

A bullet smashed a window on the second floor, just steps from the First Family's formal living room. Another lodged in a window frame, and several more pinged off the roof, sending bits of debris to the ground. At least eight bullets flew seven hundred yards across the South Lawn. Seven of them struck the Obama family's upstairs residence.

President Obama and his wife were out of town on that chilly evening. But their younger daughter, Sasha, and Michelle Obama's mother, Marian Robinson, were inside the home. Their older daughter, Malia, was expected back any moment from an outing with friends.

Secret Service officers rushed to respond. One, stationed directly under the second-floor terrace where the bullets struck, drew her .357 handgun and prepared to crack open an emergency gun box on the side of the mansion. Counter snipers on the roof, standing just twenty feet from where one bullet struck, scanned the South Lawn through their rifle scopes for signs of an attack. With no camera surveillance on the far south perimeter of the White House, it was up to the Secret Service officers who protected the White House to figure out what was going on.

Then came an order that surprised several officers on the complex. "No shots have been fired. . . . Stand down," Sgt. Wallace Strong called over his radio. The noise, the sergeant said, was just backfire from a nearby construction vehicle.

His command was the beginning of a string of blunders as the Secret Service fumbled to recognize a serious attack on the White House. Throughout that night and the rest of the weekend, Secret Service leaders continued to miss clues and make mistakes. As they gradually realized their errors, the senior leadership tried to keep the details a secret—even from their own employees.

WHEN OSCAR ORTEGA-HERNANDEZ shot at the White House just after 9 P.M., President Obama and the First Lady were in San Diego on their way to Hawaii for the Veterans Day weekend. The president was aboard an aircraft carrier in the San Diego harbor for an auspicious occasion—the first college basketball game aboard a military vessel. With the First Couple gone, the Secret Service staff at the White House slipped into what some called "casual Friday" mode.

By 8:30 that night, most of the agents and officers on duty were coming to the tail end of a quiet shift. On the White House's southern border, a few construction workers were milling about. D.C. Water utility trucks planned to use the low-traffic hours to clean sewer lines along Constitution Avenue. They had parked in the lane closed off by orange cones on the side of the street adjoining the grassy park leading to the White House's South Lawn. This is where the gunman pulled over in his black 1998 Honda Accord.

Ortega was a twenty-one-year-old high school dropout who had left his Idaho Falls home a month earlier, on what he told his family was a vacation. He and his girlfriend had just had a baby boy, but she had recently broken off the relationship. She loved Ortega but could tell something was deeply wrong. She and his friends noticed he had been acting increasingly paranoid. He would launch into tirades about the U.S. government trying to control its citizens. Friends often told him he looked like Jesus, and he had become fixated on his role as a messenger. He called President Obama "the Antichrist" and said he "had to be stopped."

Ortega arrived in Washington on November 9, after driving more than three thousand miles and making a brief stop in rural Pennsylvania to stay with friends. Sitting in his car on the Washington Mall that evening, he was ready to send his message.

He had 180 rounds of ammunition in the backseat. A Romanian-made Cugir semiautomatic rifle, similar to an AK-47, rested at an angle against the passenger side floorboards and the right front seat. He had purchased the gun for $550 at an Idaho gun shop in the spring and practiced shooting at random pieces of junk at a gun range near his home. Now, more than halfway across the country, within striking distance of the president's home, Ortega raised his weapon and pointed it out the passenger side window. He began firing.

On the rooftop of the White House, countersniper officers Todd Amman and Jeff Lourinia heard six to eight shots in quick succession. It was likely semiautomatic fire, they thought. They scurried out of their shedlike booth, readied their rifles, and scanned the southern fence line. Under the Truman Balcony, the second-floor terrace off the residence that overlooks the Washington Monument, Secret Service officer Carrie Johnson heard shots and what she thought might be debris falling overhead. She radioed the Secret Service's Joint Operations Center, at the agency's headquarters on H Street Northwest, to report she was breaking into the gun box near her post. She pulled out a shotgun and replaced the buckshot inside with a more powerful slug in case she needed to engage an attacker.

Ortega fired his shots about fifteen yards from Officers William Johnson and Milton Olivo, who were sitting in a Chevrolet Suburban on the Ellipse near Constitution Avenue but facing away from Ortega. They could smell acrid gunpowder as they jumped out of their vehicle, hearts pounding. Johnson took cover behind some flowerpots. Olivo grabbed a shotgun from the Suburban's backseat and crouched by the vehicle.

Officer William Johnson noticed something odd as he looked around the grounds—leaves had been blown away in a line-like pattern, perhaps by air from a firearm muzzle, creating a path of exposed grass pointing from Constitution Avenue north toward the White House.

Then another call came over the radio from a supervising sergeant—the one ordering agents to stand down. This led to some confusion and surprise, especially for officers close to the White House who, like Carrie Johnson, felt sure they had heard gunshots. Officer James Sevison, a canine handler in a parked cruiser on the east side of the mansion, had hopped out at the sound, drawn his weapon, and taken cover behind the First Lady's limousine. Officer Nathan Hogan, stationed nearby, had pulled out a rifle and started walking toward the South Lawn. Nevertheless, they complied with the order. They holstered their weapons and turned back to their posts.

But civilians, lacking any police training, had no doubt about what they'd seen. A woman in a taxi stopped at a nearby stoplight immediately took to Twitter to describe the actions of "this crazy guy" in a car in front of hers. "Driver in front of my cab, STOPPED and fired 5 gun shots at the White House," she wrote, adding, "It took the police a while to respond."

Another witness—a visiting neuroscientist who was riding by in an airport shuttle van—later told investigators he had seen a man shooting out of a car toward the White House.

Officer William Johnson hadn't seen Ortega or the barrel of his rifle. He didn't know about any witnesses driving down Constitution Avenue. But he felt sure he knew the sound of gunfire up close. He got on his radio to say so. "Flagship," he said, using the code name for the Secret Service command center, "shots fired."

The certainty of his report snapped officers back into action. Roving officers and members of an emergency SWAT team drew their weapons and began moving quickly to the South Grounds.

Ortega, meanwhile, was speeding down Constitution Avenue toward the Potomac River at about

60 miles per hour, according to witnesses. He narrowly missed striking a couple crossing the street before he swerved and crashed his car.

Three young women who were walking near the Vietnam Memorial heard the crash. One called 911. As they walked closer to the scene, the woman stayed on the phone with the emergency operator and narrated what they saw. The Honda was spun around to face them, headlights glaring at oncoming traffic. The car's tires were straddling the curb, with the right side of the Honda in the on-ramp to the Roosevelt Bridge and the left side lifted slightly over the concrete curb. The driver's-side door was flung open onto the grass. The radio was blaring.

The driver was gone.

Nestled against the passenger floorboards and the driver console was a semiautomatic assault rifle, with nine shell casings on the floor and seat.

McClellan Plihcik, a presidential detail agent who had been on his way to gas up his unmarked car nearby, responded to the radio report of gunshots and was the first to arrive on the scene. A homeless man told him he had seen a young white male running from the vehicle after the crash and heading north along the riverbank toward the Georgetown area.

From the Joint Operations Center, the sounds of voices competing with each other echoed over the police radios. A Secret Service dispatcher at the JOC, Officer J. Robinson, called 911 to report the sound of shots as a man's voice in the background yelled details. The dispatcher gave the D.C. police operator contradictory descriptions of vehicles and suspects. At first she reported that both a black Cadillac and a black Honda were leaving the scene. Later she mentioned a black Caddy and a yellow car, apparently a reference to a yellow construction truck parked near the grounds. Some officers mistakenly reported that Park Police were chasing the yellow car as it traveled out of the city, either on George Washington Parkway or Route 66. With the dispatcher and officer's conflicting reports, police now began looking for the wrong suspects: two Black men supposedly fleeing down Rock Creek Parkway. The man who had shot at the White House had disappeared on foot into the Washington night, with the Secret Service still trying to piece together what had just happened.

Back in the White House, key people in charge of the safety of the president's family were not initially aware that a shooting had occurred. Officers guarding the White House grounds communicate on a radio frequency, White House One, which is different from the channel used by agents who protect the First Family. The agent assigned to Sasha learned of the shooting a few minutes later from an officer posted nearby.

The White House usher on duty, whose job is attending to the First Family's needs, got delayed word as well. She immediately began to worry about

Malia, who was supposed to be arriving any minute from an outing with friends. The usher told the staff to keep Sasha and her grandmother inside. They apparently had not heard the window breaking. Malia arrived with her detail at 9:40 P.M., and agents insisted on locking all doors for the rest of the night.

The Secret Service's watch commander on duty, Capt. David Simmons, had been listening to the confusing radio chatter since the first reports of possible shots. When word came of the abandoned Honda, the captain left the new JOC at headquarters on H Street and drove to the scene at the foot of the Roosevelt Bridge.

It was technically up to Captain Simmons to decide whether the events of that night appeared to be an attack on the White House. But in the hierarchical Secret Service, no watch commander made that call alone. He checked with his bosses by phone. As Simmons surveyed the scene, he and Secret Service supervisors speculated that gang members in separate cars had gotten in a gunfight near the White House's front lawn. It was an unlikely scenario in a relatively quiet, touristy part of the nation's capital.

Sometime around 10 P.M., Simmons turned the case over to the U.S. Park Police, the agency with jurisdiction over random crimes near the White House grounds. With that, the Secret Service officially concluded there was no evidence connecting this shooting to the White House.

In the dark, nobody conducted more than a cursory inspection of the White House for evidence or damage. Ed Donovan, a chief spokesman for the agency, saw that a woman in a cab had tweeted about seeing the shooter aim directly at the White House. He forwarded her claim to the Service's twenty-four-hour protective intelligence desk that investigated potential threats. But at 11 P.M., the intelligence desk sent out an alert to all supervisors at the White House complex describing the incident as "a drug-related shooting." U.S. Park Police spokesman David Schlosser told reporters that the fact that the shooting had taken place near the White House was just a big coincidence. "The thing that makes it of interest is simply the location," he said. "You know, a bit like real estate."

At the time of the shooting, President Obama had been sitting courtside on the USS **Carl Vinson** warship in Coronado Bay, watching the fourth quarter of a basketball game between the University of North Carolina and Michigan State University on the flight deck. He was getting ready to be interviewed by ESPN at 9:05 P.M.

Not long after, the Carolina Tarheels were celebrating beating the Michigan State Spartans, 67–55. The president had finished his interview. He congratulated the players on a great game and chatted briefly with the basketball legend Magic Johnson. Forty-five minutes after the shooting, Barack and Michelle Obama climbed aboard Air Force One, bound for a trade summit in Honolulu. Director Sullivan was traveling with the president. Mickey Nelson, Sullivan's assistant director for protective operations, called the director to let him know there had been a shooting near Crown. Everything was okay, Nelson emphasized. "It doesn't look like there's any connection to the White House," he said. The First Couple was still unaware that a man had taken several shots at their residence while one of their daughters was at home and another was en route.

THE NEXT DAY, the Secret Service bosses seemed to want to put the previous night behind them.

Officer Carrie Johnson, who thought she'd heard debris fall from the Truman Balcony the night before, listened intently during the roll call before her shift on Saturday afternoon. Supervisors explained that the gunshots came from people in two cars, likely gang-bangers, shooting at each other. Johnson had told several senior officers Friday night that she thought the house had been hit. But on Saturday she did not challenge her superiors about their conclusion. She held back "for fear of being criticized," she later told investigators.

Though the Park Police was now in charge of the investigation, Sullivan urged Secret Service agents to continue to assist, amid new clues that the shooting could be connected to the White House. They used social media and other sources to locate witnesses, such as the tweeting taxi passenger. They had traced the car to Ortega and began reaching out to his family and friends, who would soon reveal troubling details. Yet the Service kept their suspicions from key law enforcement partners and even most of their own staff. Investigators inexplicably did not issue a national lookout to notify law enforcement to pick up Ortega for questioning, a routine move in such cases. If they had, Ortega could have been arrested that Saturday in Arlington County, Virginia. But police missed their chance. Police responded to a call about a man behaving oddly in local Quincy Park. They questioned Ortega but had no idea he was a suspect in a shooting, or a man who had abandoned a car on the National Mall with a semiautomatic rifle inside. They let him go.

The Park Police did not obtain a warrant for Ortega on weapons charges until that Sunday, when agents began interviewing his friends and family and learned he had become obsessed with President Obama and considered him the Antichrist. His mental health had been deteriorating for the last two years, and he believed he embodied the second coming of Jesus Christ, his girlfriend said. Now the Service dispatched Washington area agents in two-man teams to canvass the city to try to locate him. But it still made no Service-wide alert to say they had made a mistake—and that the Friday night shooting was now likely an attempted assassination.

The situation at the White House remained quiet until Tuesday morning. Most of the White House senior staff knew nothing about what the Service was piecing together. President Obama was flying onward from Hawaii to Australia. But the First Lady had returned to Washington on an overnight flight. She had gone upstairs to take a nap shortly after arriving home at five-thirty that morning.

Flying back on her plane was Secret Service director Mark Sullivan. By this time, Sullivan's agents had conducted more interviews and knew Ortega was a delusional man who had told his friends Obama was the devil and "he was going to put a stop to it." The director decided it wasn't time for the Service to share this news with the First Couple. Sullivan later said he needed more information to confirm the seriousness of the threat.

Reginald Dickson, an assistant White House usher, had come to work early to prepare the residence for the First Lady. Around noon, a housekeeper asked Dickson to come to the Truman Balcony, where she showed him the broken window and a chunk of white stone on the floor. Dickson saw the bullet hole and cracks in the antique glass of a center window, with the intact bulletproof glass on the inside. Dickson spotted a dent in another window-sill that turned out to be a bullet lodged in the wood. He called the Secret Service agent in charge of the complex.

With that, Ortega became a suspect in an

assassination attempt on the president of the United States—and he was about to become the target of a national manhunt.

Aides rushed in around noon to alert Bill Daley, the White House chief of staff, to the discovery of bullets on the second floor of the residence. The First Lady was still napping, and Daley and Deputy Chief of Staff Alyssa Mastromonaco knew it was their job to notify her and the president. They debated whether they should wake her up and give her the news. "I know these people," Mastromonaco said. "Let me handle it."

They would let Mrs. Obama sleep, they decided. Mastromonaco said she would brief the president so he could decide how to tell his wife.

Dickson, the usher, had meanwhile gone upstairs to the third floor to see how Michelle Obama was doing. He assumed she knew all about the bullets and began describing the discovery on the balcony and the clean-up. But she was aghast—and then furious. She wondered why neither Sullivan nor her own detail leader had mentioned anything about a shooting during their long flight back together from Hawaii, according to people familiar with the First Lady's reaction.

That afternoon, four days after the shooting, Secret Service investigators began interviewing officers and agents about what they had seen and heard while on duty the previous Friday night. They put out an all-points bulletin for Ortega and circulated his picture. Local police officers up and down the Eastern Seaboard were tasked with checking train and bus stations. Meanwhile, a team of FBI agents met early that evening to plan how they would take over the investigation and secure the crime scene at the White House.

At 7:45 the next morning, FBI agents arrived at the White House complex. They interviewed some of the Secret Service officers who had been on duty that Friday night and scoured the Truman Balcony and nearby grounds for casings, bullet fragments, and other evidence. They found $97,000 worth of damage to the exterior of the mansion.

The Secret Service had sent pictures of Ortega to places where he had been seen before, asking people to be on the lookout. That Tuesday morning, a hotel desk clerk at a Hampton Inn in Indiana, Pennsylvania, called police after recognizing the man by his distinctive neck tattoo. State troopers arrested Ortega on a tip the Secret Service provided and kept him in a holding cell until FBI agents could arrive to question him.

Michelle Obama was still upset when her husband arrived home five days later from Australia. The president was fuming, too, former aides said. Not only had the Secret Service stumbled in its response, their deputies had failed to immediately alert the First Lady. "When the president came back . . . then the shit really hit the fan," said one former senior aide. "He was outraged that the incident had happened and was found out the way it was. He was upset there wasn't a better briefing of the First Lady. He had gotten an earful from her."

Tensions were high when Sullivan was called to the White House for a meeting with the First Lady; Valerie Jarrett, senior adviser to the president; and other Obama aides about the incident. Michelle Obama tried to keep her outrage in check. "I'm speaking to you now not as the First Lady, but as a mother," she said slowly. But as the meeting continued, she addressed the director and his aides in such a sharp and raised voice that she could be heard through a closed door, according to people familiar with the exchange.

She had many questions. Why hadn't her daughters and mother been moved to a safer place when gunfire was first heard? Why hadn't the threat level at the White House been raised to Condition Red, which would have triggered more safety precautions for her family? How did agents and officers miss bullets from an assault rifle lodged in the walls of what was essentially her living room? One of the bullets hit the window of one of her favorite spots to read and relax, the Yellow Room. She was appalled to learn of the more "casual" security posture at the complex when POTUS was away. "Her general frustration was—'Oh! So when **he's** not at the house, what are **we**? Chopped liver?'" the former Obama agent said.

White House staff generally liked and trusted the

director, and he survived in his position despite the bungled shooting incident. But the First Lady and White House chief of staff Bill Daley stressed that this wasn't confidence-inspiring. "It was made clear to him this was a fuckup," a senior Obama adviser said.

Sullivan later disputed that Mrs. Obama raised her voice at him. But he declined to describe the meeting.

FOR MANY FORMER Secret Service officials, the 2011 shooting was a sign of far deeper troubles. The Service preferred to keep a security breach a secret, even when open discussion could improve protection for the president in the future. With the public and even with their own rank and file, Sullivan and his top deputies acted as if the shooting had never occurred. Sullivan never ordered a formal after-action review. The first time the Service sought out video surveillance footage of the area for the night of the shooting was on November 15, when the housekeeper found the bullet hole in the Yellow Room window.

The Secret Service stressed that Ortega had been bizarrely lucky in his aim. The agency never expected that a rifle could strike the residence from that distance, roughly 750 yards. But that was the problem. The Service hadn't imagined a risk that proved quite imaginable—and real.

Sullivan and his deputies found serious protection gaps as a result of the shooting. Quietly, they made changes meant to beef up security. New York City police had rafts of cameras scattered around the city to help identify and catch criminals. But Sullivan had to reluctantly acknowledge that the exposed southern border of the White House had none. In 2012, the Service purchased and installed a suite of cameras there. At the urging of the newly promoted special agent in charge, Vic Erevia, the Service increased the number of officers on the perimeter posts and added countersurveillance patrols. In typical Secret Service fashion, the agency threw bodies at a problem. In another new policy, officers at the White House complex had to clear all members of the public from the E Street area of the South Grounds whenever the Obamas used the Truman Balcony.

Ortega was charged with attempted assassination and later pleaded guilty to slightly lesser charges. He was sentenced to twenty-five years in prison.

Ortega turned out to be a deeply confused person, but also a classic presidential assassin: a young man, developing paranoid schizophrenia as he aged into his twenties, who felt compelled to take dramatic action to right some vague, ill-defined wrong. He succeeded in hitting the president's house. He just happened to show up at the White House when the president wasn't home.

Ortega's friends traced his troubles to about a year earlier, when he had become agitated watching an antigovernment film. The movie, called **The Obama Deception**, was written and produced by Alex Jones, a Texas-based conspiracy theorist and talk show host. It claimed that a cluster of wealthy families were engaged in a conspiracy with President Obama and had installed him in the White House to use the government to surveil and hurt the interests of most Americans. Soon Ortega bought a powerful rifle and began practicing his aim.

In early fall, Ortega asked a friend to record his video testimonial about his role as Jesus Christ. Ortega asked Oprah Winfrey to broadcast it to her national audience. "You see, Oprah, there is still so much more that God needs me to express to the world," he said. "It's not just a coincidence that I look like Jesus. I am the modern-day Jesus Christ that you all have been waiting for."

Ortega's attack revealed that an elite force of selfless and highly skilled patriots—willing to take a bullet for the good of the country—was still not always up to its job. "It was obviously very frightening that someone who didn't really plan it that well was able to shoot and hit the White House and people here did not know it until several days later," Daley said. "The handling of this was not good."

CHAPTER 19

"I WOKE UP TO A NIGHTMARE"

Dave Chaney was ready to retire. He still reported early to work, a habit of many agents, but he felt less zip each morning when he was getting ready. After twenty-one years with the Service, Chaney had reached the respectable but modest grade of GS-14. Now a senior supervisor, he oversaw a small headquarters division that worked with foreign countries. His unit helped train foreign security forces in how to create a safe bubble around their leaders.

In just a few months, the forty-eight-year-old supervisor could turn in his retirement papers. He was looking forward to deciding for himself how to spend his hours.

Chaney had enjoyed a special perch, not just as a Secret Service agent, but as a Secret Service legacy. He was the son of George Chaney, a World War II veteran who had protected President Eisenhower's grandchildren and President Johnson and then risen to become a well-respected head of personnel. He reaped the benefits of his dad's reputation, as the elder Chaney had hired many of the agents who became Dave Chaney's bosses.

Dave Chaney loved the Service, but not in the same way his dad's generation had. Certainly Chaney valued the brotherhood, the history he'd witnessed, and the lifetime friends he made in an all-consuming mission. He became known as the guy who jumped to take up a collection for a sick co-worker or a retirement party. But Chaney was also irreverent, joke-cracking, and clear-eyed about the Service's flaws. He noticed how the senior leadership seemed surprised every four years when a presidential campaign arrived. He watched a mass exodus of supervisors in the late 1990s—a bleeding wound the Service didn't try to patch until too late. The Service overworked a small team of horses to make ends meet—all in the name of duty and valor.

Chaney had long ago hopped off the promotion track, and for seven years as a supervisor opted not to bid for a promotion. This made him a huge exception in an agency stocked with Type A's furiously jockeying to grasp another rung of the career ladder. One day, his deputy assistant director urged Chaney to consider putting in for a higher job.

"What does the director make?" he asked his boss, noting that his wife made twice that. "You want me to transfer to Detroit? So I can get a better title? So maybe one day I can make ten thousand dollars more than I do now? No thanks."

Chaney felt strongly about this. When he was in grade school, his father had moved their entire family—five kids—from Austin to El Paso with just two years left before his retirement. His sister had to change high schools. "Why did you do it, Dad?" the younger Chaney once asked. "I wanted to retire as a special agent in charge," the elder Chaney replied. The son was dumbfounded. He had admired his father greatly, but he vowed he wouldn't do this—disrupt his child's high school experience for a better title.

Now, as Dave Chaney prepared for his own retirement, one of the best perks of being a Secret Service agent landed in his in-box: an exotic foreign trip. He had volunteered to provide extra help on President Obama's trip to Cartagena in mid-April, and headquarters emailed to say he'd been chosen to go. He'd be the jump team supervisor—a pretty easy gig. Jump team members would fly in with the president's limo and other tricked-out vehicles on two Air Force cargo planes, dubbed "car planes," about forty-eight hours before Obama. While the president was in country, they would serve as "post standers"—the worker bees who covered manage-able but boring shifts. They usually stood guard at perimeter posts or security checkpoints, all while staying in a five-star hotel in a beautiful city.

Before POTUS arrived on April 13 and after he left, the post standers were free to party. And Cartagena—with its late-night club scene—specialized in just that. "See logistics below," Chaney emailed the fifty-four guys on his newly assembled jump team on Monday, April 9, the day before they departed. "Our motto for this trip is Una Mas Cerveza por favor." Nothing wrong with partying on Uncle Sam's dime a couple of nights, the men reasoned. Not when agents and officers that year had spent so many hours standing in stairwells or cold streets on the midnight shift, walked so many miles a day on a campaign detail, or missed countless kids' games, anniversaries, and birthdays.

Cartagena also boasted a Vegas-like approach to sex. Prostitution was legal there, and the local clubs made the transaction all the more civilized by letting men pay for a woman's sexual services on their bar tab. It had become so commonplace that locals took to calling prostitutes **prepagos**—"prepaids." Some members of the jump team toyed with the idea of how to round out the trip with a bit of the city's X-rated fun.

The first cargo plane took off Tuesday night and landed at 2 A.M. Wednesday, April 11. The second plane arrived a little after 4 A.M. due to some mechanical repairs it needed at the base. In prearranged teams, the jump team guys drove their SUVs, trucks, and the president's limo, loaded with guns and detection equipment and luggage, down the ramp and out of the plane. In an unofficial motorcade, the vehicles sped the men to their home away from home for the next five days: the Hotel Caribe in the heart of Cartagena's tourist district.

Agents often joked that they brought so much gear and hardware and personnel into town for each presidential visit, their presence was hardly a secret. It was why some agents mockingly nicknamed their enormous troupe the Secret Circus.

President Obama was scheduled to arrive Friday at the Hilton Cartagena, a luxury high-rise on the farthest end of a hook-shaped stretch of pristine beachfront. The Service's advance and logistics teams had already been at the Hilton for a week, working hard to prepare for his weekend visit.

But Party Central was the Hotel Caribe, about six blocks away, at the other end of the hotel-lined beach. Of the 175 Secret Service personnel in town, 133 were staying at the Caribe. Many of the 100 military personnel, who provided extra security, counterintelligence, and bomb detection, were booked there too.

Chaney's and fellow agent Greg Stokes's jump teams arrived in the early morning hours Wednesday and crashed in their Caribe hotel rooms to get some sleep. By midday, most of them had awoken and found the Caribe's enormous pool buzzing with a spring-break vibe. Speakers blasted a mix of hip-hop and country. Some of the military guys had stocked Styrofoam coolers with beer and booze from a local liquor store and kept them next to their lounge chairs.

Some of the Secret Service jump team members hit the pool or went to the nearby grocery store for provisions. They exchanged emails about meeting up for dinner at dusk, making plans for a night on the town. Chaney and Stokes met at the pool at about 6 P.M. and left together for dinner with about eight younger agents. One of the Spanish-speaking agents led them to an unassuming local restaurant he knew from previous visits. They moved on to a well-known club nearby, Mister Babilla, for a few drinks.

But Stokes, who was single, and Chaney, who was married, had discussed another plan: visiting a strip club. An advance agent had even sent Chaney a recommendation. "Pleyclb bosque off hook!" the agent wrote, referring to a strip club and bordello in the Bosque neighborhood. Sometime around 10:30 P.M., the two supervisors got in a taxi and told the younger guys they were heading back to the hotel for the night. They left on their own, not knowing the other agents and wanting to be discreet.

Once inside the back of the cab, Stokes told the driver, "Take us where the girls are." They pulled up a few minutes later to a windowless building on the backside of Cartagena Bay that had a neon sign depicting a naked woman swinging her leg around a large anchor at the entrance. The men presumed it was the Pley Club. In fact, the club was El Paraiso del Marina—Paradise on the Water—about ten blocks away. A bouncer escorted the men to a table. No women were dancing onstage, but soon a group of them paraded by in a line and introduced themselves.

Stokes and Chaney began talking to two women, who gave their escort names of Juliana and Maria. They bought the women some drinks. The club was full of white American men—some Secret Service and some military men, Chaney noticed. He guessed it was about 11 P.M., but time was fuzzy. By now Chaney had had a mojito and at least eight beers. Stokes had about four or five beers.

Juliana smiled at Stokes. "We can spend all night together if you ask the boss," she said. She told him it would cost 200,000 pesos—about $100—plus a "tax" for her to leave the club with him.

Separately, Chaney tried figuring out Maria's price, but he had trouble understanding her because he knew very little Spanish. Stokes went to the cashier to ask about the exact fee.

When the men had paid what the women and the club required—roughly $140 each—they got into a taxi with the two prostitutes and headed back to the Caribe.

THE MEN FROM the Counter Assault Team started their night with a bottle of Grey Goose at the hotel.

"I have goose and some mixers in my room for a

pre-game," Joe Bongino wrote to his buddies Art Huntington and Todd Bratz. "How about 545 in room 710 for a few?"

All three agents were assigned to CAT, a group that had developed something of a reputation over the years. Most members kept physically and mentally honed for the mission, spending hours each month on the range and in the gym. Many had impressive physiques. Some also rated as expert marksmen. Team members likened themselves to a Special Forces unit and often adopted an alpha-male swagger to match. In the thirty-plus years since CAT was formed, however, they had never once been called upon to fire on an armed attack. And during that time, they'd also become synonymous with some of the most determined partying and skirt chasing in the Service. Some younger female White House staffers coyly discussed who among them had "earned a CAT shirt." If they had the shirt, it meant they'd slept with someone on CAT.

These three members of the team were ready to hit the town and party as soon as they touched down at the resort. After their pregame drinks in Bongino's room, they went to a steakhouse for dinner a few blocks from the hotel, returning to Bongino's room for a few more shots of Grey Goose around 10 P.M. Bratz then suggested they go to a club at the entrance to the old walled section of the city: Tu Candela, or Your Flame. The cave-like venue drew locals, tourists, and also some pretty, more discreet escorts. Once inside, the CAT guys ran into some Secret Service agents from the New York field office, and together they formed a knot at one end of the bar.

Dania Londono Suarez, a lithe twenty-four-year-old with golden highlights in her long brown hair, had come to Tu Candela with three other working girls sometime after 11:30 P.M. Suarez, a single mom with a toddler son at home, paid the bills by visiting the clubs a couple of nights a week. She prided herself on being an escort, not a **puta**—a prostitute or common streetwalker. She dressed well, controlled where and when she worked, and had higher-paying clients. With so many Americans in town, Suarez surmised it was a good night to work.

Suarez was part of a foursome that grabbed a table off the dance floor. Mariela, who worked as Suarez's pimp, and two other escorts, who went by the names Luciana and Vanessa, joined her. The women couldn't help but notice a group of ten raucous Americans who seemed to be friends, ordering round after round of drinks for one another at the bar. One of them, who appeared more drunk than the rest, was swaying and dancing on top of the bar. He grabbed a pole and mimicked the bump and grind of a stripper.

Bratz, a single guy who spoke more Spanish than his comrades, approached the women. Mariela decided to translate. She turned back to the escorts and explained in Spanish that the men were offering to buy a bottle of vodka for their table and hoped to join them. Mariela suggested Bratz bring his friends over so everyone could dance. Huntington and Bongino joined Bratz. Huntington homed in on Suarez. They paired up to dance.

Huntington didn't know then that Suarez was a professional escort. He was used to meeting women he could charm into sex the first night. And Suarez didn't know then that Huntington was a Secret Service agent. She didn't understand most of what her clients said about their work anyway.

The American men kept ordering more vodka. Suarez noticed they were downing the clear liquid "like it was water." She thought Huntington was handsome and polite, but also "full of himself." They danced, and she giggled as he repeatedly lifted his shirt to show her his taut stomach muscles.

Bongino, who was also married, danced with Luciana. As the night progressed, Luciana told Suarez she "was in a love story" with the handsome, wide-faced American. She planned to treat this as a normal date. She wasn't going to charge him.

At about 1:30 A.M., after a lot of dancing, Suarez told Huntington she had to go home. He pleaded with her to stay, as she fully expected. Suarez called over to her pimp to explain things to Huntington, again using Bratz as a translator. "If he gives me a 'little gift,' I will leave with him to the hotel," she relayed.

Suarez thought she had hooked herself a big

spender. During the evening, Huntington had given her a 50,000-peso note—worth about $30—to buy some cigarettes during the night and never asked for change. He and his friends whipped out credit cards and cash to buy the women at least three bottles of vodka and various other drinks. Suarez usually charged $200 to $500 for an overnight with an American—they simply paid better than locals. But she guessed Huntington might pay even more. Before they left, Suarez mentioned her "gift" one more time.

"How much?" Huntington asked.

She held up eight fingers, then said "dollars" twice. She wanted to be clear how much a full night of sex with her would cost. "Eight hundred" is what she tried to say in broken English. "No problem, baby. No problem," he replied. "**Vamonos.**" Huntington may have been too drunk to understand. By this time, he had tossed down about thirteen vodka drinks.

Bongino paid the remaining bar bill, and he and Huntington and the two women piled into a cab to return to the Caribe. Bratz, still talking to a woman at the bar, stayed behind at the club.

As they entered the main lobby, the two women knew the drill. Hotel security guards posted at the entrance gave them the once-over. They walked toward the front desk to register as "overnight guests," a polite term of art the local hotels used, and handed over their identification cards. Their "hosts" had to be present, and they were told they would be charged another $20 fee to bring this added guest inside. Bongino and Huntington stood by, looking befuddled by this odd bit of late-night bureaucracy.

When they were finished registering, the four headed toward the elevator bank and to the agents' respective rooms on the seventh floor. Bongino carried Luciana piggyback down the hall to room 710.

THE FRONT DESK at Hotel Caribe called room 707 early Thursday morning, sometime around 6:30 A.M. Suarez answered the phone. The reception clerk told her it was after six—time to clear out. Suarez apologized and said she would leave immediately. She well knew the hotel policy requiring prostitutes to leave first thing in the morning.

The clerk was annoyed. When she showed up for work, she found more than a dozen prostitutes' ID cards still in a little box at the front desk. That meant she had to make a lot of awkward reminder calls to the hotel's American guests.

Suarez collected her clothes to get dressed. From under the sheets, Huntington asked her to stay a little longer. Suarez said she couldn't. She said she had to take her son to "baby school."

"My cash money, baby," Suarez softly reminded him.

Huntington reached for his wallet on the floor.

He picked through the bills inside and handed her another 50,000-peso note. Suarez grew upset. He was giving her a pathetic amount, but she could see in his wallet that he didn't have anywhere near enough to pay her fee.

"No," she said. **"Mas dinero."**

"No dinero," Huntington replied.

Suarez started to cry. Huntington looked at her, startled to hear her demanding what sounded like hundreds of dollars. Later, each would remember threatening to call the cops on the other. She, if he didn't pay. He, if she didn't leave.

"No, let's go, bitch," he said finally, and pushed her toward the door.

With Suarez in the hall, Huntington closed the door behind her. He watched Suarez through the peephole as she walked over to his friend Joe Bongino's door. Huntington's head was hurting from the night before, so he slunk back to bed. He vaguely remembered having sex with Suarez the night before, but he couldn't remember the specifics. He also vaguely remembered her saying something as they left the club about wanting money for sex. But $800?

Across the hall in room 710, it was Bongino's turn for a rude awakening. Suarez had been banging on the door, and Luciana, Bongino's guest that night, had opened the door to let Suarez in. She walked into the room wailing in Spanish.

Bongino remembered having sex with the woman in front of him last night, but he couldn't remember her name. He also recognized the agitated taller woman—Suarez—as the woman Huntington had brought back to the hotel. She grabbed a pillow from Bongino's bed and clutched it to her chest. "He fucky fucky, he no pay!" she yelled.

Through a mix of Spanish and English, Suarez tried to impress on Bongino that she wasn't leaving. His buddy owed her money, and she wanted Bongino's help to get it.

Suarez grew angrier, sensing that Bongino didn't seem concerned. She pulled out her mobile phone and pretended she was dialing the police. Bongino, who had rapidly dressed for his bizarre wake-up call, recognized he had a situation to clean up. Fast.

"No police," he said. "Please, please, no police."

Bongino pounded on Huntington's door. No answer.

He called his room phone. No answer.

At 8:33 A.M., he emailed Huntington on his BlackBerry. **We need to talk ASAP open the door.**

No answer.

Bongino was pissed. Huntington had to be awake. Every now and again, he could see his shadow moving under his door.

Fed up and with tears of frustration in her eyes, Suarez was about to give up. Just before 9 A.M., she clopped away down the hall in her awkward high heels. But at the elevator bank, she found a local police officer standing post. Sniffling, she told him she was a little embarrassed but needed his help.

When she explained her dispute with an American customer, the officer left for the front desk to find a more senior English-speaking officer.

He found a Colombian police sergeant at the desk. "There's a problem on the seventh floor," the officer told his superior.

The sergeant returned with the officer and found a tall, tearful young woman complaining in the hallway with another local woman and a white American man. She said another American man in room 707 hadn't paid her fee and had been rough with her.

"Did he hit you?" the sergeant asked.

"No," she said. "Just tell him to give me $250 and I'll get out of here."

Eric Johanson, a well-respected CAT supervisor on the night shift, had heard a ruckus in the hall by this point and had stepped out of his room to see what was going on.

The hallway had gotten crowded. Two Colombian police officers in uniform and two local women were all heatedly discussing with Bongino how to get Huntington to answer his door and pay a prostitute.

The Colombian officer turned to Bongino and Johanson. "The best thing you can do is pay the woman before it gets any worse," he said.

"What do you want to do?" Johanson asked Bongino.

"I want to pay this girl to keep Art from getting arrested," he said.

Bongino had $60 in his wallet. Johanson offered to lend him $100. Suarez said that wasn't enough. She wanted $250.

"If you don't pay me now, it will cost a lot more later," she said.

Bongino dashed to the ATM in the lobby to get more money. Confused by the exchange rate, he ended up having to insert his card again and make a second withdrawal. He returned with a wad of peso notes and gave the sergeant a mix of pesos and dollars worth $250. He stressed that he and Johanson were only helping with the money to avoid unpleasantness and that they had no connection to Suarez.

The local police sergeant then handed the wad of cash to the escort. "Is everything good?" he asked her in Spanish.

"Yes. Everything is fine," Suarez replied, nodding.

As Suarez and her friend reached the ground floor and headed for the hotel exit, the Caribe's director of security approached the women and scolded them. "You violated the rules here," he said in Spanish. "You will not be allowed to return."

Upstairs, Bongino was finally free from the tense hallway standoff and able to leave to get some breakfast. Walking quickly down the hall, he passed another CAT member, who noticed Bongino's downcast face.

"Everything okay?" the agent asked Bongino.

Bongino kept walking, and his terse reply floated back over his shoulder: "I woke up to a nightmare."

———

SUAREZ'S DECISION TO seek the help of local police that Thursday morning turned a hallway dispute over fees into an international incident. Diplomatic protocol required that Colombian authorities alert the U.S. embassy if their law enforcement agents had any official "contact" with a member of the U.S. delegation. The Colombian police sergeant's hallway talk with Bongino and intervention in Suarez's complaint against Huntington clearly qualified as contact. At 9:15 A.M. Thursday, before Suarez had even left the lobby, the hotel's director of security was on the phone calling the U.S. embassy's branch office in Cartagena and aides to U.S. ambassador Michael McKinley.

Over the phone, the Caribe security director told McKinley's security officer about the local police having to intervene with a U.S. Secret Service agent in room 707. Two members of the embassy security team quickly drove over to the Hotel Caribe for a full debrief. When they got there around 10 A.M., the hotel's director of security gave a more detailed account of the prostitute's complaint.

Then he launched into his own much longer and more detailed list of complaints. On top of the standoff over the escort's payment, the security director was fuming about the Americans' general pattern of obnoxious behavior. Caribe staff had reported that K-9 officers were letting their bomb-sniffing dogs defecate on the hotel's lawn, urinate on carpets, and even sleep in hotel beds. Some guests were complaining about the loud noise and alcohol-fueled antics at the pool—mostly caused by military servicemen. On top of that, his morning reception clerk had counted eight guests who kept prostitutes in their rooms after the cutoff hour of 6 A.M. He handed over his handwritten list of those eight names.

With that formal in-person notification, the Service's sordid little secret spread rapidly. The two military agents conferred with Perry Holloway, Ambassador McKinley's right-hand man as the deputy chief of mission. They all agreed: They had to notify the Secret Service. Just after 11:30 A.M., the embassy security officer drove to the Hilton and found Lonn Kalama, a supervisory agent based in Bogotá whom he knew.

"We have a problem," the officer told him.

Kalama then raced to find the senior agent with overall responsibility for the Secret Service team in Cartagena—Paula Reid. It was easy for him to find the five-foot-six, ramrod-straight supervisor in a crowd of Secret Service agents in the Hilton lobby— she was an African American woman in a sea of white men. While Reid listened in shock, Holloway, McKinley's deputy chief of mission, walked up to Reid with a furrowed brow.

"This is very, very serious," he warned. Any news about multiple agents hiring prostitutes would severely embarrass President Obama and the U.S. government, he said.

Reid nodded and frowned, and pledged she was going to get to the bottom of this.

Holloway continued. Secretary of State Hillary Clinton was going to be livid, he said. She was scheduled to arrive the next day. Secretary Clinton considered this kind of bad-boy misconduct one of her top concerns about U.S. personnel working overseas, he said. "If State Department employees did this," Holloway declared, "they would be shipped home immediately."

Reid had weathered a lot in her two decades on the job, but nothing that would compare to this mess. She quickly called a huddle with her staff, asking them to summon the two other senior supervisors on the trip to join. At 12:30 P.M., she briefed them on the Huntington incident and the list of agents who possibly brought prostitutes to their rooms. She asked a staff member of her team to confirm the Caribe's guest records, checking which agents had been in which rooms.

Reid wasn't shocked that agents would hook up with women on a work trip, but she was taken aback at the toxic combination of so many people boozing it up and carousing with prostitutes, and the carelessness that had allowed the incident to become public. She took a deep breath and called her boss in Washington. There was no way to sugarcoat the brewing scandal. Reid's boss, also a woman, heard the first few facts and quickly concluded that this was above even her pay grade. She told Reid to call David O'Connor, an assistant director over all the field offices.

O'Connor listened to Reid's account. "What the hell were these guys thinking?" O'Connor said.

Reid said she planned to begin interviewing agents and would get back to him when she had a fuller picture.

O'Connor hung up. He walked down the hall to get Mickey Nelson, the assistant director over protection. Together they would break the bad news to the director, Mark Sullivan.

DIRECTOR SULLIVAN CALLED Reid after learning what was going on from his assistants. She repeated the facts she had in hand. This was a diplomatic nightmare, but so far it was one that hadn't gone public and that the Service hoped to contain. Reid explained to the director that the biggest threat right now was the embassy's anger. Ambassador McKinley's number two had warned her that the agents should be shipped out. Sullivan listened, saying that that might be necessary. Reid said she was about to start interviewing the men involved, and they agreed she would pass along updates on what she found.

At roughly the same time, Chaney and Stokes both received an email telling them to report

"ASAP" to Reid at the command center at the Hilton. They suspected, based on the rumors going around about a CAT guy getting into a dispute with a prostitute, that they might be asked about the incident. Neither man was that concerned about getting in trouble with the Service over their own one-night stands, a common event on such trips. Still, Chaney hoped Reid wouldn't find out about **his** prostitute. He didn't want his wife, who had been his rock through some difficult years on the job, to have to learn any of this.

Reid called Chaney first into room 819, a suite the Service had converted into a makeshift office. A former supervisor on President Obama's detail, Reid had a reputation as a standoffish agent and a rigid boss. One of her colleagues said she "read the Secret Service manual like fundamentalists read the Bible." But Reid had a soft spot for Chaney. They were close friends from the Secret Service training academy. She had greeted Chaney with a warm hello when they first crossed paths on the Cartagena trip, earlier that same morning.

"Look, Dave, before we start this, I have to report to the ambassador in a little while," she said, looking him squarely in the eye. "I need to know everything that happened so I'm not looking like a fool and having to correct myself later."

That did it. Chaney copped to everything: The dinner with a cluster of agents. The mojito and the many beers that followed. The taxi ride with

Stokes to a strip club. The fees they paid the club to bring the prostitutes back to the Caribe. Everything.

Reid asked him whether the woman he took to his room could have learned sensitive details about Obama's visit. He explained he never told the woman he was an agent, and he had no sensitive security information lying around his room. "I'm sorry I put you all through this," Chaney said as she ushered him out of the room.

Then it was time to interview Stokes. "This is a big shitstorm, Greg," she began.

Stokes was adamant that he hadn't violated any rules or regulations. He was single. Prostitution was legal in Cartagena. He hadn't told the woman what he did for a living. He knew agents and supervisors on the job who had done this much before—and some who had done a lot worse. He soon told Reid the full story of their night out, and it was largely a carbon copy of Chaney's account.

MICHAEL MCKINLEY, THE U.S. ambassador to Colombia, was mostly worried this large-scale indiscretion by the president's protectors—on the eve of the president's arrival, no less—would leak out. McKinley, an Oxford-educated diplomat who had spent most of his childhood and career in South and Central America, knew that if it did, it could very well jeopardize his team's careful preparation for a thoughtful exchange with Latin American leaders. The U.S. government had pledged in international conferences to help fight sexploitation and female sex trafficking. Now a bunch of agents threatened to make their government look like a bunch of hypocrites.

McKinley, who was busy welcoming members of Congress as they arrived for the summit, kept getting periodic updates from his staff that afternoon. With each new report, the number of U.S. employees who'd entertained women in their taxpayer-funded rooms rose. In scouring hotel guest logs, U.S. military leaders in the Southern Command learned that five of its members had registered overnight guests. Later they realized the number was closer to ten, including men from Special Forces and explosive ordnance teams. Eventually, a total of twenty-two U.S. delegation members were implicated—twelve Secret Service and ten military.

After the 2:30 P.M. meeting ended at the Hotel Caribe, one of McKinley's security officers called to warn Reid. McKinley wanted a meeting to discuss whether the agents were going to be allowed to stay in country. "The ambassador was extremely angered," he said.

The Service assured the embassy staff they weren't trying to cover anything up. Reid was busy investigating so the Service could decide what to do. The military, meanwhile, insisted it had to keep the implicated men on the ground because it needed their specialized bomb detection and security training for the president's protection.

Around 4 P.M., Holloway, the ambassador's deputy chief of missions, got a call from a **Los Angeles Times** reporter. He wanted to know if Holloway knew anything about the Secret Service getting into trouble with prostitutes. Holloway quickly got off the call without giving an answer. McKinley girded for the story to break.

Between 3 P.M. and 10 P.M., Reid had interviewed twelve men, all of whom, according to Caribe and Hilton records, had signed local women in to their rooms as overnight guests. In addition to the two jump team leaders and the three CAT members, Reid also interviewed three Washington field office agents, three officers on a counter-sniper team, and one magnetometer officer.

That magnetometer officer insisted Reid had the wrong guy. He had been on duty on the midnight shift from Wednesday night to Thursday morning. A few men acknowledged bringing women back to their rooms but denied having sex with them. One relatively new agent had visited a club called Isis, which turned out to be a bordello, with two other agents. The new agent said he thought the two women he brought back to the hotel were just out for some fun. He insisted he kicked them out of his room when they told him they wanted money for sex. Three men, including Bongino, said they'd had sex with the women they invited to their rooms but that these were harmless one-night stands for which they had paid nothing.

Cavorting with foreign prostitutes sure looked

like a stupid lapse of judgment for men holding security clearances and preparing for the president's arrival. But the Secret Service manual didn't specify the severity of the violation, or the proper punishment. Was a one-night stand with a foreign national forbidden—whether you paid or not? Did it make it worse if the agent or officer was married? The Service would have to sort that out back at headquarters. Sullivan told Reid to fly all the men who were under investigation back home to D.C. the next morning.

AT MIDNIGHT, CHANEY, Stokes, Huntington, Bongino, and eight more Secret Service agents and officers got an email from the logistics team telling them to pack up and report to the Caribe lobby at 8 A.M. Friday. They were being shipped home.

At a second layover, in Miami, the acting top supervisor of the Miami field office, Vance Luce, greeted Chaney as he disembarked. "Dave, I hate to be the bearer of bad news, but you are to report to inspection at ten A.M. Saturday," the Miami chief said. "You need to report with your badge and your gun."

With that, Chaney knew they were all going to be put on administrative leave pending a full investigation. What might come after that? Chaney had a bad feeling that this wasn't going to end with a slap on the wrist, like most Secret Service investigations.

Once on the ground in Miami, Stokes spoke

on the phone with his supervisor at the Rowley Training Center. "Just hang tight, Greg," the boss said. "Weather the storm. You're probably going to do some days on the beach."

At different times on the long flight home, the younger guys on the plane came up to Stokes and Chaney to ask different versions of the same question: "Is everything going to be okay?" Stokes, a pugnacious agent from the Boston area who ran the canine unit, shrugged it off. In his mind, there was a long list of agents and supervisors who'd gotten in worse scrapes: guys who'd gotten DWIs, had stolen agency money, had been accused of statutory rape. Most got just a short suspension or a letter to their file and stayed on the job.

"This is probably going to blow over," Stokes told them.

"Nah, this is not going to be okay," Chaney said. "A U.S. ambassador is involved. Twenty-two guys on a presidential trip. This is big."

The two friends did agree on one thing: They were worried about Art Huntington. Chaney and Stokes kept checking on the agent, who was barely speaking to anyone and wore the expression of a wounded animal.

On his ride home that evening from the airport, Chaney thought about the mess he had gotten himself into—**It would be so easy to drive into those barriers,** he thought—but he also knew he would never do it.

The first thing he did after he closed his front door behind him was walk upstairs to his bedroom and tell his wife everything. Within hours, **The Washington Post** published a breaking news alert: U.S. SECRET SERVICE AGENTS RECALLED FROM COLOMBIA.

CHAPTER 20

SULLIVAN'S STRUGGLES

Director Sullivan had survived some headline-grabbing screw-ups before. Whenever he'd found himself under the gun in the past, he'd turn on his guileless "aw shucks" charm. His manner telegraphed trustworthiness rather than cover-up. Like some previous directors, he was also pretty good at stroking politicians' egos.

After an uninvited couple sneaked past the Secret Service into a 2009 White House dinner—and shook hands with President Obama—Sullivan made a series of supplicant visits to lawmakers' offices to brief them personally. He shared the details of his team's findings on how protocol broke down at a White House entry checkpoint. Lawmakers then went on television to show how important and "in the know" they were, telling viewers of the one-on-one download they'd received from the director.

Congressional staffers dubbed his rounds on Capitol Hill "the Mark Sullivan self-preservation tour."

Though the public had no idea, Sullivan had also survived the First Lady's anger in 2011 over the agency's botched handling of the November shooting at the White House. Sullivan had promised Michelle Obama that nothing like that would ever happen again.

This time, though, the director had reason to fear he didn't have any more professional lives left. The words "Secret Service" and "hookers" now led the front page of every newspaper and scrolled across the chyron at the bottom of every cable television news program.

Ed Donovan, the Service's top spokesman, told Sullivan and his senior deputies the Cartagena story was hot now, but it would flame out. A two-day story at the worst, he said.

Sullivan wished that were the case, but he didn't have much faith the furor would die down. On Saturday, he approved a statement to the press announcing that the Service had put eleven men on leave pending an investigation. At the same time, the statement oddly—and some would argue prematurely—concluded that the men had violated the service's "zero-tolerance policy on personal misconduct."

When the statement was released, some of the men were still denying ever having hired prostitutes. Had they engaged in misconduct simply because they'd gone drinking off duty? If so, nearly every Secret Service agent and supervisor was in the crosshairs.

Still, there was no doubt the salacious image of agents carousing with prostitutes had splashed mud on the president at his own summit. News organizations that Saturday hastily dispatched teams of reporters to Cartagena. They bypassed the summit and instead taxied to the red-light district to interview bartenders, escorts, and cabdrivers for any sordid details they might have seen or heard. White House chief of staff Jack Lew told Sullivan there had to be consequences for embarrassing the president. Some heads might have to roll on this one.

On Sunday, Obama held his first joint press conference with Colombia's president, Juan Manuel Santos. The first reporter to get a question in immediately asked about Hookergate: "I wanted to ask quickly about the issue that has sort of hung over this Summit for the Americas, is the controversy that involved members of the detail that is sworn to protect you," **New York Times** reporter Jackie Calmes asked Obama. "Were you angry when you heard about this as you came here?"

President Santos looked over at the world's most powerful leader sympathetically. Obama looked down at the lectern to gather his thoughts, first saying a few words about his hopes for expanded freedom in Cuba. "What happened here in Colombia is being investigated by the director of the Secret Service. I expect that investigation to be thorough and I expect it to be rigorous," he finally said. "If it turns out that some of the allegations that have been made in the press are confirmed, then of course I'll be angry—because my attitude with respect to the Secret Service personnel is no different than what I expect out of my delegation that's sitting here. We're representing the people of the United States. And when we travel to another country, I expect us to observe the highest standards because we're not just representing ourselves, we're here on behalf of our people. And that means that we conduct ourselves with the utmost dignity and probity."

He paused, his face tightening. "And obviously what's been reported doesn't match up with those standards."

Early Monday morning, all the platoon leaders were called to the ramparts at headquarters. A haggard Director Sullivan asked the members of his Executive Resources Board to strategize a way out of the disaster. The board was made up of all eight of Sullivan's assistant directors and his deputy director.

Sullivan told his team that he was getting calls from the Hill for heads to roll, the White House was pissed, and they had to act swiftly to control the potential damage and demonstrate how seriously the Service took this misconduct. He put nearly the entire unit of internal investigators on the case, sending a team led by Rob Merletti, a highly respected investigator and the former director's nephew, to Cartagena. But the polygraphers, security clearance staff, and inspectors were shocked at how fast they were being pushed to get answers, and how rapidly the bosses were making critical decisions about men's careers. For years, the Service had slow-walked investigations of internal misconduct and often turned a blind eye altogether to the misdeeds of favored agents. But those old car crashes, allegations of statutory rape, sexual misconduct, and claims of serial sexual harassment hadn't leaked to the press. Now that this dirty laundry had been aired, Sullivan needed to persuade lawmakers this was an honorable agency with just a few bad apples that he was more than willing to throw into the trash.

The board hashed over the men's various accounts of their night out in Cartagena. Some still denied having sex with women they brought to their rooms, but most acknowledged they did. Some admitted paying the women; others insisted they paid nothing. The Service didn't know for sure who was lying, but they felt they would learn soon—they'd hook them up to polygraph machines starting the next morning.

Before they'd gathered all the facts, the board tackled the thorny matter of which acts were fireable offenses. Firing was something, frankly, the Service rarely did, and sex with a stranger in a foreign land was hardly unheard of. In fact, at a security briefing just a month earlier, a top supervisor told the entire Washington field office staff that they didn't have to report one-night stands with foreign nationals on trips—they had to notify their bosses only if the relationship continued beyond one night.

To help navigate these tricky waters, Sullivan turned to David O'Connor, a tough-edged Irish agent from Boston. O'Connor had twenty-six years on the job, and had done time in nearly every office in the Service, from counterfeit ring investigations in Newark to the Clinton family detail to overseeing security for the 2008 presidential campaign. He had just been promoted to be the assistant director in charge of all field offices—one of the two most important AD jobs. He raised the central question: "Do we have grounds to remove these guys or not?" he asked the table.

The Service's longtime attorney Donna Cahill didn't say yes or no exactly. She said paying prostitutes was illegal in the States, and a violation of the agency manual wherever it occurred. A onetime misconduct violation didn't normally trigger removal. But some sexual behavior and personal conduct could be used as grounds for stripping someone of their security clearance—if it showed "questionable judgment" and "lack of discretion." When it brought discredit—bad press—to the agency, that was an aggravating factor. Revoking a clearance was a sledgehammer, a surefire way to bounce someone from the agency. Agents and officers couldn't work for the Service without a top-secret clearance.

The investigation was in its early stages. But even then, Sullivan and the board agreed that the men proven to have paid for prostitutes would get the boot, and the ones who had one-night stands might be disciplined. The Service would urge the former group to resign quickly, informing them that if they didn't, they would soon lose their security clearance and job anyway.

O'Connor, nicknamed the Enforcer, was known for his exacting standards. Sullivan trusted him more than any of his other deputies. The director asked him to sit down with several of the agents. The unspoken assumption: O'Connor would have the best shot at getting the guys to resign without a fight.

The Service was a small family. Many of the bosses had worked alongside one or more of the guys now jammed up. The loss of a clearance raised the specter that some of them would never work again as an 1811—a federal investigative agent.

Mike Merritt, an assistant director over administration, acknowledged that the agents' behavior in Cartagena had been stupid and brazen. But he warned Sullivan and his fellow assistant directors that firing employees because they paid for sex on the road could open the Secret Service to more humiliating scrutiny. He stressed the punishment had to be consistent with how they'd disciplined previous agents who'd done the same thing. "Remember, we need to be careful here," he said. "If we treat these people differently, some are going to get pissed off, and the skeletons will come out of the closet."

From then on, Sullivan barred Merritt from any discussions of the subject. But his warning couldn't have been more prescient.

One by one, the Cartagena jump team was called in for a tough talk. On Tuesday morning, Chaney entered the windowless conference room at headquarters where O'Connor waited. O'Connor normally wore a fierce expression, but he looked slightly less ferocious today, and more somber. Chaney took it as a sign of respect for his two decades of service.

O'Connor said he was sorry about the reason that brought them together. He pushed a single piece of paper across the desk. It was a proposed legal agreement, just three paragraphs. It spelled out that Chaney would agree to retire on a set date in August—after taking some accumulated leave— and the Service would pursue no disciplinary action against him. Chaney raced to read the key words then reread from the top more carefully. After more than a minute, he looked up at O'Connor and asked, "This would help you guys out?"

O'Connor's tough face melted a little hearing Chaney's question. "It says volumes about you that you ask that, Dave," O'Connor said. "And yes. Yes, it would." O'Connor told Chaney he had one hour to decide.

Chaney didn't need it. He signed the paper. He would retire and get his pension. He handed over his gun and badge and walked down to his car in the lot outside. Less than seventy-two hours after returning from Cartagena, Chaney was effectively out of the Secret Service.

That same Tuesday, Stokes was told to report at 1 P.M. to headquarters. Like Chaney, he entered the room where O'Connor sat in wait. Stokes and O'Connor knew each other well—at least twenty years. They had both grown up in and around Boston, part of an unofficial Boston fraternity in the Service.

But that fraternity could help only so much. Unlike Chaney, Stokes was four years away from retirement, not four months. "Greg, I've never had to do this in my entire career," O'Connor began. "I'd give anything not to be here now."

He pushed a piece of paper across the desk to Stokes. The words on the paper that caught his eye were "removal . . . for cause." It was a proposal for termination. Stokes's head was spinning.

"I have to ask you for your resignation," O'Connor said.

"Dave, I get it. This is serious. Presidential trip. But for you guys to ask me for my resignation? No. It ain't going to happen."

"I understand," O'Connor said. This was a

man's career and honor at stake, so close to the finish line.

Stokes pulled a green 3x5 index card out of the breast pocket of his jacket. On it was a Bible reference. **John 8:7.** He began the passage from memory: "He that is without sin among you . . ."

O'Connor, a fellow Catholic, finished the verse, but louder and faster: "let him be the first to cast a stone."

O'Connor sat back in his chair. He had been feeling sorry for Stokes, but now he was angry. Was Stokes accusing him of something? "What the fuck are you saying, Greg?" O'Connor asked.

Stokes looked surprised—he wasn't talking about O'Connor personally. He just wanted to send a message to the higher-ups in the Service that he had knowledge about far worse misconduct. He considered it leverage, not a threat. "You take this upstairs and you show every one of them," Stokes told O'Connor. "Take it to the director. Tell them: I would really recommend you think about this."

O'Connor took the elevator up to the eighth floor and Sullivan's office. They hashed it out for the next several minutes. What kind of threat was Stokes really making? The truth was that Stokes was bluffing at this point. He believed the Service would never really fire him, if they were just reminded of all the truly serious misconduct they had covered up and excused.

WHILE COPING WITH the furor over Cartagena from outside the agency, Sullivan faced a major loyalty problem inside his own ranks as well. A small tribe within the eighth-floor management team considered Sullivan a weak imitation of directors from the past, and they didn't try hard to hide it. Rick Elias, who oversaw protective intelligence for the Service, and his deputy, Craig Magaw, were leading members of that tribe. They hailed from an elite fraternity within the agency who considered the Secret Service a family business they were destined to control. Elias, a brainy, bearded professor type, was the aloof brother-in-law of Brian Stafford, the former director under President Clinton. Craig Magaw was the son of John Magaw, who had been a director briefly under President Bush.

Both these former directors, Brian Stafford and John Magaw, had a chilly relationship with Sullivan. They privately groused to alums that he didn't run the place as shipshape as they had. He focused too much on politicking and diversity hires. On top of their families' bond, Rick Elias and Craig Magaw both nursed more personal grudges against Sullivan as well. They felt he hadn't given them the promotions and power they deserved.

A few years earlier, Magaw's father had called Sullivan up urging him to make his son Craig the head of the president's detail. Officials believed the elder Magaw hoped to lay down the landing lights for his son to be director—following his same path.

Sullivan was surprised, but respectfully suggested the son wasn't ready yet. The two men had barely spoken to each other since. Now, with a sizable dose of schadenfreude, Elias and the younger Magaw watched the Cartagena scandal dominate the news. Sullivan was in danger of losing his job. And these two critics in his midst knew something that could make Sullivan even more vulnerable.

Elias's Intelligence Division had asked the CIA to run the names of the Cartagena prostitutes through a CIA database called CENTS (CIA Electronic Name Trace System) and had gotten a "hit" on one woman whom an agent had brought back to his room. The item described in two or three lines that a person with her name was of interest to the intelligence community because of a past bank account traced to money laundering for a drug cartel.

A hit with the CIA tracing system was pretty rare. In the many thousands of names that the Service asked the CIA to run through its database, agents had seen only a couple come back with a positive hit. "Even one is concerning," Sullivan would later explain.

When Magaw and Elias learned about the problem with one woman's name around April 19, Elias went to Sullivan's office to brief him. Meanwhile, on that same Thursday, two of Rob Merletti's inspectors learned another inconvenient fact. They paid a visit to the local Hilton's business office and obtained the names of three U.S. personnel who the hotel said had presented prostitutes to the front desk as their overnight guests. One was a CAT agent. Another was a military official assigned to the White House Communications Agency. A third, the hotel reported to investigators, was a White House advance staff volunteer who helped with presidential travel.

The last one surprised the inspectors. So far the prostitution scandal had embroiled the Service, the Defense Department, and the DEA. Now the White House too? Merletti heard the news and quickly sent word up the chain of command to the director.

Sullivan then alerted the White House to the discovery that a White House advance staffer had been identified in the hotel logs. But White House Counsel Kathy Ruemmler and Obama's deputy chief of staff Alyssa Mastromonaco both made it clear to Sullivan in different ways that the Cartagena sex scandal had tarred other agencies, but it did not involve the White House. First, the advance staffer wasn't technically part of the Executive Office of the President, the real White House staff, Mastromonaco said. Ruemmler also noted that her office had interviewed him and concluded he was telling the truth when he said there must be a mistake.

Nevertheless, Sullivan faced several questions about the matter from the Hill. In April, Representative

Pete King, chair of the House Homeland Security Committee, sent the Secret Service a list of fifty questions about the scandal. In one, he asked whether any members of the president's staff had been linked to the prostitution scandal.

Sullivan wrote back his answer on May 1: "No. The USSS has uncovered no information suggesting that any member of the EOP was involved in the incident." The answer was technically accurate—and a dodge.

On May 10, Sullivan gave a closed-door briefing to members of the Senate Homeland Security Committee. The toll of the past few weeks had begun to show on the director's face. The leader who once could so easily pour on the charm now had a bewildered look at some of the questions fired his way.

He focused on his response to the scandal thus far. He told them that everyone who'd paid a prostitute would lose his clearance and his job. Senator Ron Johnson, a Homeland Security subcommittee chair, wanted to know whether men, especially married men, who simply had a one-night stand with a foreign woman would be punished. Sullivan explained that that wasn't a fireable offense.

Republican senator Susan Collins of Maine called this kind of behavior "every bit as troubling." Senator Lieberman agreed, noting that adultery was an offense in the military and would make agents susceptible to blackmail. Sullivan said he felt he could try to root out some of the agency's macho boorishness by increasing the percentage of women—now just 11 percent—in the Service.

Johnson warned Sullivan about any attempts to bury other embarrassing information. His comments proved prescient. "The worst outcome would be if something were to be revealed months later," he told Sullivan. "You need to rip the whole Band-Aid off."

ON MAY 23, Sullivan was scheduled to testify publicly for the first time about the scandal. That morning, the director entered the cavernous wood-paneled hearing room in the Dirksen Senate Office Building and was immediately engulfed. If he had any doubt before, now he could see: This was the Secret Service's Watergate, Tailhook, and Clinton-Lewinsky scandals all rolled into one.

More than forty cameramen and photographers stood up at once from the well of the room. A wave of flashes and clicks kept pulsing at Sullivan for several minutes. He looked understandably nervous.

As the hearing got rolling, Senator Joe Lieberman, the chairman, asked Sullivan what he thought of a **Washington Post** story that described the Service as having an informal motto of "Wheels up, rings off" while out on the road—a reference to the libertine celebrations that often commenced when the president's plane had lifted off to wing him home and dozens of agents remained behind.

Sullivan shook his head. "You know, the thought or the notion that this type of behavior is condoned or authorized is just absurd, in my uh, opinion," Sullivan said. "I've been an agent for twenty-nine years now. I began my career for seven years in Detroit. I've worked for—I was on the White House detail twice. I've worked for a lot of men and women in this organization. I never one time had any supervisor or any other agent tell me that this type of behavior is, uh, condoned. I know I've never told any of our employees that it is, uh, condoned."

Actually, Sullivan and his executive team knew more about the Vegas-like behavior lurking in the Service's culture than they let on.

The director didn't mention a relatively junior agent who, eighteen months earlier, had gotten so drunk with local women believed to be prostitutes that he threw a major wrench into President Obama's four-country tour of Asia. During a layover in Thailand, investigators found, the agent lingered in what his fellow agents described as a brothel and showed up at the airport the next day reeking of alcohol and four hours late for the next leg of the trip. The younger agent delayed a team of fellow agents who were supposed to be winging their way to the president's next stop in South Korea. A supervisor, a by-the-book CAT agent, had to stay behind in country to make sure the agent returned home safely. His recommended punishment was watered down when a top head-quarters deputy overruled the agent's immediate supervisor.

Nor did the director mention an agent on President Obama's detail whom the Service had very recently investigated. After an ex-girlfriend called to report his secret life on the road, the Service discov-ered he had used his presidential work travel to facilitate his appetite for random group sex hookups. The detail agent had posted lewd videos of himself having sex on an adult swinger site. Then he secretly arranged to meet swinging couples and small groups for sex on the road—connecting online with like-minded strangers just before he arrived in a city with the president or for another assignment.

The director didn't mention, either, an old Secret Service tradition among some site agents of stocking hotel bathtubs with ice and booze—all for their colleagues' arrival before the president touched down in a city.

The chairman, Senator Lieberman, asked Sullivan whether any of the men implicated in Cartagena had done something like this before. "Let me ask you, with respect to your own investi-gation thus far and the individuals alleged to have behaved improperly, were they asked whether they had engaged in similar conduct on other occa-sions?" Lieberman questioned.

"Yes, sir, they were," Sullivan said.

"And what was their answer?" Lieberman asked.

"Their answer was that they had not," Sullivan said.

He wasn't telling the full story. Two agents admitted they'd met up with foreign women for casual sex on presidential trips, their interview records show. Huntington said he had improperly hid the fact that he had sex with foreign nationals and other women on trips to Italy, Ireland, Russia, and the Republic of Korea. Two agents implicated in Cartagena would later admit to investigators that they had previously engaged or assisted in identical behavior on the road. One had hired prostitutes while on work assignment in El Salvador and Panama. A CAT agent fluent in Spanish revealed that fellow agents had frequently bought him drinks on past trips—in exchange for his serving as their translator with prostitutes and negotiating their fees. The CAT agent had also told investigators about a time he shared a cab with his boss back to the agents' hotel, and the supervisor alerted the front desk to send up a female visitor he was expecting for the night.

Then it was Senator Collins's turn to ask some questions. She wanted to know about the risk that these women in the agents' rooms in Hotel Caribe might have been spies or worse. "Have you now been able to definitively conclude that the women were not associated with—that they were not foreign agents? That they did not work for drug cartels? That they were not involved in human trafficking?" Sullivan said the Service had worked with the intelligence community to thoroughly check the women's backgrounds. "All of the information that we have received back has concluded that there was no connection either from a counterintelligence perspective or a criminal perspective," he said.

Sullivan's answers would come back to haunt him. Whether he was misinformed or following a Secret Service habit of papering over bad news, some of the things he said weren't true. One of Sullivan's central goals in the hearing was to assure lawmakers that the Service didn't foster a culture of boozing and womanizing—and that he wouldn't tolerate it now. But the chairman and the ranking member, the key people he had to convince, didn't buy it.

Senator Collins gave Sullivan her own read of the facts from the dais that day: "Two of the participants were supervisors—one with twenty-two years of service and the other with twenty-one," she said. "That surely sends a message to the rank and file that this kind of activity is tolerated on the road. The numbers involved, as well as the participation of two senior supervisors, lead me to believe that this was not a one-time event."

She had confided to her staff before the hearing that she thought the director was just naïve about the dysfunction in his agency and didn't believe he was intentionally lying. "He has a difficult time coming to grips with the fact that he has a broader problem than just this one incident," Collins told reporters as she left the hearing. "He kept saying over and over again that he basically does think this is an isolated incident, and I don't think he has any basis for that conclusion."

Many rank-and-file agents shook their heads watching Sullivan's live testimony in the down room as he said he was "dumbfounded" by the bad-boy behavior of his agents. They all knew better. With their own eyes, they had seen their super-visors' and colleagues' romper-room antics on trips for years before Cartagena.

One agent thought a few years back to a drunken detail supervisor at a wheels-up party, the traditional celebration that advance agents and post standers had after the president departed an official visit. This particularly raucous one was in a cavernous bar in another South American resort. Grinning and slurring his words, the supervisor congratulated the brand-new baby agents working the detail on the perks of being a Secret Service agent.

"You guys don't know how lucky you are," he told them. "You are going to fuck your way across the globe."

CHAPTER 21

OUTED

The way Greg Stokes saw it, he had only one card left to play if he wanted to get his job back.

The Secret Service discipline process gave Stokes a final chance to make his case in August—an informal hearing at which he could verbally appeal the agency's decision to revoke his security clearance and take away his job. Stokes's lawyer, Larry Berger, warned the agent the night before that the Secret Service had grounds to fire him and, given the national embarrassment they suffered, plenty of motivation. Stokes could plead for leniency in the hearing, but his chances of success were slim.

"This is a very difficult case, Greg," Berger said.

Stokes wasn't ready to give up. He told Berger to plead with his bosses to reassign him to the Department of Homeland Security, even in a lowly position, just anywhere he could finish his last few

years until retirement. He knew of several agents the
Service had caught in worse misdeeds and protected
until they could retire. He also knew that an intelligence supervisor who had self-reported getting a
sexual massage from a prostitute while in Cartagena
had been able to hold off the Service from taking his
clearance. The threat of more disclosures appeared to
have played a role. The supervisor's lawyer warned
senior management that the intelligence supervisor
knew compromising information about one of the
highest-ranking supervisors on the Cartagena trip,
Nelson Garabito, being involved in similar activity.
Garabito, who oversaw sensitive intelligence at headquarters, told investigators that the claims of his
engaging with prostitutes were baseless and encouraged them to check the hotel video and his room key
records to verify his innocence. Investigators couldn't
do a full investigation and would conclude they
could not substantiate the allegations. Word spread
to a cluster of agents that headquarters was panicky
about more bad news eruptions, especially involving
a top supervisor.

The night before the hearing, Stokes told Berger
he was going to put the eighth floor on notice about
all the buried bodies he could identify. He planned
to lay out the Service's hypocrisy and share his
inventory of secrets that Sullivan and the Service
had tried to keep under wraps. He hoped his
examples would make the eighth floor reconsider
flushing his career down the drain simply to make
the director look like a responsible leader.

Stokes felt like a cornered animal. His name had been leaked to the press and quickly spread through the Internet as four continents devoured the story of the presidential guards caught in a sex scandal. He feared he'd never find another job. Most of the agents and officers caught up in the Cartagena mess had worked for the Service from two to ten years. But Stokes had put in twenty-one years—he was just four years shy of retiring and getting his full pension.

The morning of September 13, Stokes arrived for his hearing with Pete McCauley, the deputy assistant director over the Security Clearance Division. Stokes had been scheduled to make his appeal in August, but his mother died just before the date, and the Service pushed the hearing to September.

McCauley, a respected former Clinton detail agent, had known Stokes for fifteen years. But he barely looked up at Stokes as he crossed the threshold into the conference room. "Glad you could come in today, Greg," McCauley said. "I guess you had a death in the family." McCauley sat down. He didn't ask Stokes who died. **Cold,** Stokes thought.

Berger began with some prepared remarks. Stokes was a decorated, can-do agent, he said. He had just helped the Service with a highly acclaimed project to tackle one of its biggest fears: package bombs. A canine expert, Stokes helped devise a $2.3 million method to screen for hard-to-spot nonmetallic bombs at the White House. Berger

said Stokes had been honest about hiring a prostitute in Cartagena. Berger said the supervisor had
created no security risk there, and the grounds for
revoking his clearance were legally dubious.

"If you look at the whole picture, the bird's-eye
view, you have an eminently salvageable career here.
It is absolutely no reason to revoke a security clearance in a case like this," Berger told McCauley.
Stokes had made a mistake and deserved discipline,
his lawyer said, but not banishment. "And we're
concerned about how differently others have been
treated in the recent past," Berger added, diplo-
matically.

Now came Stokes's turn to speak. He looked
directly at McCauley, and while the stenographer
clicked away on her machine, he began to remind
the veteran supervisor of far more egregious conduct.

Stokes mentioned the name of a notorious supervisor whom headquarters had moved from field
office to field office, usually after female employees
accused him of sexual harassment. His story was
legendary. "Let's talk about him for a moment, shall
we?" Stokes said. "That's one of our favorites."
Stokes reminded McCauley that this top supervisor
accused of sexual harrassment was never referred to
local authorities on reports he grabbed one woman's
breasts in the office, which should have been investigated as a sexual assault. The supervisor had denied
the claims as being exaggerated by his foes. He
had been put on paid leave for well over a year and

recently been allowed to retire after agreeing not to join the Black agents' lawsuit against the Service.

"Is that a little disparate?" Stokes asked, comparing the supervisor's gentle treatment to his own. "I believe it might be."

"Yeah," Stokes said. Then he recounted the experience of a married supervisor based in a European office who was caught having sex with a foreign national in a secured area of the embassy offices there. The Service had to ship the senior supervisor back to the States because the ambassador's staff, who'd warned him once already, were outraged when they caught him doing it again. "Has **he** been referred for security clearance revocation?" Stokes asked of the supervisor. "No."

Stokes then brought up a longtime friend of McCauley's. He said the Service should remember "certain agents who were on the detail under the Clinton administration who had open affairs and then were sued for divorce by the spouse on the grounds of adultery." He spooled out the details he and dozens of agents had discussed about Alvin "A.T." Smith, the former head of First Lady Hillary Clinton's detail. "Yet that person was never found to be in violation of any sexual behavior. . . . And he was on the president's detail in a supervisory role at that time, in fact."

The man he was talking about—Smith—was now deputy director, the Secret Service's number two boss. And the man in charge of deciding discipline for the Cartagena men. During Smith's time working on the Clinton detail, his wife accused him in court filings of adultery. Fellow agents gave sworn statements saying it was common knowledge among Service leadership that Smith was having an open affair with President Clinton's staffer and distant cousin, Catherine Cornelius, who ran the White House travel office. Smith ended up divorcing his wife and getting remarried—to Cornelius. Now, two presidents later, the director had assigned Smith to oversee discipline for the men implicated in sexual misconduct in Cartagena.

As Stokes spoke about other agents who had gotten away with much worse conduct, he projected a strange sense of calm, but inside he was petrified. McCauley was no longer looking Stokes in the eyes. The stenographer kept clicking away at her keyboard to keep up. Stokes took a deep breath. He had saved his most damning example for last: a top supervisor on the president's detail.

"You've got an ASAIC on the presidential protective division who's had a long-standing extramarital affair with a foreign national," he said. Stokes said he had been told the special agent in charge of presidential protection knew about it and hadn't reported it.

At this, McCauley rolled his shoulders forward and tilted his head down to the desk. He gave out a heavy sigh. Stokes was poking the Service in a very vulnerable spot.

He never said his name, but Stokes was referring

to Rafael "Rafi" Prieto, a prominent GS-15 supervisor on the president's detail. Prieto was no random
shift agent. He stood on President Obama's shoulder day in and day out. The president greeted Rafi
by name. And yet several senior supervisors in
Washington and New York knew Prieto was leading a double life with another woman—an affair
that likely violated the standards for his security
clearance. But they let it go. They liked Prieto, a
highly regarded supervisor and a soft-spoken and
elegant man whose family had fled Castro's Cuba.
For his part, Prieto seemed comfortable that his
peers and bosses would look the other way about
his rule breaking.

Just a few months before the Cartagena trip,
Prieto had brought his girlfriend, a Mexican national,
to a small promotion party for another high-ranking
Hispanic supervisor at an exclusive Alexandria cigar
club. The guests, most of them GS-15s and Senior
Executive Service bosses in the Service, included Vic
Erevia, the powerful head of Obama's detail. The
club member hosting the party was a top supervisor
running the division that oversaw security clearance
violations.

"That's Rafi's mistress," an agent explained to
another guest when he asked about the gorgeous
young woman with long black hair. "His wife lives
in New York with the kids. He lives here with her."

In his hearing, Stokes now demanded the agency
answer for its inconsistency in meting out

punishment. Why was it okay for this detail super-visor to conduct a clandestine long-term affair with a foreign national—violating rules that re-quired him to report it—and yet still be trusted to stand next to the president? Why, in the meantime, did the director and his deputies claim that Stokes's very public one-night stand with a foreign national was so dangerous the Service had to fire him? Stokes liked Prieto and simply hoped that this private threat would stop his own firing.

"Oh, yeah," Stokes said as he left the hearing. "You tell the boys upstairs to think hard about that."

MCCAULEY RELAYED THE outcome of Stokes's inter-view up the chain of command, first to Smith, his friend and boss. It had a chilling effect on the eighth floor. Word had already spread through the gossipy Service that Stokes was furious and ready to start naming names. The hearing seemed to confirm it, and put Sullivan and his deputies on edge—leaving them to imagine what sordid details might leak out.

Stokes had the receipts. Indeed, the Service had historically protected and covered for supervisors who engaged in gross misconduct, even those who broke the law.

"There are always two sets of rules [for discipline] in the Service," a former supervisor on the Clinton detail explained. "There's a rule for thirteens and below. There's a rule for fourteens and above. The rules are totally different. I'll tell you why. If you sting a fourteen, some of them know where the bodies are buried."

If any of the bad-boy behavior Stokes mentioned actually hit the news, it could torpedo the director's credibility. In his public testimony in May and in nearly a dozen one-on-one meetings with lawmakers, Sullivan had repeatedly assured Congress that the drunken girl-chasing in Cartagena was an aberration. The Service had no culture problem, he insisted, no pattern of sexual escapades or bad behavior on the road.

Word quickly reached Erevia. Years earlier he had survived his own relatively short-lived embarrassing moment in the spotlight when his racial stereotyping in a private email to two friends was uncovered in a discrimination lawsuit. Now, in addition to being the top boss on the president's detail, Erevia was also the unofficial dean of its Hispanic agents. Just like other senior agents who were Black, or from the South, or from the New York field office, Erevia looked out for his tribe. With the new senior position he'd gained since joining Obama's campaign detail, he had established a notable track record of helping Hispanic agents get promoted.

With Erevia's backing, the reserved and solicitous Prieto had risen quickly on the detail. A child of Cuban-born parents who moved to Spain and then settled in California, he had grown up with a refined bearing but in poor circumstances. His father worked in a plant that made airplane parts. His own first job was in a paintbrush factory. In joining the elite presidential detail, he had reached a career pinnacle. But in the meantime, his personal life had taken a complicating turn. He was living separately from his wife of twenty years, who was working and raising their two children in New York. He called Washington home and spent most of his free time there with a very attractive young Mexican woman. Now it looked as though all that he had accomplished in both his career and his personal life could come crashing down.

One of his more senior friends warned Prieto what Stokes had said. The possibility that other senior managers would discover his relationship put Prieto in a terrible bind. Not only had he hidden his relationship in violation of the rules, he'd made things far worse with another set of lies he'd just put in writing. In June, Prieto had turned in routine forms for the five-year update of his security clearance. Usually agents had little of significance to report, but they had to answer the questions on the update forms anyway. Had they gotten divorced or married or had children? Had they moved? Taken on any big debts? They were supposed to report immediately any contact they had with foreign nationals.

Prieto had sworn with his signature, under

penalty of perjury or termination, that he had no social contacts with foreign nationals. Except he was in a long-term relationship with one. And he'd been having sex occasionally with a few others.

Prieto's update forms were still sitting in the Service's Security Clearance Division in September, waiting for an examiner to review them and issue Prieto a fresh top-secret clearance for another five years. Another presidential protection supervisor called over to the Security Clearance Division, asking to swing by and pick up Prieto's forms. "He needs to get that paperwork back," the person said. "He needs to make some small changes."

The changes weren't so small. When he returned his revised forms, Prieto reported something new: contact with a foreign national. He would label it "personal" on the forms.

Robin DeProspero-Philpot, a thirty-year veteran of the Service, had effectively run the Security Clearance Division for more than a decade, earning agency-wide respect for her willingness to tackle touchy security clearance problems with employees. DeProspero-Philpot made the recommendations about whether an agent should lose their clearance for bad judgment and whether or when they should get it back. She also guided the Service in determining whether a job applicant should never get one at all, and whether they should be disqualified for anything from drug use to fudging the facts.

Directors and assistant directors came to rely on

her. They trusted her judgment, even when they grumbled about it. Often they were secretly glad to have someone else willing to make the harsh calls. A petite blonde with a stubborn will, DeProspero-Philpot strove to use a consistent yardstick in handing down her rulings. She joked with friends that behind her back, some in the agency didn't use her mouthful of a hyphenated name. Instead, they referred to her by a simpler term: "That bitch that took my clearance." But she didn't get rattled by it. People told her she was just like her dad, Bobby D: all business.

The Prieto case, however, was unlike any other that DeProspero-Philpot had ever faced. When she learned of his newly reported foreign contacts, it set off all sorts of internal alarms. Because Prieto was married and now disclosing a long-unreported affair with a foreign national, she believed he was inevitably going to face some kind of Service investigation— and likely some kind of punishment. She also figured that if he'd shared any classified information with his girlfriend over the years, he could be guilty of a crime.

DeProspero-Philpot felt strongly that the Inspection Division—the internal affairs branch of the Service—should take the lead in investigating what Prieto had been doing. But the Inspection Division showed no interest in launching a probe of Prieto. Top inspectors called a special meeting at which they urged DeProspero-Philpot to interview Prieto instead and treat it as a security clearance review. "After Cartagena, they were like, 'Oh my God, please don't let any more come out,'" she said of the Secret Service's eighth floor. 'We don't want to learn anything else bad. Oh, please don't make me.'"

DeProspero-Philpot agreed to handle the interview—a major departure from standard procedure, in her view. She told McCauley, the deputy assistant director of the division, that she was actually a little worried about what she might find.

She called Prieto to set a date for an interview. She reminded him that after he answered her questions in a preliminary interview, he would be polygraphed to test his candor. He agreed to come in on October 23, a week when he wasn't traveling with Obama on his reelection campaign. "The most important thing is to be truthful," she said gently when they sat down in the interview room.

Prieto admitted to a relationship with one woman, and that it had been going on for some time—for years. With tears in his eyes, he stressed over and over that he loved her very much. When the security chief asked, he denied relationships with any other foreign nationals or any other women.

Then came the national security polygraph. When Prieto was asked a few key questions about whether he had ever shared classified information, the polygrapher saw larger swings in his vital signs. He was struggling, tense. The readings were inconclusive. They signaled that something was funky about Prieto's story. The polygrapher came over to DeProspero-Philpot's office, shaking his head. "He's hiding something," he said.

Now DeProspero-Philpot felt she had to conduct a second test. Prieto, always polite and gracious, showed no anger and agreed to another round. He said quietly that he was sure there must be some error.

Three days later, on Friday, October 26, DeProspero-Philpot's division conducted a second polygraph test. She urged Prieto, "Please just come clean. If you don't tell the whole truth, I can't help you." She explained methodically that if he told the whole truth, told his wife, and discontinued his relationship, he would reduce the risk of his contact. He would no longer be hiding something, and thus no longer vulnerable to blackmail or manipulation.

Prieto repeatedly assured the security officer that he was being truthful. He thanked her again for the care she took to explain each step to him.

The polygrapher began. Soon he got to the more detailed questions about whether Prieto had shared or mishandled classified information. He had admitted that his girlfriend had stayed with him at the hotel when he traveled with the president. Did he leave the president's site security information out in the hotel when she was there? Did he let her, even inadvertently, see any of the top-secret details of how the team shielded the president? He said no.

He failed a second time.

Here it was: DeProspero-Philpot's worst fear. Prieto appeared to be concealing something—even beyond his long-secret affair with a Mexican national. How bad was the stuff he wouldn't share? Now the Inspection Division had no choice. It had to investigate.

That Friday afternoon, DeProspero-Philpot got on a conference call with the Service's counsel and the deputy assistant director for protection. They needed to put Prieto on administrative leave pending a full investigation. Erevia was spitting mad. He lobbied Sullivan to give Prieto a chance to quietly clear his name. Erevia reminded the director that Prieto had been a stellar go-to supervisor for the Obama detail.

Sullivan agreed about Prieto's work but sided with his security chief. An internal team of investigators was still combing through the Service's records in the wake of the Cartagena scandal. There could be no special favors.

The Security Clearance Division made Prieto an official "Do Not Admit" that Friday afternoon—the Service equivalent of a scarlet letter. A company-wide email went out alerting thousands of employees that one of the highest-ranking members of Obama's detail was barred from all Secret Service–controlled facilities, including the White House.

Mike White, one of the longest-serving supervisors on the detail, had been with Obama since the start of his campaign. He went to Prieto's home that day to pick up his badge and gun and formally serve him with notice of his suspended clearance. He stayed a little while to get a read on his friend's mental state. White also called the deputy special agent in charge of the detail. White reported that Prieto seemed okay.

Sometime late that Friday night, receipts would later show, Prieto headed to the Home Depot on Rhode Island Avenue. He bought rolls of duct tape, packs of cardboard, and some small hoses.

His close friend on the detail, Neil Hegarty, called and texted Prieto to see how he was doing, but he never got an answer. Others tried calling too. Hegarty fretted about the silence. That Saturday, he tried again. But Rafi never picked up. Anxious, Hegarty drove over to his Mount Pleasant row house on Kenyon Street. Prieto paid rent to share the house with a diplomatic security agent at the State Department. His roommate was traveling at the time. When Hegarty neared the narrow alley behind Prieto's house, he heard something humming in the detached brick garage.

Behind the white garage door, Rafi was dead in the passenger seat of a 2009 Toyota FJ Cruiser he'd just bought from a friend. A laptop computer sat on the front seat, opened to pictures of his two young sons. Brookstone earbuds still hung from his ears, attached to his iPod.

The small SUV's engine had been running as long as twelve hours. Prieto had thoughtfully, painstakingly taken his own life here, on his own terms. He'd taped panels of cardboard at the bottom of the garage door to keep the noxious exhaust trapped inside with him.

Hegarty felt sick. He called some fellow detail members and 911. An ambulance and fire truck arrived, but there was nothing they could do. Several of Prieto's friends rushed to the scene. A supervisor who had worked with Prieto got word of his suicide and walked through Prieto's house looking for clues about his final moments and state of mind, agents said later. The D.C. medical examiner arrived and took pictures, and eventually the rescue crew loaded up his body on a stretcher so they could perform an autopsy back at the city morgue.

Prieto's death set off tremors at headquarters and eventually shook the whole Service. Prieto had a loyal band of friends in important places, starting with aides to the president, the president's detail, and also going back to his old days in the powerful New York field office, where he had worked on former president Bill Clinton's detail. In the White House, Obama was stunned when aides shared the news. He'd had no indication that Prieto was struggling with something so personally painful, and he knew nothing of his security clearance investigation.

Greg Stokes hadn't been close to Prieto, but he had worked with him years before on an assignment or two. He was speechless when he heard the news from another agent, then broke down crying on the phone.

As word of Prieto's suicide ricocheted across the Service on Saturday night and Sunday, many agents, including Erevia, blamed the director. If headquarters hadn't shamed Prieto by making him a Do Not Admit, he might not have felt so despondent. "I don't think Vic is ever going to forgive me," Sullivan told a colleague later.

Word trickled down to Stokes from friends that senior headquarters officials were telling others in the agency that Prieto's death was Stokes's fault, not theirs. He heard from colleagues on the White House detail and in New York that they were explaining that they'd had no choice but to investigate Prieto after Stokes brought up his likely security violations. Stokes was furious. All he had done was confront supervisors with their own double standard.

DeProspero-Philpot heard through the Secret Service grapevine that Sullivan was also criticizing how she had handled Prieto's case. She felt a great weight on her shoulders about his death, but she also felt she'd done the right thing. She insisted on scheduling a meeting with the director. When she met with Sullivan, she got no comfort. He was testy. Why did she have to do a second polygraph so soon after the first? he asked. He questioned if that followed protocol. Why dig so urgently? "Come on, Robin," Sullivan asked her. "Did you really think he was a security risk?"

She was stunned at Sullivan's about-face. How

could the director now be so cavalier about an agent who'd been lying to the Service and who might have mishandled its most sensitive secrets?

At Prieto's memorial service, his family stood numb and red-eyed in the Catholic church on the Lower East Side. The collective grief of relatives, friends, and co-workers filled the sanctuary. But the tension and recrimination within the Secret Service family hung palpably in the air, too.

Both Sullivan and Stokes had wanted to attend Prieto's funeral, and with some trepidation, they decided they had a duty to go. Sullivan hoped that by showing up he would temper the New York office's desire to blame him. Still, when the director entered, agents quietly muttered behind his back.

Stokes also insisted on going, a cauldron of emotions. He was devastated that Prieto had killed himself; he was furious that headquarters was blaming him for something Prieto's supervisors had known about and should have dealt with long ago. Stokes got worse treatment at the church than even Sullivan, however. A cluster of Prieto's New York buddies glared at him as he passed their rear pews after communion.

But no one in the church that day, not even Stokes, knew the full truth about Rafi. As it happened, Prieto had been lying about much more than one love affair.

Three weeks after his death, the Department of Homeland Security's inspector general and the Secret Service launched a joint investigation to determine exactly what Prieto had been keeping from them. His secret life soon came spilling out from the pixelated data of ten different electronic devices. In addition to his Secret Service–issued laptop and BlackBerry, Prieto had access to two heavily encrypted personal BlackBerrys, three personal laptops, and three other data storage devices.

Investigators couldn't break through the encryption on his personal phones. But using files synchronized between his phone and other devices, they eventually discovered he used them to privately communicate with various women, including several from foreign countries. He appeared to have a habit of visually documenting his love life. He'd kept racy photographs and videos of a number of women whom he appeared to have either dated or met for a brief fling.

Prieto had also been secretly taking personal trips out of the country without reporting them as required. He'd sworn to the Secret Service that he'd never left the States for a personal reason in the last seven years. He'd said his only foreign trips were for work with the president. But in that time, investigators found, he'd actually taken twenty foreign trips for unexplained personal reasons. And some of the women he was associating with on those trips gave the Secret Service enough pause that they sought the help of the CIA to check their backgrounds. One was from a former Communist Eastern Bloc country, which raised some eyebrows.

Another woman's background made investigators cringe: She was of Middle Eastern descent, from Iran, a repressive theocracy and an enemy of the United States. Investigators initially feared she or her family had ties to her country's government, which the State Department ranks as one of the world's leading sponsors of terrorism. But U.S. intelligence analysts looked into both women and could find no evidence that either one had ties to foreign intelligence services.

Prieto had been read into some, though not all, of the most sensitive top-secret programs that protected the White House and the president. He knew the hidden "safe places" where you were supposed to take the president in a time of emergency—and how to get in and out of them. He knew about a web of classified military and NSA tools that shielded the president when he traveled abroad.

And yet Prieto had also led a secret life in the highest-profile job a Secret Service agent could have. He had been able to do this under the noses of a team of trained observers.

By all accounts, Prieto was a gentle soul who deeply loved America. Though he'd used terrible judgment in his personal life, and exposed himself to blackmail, he'd adored his job. Investigators interviewed nineteen fellow agents, family members, and friends, and every last one said Rafi was a patriot who would never have turned traitor. But what if he'd casually shared presidential secrets with one of these women? The Secret Service couldn't know for sure.

None of Prieto's peers or supervisors had pressed him about the relationship with one foreign woman, so they didn't learn about any others. "It's horrifying," one of the Secret Service's former top officials said of the discovery of Prieto's multiple foreign contacts. "And the special agent in charge of the president's detail, Vic Erevia, is turning a blind eye to it." Erevia had insisted he didn't know the woman was Prieto's girlfriend.

Stokes had been unfairly branded as the guy who outed Prieto, and he was devastated by the suicide and the accusations. He'd never mentioned Prieto's name and had only pressed supervisors to face their hypocrisy: They tolerated and covered up all sorts of private misconduct and then the director took the agents publicly caught in misbehavior to the gallows as proof of his good stewardship. In reality, Prieto's cover story had already begun to unravel. Several supervisors knew about the double life Prieto had been concealing from his wife and the Service for years. Prieto took his own life, his friends said, because his sense of self-worth was so tightly wound around his identity as a Secret Service agent.

Stokes was ultimately stripped of his Secret Service identity too. For spending one night with a prostitute in Cartagena, Stokes was told he would have to leave the Service. For many months Stokes fought and appealed the agency's decision to take away his clearance, but eventually lost the legal battle. He was terminated as an agent just two years before he was eligible to retire and lost his right to a government pension.

CHAPTER 22

A NEW SHERIFF IN TOWN

Rachel Weaver thought she smelled a cover-up. The determined staff director for Senator Ron Johnson of Wisconsin, the ranking Republican on a Homeland Security subcommittee, had a voracious curiosity and a good bullshit detector. After most of Washington had moved on to the next hot topic, she resolved to find out what was really going on inside the Secret Service. She was after the truth, but her own and her boss's politics added an incentive. They were Republicans questioning the Obama administration's accountability.

That early fall of 2012, the coming presidential election vacuumed up much of Washington's energy and dominated the news. Polls that month showed President Obama with a narrow lead against his Republican challenger Mitt Romney. The Secret Service's hooker scandal in the spring had now fallen off the front pages and cable news roundups.

Behind closed doors, however, Secret Service headquarters was a boiling cauldron. Greg Stokes and others angry about the harsh punishment and double standard for the agents caught in Cartagena had been threatening to go to the press. Meanwhile, Director Sullivan and his top deputies were extremely anxious about a broad Department of Homeland Security investigation looking at Secret Service punishment decisions that threatened to unveil much of the Service's past misconduct. The inspector general's fifty-member team had gone further than the Service expected and pulled dozens of old internal investigations of agents and officers over alleged conduct and policy violations. Some of the files contained evidence that agents had engaged in disturbing and salacious behavior. They also included accusations of domestic abuse, statutory rape, viewing pornography at work, and sexually harassing subordinates. A lead investigator brought in from Miami, David Nieland, started to question the end results of these cases. Some personnel had received light punishment when investigators confirmed violations that should have been grounds for termination.

Director Sullivan was genuinely fearful about his own exposure. The investigation had taken a sideways detour into whistleblowers' claims that the director had lied to Congress when he said they'd found no criminal or national security concerns about the prostitutes in Cartagena. Sullivan felt the allegations were baseless. Still, he had to hire a lawyer. Investigators planned to refer their findings to the Justice Department so they could determine whether to open a full-blown criminal probe.

Weaver didn't know any of that, but she was about to uncover it. Back in May, when Congress was still grappling with the Cartagena scandal, Weaver had attended a closed-door briefing with Director Sullivan as he assured her boss, Republican senator Ron Johnson of Wisconsin, and fellow lawmakers that serious steps were being taken to punish the culprits and make sure that sort of incident never happened again. Johnson was then the ranking member of a Homeland Security subcommittee closely following the Service's handling of the Cartagena affair. Weaver remembered thinking that Sullivan and his deputies had given a lot of information in their briefings without saying much of anything. They provided a lot of numbers and exact times: the second car plane landed at this hour, there were this many agents in Colombia, this group of agents were interviewed on these dates. Though the briefings gave the impression of transparency, none of those minutiae really told the lawmakers what had happened.

Now, months later, Weaver was curious what the inspector general's team had found. Did they think the Service leadership had tolerated sexual hijinks in the past? Had they learned anything new that Sullivan had not shared about Cartagena?

On the morning of September 25, the inspector general's lead investigators came to the Hill at Weaver's urging to brief the Homeland Security committee staff. Weaver had prepared a list of detailed questions. But the investigators working for Acting Inspector General Charles Edwards sheepishly explained that they lacked many of the answers. These investigators now had been on the case for five months but hadn't been allowed to look at billing records for the Cartagena hotels, or to interview the hotel staff, the strip club owners, or the prostitutes whom the Secret Service agents brought to their rooms. The Justice Department had refused to green-light investigative work in a foreign country, saying they weren't conducting a criminal probe.

Meanwhile, investigators working for Edwards heard that Secret Service supervisors had been discouraged from cooperating. About thirty-two agents, including ten senior headquarters officials, had refused to be interviewed. It sounded to Weaver as though the IG team had gotten played by being stiff-armed on records and interviews.

She was also a Republican suspicious of the political motivations of the Obama White House and certainly looking to catch them if they were covering up something. Was the incumbent administration trying to fend off any unflattering news during the final months of Obama's reelection campaign, she wondered.

Weaver was a street fighter in stylish feminine clothing. At thirty-three years old, she was a tall, attractive, long-haired blonde who wore high heels and sported the retro cat's-eye glasses of a person wanting to look both serious and fashionable. In the male-dominated bastion of Capitol Hill, lawmakers typically treated pretty young females as worker-bee eye candy. But Weaver wasn't looking to endear herself to anyone. An evangelical Christian, she'd grown up the oldest of four in a modest, blue-collar home in Sacramento—the daughter of a pool contractor. She'd been the first person in her family to go to college. After graduating Sacramento State, she kept going, getting a master's degree in security policy studies at George Washington University while also working on Capitol Hill as an intern for her hometown congressman. Her career hero was Condoleezza Rice.

Weaver had earned her way into this committee job and was focused on making the country more secure. She told Edwards's lead supervisor on the investigation that she wanted to see his team's draft report. The investigator checked into it and said Edwards would allow her and other key committee staff to review a confidential draft at their headquarters. They could not have a copy.

Weaver was the only staffer who took up the offer to come read the draft report. Her counterpart in the ranking Democrat's office said he was busy with something else. The morning of October 2,

Weaver went to the inspector general's office, and Charles Edwards greeted her at the entrance. The round-faced man with a formal manner escorted her to a second-floor conference room with no windows. The draft report, thick as a metropolitan telephone book, was plunked down in the middle of a long table. He showed her a laptop on which she could review sensitive attachments and documents cited as supporting materials for the report. Edwards explained that she was not allowed to take any notes.

"I'm sorry. I must take notes," Weaver replied politely. Edwards and Weaver stared at each other for a moment. "I have to brief my boss. I can't remember all this," she said, pointing to the thick stack of papers on the table. Edwards relented. He agreed that Weaver could take notes, and then excused himself.

In Weaver's mind, Edwards was only letting her and other committee staff review the Cartagena report in the hope of creating warm relations with key lawmakers. He was angling for the permanent inspector general job. This strategy would end up backfiring spectacularly.

Weaver chose a chair, flipped open the first page of the draft report, and dug into her chore. She'd only reached the middle of page 2, and already she'd found something interesting.

"OIG received reports that USSS employees had engaged in similar misconduct on other occasions," it read. But Director Sullivan had insisted to Congress that Cartagena was an aberrant, one-time incident. She kept reading. A few lines down, she saw "OIG confirmed incidents of prostitution solicitation during official visits in El Salvador and Panama." Sullivan had told Congress that the Service sent teams to check into reports of agents hiring prostitutes in El Salvador and found they were false.

A couple of paragraphs farther on, she read the interview of an agent who'd worked advance in Cartagena. He said that on trips to Spanish-speaking countries, his fellow agents routinely used him to translate with prostitutes and negotiate fees for them because he was fluent in Spanish. He said he also returned to his hotel one night in a cab with a top-level boss, and that supervisor told the front desk he was expecting a female for the evening and to please send her up.

Weaver was shocked, but she soon found information that shook her even more. Edwards's investigators had found documents illustrating that a check of intelligence community records had raised concerns about one of the prostitutes in Cartagena. Edwards's team wrote in their draft that his office had begun investigating whether Director Mark Sullivan had made false statements to Congress. "USSS officials knew" that a CIA report had flagged one of the prostitutes as possibly being linked to a criminal cartel, the draft report said. But Sullivan had told Congress there was no derogatory information found about any of the women.

It was hard to believe a politically savvy and cautious government official like Sullivan would knowingly lie to Congress. But clearly, Weaver thought, Sullivan hadn't told the full truth on several scores.

There was one final paragraph in the report that grabbed Weaver's attention. It had little to do with Secret Service. But she quickly recognized that in the midst of Obama's reelection campaign, it was a stick of political dynamite.

Investigators said Secret Service personnel reported that they'd discovered a member of the White House advance team was listed as having brought a prostitute to his room overnight while working the Cartagena trip. The report cited records provided by the Hilton hotel and Secret Service investigators' interviews with senior Hilton officials as evidence implicating the advance staffer. This member of the White House advance team was the son of a prominent Obama donor and lobbyist who had partnered with the White House on several of its high-profile policy goals. Weaver thought the staffer's identity didn't matter; Obama's senior advisers would never want the phrase "White House" to be tied to the Cartagena prostitution mess.

In letters to lawmakers, in congressional testimony, and in public press conferences, Sullivan and

White House officials had repeatedly insisted there was no evidence of White House personnel being involved in the Cartagena incident.

Senator Ron Johnson was elated. Because of his staff director's pluck, the first-term Republican senator was sitting on a pile of juicy material that nobody else had. It suggested that the Obama administration had misled Congress.

On October 19, Senator Johnson issued a press release with a nine-page memo Weaver drafted. It outlined the major chasm between what Sullivan and the White House claimed and what the investigators found. The discrepancies, Johnson said, "suggest the administration misled or withheld information from Congress." A few news organizations got an early peek at the evidence contradicting the official Obama administration account. Breitbart News led the story with the headline DHS ALLEGES PERJURY. CNN played it with less edge: "A new investigation reportedly contradicts prior official testimony."

Johnson should have felt like a GOP hero. He'd produced evidence indicating the Obama administration had been trying to cover up any hint that White House staff were connected to the prostitution scandal—and released it on the eve of the election. Chairman Lieberman, a Democratic-leaning senator, attacked the release as an "unauthorized leak" that was grossly unfair to Sullivan. But Johnson's fellow Republican, ranking member

Susan Collins, was also furious. She called Edwards demanding answers. How had a staffer for a lower-ranking committee member gotten hold of the draft report before her? Following the pattern of many lawmakers responsible for overseeing the Secret Service, Collins had little interest in deeply probing this agency of self-sacrificing patriots.

Johnson found himself pilloried by his Republican superior on the committee. But Weaver was just getting started.

PRESIDENT OBAMA SEIZED victory and a second term in the White House, winning slightly more than 51 percent of the vote in the November 2012 election. Meanwhile, Director Sullivan was hoping to leave the administration with credit for the good work he had done rather than just the blame for Cartagena. As 2012 wound to a close, Sullivan felt he had weathered the equivalent of a Category 3 storm for seven straight months. Each week brought a new torrent of investigators' questions, lawmakers demanding answers, and second-guessing from all camps, including from his own deputies. He'd suffered an insurrection; some of his own lieutenants had told internal investigators that the director had lied to Congress about whether any of the Cartagena prostitutes posed an intelligence or criminal concern—a felony—raising the specter of a criminal investigation. Two of Sullivan's trusted deputies told investigators that when they briefed Sullivan the day before his hearing, they told him they highly doubted the hit was a true match to the prostitute, but they were still trying to verify the information. Sullivan would later produce a declaration from his chief of staff that one briefer told Sullivan the "hit" was most likely false and said: "It's not our girl." Asked why he made such a conclusive statement to Congress if the information was still being checked, Sullivan told internal investigators: "I don't know. I just answer what they tell me." In the end, investigators concluded they did not have evidence to show Sullivan knowingly lied.

NOW, AS THE Christmas holidays neared, Sullivan charted his exit amid some good news. The Justice Department had concluded that the facts about Sullivan's testimony didn't merit a criminal probe. Also, a new draft report by the inspector general concluded that Sullivan had acted "expeditiously and thoroughly" to investigate the misconduct in the Cartagena incident.

The director knew that his name and thirty-year career might forever be linked in history to the humiliating bad-boy behavior of Secret Service agents in Cartagena. But he hoped this last report would snuff out any speculation that the scandal was forcing him to leave the agency. Sullivan had been discreetly planning to form a security consulting company with Homeland Security Secretary Janet Napolitano's chief of staff, Noah Kroloff. Sullivan had struggled at times to win the money the Service needed to modernize. Now the pair of government executives had found a wealthy partner willing to stake their new security company through which they would sell their advice and internal know-how to corporate clients and contractors seeking to win federal dollars and influence policy.

Sullivan notified Secretary Napolitano and the White House of his plan to retire at the end of February and offered to recommend a handful of top contenders to be his successor. He suggested four candidates. But he was really recommending only one.

He privately lobbied Kroloff to select his first choice, David O'Connor. O'Connor, fifty-seven, from Boston, had cut his teeth on protection during the Clinton White House years. He had won broad respect for his rigor as an agent, yet his management style evoked strong, divergent feelings among the rank and file. Some agents considered O'Connor an unforgiving boss and a fearsome presence. Some felt he set a high bar and was the best leader they'd ever worked for.

Sullivan separately told the contenders—Deputy Director A. T. Smith, his chief of staff, Julia Pierson, and assistant director Faron Paramore—that each was on a short list he had recommended to the White House. Sullivan asked them not to discuss it with others in order to ensure a fair process. Smith, as deputy director, took comfort in the belief that he was the natural heir apparent. Pierson, whom Sullivan had sidelined to the chief of staff job, shrugged off Sullivan's recommendation, figuring she was tossed in as the token female. Word quickly spread that three candidates had made it to the second round and had come to the West Wing for an interview: O'Connor, Smith, and Pierson. In a first for the interview for a Secret Service director, the interview panel was made up entirely of women: White House counsel Kathy Ruemmler, White House deputy chief of staff Alyssa Mastromonaco, Obama senior adviser Valerie Jarrett, and the First Lady's chief of staff, Tina Tchen.

The West Wing panel was impressed with the straight-talking O'Connor. He had successfully managed some complicated high-wire assignments, including the party conventions, the massive presidential campaign, and the pope's visit. Smith turned the panel members off. One aide thought he looked disappointed in his interviewers. In late February, only O'Connor and Pierson got to the third round: a meeting with the president.

Obama was holding Pierson's résumé in his hand when she walked into the Oval Office. The president asked Pierson to explain what drew her to the Secret Service. He never asked about her ideas for the agency. He was curious about something else.

"What has it been like to be a woman in the Secret Service?" the president asked.

Pierson locked eyes with the first Black president. Almost instinctively, she replied, "You know."

She regretted it straightaway, fretting that it was too direct a thing to say. But Obama nodded and looked down, seeming to understand.

About two weeks later, Kroloff called Pierson in the morning to tell her the president had chosen the twenty-third director of the Secret Service: David O'Connor. "You did a great job in the interview and we appreciate your participation. You're a great candidate, and don't let this get to you," Kroloff told her. A special alert went from headquarters to the agents in charge of major divisions to prepare them: O'Connor would be the next director. Word spread rapidly through the agency on that Friday, March 1. By Monday, Reuters had reported—citing anonymous sources—that he was the expected choice.

But by Wednesday that week, Reuters had a new take on the story. They revived old reporting from 2008 about the racist email O'Connor had received at work from his brother. The five-year-old story was something anyone could find in a Google search. But it was unwelcome news to the Obama White House and to Secretary Napolitano. Many in the agency, including O'Connor, believed Smith had orchestrated the story to attack him.

That same day, the National Organization for

Black Law Enforcement Officers wrote to the White House chief of staff urging them not to choose O'Connor. The group, with more than twenty-five hundred members, warned "nothing will change" with Secret Service minority hiring or morale if the White House put O'Connor in charge. Interestingly, the group urged the White House to choose A. T. Smith instead.

Obama's chief defender, adviser Valerie Jarrett, was furious. Once again, the Secret Service had made the president and his White House operation look foolish. Team Obama was already facing criticism for a lack of diversity in its second-term appointments. Jarrett disliked leaks more than anyone else in the West Wing. She had ample reason to conclude that Smith was the architect behind the stories, and she certainly wasn't going to reward that kind of slick move. The White House search for a new director went dark. A few days later, Napolitano called O'Connor. She asked if he would consider withdrawing his name from the running.

"I've already considered it," he said tersely. "I'm out." O'Connor was furious at having an old—and what he considered unfair—smear recycled in the national news. Someone hoping to block him from the director's job had tried to brand him as a racist, and that someone, he felt with certainty, was Smith.

Two weeks later, on March 26, Smith was leading a senior executive meeting when an administrative assistant stepped into the director's conference room. The aide told Pierson she had an important call she needed to step out to take. When Pierson got to her office, the voice on the other end of the line was Janet Napolitano's.

"Julie, this is Janet," she said. "A little later today, the president is going to announce the selection of the twenty-third director." There was a pause. "You're going to be the next director of the Secret Service."

Pierson said nothing for a few moments, then thank you, then goodbye. She was shocked. She sat at her desk a minute, letting the honor sink in. She chuckled to herself, and then called her mother in Florida.

She would be the first female director in the Secret Service's 148 years.

CHAPTER 23

A LISTING SHIP

O ther than a dinner out with a small group of friends at the Carlyle in nearby Shirlington, Virginia, Julia Pierson didn't really take time to celebrate this all-time career high. She started work two days after the president's announcement of the Secret Service's first female director. Lawmakers applauded what Homeland Security chairman Tom Carper called a "proud milestone" in the agency's history. In truth, the White House and lawmakers were crossing their fingers and hoping a woman would put all the Service's bad-boy problems to rest.

"During the Colombia prostitution scandal, the Secret Service lost the trust of many Americans and failed to live up to the high expectations placed on it," said Senator Chuck Grassley, the ranking Republican on the Judiciary Committee. "Ms. Pierson has a lot of work ahead of her to create a culture that respects the important job the agency is tasked with. I hope she succeeds in restoring lost credibility [to] the Secret Service."

In her first days on the job, Pierson wasn't focused on misconduct. She was worried about money. On day two, she made an appointment to visit David Haun, a longtime career manager and deputy associate director at the White House's Office of Management and Budget. The somewhat intimidating White House budget master had helped oversee the Secret Service's budget for three decades. He had never been very impressed by the agency's justifications for its spending.

When she sat down with Haun in his office, it was her second week on the job. She knew him well from her time as chief of staff, and she knew the depth of the Secret Service's budget hole even better. This blunt conversation couldn't wait. "I'm here because I need to declare bankruptcy," she told him.

Haun and a DHS budget officer listening in remotely chuckled, not sure if she was kidding. "No," the director said. "I'm serious. I'm here to tell you we are beyond our tipping point. We have made decisions that have impacted our operations and our staffing. I'm declaring bankruptcy on behalf of the Secret Service."

She laid out the problem. To meet mandated budget cuts, the Service hadn't hired anybody since 2011. The agency was down more than six hundred employees below the number Congress had authorized them to hire—the bare-bones number they needed for a growing list of missions. The waves of Uniformed Division officer resignations—as many as a hundred a year—could no longer be ignored. Officers were fleeing simply because they were tired of working more than half of their days off, with no end in sight.

The day she walked on the job, Pierson said, she found that eighty-six supervisory positions were vacant. Sullivan had left them open to save money on relocating supervisors to the offices where they were needed. Another eighty-five agents on the president's and vice president's protective details and special operators on the detail needed to be transferred and replaced immediately. They had been doing their pressure-cooker jobs longer than six years at this point, but they should have rotated out after four years. Forcing them to stay helped save money—the cost to move them out and move their replacements in to Washington, D.C.—but the extended assignments were, to use the director's catchphrase, "cruel and unusual."

Pierson told Haun and her department budget chief she needed money ASAP to restart hiring. She had hundreds of staff positions to fill, holes that increased the chance of error—and of catastrophe.

Haun grasped the urgency now. But, he cautioned, he couldn't snap his fingers and come up with money. The federal government was in the middle of determining the 2015 fiscal year budget. The ink on the 2014 fiscal year budget plan was already dry and awaiting the president's signature, he said. That meant she wouldn't be able to lasso any money for her current staffing crisis until the start of fiscal year 2015, about eighteen months away.

Pierson's blunt talk about filing for Chapter 11 protection, however, made an immediate impression. The department's budget officer scrounged around and found Pierson $37 million he decided to "reprogram" from Homeland Security's larger components, mostly the U.S. Coast Guard. The money hit the Service's bank account in August. With money in the bank, Pierson made her first list of promotions in late August, filling seventy-six empty supervisor positions and transferring another sixty-five exhausted agents off their Washington details. The money wasn't enough to completely plug the slow leak in the boat, but it helped keep it temporarily above water.

Next she set her sights on cranking up the Service's frozen hiring system. She suggested the recruiting team set a goal of hiring forty-eight people—especially officers, who desperately needed reinforcements at the White House—in time for them to start the Secret Service's academy training in October.

But the remnants of the Cartagena scandal, and a determined Hill staffer, continued to stalk the agency and its new director. On top of that, a fresh round of bad-boy behavior and stupidity was soon to erupt. In mid-June, a little more than two months after she started, Pierson had to tackle her first major misconduct case. It didn't go smoothly.

It was 3:30 A.M. on a Wednesday in mid-June when a concerned security official at the landmark Hay-Adams hotel called the Secret Service. The hotel official said a female guest was complaining about a Secret Service agent who had gone upstairs with her to her room after a night of heavy drinking at the hotel's "Off the Record" bar. She had become panicky after they got to her room and she realized he had a gun. He offered to take the round out of the chamber. Soon after, she told him she wanted him to leave and asked a hotel security guard to escort him out, records show. But the agent later came back.

The man was a high-ranking Secret Service supervisor named Ignacio Zamora, Jr., a member of the agency for two decades who worked on President Obama's protective detail. Zamora, better known inside the Service as Nacho, had agreed to leave the woman's room at around 2 A.M., but soon doubled back. He asked the hotel security guard on duty if he could return to the room so he could get a money clip he left behind. The real reason: He had taken the bullet out of his gun while in her room and now needed to get it back. Zamora denied being with the Secret Service when the security officer asked. When the officer went to talk to the female guest, Zamora became anxious and left the hotel, raising the hotel's suspicions even more. Zamora, who had drunk enough that he and the female hotel guest decided he shouldn't drive, was scheduled to report to the White House for work in just a few more hours.

Zamora's boss was Vic Erevia, who had been Obama's longtime detail leader and was now assistant director over all protective operations. Just before Sullivan left as director, he'd promoted Erevia to this powerful eighth-floor job at the president's urging. Obama told Sullivan he thought Erevia should be the director one day. Sullivan politely explained that he wasn't ready for that yet. But Sullivan did recognize Erevia's dedication by giving Erevia his first senior management role in headquarters, another rung closer to director.

When Pierson heard about Zamora's alcohol-fueled escapade the morning after, she told Erevia she wanted Zamora transferred out of presidential protection that day. She wanted him to report to a headquarters administrative job, where he'd be on a shorter leash. "He needs to know he's on a time-out," she said. He had shown poor judgment off duty, and he needed to prove himself anew.

Erevia had gone easier on Zamora than Pierson was expecting, giving him a memorandum of counseling, which came with no discipline at all but created a record for future discipline if he crossed the line again. Erevia should already have been on alert about other possible trouble with Nacho. Agents on Obama's protective detail had been alleging since 2011 that Zamora appeared to be having an affair with a female agent who reported to him. In March 2013, Erevia's deputy Rob Buster had confronted Nacho about these rumors, which Zamora denied, and counseled him about the problematic perception that he was engaged in an illicit relationship with a subordinate.

A month after the Hay-Adams incident, in mid-July, Pierson received a new report of misconduct in an unexpected call from the assistant inspector general at the Department of Homeland Security. Carlton Mann had surely delivered unpleasant news before, but this felt more delicate. Mann told the Secret Service director that his office had turned up a problem after getting a hotline tip about George Luczko, her assistant director over internal affairs. Luczko was the most senior executive in charge of ferreting out misconduct in the Secret Service—and the same man that Mark Sullivan had promoted to assistant director after discovering he had sent sexually graphic content on work computers.

A tipster had told the inspector general's office that Luczko was misusing his government car to meet and carry on romantic relationships with younger women from foreign countries. So they decided to have a surveillance team follow him. Twice they tailed him, and twice they found him using his Secret Service car for what appeared to be private dinners and meetings with foreign women. One of the women later told investigators she didn't feel comfortable discussing whether her relationship with Luczko was intimate.

The Secret Service considered it an open-and-shut case of misconduct for agents to use their government car for personal business. Also, Luczko ran the department that had reminded agents repeatedly after Cartagena that they had to report such contact within seventy-two hours. Pierson brought Luczko into her office and told him about the inspector general's tail and what they had learned. She told Luczko he needed to think hard about retiring with dignity. He resisted at first, complaining it wasn't fair. Misusing his car probably warranted a thirty-day suspension, he said. She said no. "I'm not going to be able to leave you in your position," she said. "If you appeal, it's going to be ugly."

Luczko relented. He agreed to retire at the end of August. Through a Secret Service spokesperson, Luczko denied ever having inappropriate relationships with any foreign nationals and said all his contact with foreign nationals was reported through the required channels.

That October, Director Pierson learned about more troubling claims involving Zamora and another top supervisor. The Washington Post contacted her press shop that month after learning about the Hay-Adams incident and also about allegations that

Zamora and presidential detail supervisor Tim Barraclough had each been separately sending sexually suggestive texts to a female subordinate on the detail, Christine Farber. All three were married. Spurred by the questions, Pierson had her internal investigators pull all the electronic communications for the two supervisors and the agent, starting the next day. The emails and texts they reviewed over the next week suggested a tawdry situation. The conversations gave the impression they were carrying on workplace flings, or indulging in heavy flirtation, while using government equipment.

Farber called Zamora "sweetie" and "baby." She also called him "my 6," a reference to his number in the detail roster. In another set of texts Barraclough's estranged wife told investigators she had documented, Farber called Barraclough "my doughnut" and he called Farber "babydoll."

Zamora told Farber in an August 2012 email that she shouldn't worry about another woman. "I'm sure [she] doesn't feel the same way about me as you do, so no need to be jealous!" Farber replied: "Haha . . . Bby, imu!" A few days later, the two signed off for the night in intimate texts. "Gdnt bby," Farber wrote Zamora. "Swt dreams sweet girl," Zamora replied. "Love when you call me that," Farber texted. The three agents exchanged unusually personal information. In March 2013, for example, Farber kept Zamora up to date on her menstrual cycle. "I need my 6 so bad today," she wrote, using his nickname. "And my monthly visitor came early!"

A few days later, Farber and Barraclough exchanged a cozy chat about her decision not to shower. "Still on couch. I need to take a shower, but I don't feel like it."

"Mmmmmmm," Barraclough replied.

"Bad tj," she wrote back, using his nickname.

In August 2013, not long after the Hay-Adams incident, Farber texted Zamora: "OMG . . . soooooooooooo hny."

All three insisted to investigators they were not having affairs with their co-workers. Farber acknowledged that some might interpret her conversations with her bosses as sexual if they didn't know all the facts. She later told investigators she was just a "friendly, flirtatious" person because of her personality and Hispanic heritage. She admitted she kissed and hugged her male bosses, but it wasn't sexual. She said that when she wrote "hny," she meant "hungry."

Farber told inspectors that she and Barraclough had become close in 2009 and they had worked together on Secretary Napolitano's protective detail. But she said she felt guilty about some of their racy texts to each other back then, and they were less close now.

Their texts and emails in 2013 suggested otherwise.

"You still mean the world to me," Barraclough wrote Farber in April 2013.

"Really! Promise?" she asked.

"Just like I promise you are soooo h*t!" Barraclough said.

Barraclough's wife provided investigators with more reason to probe the Obama detail agents. She gave them her written description of the lovey-dovey-sounding texts she said she found between her husband and Farber from 2009. At the time, Mrs. Barraclough was pregnant with their fifth child.

In his wife's recounting of those older texts, Farber had called Tim Barraclough "lover" and Tim Barraclough described to Farber how he dreamed of her and wished he could hold her.

Mrs. Barraclough told investigators she had confronted her husband and Farber in 2010 about these earlier messages dating back to 2009 when she discovered them on his cellphone. Mrs. Barraclough told investigators that her husband admitted the affair and begged her not to tell the Secret Service, warning that they could lose their jobs. Her husband promised her the affair was over, she said. But Agent Barraclough told investigators he had recently separated from his wife due to the turmoil in their marriage. He said some of the texts his wife mentioned sounded familiar; others seemed contrived. He would later dispute all of her claims.

The Secret Service had had its own warning signs. In March 2013, Rob Buster, the head of the president's detail, had confronted Zamora about rumors circulating through the protective detail that he was having an affair with Farber. Some agents had seen them openly flirting and hugging, in the office and on trips. Farber and Zamora said they were demonstrative people, but simply close friends and their texts were entirely innocent.

Two years earlier, in 2011, Barraclough had been suspended for a few days for a sexting relationship with a female family friend. The Secret Service discovered the relationship when the woman sent pictures of herself to his work email. In some, she appeared to be masturbating on a bed. In others, she posed nude or in revealing lingerie.

Now Zamora and Barraclough were under scrutiny again, but under a new director who considered it her mission to root out misconduct. When investigators pressed Farber about agents' complaints that she was having an affair with a supervisor, she said she feared this office gossip was the product of competitive agents seeking to hurt her career. The macho Secret Service wasn't an easy place for women to advance. Farber would later contend that she employed her bantering style of communication in order to better fit in among her peers, employing it as a means of survival in a toxic work environment, and that her texts and answers to investigators reflected this need to survive. Some top supervisors doubted the agents' denials of an affair, given the tone of their exchanges. But all the Service could definitively prove was that the supervisors had engaged in inappropriate behavior with a subordinate.

Director Pierson, however, decided to make sure they'd all be removed from the elite assignment of the president's protective team. Zamora had already been reassigned to a lateral position at headquarters, the same rank but a step down from the elite protective division. He was later suspended for fourteen days. Barraclough lost a promotion his bosses had recommended him for, to run an Arizona field office. Farber, who happened to be several months pregnant, resisted being transferred to New York. She had earlier told investigators she wanted to be reconnected with her husband, who was based in New York, but now she said it was unfair. Pierson passed down word that she didn't really have a choice. Farber went to New York.

Her removal pleased several of her male Type A peers on the detail. Like most agents, they closely watched the careers of their contemporaries—people who graduated from the academy in the same year. Detail members noticed Farber getting prestigious assignments in quick succession. Some agents groused when Zamora pushed to make Farber a lead-qualified agent on the detail, arguing she wasn't ready for that role. Zamora insisted to investigators that he'd given Farber no special treatment.

BY THE END of 2013, Pierson was growing concerned about why it was taking so long for the Service's recruiting teams to hire job applicants. She wanted to start filling up academy classes so the new hires could begin working in a few months. But so far, they'd offered jobs to fewer than twenty people, mostly officers.

The logjam? A new hiring system that had never been tested before.

Since as far back as Kennedy's era, the special agents in charge of field offices largely decided who made the cut to be a Secret Service agent. That led to hiring a lot of new recruits who closely resembled the bosses, and white males dominated those ranks. The system wasn't objective, but it did have a huge plus. The seasoned supervisory agent often had a reliable nose for candidates who would wash out in the rigorous application process. Maybe the person expressed some mild reservation about the time commitment. Perhaps they had a college drug history they hoped to hide. The senior field bosses weeded out a lot of chaff and tossed their applications in the trash at that first meeting so the Service could focus on the most promising candidates.

But that changed in 2010, when the Service overhauled its hiring process. Former director Sullivan had agreed that, due to the racial discrimination case, the Service needed to create a fairer system that encouraged more diverse candidates. Sullivan agreed to toss out three hundred files of pending applicants who had all been painstakingly prescreened and were likely hires. The goal was to start with a clean slate. The new system they devised would allow people to apply on the federal government's USJOBS website. And they would go through each step before they could be rejected.

Of course, no one had actually used the system. No sooner had the Human Resources Division crafted the plan than Sullivan had ordered a Service-wide hiring freeze in 2011.

But by January 2014, with the hiring freeze over, field office supervisors were griping that they were drowning, having to interview hundreds of online applicants in their area who couldn't possibly pass muster as agents. They'd met with people who didn't know what the Secret Service did. They met one four-hundred-pound man, another with a prosthetic arm. Applicants showed up in gym shorts. Some said they couldn't agree to a required home interview because their roommates didn't like having cops around. These interviews sucked up supervisors' valuable time—with almost no results.

The Secret Service was tasked with screening thirty-five thousand applicants. It was able to look at only a fraction of these. Almost all they considered would wash out, unable to meet the basic fitness and security standards. The Service hired only eighteen from that group.

Meanwhile, agents on details and officers at the White House kept doing their jobs without a breather. Officers were working half their days off. Agents and officers had to give up regular in-service training. They simply didn't have time for training on top of their normal shifts. The already low morale continued to sink. The exhaustion level in many jobs was dangerously high.

"We kept hearing 'The cavalry is coming, the cavalry is almost here,'" said former agent Jonathan Wackrow. "Really? When will that be?"

THE MORNING OF March 7, 2014, assistant director Vic Erevia called the director at home at about 7 A.M. to let her know about a car accident. Two counter-sniper officers had been in a minor crash in the Florida Keys the night before. They'd arrived a day early—Wednesday, March 6—to be in place to receive the president and his family when they were scheduled to arrive that Thursday for a long weekend vacation in sunny Islamorada. "The vehicle was totaled, but they're okay and they're going to stay and work the president's visit," Erevia explained.

Pierson asked a lot of questions. Was everybody physically okay? Have they been checked out at a hospital? No, they were fine, he said. Toward the end of the conversation, Pierson thought of one last thing. "Vic, what time was the accident?" she asked.

Erevia was quiet for a moment. "Um, it was about two o'clock in the morning, Director," Erevia said finally.

"Vic, the president's not in Islamorada yet. He gets there later today," she said. "Is there a reason these officers were out at two o'clock in the morning?" He said he heard they were coming back late from dinner. But Pierson smelled a DUI six states away.

"Okay, I'll tell you what, Vic," she said. "Tell those two officers to stand down. They're not working today." She ordered an inspection team to go down and sort out what happened.

The true tale the investigators unspooled after interviewing two dozen people was a wild one. About ten officers serving on the counter-sniper and surveillance team had headed out for dinner the Wednesday night before the Obamas' arrival. But around 9:30 P.M., they gathered at a rowdy sports bar. They spent the next few hours downing Coronas and shots of tequila and Fireball into the early hours of the morning.

Their team leader had been compiling rosters and time sheets in his hotel room at the tony beachfront Cheeca Lodge & Spa Resort and became concerned around 11:15 P.M. when none of his team had returned. All of them had to report for duty early the next morning. The officers were in danger of violating the ten-hour rule, which banned drinking within ten hours before reporting for duty. The team leader hopped into his rented Suburban, drove north a few miles on the beach highway to the sports bar, and tried to persuade the officers to call it a night. But the officers playfully refused to leave, and someone called out for more tequila shots. The team leader suggested a compromise. One more round of shots and then everybody would leave. They did their round, but as the team leader was sipping his soda and talking, he noticed that another set of filled shot glasses had appeared on the bar. To keep people from drinking, the team leader poured one shot into another glass and quickly handed another shot glass to a customer passing by. Still the drinking continued.

The team leader finally gave up at 12:45 P.M. Only one officer agreed to go back to the hotel with him. As they drove toward the hotel, though, the younger officer threw up his crabcake dinner and drinks all over the Suburban.

The team leader's nightmare didn't end there. Before he could get the vomit cleaned up, he got a call from Officer Mathew Reyes at about 1:25 A.M. Reyes said he had been in a car accident across the street from the Cheeca Lodge. He and a fellow officer had been getting sandwiches and Gatorade for the next day at a nearby grocery called the Trading Post. Reyes had pulled out of the store parking lot to cross the main island highway and immediately enter the hotel driveway across the road. But he forgot to turn on his headlights and didn't check well for traffic. As soon as he pulled out, a Publix tractor-trailer traveling down the highway slammed into the left side of the van. The truck pushed the van several feet down the highway before they came to a stop. No one was injured, but the van midsection was crushed and it couldn't be driven safely.

A Florida Highway Patrol trooper arrived at the scene about an hour later. The team leader, according to one officer, greeted the trooper and explained they were with the Secret Service. The trooper smelled a light odor of alcohol on Reyes's breath but didn't test his blood alcohol level. Instead, he asked the officer to follow with his eyes a pen he held in the air. The trooper concluded the Secret Service officer didn't show signs of being impaired. He gave the visiting security officer a ticket for causing the accident. Reyes admitted to having drunk beer, two scotch and sodas, and some liquor shots—at most six drinks over the course of the evening. Nothing too excessive for several hours, he said. He said he was sober to drive.

Pierson knew in her gut that alcohol was the culprit, even if the trooper said Reyes passed a field sobriety test an hour after his accident. She couldn't believe the stupidity. Young officers in a four-star oceanfront resort on the government's dime, bored and looking for something to do for one night, decided they had to do tequila shots till somebody threw up.

Pierson wanted headquarters to send a signal. The officers on the Keys trip received much stiffer punishments than others had suffered in the past for the same kind of drunken behavior. Several counter snipers were suspended for more than a month, some for a week, and the officers involved in the car accident lost their coveted spots on specialized tactical units and were bucked back down to patrolling the White House complex.

Pierson called an all-supervisor meeting on March 13 with the Special Operations Division. This division oversaw the Counter Assault and Counter Sniper teams, which were most often implicated in the blackout drinking, bar brawls, and car accidents. She began the meeting describing the crash in the Florida Keys. "All of us know what was going on," she said. "The challenge here is, if this was a football team, would your guys be out at two o'clock in the morning and ready to play the next day? No, they wouldn't. It puts everyone and our mission at risk."

Supervisors had to make sure their agents and officers knew the binge drinking and road-warrior antics had to end, she said. Then the director made a not-so-veiled threat. "If this leadership team doesn't work, I'm going to continue to make changes until we get a team that does work," she said.

The first big test came on Saturday, March 22. More than a hundred agents and officers descended on the Netherlands to help provide security for President Obama's coming visit. The president would arrive in about thirty-six hours. At about seven o'clock that Saturday night, Counter Assault Team leader George Hartford escorted his agents from their hotel to dinner in a touristy section of The

Hague. He had gotten a briefing from his supervisor and knew Pierson was ticked about a group of officers who got shit-faced in the Keys. He had Florida on his mind as he prepared to return to the hotel around 9:30 P.M.

The team leader gave his agents a collegial warning: **Have another Heineken or two. Then go to sleep. No craziness,** he told them. Scrutiny on the Service and CAT was high. He reminded the group that the manpower briefing was at 10 A.M. Sunday. He said good night.

But some agents still couldn't resist the chance to party. At about 5:30 A.M., a Marine stationed in the hotel that would soon welcome President Obama was doing his normal patrols. A hotel employee alerted him to a thirty-four-year-old man passed out on the hallway floor outside his room. It appeared he'd tried to use his key card and simply collapsed. The badge in his pocket identified him as a special agent of the Secret Service. The hotel worker and some other agents lifted the unconscious agent and put him in his own bed. Within the hour, Hartford got a call about the hallway scene. He was soon banging on the drunk agent's door, trying to find out what the hell had happened the previous night.

Pierson got word about the passed-out agent before she boarded Air Force One. She was scheduled to travel with the president for the trip on Monday.

The next day, March 25, Pierson met with

President Obama in his hotel suite in Belgium to brief him on the embarrassing incident. She explained that she had ordered the agent who'd passed out and his two drinking buddies back to the States. She laid out some steps she planned to take with their supervisors. Then it was the president's turn.

He began sternly listing, in methodical order, every ugly Secret Service headline since his inauguration. He started with the dinner crashers and kept right on going without a breath. "And these are just the screw-ups that happened during my administration," he said. "This is a Secret Service problem, not a President Obama problem." He controlled his temper, but she could feel it in the room. "You know what?" Obama said. "The problem with the Secret Service is you don't have enough women in the Secret Service."

Pierson looked at him. "I'm working on it," she said.

On Friday, Pierson flew back to the States, stewing about what had just happened for fifteen hours in a cramped seat. She landed at Dulles at 3:30 P.M. and ordered an all-hands meeting for senior executives and GS-15s at five o'clock. It wasn't a popular time for a meeting, but she didn't care. She started by stating how valuable the Special Operations Division was to the Service, but immediately went on to note that at the moment it was serially embarrassing the president, the director, and the whole

Service. "I'm not going to let SOD tarnish the star and you shouldn't let SOD tarnish the star," she said. Then she told them to get ready for some changes in management.

Pierson removed Dan Donohue from his job overseeing Special Operations. She concluded he had a friendly, go-along personality and had made no consistent effort to curb these misconduct eruptions. But the transfer shocked the Service's top managers. Donohue was well liked and well connected, and the brother-in-law of Mike White, a senior leader on Obama's detail. Erevia told Pierson it was a mistake.

It dawned on Pierson that Erevia, at the time President Obama's favorite person in the Secret Service, just couldn't seem to get with the program. The Service needed accountability, not more brotherhood and cover-up. She believed he had tried to go soft on punishing Zamora. He'd tried to soft-pedal the Keys incident as a simple car accident. And now Erevia was resisting her efforts to hold managers accountable. This was strike three. Pierson told Erevia she was transferring him out of his job as assistant director of Protective Operations.

"Nobody wants to say it . . . but the Secret Service has a culture problem," she would later explain. "It's really a culture of managers failing to want to recognize a problem and deal with it. And it's also a culture of not wanting to report up bad news and circle the wagons" instead.

Pierson's decision to impose consequences on

senior managers shook the Secret Service firmament. People couldn't remember the last time that had happened, other than in a director's power play. She had had the guts to specifically target the Counter Assault Team, the Secret Service's last all-male bastion and a source of macho pride for many detail agents and prominent alumni.

But Pierson shared one of the weaknesses of Sullivan's tenure as director. Several on her team lacked the expertise and strong management skills to help her implement her vision for the Service. Now some in her midst would work hard to undermine her. "She had a weak team," said one of her deputies. "The people gunning for her were smart."

The week after the Netherlands and the president's scolding, Pierson had a regularly scheduled Monday meeting with the new inspector general on March 31. She and John Roth weren't chums, but they sized each other up as worthy of professional respect. Pierson looked at Roth, a former federal prosecutor, and saw a man serious about thorough, independent investigations from whom she wasn't going to hide the facts. Roth listened to Pierson and could tell she deeply cared about the Service and was trying her best to fix it.

Pierson told Roth the passed-out agent would likely lose his job and the other two would likely face some temporary suspension. She vented about how lately she only met with the president to apologize for some new eruption of frat boy behavior. She shared how disgusted President Obama was with the Secret Service at the moment.

"We fired a bunch of people who got caught in Cartagena. We're going to fire some people here. I just don't understand why they aren't getting it . . ." she told him, her voice trailing off. "I am one drunk driving incident away from getting fired."

WHILE JULIA PIERSON was trapped in a game of whack-a-mole, identifying one systemic problem in the Service only to have another pop up elsewhere, Rachel Weaver, staff director for Senator Ron Johnson, the ranking Republican on a Homeland Security subcommittee, was busy prying open the Service's closet of secrets.

Weaver had been pushing to get hold of the Secret Service's internal investigative report on Cartagena for six months before Pierson got her job. Director Sullivan and Secretary Napolitano had successfully stonewalled the minority staffer, but Weaver wasn't giving up, especially after Sullivan stepped down.

"Who is this Rachel Weaver, anyway?" a leader of the Service's congressional affairs team asked a friendly Democratic committee staffer one day. "What did we ever do to her?"

The Secret Service had enjoyed a protected status on Capitol Hill. It rarely faced hardball questions. Senior lawmakers, several of them potential presidential candidates (whether in reality or in their own head), greeted the directors and their deputies as collegial chums. Congress hadn't asked the Government Accountability Office to probe a Secret Service program for more than a decade. But Weaver had evidence suggesting that the Service and Sullivan had misled the public and Congress about Cartagena and wondered what else the Service was hiding. So Weaver had been politely relentless in pushing the committee to get the inspector general's finished report on Cartagena.

At a tense April 9 meeting, Weaver's boss, Senator Johnson, angrily pressed Director Pierson and Committee Chairman Tom Carper to deliver the final report. Pierson said she'd been director for only a few weeks and didn't have all of it herself.

Pierson considered Carper a friendly advocate. When they were alone after the meeting, she told him the Service needed a breather from bad publicity about sex scandals. She needed to focus on hiring and training, and to get her staff refocused on the mission. She recalled that Carper had served in the Navy. "How long did it take the Navy to get back to normal after Tailhook?" she asked, as Carper nodded that he understood. "That's what I need," she said. "I need some time."

By early May, Weaver's phone was ringing regularly with calls from whistleblowers from both the Secret Service and the inspector general's office. Those whistleblowers would include people supremely unhappy with Pierson, including some from the highest levels of her executive team, working alongside her every day.

Weaver had a breakthrough when she was introduced to one of the Acting Inspector General Edwards's investigators. He said an Edwards deputy had ordered the deletion of key findings from the Cartagena investigation, and also the removal of references to other agents hiring prostitutes in the past and to evidence that a White House volunteer had brought a prostitute to his room. Another set of Edwards's employees told Weaver they had evidence that Edwards had had staff write his dissertation and had pushed to get his wife hired at the agency. That summer, at Weaver's urging, Johnson convinced his subcommittee chairwoman, Democratic senator Claire McCaskill of Missouri, that they had to open a joint investigation of Edwards.

Meanwhile, Weaver was immersing herself in the world of the Secret Service and was surprised to discover the story was more complicated than she first believed. She interviewed dozens of agents, including many who had been implicated in the Cartagena scandal. They were all shell-shocked at their punishment, having witnessed peers and supervisors engage in bad-boy behavior for years with no consequences. She listened to their stories of much worse misconduct that had never been reported or punished.

"I'm spending my entire day on the phone with these guys," Weaver said. "I'm starting to feel really sorry for them. I'm developing relationships with them to a certain [extent], which is the last thing I thought—that I would feel sorry for them."

Most had lost their jobs. Now some were overdue on mortgage payments, burning through their retirement savings, or trying to patch their marriages back together. She realized the Service had two sets of rules: one for well-connected supervisors and another for the rank and file. Many of the guys she interviewed had become expendable when Director Sullivan and his team were facing public heat over Cartagena.

Starting in late 2013, however, Ron Johnson's interest in the Secret Service was beginning to wane. Weaver was exhausted from her investigations and pregnant twins. She was ordered to stay home on bed rest for the last trimester.

Working on her laptop on the third floor of her Alexandria townhome, Weaver battled to get Chairwoman Claire McCaskill's staff to agree to publish the details of what the committee had found: first, that Acting Inspector General Edwards had softened his reports as he tried to please Obama appointees, and second, that the Secret Service had misled Congress about the misconduct it had tolerated and covered up. The Republican and Democratic staffs haggled over every phrase that might embarrass the White House. But the final report, while covering only a tiny fraction of what Weaver had uncovered about the Secret Service, did clearly document one thing: Edwards was not an independent or ethical inspector general. It was published April 24, 2014. He stepped down before the report's public release. Two weeks later, on May 9, Weaver delivered two healthy babies, a boy and a girl.

In October 2014, just as Weaver was nearing the end of her maternity leave, her phone rang. It was a miracle that she picked up. With her twins taking turns crying and demanding to be fed, she rarely answered the phone. Jason Chaffetz, a telegenic, ambitious Republican congressman from Utah, was on the line and asked her to come to his office for a chat. He had designs to replace Darrell Issa, who was stepping down as chairman of the House Oversight Committee at the end of the year. He was interested in hiring her to help him with that, and with investigations generally. He had noticed how she had grabbed the Secret Service by the teeth and wouldn't let go.

"So how many whistleblowers do you have, anyway?" he asked her.

Weaver was elated at the idea of a boss who was interested in dogged investigations, and in a subject she had studied intensely. She started working for Chaffetz from home the first week of September 2014.

Timing is everything in life, and something unfathomable was about to happen in downtown Washington. It would rock the White House and make Weaver the expert on the most important subject in town.

CHAPTER 24

"HE'S IN THE HOUSE"

At around 6 P.M. on a warm Friday evening in September, most of Washington had begun to shut down their computers, pack up their things at work, and officially commence their weekend.

President Obama still had a few senior staff meetings before he, too, would head out for a weekend getaway at Camp David. He was scheduled to depart the White House with his two teenaged daughters in an hour, flying to meet his wife at the presidential retreat in Maryland's Catoctin Mountains.

Six blocks south, though, a former Army scout had just arrived in the city. Suffering from delusions and panicky dreams, Omar Jose Gonzalez could feel the adrenaline in his veins. He was itching to set off on his important mission.

Gonzalez parked his 1996 Ford Bronco off

Fifteenth Street near the Holocaust Museum, cracked his windows a little, and hopped out. The disabled Iraq War veteran had lost his wife and his home near Fort Hood, Texas, and had been living in his car, short-term motels, and campgrounds for the last several months. Part of his foot was missing after the Humvee he was riding in rolled over a roadside bomb in Baghdad. His family felt he had been struggling to keep hold of reality after he returned from three tours and eventually retired with a disability in 2012. A cavalry scout, he described watching friends getting blown up. At his home near Fort Hood, he kept guns leaning behind the doors. He feared children he didn't know and warned his wife they could be deadly.

As he set off for the White House on foot, he left hints of a life that was unraveling: two dogs in the Bronco's backseat, jars filled with his urine on the floorboards, and eight hundred rounds of ammunition, two hatchets, and a machete in the trunk.

At 6:25 P.M., Gonzalez reached the southeastern corner of the White House's fenced grounds and began casing the perimeter for a way in. The forty-two-year-old soldier marched up the western border on Seventeenth Street, then along the north fence on the Pennsylvania Avenue pedestrian plaza, then down Fifteenth Street on the east.

Four Secret Service officers who patrolled the compound for trouble—two on bikes and two on foot—noticed Gonzalez at different points in his walk. A few even recognized the caramel-complexioned man with a shaved head from a visit the previous month. That day, he had been walking along the south fence line with a hatchet tucked into his pants belt. He said he used it for camping and stowed it in his car. Today, in his dark T-shirt and baggy cargo pants, he didn't appear to be carrying anything or behaving oddly. They let him pass.

Gonzalez doubled back to the north fence line, where most tourists were content to snap photos. But this Army vet knew he had to get inside. He had a life-or-death matter he had to discuss with the president.

As dusk fell, two starkly different scenes played out on opposite sides of the White House grounds. On the South Lawn, order and serenity ruled. An orchestrated routine that the Secret Service had rehearsed over and over repeated itself. On the North Lawn, a modest problem set off a series of cascading disasters. Every last one of the Secret Service's defenses disintegrated. And officers sworn to tell the truth would lie about the mistakes they made.

Around 7:05 P.M., President Obama stepped out of the Oval Office into the soft evening air. A briefcase of weekend reading in his hand, he strolled down the West Colonnade with his deputy chief of staff, Anita Breckinridge, then said goodbye to go meet his daughters.

Four suited Secret Service agents shielded Barack Obama's flank and back as he walked from the South Portico's ground-floor exit to his waiting helicopter in the grass. Malia and Sasha, along with a school friend, followed close behind their dad, canvas backpacks of schoolwork strapped to their shoulders.

Most of the Secret Service's traveling shift that would accompany Obama the next three days had already left for the Anacostia Naval Station. They were catching their own helicopter ride north and would receive the president when he arrived at the retreat. Now agents on the temporary "make-up" shift took their positions around the family to ensure they departed safely.

One of the presidential detail agents who often protected the Obama daughters, Stavros "Nick" Nikolakakos, an expert marksman and fitness fanatic of Greek descent, had spent a chunk of his career preparing for a high-stakes shootout. But he wasn't expecting much excitement tonight. Before the First Daughters' detail, the black-haired Bronx native had worked as the top-ranked sharpshooter on CAT, the Secret Service's elite Counter Assault Team. The daughter detail was relatively ho-hum compared to that, but it was a good route to rise to the president's detail.

This Friday evening, on the access-controlled White House compound, Nikolakakos and his fellow agents searched for any movement, sharp sound, or odd shape, their eyes darting back and forth. Meanwhile, Obama looked eager to escape the capital after another draining week. He gave a short wave to the skeletal Friday night press pool, wishing them a good weekend.

His daughters, sixteen and thirteen, walked on toward the helicopter, keeping their eyes forward, turned away from the flashing cameras. The agents halted at the end of the paved walk, staying out of the picture frame. The famous family stepped onto the grass alone and the cameras whirred. When the Obamas reached the white-topped green helicopter, the president ushered his daughters and guest up the short accordion stairway, then climbed aboard behind them.

The president's walk to Marine One and departure from the South Grounds had become a well-choreographed movement in the modern era, repeated several times a week as he dashed from city to city. This serene image, captured hundreds of times, was as close as the president could get to appearing a carefree everyman strolling across his backyard without any bodyguards or guns in view. In reality, a small militia stood at the ready.

Obama's Secret Service protectors feared that helicopter departures provided a choice opportunity for enemies to attack. Marine One's lumbering liftoff from the lawn—clocking the same speed as the helicopters that had carried President Eisenhower in the 1950s—made the president a sitting duck for his enemies in the sixty to ninety seconds it took for the helicopter to rise and begin its flight path.

So, as they'd done for hundreds of POTUS helo lifts before, Secret Service officers in uniform and plain clothes fanned out from the South Portico to Constitution Avenue. They scanned the adjoining streets and crowds on the nearby Ellipse for anyone who might pull out a rifle or grenade launcher to try to take down the president's slow-moving aircraft. Counter-sniper officers posted on the White House roof checked their sight lines on the South Grounds and nearby roofs and balconies for unusual movements. Four officers on the Emergency Response Team, wearing all-black tactical gear and Kevlar vests, lurked on the southwestern side of the grounds. They stayed close enough to tackle any intruder who got close to the landing zone.

"Renegade departing Crown," agents heard over their earpieces, the president's familiar code name.

Like other agents standing by, Nikolakakos knew the First Family would be helicoptering northward in a minute, his shift would end, and he could give his guard-dog reflexes a rest. Marine One lifted off without a hitch, albeit a few minutes late, at 7:16 P.M.

The president left in the nick of time. In three minutes, all hell would break loose.

With Marine One airborne, all 154 Secret Service agents, officers, and supervisors working to protect the complex that night started breathing a little easier.

It was simply a natural reaction when Obama left the premises: The Boss was on somebody else's watch now. On the South Lawn, members of the Counter Assault Team now started stripping off their hot tactical gear and loading it into SUVs parked on the nearby south drive. Some took out their earpieces—no need to monitor the radio now.

Agent Nikolakakos walked with a shift supervisor toward the house and into the Diplomatic Room. Both men needed to collect some of their belongings from Staircase, the detail agents' down room under the First Family residence.

On the north side, Officer Clifton Monger, an experienced canine officer stationed with his dog in a van just west of the North Portico, grabbed his cellphone to make a personal call. The former Marine no longer was solely focused on the White House radio frequency but thought he could monitor it with one ear. He had left a second tactical radio, one he used to communicate with his emergency response team, in his locker.

Officer Sean Hughes, a lanky, brown-haired newbie who was guarding the front door at the North Portico, left his post to talk to his friend stationed just inside the house. Officer Phylicia Brice had graduated from officer school together with Hughes a few months earlier. She was headed to New York to help with the upcoming United Nations Assembly, so Hughes was offering her some suggestions for places to eat and visit in the Big Apple.

At 7:19 P.M., while Monger was on a call and Hughes and Brice were chatting, Gonzalez hopped onto a three-foot-high concrete wall abutting a section of the White House's black iron fence. This section of fence was under repair and missing its spiky decorative finials. From the concrete barrier, Gonzalez easily hoisted himself onto the seven-foot-six-inch fence and straddled the flat top. A short bald officer stationed just twelve feet away spotted him and yelled at Gonzalez to stop. He missed grabbing him by an arm's length. Gonzalez swung his leg over and landed on the White House grounds in one swift motion.

He was the fifth fence jumper that year, part of an increasing nuisance for the Secret Service officers guarding the complex. Most of them were mentally troubled people. All were easily stopped within a few yards of where they landed, usually by the canine.

On this Friday night, though, nearly every single thing that could go wrong did.

As Gonzalez crossed the fence line, his body passed through an infrared beam similar to an invisible dog fence. He also set off a ground sensor soon after he landed. Both sounded an "alarm break" at the Secret Service's Joint Operations Center on the ninth floor of Secret Service headquarters on G Street. The team there was supposed to coordinate the response to emergencies and threats at the White House six blocks away.

An alarm and a flashing red light on the JOC

console gave the location where the intruder had entered. Gonzalez had cleared the fence near Charlie 4, Zone 312—just east of the complex's main visitor gate on Pennsylvania Avenue.

Kenneth Havens, a Secret Service officer in charge of alarms at the JOC that night, heard a muffled radio transmission: "Jumper! . . . north fence line." Havens wanted to be sure officers heard the location, so they could nab him. He pushed the radio console's microphone for White House One, the frequency for all officers on the complex.

"Got a jumper," Havens said. "North ground center fence jumper. North fence line fence jumper. North fence line."

This was failure number one of the night. Other than the phrase "got a jumper," none of Havens's broadcast reached the officers. Unbeknownst to him or many others in the JOC, the sophisticated radio console the Service bought four years ago for the command center hadn't been set to automatically override other officers' calls. One officer had "keyed" his radio—depressed a button to speak— just before Haven and canceled his transmissions to everyone.

Gonzalez meanwhile proceeded in a curved route toward the east side of the driveway in front of the mansion, running with a limp.

Two officers on the Emergency Response Team, the tactical team wearing black vests and in charge of putting down trouble, were standing guard inside the Charlie 2A booth immediately to the east of the North Portico. Here was failure number two.

Someone had removed the speakers from the booth's alarm system. Officers had been joking that summer about officers somehow "liberating" high-end speakers from fixed posts on the ground. So the two ERT officers received no broadcast alerts about what was happening.

Even with that glitch, the two men picked up the telltale signs of a jumper. They heard yelling from the north fence line officers. They saw floodlights come on at key guard booths, a standard signal in the case of a jumper.

The men came out of their booth within five seconds, moving quickly toward the north driveway, and readied their long guns for what might come. Though they couldn't see him yet, they were in the perfect spot to intercept Gonzalez.

Next came failure number three. The emergency response officers were thinking: **We don't have to rush this guy.** They'd been trained to let the dog handle jumpers.

The Belgian Malinois, the Secret Service's fail-safe method for neutralizing fence jumpers, was bred to home in on a designated enemy and launch like a missile to take down that prey. Known as the leaner, meaner German shepherds, these dogs had taken down nearly every jumper on the grounds. Canine handlers were trained to release the dogs within six to seven seconds of any perimeter breach.

Within the same five seconds it took the ERT officers to come out of their booth, Officer Hughes had run back out to his abandoned post at the front door. Hughes squinted to see through the bright lights shining down from the portico. Black trucks and hedges blocked his vision, but he could make out officers moving toward the North Lawn.

Now eight seconds after the jump, Hughes drew his 9-millimeter P229 pistol out of his hip holster and backed away from the front door. He remembered from academy training that the canine and the ERT were supposed to tackle any jumper. He had also heard in training that the dog could get confused about whom to attack and he wanted to reduce the risk of that by staying clear. But that training presumed that a Malinois with big teeth was bounding his way.

At the eleven-second mark, Gonzalez came chugging into view, curving around the east side of the fountain in the center of the circular drive. **Where the hell is the dog?** one ERT officer thought.

Failure number four was something nobody would have predicted: The dog was so late he missed the whole incident.

The Malinois on duty that night had been resting in a comfy crate in the back of a parked van next to the portico when Gonzalez made his jump. Monger, his handler, was on his phone. Officers were supposed to monitor their radio closely at all times, but they had so little free time that quick personal calls were allowed. Despite years of trying to hire enough officers, the White House still suffered from a manpower shortage, and officers were still being called in and ordered to work extra shifts. On average, they still worked half their days off.

Another ERT officer on the west side of the North Lawn who was closest to stopping Gonzalez didn't run to grab him. He instead ran to get Monger and the dog. Monger learned there was a jumper when he glanced through his van window and saw an officer running outside. He hopped out of his vehicle, unlocked the Malinois from his crate, and started running with his dog on a long leash.

It was now thirteen seconds since Gonzalez's jump. The intruder had a big head start on what was supposed to be the White House's crack security team.

Canine handler Monger and his dog came from the west and reached the grassy lawn in front of the North Portico fifteen seconds after the jump. Monger hadn't had time to make sure the dog locked on to the jumper. He couldn't successfully sic the dog unless it'd already been trained on a single target. The two ERT officers from the Charlie post on the east side had rushed over in an L formation to try to corner Gonzalez. But Gonzalez surprised them all by plowing into the thick, century-old boxwood hedge that surrounded the front of the portico platform.

On the raised marble landing, Hughes kept his

service pistol at chest level and took cover behind a pillar at the far east corner of the portico. He saw rustling in the shrubs below and thought it might be a scuffle.

But Gonzalez—a broad-shouldered bald man with light brown skin and wide eyes—was only wrestling with the bushes. He stepped out of the dense shrubs and lumbered up onto the western steps of the stone portico. "Stop now! Get down! Stop!" Hughes yelled at the intruder at the top of his voice.

Failure number five was captured on CNN's live feed aimed at the White House's front door. Hughes was taking cover more than fifteen feet from that door. Nothing blocked Gonzalez's path into the president's house other than the risk of Hughes's shooting him. Gonzalez stepped up to the white-framed threshold, seeming to look through Hughes. The officer didn't move. The Service had not trained him for this possibility—a man standing at the White House's front door—but he didn't think he should shoot to kill. He later explained that he believed the jumper wasn't armed, the doors were locked, and the priority was to let the dog take the man down and avoid being attacked by the canine himself.

Failure number six unfolded inside the White House. On the other side of the door, in the vestibule, Officer Phylicia Brice had never received the advance warning of the menace outside. The "crash box," installed at all booths and standard posts, was supposed to sound an alarm for intruders. But the box at Brice's post and others inside the mansion had been muted at the request of the White House usher's office more than a year earlier. Frequent false alarms tended to disrupt events inside. So Brice never heard any emergency broadcasts. Seconds before Gonzalez reached the door, she realized this was an emergency when she looked out the window and saw Hughes with his sidearm drawn.

Failure number seven was that because Brice didn't get any warning of the jumper, she didn't have time to properly lock the doors. She pulled them shut but wasn't able to latch them with the heavy-set pins when Gonzalez yelled from outside, "Let me in!" He gave the two decorative wooden doors a firm push with both hands, and they flew open. He came crashing in and knocked Brice to the ground.

In twenty-nine seconds, Gonzalez had made his way from a public sidewalk to inside the White House. He had gotten directly past eight trained security professionals on a compound staffed with 154 men and women in total.

Brice jumped back up and tried to tackle Gonzalez, but at roughly five foot five, she was no match for his much bigger frame. She yelled at him to stop. He didn't and kept walking briskly toward the East Room. She pursued him and reached for her baton to hit him, but she grabbed her flashlight by mistake.

The delay let Gonzalez walk into the East Room, a grand ballroom that had hosted some of the country's most historic ceremonies. Brice threw her flashlight to the floor and pulled her handgun on Gonzalez, but he continued to ignore her commands that he stop. He turned back into the grand hall and toward the State Floor.

Failure number eight was the result of assumption. While Brice was struggling to control the intruder, the ERT officers outside didn't rush inside to give her backup. They paused outside the door. This unique SWAT team, trained to put down all manner of threats, believed the CAT team was responsible for handling emergencies inside the White House, while they handled the outside. The only problem was that the CAT team, then loading their gear after the president's departure, was not monitoring their radios. They had no clue about the jumper.

Failure number nine was the result of bad communication. Like CAT, PPD agent Nikolakakos and supervisor Joshua Pruett had little warning about the intruder. Agents on the president's protective detail used a different radio frequency than the one for officers protecting the White House. Mostly, they couldn't be bothered with the volume of White House traffic. But in some rare cases it mattered, and they missed what was happening.

The two agents got their first signal of trouble when they heard muffled yelling echoing down toward Staircase from one level above. Luckily, the whole building was an echo chamber. Both agents bounded out of the down room, where agents gathered between assignments and trips, and up the stairs leading to the East Room, where they found the true hero of the day—Officer Michael Graham—on top of Gonzalez. Graham had lunged at the intruder to bring him to the ground, but Gonzalez was still wrestling to get free.

Nikolakakos helped Graham by grabbing the intruder's arms. Meanwhile Pruett kept his gun drawn on Gonzalez. Nikolakakos cuffed Gonzalez's wrists behind his back and began a cursory search for any explosives or other weapons. The agent dug into the Army veteran's pocket. Some chewing tobacco tumbled out. Then Nikolakakos felt something metal and pulled out a folding knife with a three-and-a-half-inch blade.

The three men looked at one another in disgust, at the insanity of anyone getting through hundreds of millions of dollars' worth of security technology, rings of duplicative security systems, and that many Secret Service guards. Here a fence jumper had made it deep inside the mansion and right up to the steps of the president's private living quarters. And he was armed.

"Jesus Christ," one of the agents said. "The guy's got a knife."

———

JUST AFTER 7 P.M. that Friday, Julia Pierson steered her government Jeep into the on-ramp for I-395 South, curving around the Jefferson Memorial. She was giving her assistant a ride home so they could talk over a to-do list of priority tasks for the coming week. She wanted to get home to her Alexandria townhouse, pack, and get some sleep before rising at 6 A.M. and catching the 8 A.M. shuttle to New York. But as Pierson approached the Pentagon, some sharp voices crackled over her Service radio. She almost always traveled with the radio tuned to White House One, the frequency used by the Uniformed Division officers at the complex.

"North fence line," she heard one officer call out at about 7:20 P.M. "Got a jumper," another voice announced. The director kept driving, but her ears perked up to hear how this fence jumping—an increasingly frequent occurrence at the complex—would play out. Sounds of commotion, partial phrases, and some cross-chatter spilled into the Jeep for the next sixty seconds. Pierson and her assistant were startled to hear the report that came over the air next: "He's in the house . . . . He's entered the house."

Pierson flipped on the flashing lights atop her Jeep and veered quickly to the next exit ramp on her left so she could make a U-turn. She knew she needed to whip back around to the White House for this.

She sat locked to the JOC radio frequency on

the short drive back, hanging on each clue uttered as officers reported new details about the breach. Within another two minutes, they heard a supervisor formally report that the jumper was on the ground and handcuffed. It was cold comfort for Pierson. The intruder had been arrested inside the White House, a building that was supposed to be one of the most secure in the country.

The director parked her Jeep on Seventeenth Street minutes later at the corner in front of the Old Executive Office Building near Pennsylvania Avenue. She found her chief of staff, Mike Biermann, walking her way on the pedestrian plaza. They took turns shaking their heads in shared disbelief. Then she asked Biermann what he knew about what had just happened.

About fifty feet in front of Pierson, the captured intruder sat in the backseat of a Secret Service officer's white cruiser on Pennsylvania Avenue. Agents from the Washington field office inside the car asked Omar Gonzalez why he broke into the White House. Gonzalez said he had to alert the president that the atmosphere was collapsing.

"What do you mean?" an interviewing agent asked Gonzalez.

"You know, the air, the environment," Gonzalez said. "The planes are even having to fly lower to the ground."

Gonzalez suddenly became manic, talking rapidly about his heart problems and insisting he had

to get to a hospital. When agents helped him out
of the car, he collapsed on the pavement. Pierson
watched her officers kneel on the street and apply
an oxygen mask to help this man who had humiliated them and their security defenses. As officers
worked to revive Gonzalez, an ambulance arrived
and took him away with his agent chaperone.

Meanwhile, Rob Buster, the bald, bespectacled
head of the president's detail, and his deputy, Marc
Connolly, came out of the West Wing to brief Pierson
on the pedestrian plaza. Connolly had responsibility
for overall security at the White House complex, and
uniformed officers here ultimately reported to him.
He told the director that radio problems and confusion had delayed officers in responding to the jumper.

Connolly had just yelled that less politely over
the phone at a senior official who oversaw all technical security. He insisted the fence alarms must
have failed to sound at key spots. "Your goddamned
fence alarms caused this," Connolly said, according
to two witnesses. "I'm tired of these failures."
Connolly didn't realize the true source of the problem that night.

The director didn't know precisely what had
failed at this point either. But she was taken aback
to hear Connolly partly blame poor radio communications. She thought, **I was on 395 at the
Pentagon and I heard it loud and clear.**

Buster could at least take pride in the fact that
his guys had helped. He told Pierson that two

presidential detail agents gathering their gear at the ground floor had heard a ruckus and run upstairs to help Officer Graham subdue Gonzalez. Buster also explained that the president was aware of what had happened. Buster had told the senior detail leader traveling with Obama, Hector Hernandez, to brief the president in the helicopter halfway to Camp David.

A Uniformed Division sergeant on the complex walked up to show Pierson the jumper's path. He showed her the section of fence Gonzalez climbed over, then his path to the east side of the fountain and through the boxwoods.

Here the officer paused. He said Gonzalez some-how miraculously beat both the attack canines stationed on the east side of the portico, the nearby emergency response team on the west side of the portico, and the officer in charge of the front door. He explained how one officer inside had success-fully brought Gonzalez down, with help from two presidential detail agents.

"Was he armed?" Pierson asked.

"No, ma'am," the sergeant said.

"Good," she said.

The sergeant walked Pierson to the scene of the scuffle and arrest, a section of the Cross Hall within sight of the North Portico door. A small pile of chewing tobacco, which had fallen out of the jumper's pocket when the officers searched him for weapons, marked the spot.

JUST BEFORE 8 P.M., Christian Marrone, the hard-charging chief of staff for the Department of Homeland Security, stood in the meticulously maintained flower beds in front of his Arlington home and pulled a few errant weeds. He had just finished a Friday night dinner with his wife and young kids—a rarity for him. Often the children were in bed when he got home. There were very few easy days running a behemoth department devoted to protecting the homeland, with 240,000 employees in seven disjointed agencies and a dozen smaller components. His wife, Nicole, followed a tight schedule to give their young daughters some healthy structure. She was now inside putting their four-year-old and six-year-old to bed.

Marrone's cellphone buzzed in his pocket and he immediately recognized the number: Julia Pierson's cell. She didn't typically call on weekends, but she did alert him to even fairly modest incidents. Marrone appreciated that she kept him in the loop.

"We have a problem," Pierson began.

"What's the matter?" Marrone asked, tensing slightly.

"Christian, just listen," she said. "I'm out here on Pennsylvania Avenue. We had somebody jump over the fence."

"Oh-kaayy," Marrone said, relaxing a bit. Pierson

called him about every jumper, even though the people were usually harmless and Secret Service officers quickly collared them. These fence jumpers were becoming a more frequent nuisance, though. Five of them in just the last eighteen months.

"This one's different," Pierson said. "He jumped over the fence and got into the house."

"What house?" Marrone asked, confused.

"The White House," she said flatly.

The chief of staff paused, dumbstruck. "You got to be fucking kidding me," he said.

Six or seven questions rushed into Marrone's head at once: Was the president or his family home? How did it happen?

He had another question that Pierson found odd: "Who are you going to fire?"

"Look, I'm down here now," Pierson said. "I don't have all the facts yet, let me get all the facts . . ."

This was now officially a Washington shitshow, Marrone thought. He told Pierson to piece together what happened, because she would need to brief the secretary within the next half hour. Sometime tonight, he knew, White House chief of staff Denis McDonough would call his boss looking for an explanation for this fairly serious screw-up.

Marrone hung up and hustled back into his house to dial his boss Secretary Jeh Johnson's mobile phone. As he heard Johnson's voice come on the line, Marrone saw the electric red Breaking News chyron on the bottom of the television screen and a CNN reporter doing a live standup outside the White House.

Marrone shared the bare-bones report of the situation with his friend and boss, the cabinet member ultimately responsible for Obama's safety. For the first time in the modern era, a person had jumped the White House fence and gotten all the way inside the home of the First Family.

"You are not serious," Johnson said. "What—"

"Turn on the news, Jeh," he said, rubbing one side of his face with his hand. "It's all over the news."

STANDING ON PENNSYLVANIA AVENUE, Pierson answered a call from Anita Breckenridge, the White House deputy chief of staff. "Everyone's looking to me to tell them what's going on," Breckenridge told her. McDonough and the rest of the senior staff had been indefinitely detained in their offices during the lockdown.

The thirty-six-year-old Breckenridge, who until recently had been Obama's scheduler, was getting mildly peeved. She couldn't get answers from Buster. He had been listening to his earpiece and was too busy to talk to her very long. But she needed real-time information, and she didn't care who gave it to her.

Pierson understood that Buster was in crisis response mode—focused on whether Gonzalez was a diversionary tactic and whether there could be a more serious attack coming. She knew Buster and the new deputy didn't have the smoothest relationship yet, and this chaotic night didn't make it easier. But Pierson stuck to the facts she could relay. The jumper appeared to have mental problems, she told Breckenridge. He was unarmed. He was in custody.

Breckenridge had started the call with irritation in her voice. Now she sounded a little shaken. This breach was different. It felt intensely personal for some staff, almost as if their homes had been burglarized.

"Julia, how could this happen?" Breckenridge asked.

Pierson wondered the same thing. She watched as the officers on duty that night were relieved of duty and escorted to headquarters. They had to give their statements to internal inspectors about what they had seen that night, and what they had—or had not—done.

The director stepped out onto the North Portico to head back to the fence line and saw the ERT's replacement squad standing outside on the lawn facing the front door. Most were looking down sheepishly, embarrassed for their unit. On this night of an unprecedented security failure at Crown, she gave this nearly vanquished team the halftime pep talk.

"We need to stay focused," she told the replacements. "Focus on what your duties are tonight.

We're going to get through this. Stay alert, stay vigilant."

She walked out the Pennsylvania Avenue gate and had her assistant dial up all her assistant directors for a conference call. On the call, Pierson cited some evidence of human failures—especially the two officers who had failed to block Gonzalez at the front door. Still, she said, she didn't have a full picture of why things had gone so wrong.

For the time being, she ordered extra officers on the complex to shore up security the next day, and an additional canine team. Officers needed to set up an extra bike rack barricade on the northern perimeter to keep pedestrians farther back from the fence. She put Richard Coughlin, a no-nonsense inspector and then the deputy assistant director over the Office of Professional Responsibility, in charge of figuring out what had happened.

The worst part of the night for the director came when she returned to Secret Service headquarters at 950 H Street at about 11 P.M. She and several assistant directors—Jane Murphy for government relations, Dale Pupillo for protective operations, Mark Copanzzi for technical security, and Kevin Simpson, the chief of uniform division—stood around the duty desk in the Intelligence Division and watched the surveillance video of Gonzalez from start to finish.

Pierson saw a forty-two-year-old man with a noticeable limp, wearing plastic Crocs and lumbering across thirty yards of White House lawn. She saw no one standing outside the front door—an abandoned post. She saw ERT officers stand by for precious seconds as a jumper approached, then a flurry of animal and human legs that all came running too late.

With their jaws clenched, she and her aides watched Gonzalez walk through the unlocked front door as if he had been invited. Some of her deputies looked over to see the director's reaction. Pierson held her hand to her chin.

I feel like I'm going to be sick, she thought.

THE WEEK AFTER the jumper got inside the White House only brought Pierson more bad news about Gonzalez and her agency's inability to stop him. On Sunday, as she toured her agents' security preparations for the United Nations General Assembly in New York, she learned from her investigator that the jumper had actually made it all the way to the Green Room. That was much farther than her top deputies had told her. **Why am I only learning this now?** Pierson thought. On Monday and Tuesday, aides kept passing her messages from the chairman of the House Oversight Committee insisting she appear for a public hearing the following week about Gonzalez's breach.

Throughout the week, Pierson was also learning about numerous warnings the Secret Service had received—and seemingly ignored—about Gonzalez in the months before the jump. Police in Roanoke had warned the Service in July that Gonzalez, an Iraq War vet who was being treated for paranoia, kept a map of the White House and a sawed-off shotgun in his truck. Local authorities shared this discovery after Gonzalez had led them on a crazed high-speed chase down a Virginia highway median. In August, Secret Service officers interviewed Gonzalez when they noticed him marching along the White House fence line with a machete, but they let him go when he said he was just camping. Officers had recognized him as "the hatchet man" when they saw him again on the fence line on the night of September 17, but again they let him pass. On Friday, she met with the assistant director over the protective intelligence unit, Craig Magaw, and a member of his team. She asked why the Service hadn't been monitoring Gonzalez after learning of his unhealthy obsession with the White House and bizarre behavior. Magaw brought Michelle Keeney, a senior threat assessment researcher in his division, to discuss their handling of Gonzalez.

Keeney agreed that Gonzalez was a textbook case of a person that posed a potential threat to the president, but she had only learned of his case and his focus on the White House after the fence jump. The discussion didn't assuage Pierson's concerns about the lack of urgency within the larger Service. The director feared the Service's Intelligence

Division and the broader system to identify threats like Gonzalez were malfunctioning somehow.

Later that Friday, Pierson and Buster sat down with President Obama in the Oval Office. Pierson's goal was to lay out the mistakes that had allowed the jumper to get so far, and to explain what the Service was doing to prevent any similar breach. She hoped to convince him the Service could still keep him and his family safe. She kept thinking: **Every single time I meet with the President, it's to explain another major screw-up.**

Pierson laid out first what she knew had gone wrong, and then the security reinforcements she was making around the White House perimeter. Obama tersely reminded Buster he had a duty to keep Obama's deputy, Breckenridge, informed. Otherwise, the president spent much of their time together silently nodding, an all-business executive resting his closed fist on his mouth. Gone was the president who greeted his detail agents as "the boys" and called out with a teasing joke. Obama wrapped up the meeting with a glum expression.

"For the record," he said with stern emphasis, "I **still** have full confidence in the Secret Service."

The well-worn presidential phrase carried no reassurance. Instead, President Obama seemed to be issuing a warning: **I can only be patient for so long. You guys better get your act together.**

That weekend Pierson prepared for the congressional hearing with a mock interview panel led by

Marrone and her aides. She knew her facts cold, but she also felt boxed in. Marrone coached her that she shouldn't try to excuse the breaches by pointing to the budget cuts the Service had suffered. She knew she wouldn't attack her own workforce. Where did that leave her in explaining what had weakened the Service? At the end of the Sunday prep session, she only felt more rattled.

JASON CHAFFETZ COULDN'T believe it when he heard it the first time. If this was true, he had a bombshell on his hands.

That Sunday evening, the young Utah Republican was driving back from a relaxing weekend in Grand Teton National Park near Jackson Hole, enjoying a favorite hobby, photographing the breathtaking landscape. He tried to keep focused on driving and also absorb the incredible story now being piped into his truck dashboard. A new Deep Throat, a skittish senior Secret Service official, had relayed a story to his senior staffer, Rachel Weaver, and what he had to say was important enough to cause her to patch him through to the congressman.

"I can never be identified," he told Chaffetz. "We had an incident a few days before the jumper. The president went out to Atlanta, to the Centers for Disease Control. There was a person there that was without clearance that was allowed to ride in the elevator with the President."

"And he had a gun," the official added.

This was very bad, the agent explained. A private security guard at the CDC's Atlanta campus was tasked with escorting President Obama in an elevator when he visited to thank federal employees for their work combating the Ebola virus. The Service is required to run background checks on every person who gets close to the president—even the waiters and staff at the hotels he visits. No one is allowed to be armed near the president except Secret Service agents and the select sworn law enforcement officers who are part of the Service's security plan. In the case of the guard, he was armed, and the Secret Service never checked his background.

The Service discovered its mistake almost by happenstance, then checked the man's arrest record. He'd been charged with battery and assault but never convicted. In another case later dropped, he had been accused of reckless firing of his weapon.

"What? Are you serious?" Chaffetz asked.

Deep Throat said he was, then added another detail:

"Funny thing was, that day, Director Pierson or someone in her office sent one of her agents to Atlanta to quietly investigate," he said. "They wanted to make sure you and the public never heard about it."

"Huh," Chaffetz snorted.

Chaffetz thanked the official, and another agent

on the line who had brought the official to Weaver, and said goodbye. Chaffetz stayed on a line with Weaver a few more minutes to strategize. As an Oversight Committee subcommittee chairman, he had an idea for how to test Pierson at the upcoming hearing.

"Now we'll see," he said. "Is she going to be truthful or is she going to lie?"

At the opening of Tuesday's hearing, Oversight Committee chairman Darrell Issa began by recounting a series of scandals that had succeeded in tarnishing the Secret Service's once impeccable record. "The fact is the system broke down on September 19, as it did when the Salahis crashed the state dinner in 2009, as it did when Oscar Hernandez successfully shot the White House on November 11, 2011, as it did in Cartagena when agents paid for prostitutes and compromised security, as it did in the Netherlands in 2014," Issa said. "We cannot further allow this."

Issa said he'd always trusted the Secret Service but now had doubts about the agency's candor. He complained he had to learn from a **Washington Post** story that the Service's claim of having arrested the jumper just inside the White House's front door was false. Omar Gonzalez actually made it deep inside the White House, he said—"what is supposed to be the hardest target in the world."

Elijah Cummings, a Maryland lawmaker and ranking Democrat on the committee, had been holding his breath since 2007, when Senator Barack Obama began running for president. He knew about the racist wackos who threatened to use Obama for target practice, and he had long feared for his safety. An armed man's ability to burst into the First Family's home shook Cummings anew. But stories in **The Washington Post** about the Service's covering up details of the jumper and failing to investigate a 2011 shooting at the White House made him angry. With a preacher's fiery admonition, he warned that the bungling of the 2011 shooting suggested a grave disease festering in the Service.

"Ladies and gentlemen, something is awfully wrong with that picture," he said. "The Secret Service is supposed to be the most elite protection force in the world. Yet four days went by before they discovered the White House had been shot seven times."

Over the course of the three-and-a-half-hour hearing, Pierson ended up being grilled on every security mistake and misstatement the Service had made in the last five years, most of them under the previous director. Some of her answers sounded bureaucratic and wooden. She was mindful of being a woman and not showing emotion. She kept her cool, but the result left members feeling chilly. One member accused her of showing no outrage about what had gone wrong or any commitment to fixing it. Another said he wished she cared as much about protecting the president as she did about protecting her own job.

Then came Chaffetz's turn. He began by asking Pierson if every serious security breach triggers a review. Her answer was yes. Would the president be informed about each one?, Chaffetz asked.

"I would assume the president of the United States is informed," she replied. "I don't know."

"What percentage of the time do you inform the president if his personal security is [sic] in any way, shape or form been breached?" Chaffetz asked.

"One hundred percent of the time we would advise the president," she said.

"You would advise the president?" he asked.

"Yes," she said. She spoke reflexively for the agency. In fact, unless it was an extreme case, Pierson wouldn't personally brief the president. In most security incidents, his detail agent briefed his deputy chief of staff. Chaffetz knew from his Deep Throat inside the agency that Pierson had never told the president or the White House about the unscreened elevator guard in Atlanta.

I have her now, Chaffetz thought.

AT AROUND 4:00 P.M., Pierson sat alone in her office, feeling pummeled and exhausted by nearly four hours of lawmakers' accusations and questions. Then Ed Donovan, the agency's chief spokesman, and his boss, Jane Murphy, the assistant director for government and public affairs, walked in hurriedly, looking exasperated as they stood in front of her desk.

Donovan said he was getting press questions about an incident roughly a week earlier in Atlanta. Reporters at the **Washington Examiner** and **Washington Post** wanted to know why the president had been on an elevator with an armed guard who hadn't been screened.

Pierson said yes, it was true, and gave a quick summary of the advance agent's failure to provide the names of people working at the event so they could be screened. "Why didn't we know about it?" Murphy, upset, asked her boss. Pierson apologized, saying she had discussed it with Buster and Smith and launched a fact-finding investigation but had forgotten to mention it to them. Then Pierson's desk phone rang. It was Christian Marrone. He was talking fast, pumped up on a mixture of adrenaline and irritation.

"Are you aware of an armed guard being on the elevator with the president in Atlanta?" he spat out quickly. "The CDC?"

Pierson took a breath.

"Yes," she began. She was about to explain the investigation she had launched, but it was too late. Marrone had already hung up.

Marrone now had to call back his press office and also prepare the White House and Secretary Johnson. He was completely disgusted. He had championed Pierson, given her a Joe Paterno–style pep talk earlier that day, and defended her at many turns. Now he was on clean-up duty after being left in the dark. The **Washington Examiner** and the **Post** both published stories describing the failure to prescreen an armed person who had stood inches from the president. It was a terrible blunder in a kind of rote security protocol that Secret Service agents could do in their sleep.

Obama's senior White House aides, Secretary Johnson, and Marrone had only begun to absorb the bruising hearing Pierson had endured. Now they had to quickly grapple with another horrible headline about the Secret Service. For all of them, the CDC story was the final straw. But there was an important puzzle piece everyone was missing.

Julie Pierson wasn't looking for more bad press. But she hadn't tried to hide this screw-up from the president.

IT WAS HARD to imagine the director's brutal day getting even worse. But the CDC stories had done it. Pierson felt physically assaulted. The stories felt hyped and terribly unfair. First of all, she wasn't trying to conceal anything. She had asked Rob Buster, Obama's detail leader, to notify the White House about the problem with the guard that same day.

That night, she called Jeh Johnson, hoping to clear the matter up. The secretary was on a plane back to Washington from Ottawa and called her back when he deplaned around 8:30 P.M. Pierson told him the hearing had been "difficult"—an understatement—but she wanted to explain something the newspapers hadn't said about the CDC incident. She told Johnson she had asked Buster to brief Obama on the elevator guard incident.

The secretary listened silently.

Pierson asked his opinion about who might be leaking these incidents to the **Post**. Johnson detested leaks. He had a strong hunch that a few senior deputies in headquarters who didn't like Pierson were actively trying to torpedo the director. But in the end, who was leaking this stuff and who had failed to brief Obama about the elevator guard—none of it mattered. Pierson was genuinely devoted to the Service mission, Johnson could see, and she had a good business plan for the agency. But the tally of screw-ups continued to mount. The White House had been caught unaware of the CDC incident. The leaks and internal feuding were getting out of hand. Pierson's inability to find her voice at the congressional hearing had weakened lawmakers' and the administration's already low confidence in the Service.

The difficult decision had already been made. The secretary had talked to Marrone at about 5:00 P.M. and they agreed Pierson had to go. The

White House told Marrone they were already lining up a temporary replacement who could be named the next day. The president wanted his former detail leader, Joe Clancy.

On the phone that night, Johnson chose not to tell Pierson she was about to be forced out. She had just taken one of the most brutal thrashings Washington had seen in a long while.

"This is a problem, Julie. A real problem," he said of the president's being taken by surprise about the CDC guard. "We're going to have to talk about it and I'll get back to you."

A day later, the White House announced that Pierson had resigned, something she was forced to do that morning, and that she would be replaced by Clancy. Many in the public rightly assumed she got canned for having one too many bad things happen on her watch, but wrongly assumed she'd tried to hide something from the president.

Johnson knew better. He knew that a series of Secret Service deputies had failed Pierson and that some had actively worked against her to leak bad news. On the day of her resignation, he told his staff to take him to Secret Service headquarters and order all the assistant directors to meet him in the main conference room, where he proceeded to give them a tongue-lashing.

"Today is rock bottom and every day after this we are going up," Johnson said. "She took the fall for all of you. But you all bear the responsibility.

You better get your asses in gear or you're out. Now one of you, go ahead and leak this, since you leak everything else."

They hung their heads and watched Johnson walk out.

SLIDING BACKWARD

THE TRUMP YEARS (2016–2021)

CHAPTER 25
CLANCY'S TURN

Jeh Johnson had a job opening he believed only a four-star general could fill.

President Obama had accepted the resignation of Secret Service Director Julia Pierson amid a flurry of failures that singed the agency, and amid depressing but clear signs that her male peers were trying to torpedo her by leaking some of them. In November 2014, the secretary of homeland security wanted a demanding leader who could exert some control over the Secret Service and stop it from plunging the Obama administration into embarrassing headlines. From his old job as counsel in the Defense Department, Johnson had come to value the leadership presence that generals exuded. Not only were they able to command action from their subordinates, the best ones were able to build an esprit de corps that made soldiers race to follow them into battle and seek to prove their worth. He had watched with disappointment as Pierson had struggled to steer the agency through the shoals amid a secret mutiny against her.

But nobody in the military's top brass was biting at this job announcement. The agency's $2 billion budget looked puny compared to even modest Pentagon programs. On top of that, the Service was facing a well-documented string of misconduct and mismanagement problems and could expect continuing aggressive oversight from a congressional committee whose members had elevated their public profiles by calling out the agency's failures.

When the new year opened in January 2015, Johnson was trying to size up his prospective candidates for the director's job. He had been privately conferring with Larry Cockell, a standout manager in the Clinton era and a previous candidate for director, urging him to consider returning for the top job. Cockell, then earning a handsome salary as a security executive for Time Warner, was well known for both buttoned-down leadership and strategic planning. But he quickly backed out of the running when he heard from the Service rumor mill that Joseph Clancy, appointed initially as a temporary placeholder, was interested in applying for the permanent job. Johnson didn't think Clancy was the best choice, given the agency's need for fresh eyes, but Cockell knew that the importance of a president's comfort with his director would trump all.

Johnson, who didn't have two decades watching the relationship between presidents and their agents, ultimately believed he had found an ideal candidate to recommend. Sean Joyce had recently left his post as deputy director of the FBI. He had the law enforcement chops, and he specialized in "back-of-the-house" operations where the Service sorely needed help.

But after Clancy quietly told President Obama one day when they were alone that he was interested in staying on, the decision was all but made. Having his first detail leader back in charge sounded great to the president—and to Michelle Obama. Cockell's instincts had been right.

In the first week of February, Johnson's deputy called a former police chief under consideration to tell him he need not come to Washington for a previously discussed interview. The president had already chosen someone.

It was Clancy. But to get the White House's full blessing, Clancy had to do something he wasn't eager to do. As an acting director, he had chosen for his deputy Alvin "A.T." Smith, an agent he had worked alongside for years but who was a divisive figure in the Service. Clancy's support of Smith had infuriated the portion of the Service that loathed Smith. More important, it had rankled Republican representative Jason Chaffetz, who was investigating Smith's role in several embarrassing security lapses. Keeping Smith as his top lieutenant would guarantee the Service, and the Obama administration, a continued unflattering glare from Chaffetz's Oversight Committee.

On February 9, Clancy announced that he was removing Smith from his job as deputy director. In mid-February, President Obama announced Clancy as his permanent new director, rejecting the recommendation of the expert panel he had personally appointed to suggest reforms to fix the Service. The panel, including two lawyers who had worked for Obama, urged the president to choose an outsider as the next leader, saying it was the only way to get the Service to ditch its old, insular ways. "Only a director from outside the Secret Service, removed from organizational traditions and personal relationships, will be able to do the honest top-to-bottom reassessment this will require," the report found.

But Clancy's connection to Obama and his reputation as Mr. Clean helped his candidacy. From 2009 to his retirement in 2011, he had served as the head of Obama's detail and was thus often the first face Obama saw when his workday began. There was no chance in hell of any ethical skeletons in his closet. Clancy had been faithfully married to the same woman for thirty-one years. While rumors of affairs and womanizing swirled around some senior male supervisors, Clancy was a Boy Scout who routinely turned down the after-work drink with the boys.

Even Clancy's fans worried about his ability to right the ship, however. At sixty-one, he had never worked in headquarters, so he lacked experience in back-of-the-house operations. He avoided confrontation, and throughout his career had warned subordinates not to try to improve on the old, proven ways. He had long-standing bonds with the leadership group that had brought the agency to this worrisome precipice. His Service nickname was Father Joe, a nod to his interest in the priesthood as a young man but also to his gentle mentoring. Yet the very qualities that made Clancy so respected and well liked also made him a less than ideal choice to reform an agency characterized by arrogant defiance.

"You can't find a better person with more integrity," said his former Philadelphia colleague. "You can't. But he's not that pit bull." And at this juncture in the Service's gradual slide, the Service needed an attack dog.

The twenty-fourth director of the Secret Service had had only two weeks to bask in his big promotion before a brand-new pile of misconduct and embarrassment hit the fan. A disturbing breach of ethics and security—involving one of his friends and highest-ranked supervisors—would have Clancy and the Service playing red-faced defense once again.

THE MARCH 4 party to celebrate Ed Donovan's retirement started at five-thirty at the dark Irish bar in

Chinatown called Fado. It seemed fitting. Donovan and most of his crew, as well as so many Secret Service agents before them, were Irish. The bar's Gaelic name, loosely translated, meant "once upon a time" and was used to start most old Irish stories. The thirty to forty guests had come for their friend, but they were also raising toasts to the victory of the Secret Service of old. Pierson, the agency's experiment with its first female director, was gone. Obama had elevated "Father Joe" Clancy, an insider they knew well who was the very definition of old guard, rather than choosing an outsider.

Donovan and his wife had arranged a buffet of pub food as well as an open bar of wine and beer. Agents, along with a few civilian staffers, greeted Donovan inside, cracking jokes and razzing the beefy former New York agent for his luck in rising through more than two decades on the job, especially defending the agency's reputation in the press shop the last several years during Cartagena, the White House shooting, and the jumper. Donovan had a great big loud bark but was also generally respected by reporters. Donovan had badly wanted to move out of the press office, but he was so good at dealing with the press and navigating rough waters that then director Sullivan didn't want to let him leave his post. When Donovan's wife shut down the open bar two hours later, at 7:30 P.M., she paid the $729 tab for the buffet, along with a bill for fifty-three beers, seven glasses of wine, and three sodas.

Two of Donovan's close friends who had worked in the press office lingered far later at the bar. George Ogilvie, a GS-14 supervisor who then oversaw the protection squad in the Washington field office, opened a tab on his credit card at 7:44 P.M., following the tradition that the junior man pays for the drinks. He had nearly twenty years on the job. His drinking partner was the older and presumably wiser Marc Connolly. Connolly, an agent for twenty-seven years, was a senior executive who had been promoted to become the number two in charge of the Obamas' detail in 2012. Two civilian press office staffers joined Ogilvie and Connolly at the bar for a time, then left.

For the next three hours, the two men sat and drank at Fado and told stories of the good old days at the Secret Service. By 10:45 P.M., they agreed it was time to call it a night. In addition to the three drinks he'd bought for the two staffers, Ogilvie's bar bill listed eight scotches, three beers, two vodka drinks, and a glass of wine; he later said he had three of those drinks. Ogilvie offered to drive Connolly, who had drunk more than he had, in his government-issued car back to the White House, where Connolly had parked his government-issued car.

Though Connolly had overall responsibility for security at the White House complex, neither he nor Ogilvie had been paying attention to their government BlackBerrys. A little before 10:30 P.M., the White House had moved to the heightened security of Condition Yellow, indicating that personnel should be alert for potential danger and triggering the closure of the E Street entrance on Fifteenth Street. As Ogilvie was paying the bar tab fifteen minutes later, the JOC had put out an email alert to all supervisors—and called Director Clancy at home—to explain that the White House had gone to Condition Yellow because a woman had thrown a suspicious package near the guardhouse at the E Street entrance and yelled "Bomb." The local police bomb detonation team had been summoned to determine whether it was a real explosive or a false alarm. To protect their own officers and the public, the Secret Service vacated the entrance, using barrel cones to block it, and then stationed officers farther north on Fifteenth Street to reroute traffic away from this two-block section closest to the package.

Oblivious to the drama, Ogilvie was heading straight for the E Street entrance to the White House grounds. A Secret Service officer rerouting cars on Fifteenth Street tried to wave Ogilvie's car to a stop, but Ogilvie blew past him. The supervisor continued driving his car toward the now vacated guardhouse. There, Ogilvie had to make a wide turn to try to go around a large plastic traffic barrel. He backed up and drove forward twice to get a better angle to pass, but he eventually gave up and slowly used his right front fender and the passenger side of his car to shove the barrel out of his way.

As his car entered the area of the White House grounds that had been evacuated for a bomb investigation, Ogilvie's driver side tires rolled within a few feet of the mystery package. Like all cars entering the White House grounds, he now had to wait for officers to screen his vehicle before they would lower a retractable metal barrier and allow him to drive farther onto the complex.

A supervisor at the JOC watching Ogilvie's SUV enter the locked-down E Street entrance on live surveillance video radioed to Uniformed Division officers to go check on the agents parked near the retractable barrier. The officers were somewhat uncomfortable, not wanting to get closer to a possible bomb until it had been inspected, but all three complied and walked up to the car. Ogilvie and Connolly lifted their Secret Service badges as the men approached.

"How'd you get in here?" the lead officer asked the agents.

The agents were silent. The officer asked Ogilvie and Connolly two more times, again getting no answer, as if the agents were playing a game. Ogilvie kept his head pressed hard to the back of his seat, with his eyes wide, as if trying not to blink. Connolly, in the passenger seat, looked glassy-eyed and disheveled and said nothing. Ogilvie eventually replied when the officer asked a fourth time.

"No one stopped us," he said. Ogilvie lied and said they were coming from headquarters. In fact, they'd been drinking in a bar for the last five hours. "Where are the post officers and the K-9?" Connolly wanted to know, appearing to be upset that they weren't being cleared to drive on past the barrier. The officers explained: This entrance was closed due to a suspicious package.

It was a few minutes after 11 P.M., and several emails had already been sent to Connolly and other supervisors about the package and heightened security at the White House. Connolly, the man in charge of overall White House security, had no idea about it. Instead, he and his drinking buddy had driven into an area that had been shut down due to the risk of a possible bomb blast.

The officers suspected the agents had been drinking because they weren't making any sense. One of the three officers decided to call the watch commander, Capt. Michael Braun, the highest-ranking officer on the grounds that night. "We have a situation," the officer told Braun. "We have Connolly and Ogilvie down here. They could be drunk."

Captain Braun, who ultimately answered to Connolly but was several rungs below him in the chain of command, called his boss. He wanted to confer about a problem he and fellow Secret Service officers had never encountered before: a likely inebriated and upset supervisor of the president's detail who had ridden back to the White House in a government car driven by another agent who might also be drunk, through a roadblock and into an active investigation scene. After the call, Braun came down to the entrance to eyeball the situation for himself and told the three officers to stand down. Reaching Ogilvie's SUV, Braun smelled a faint odor of booze. He noticed Connolly had a flushed face and glazed-over eyes and had his cellphone pressed to his ear.

"Have you guys been drinking?" Braun asked Ogilvie.

"What?" Ogilvie said.

Braun asked again. Ogilvie turned in Connolly's direction, then nodded slowly and said "Yes" in a low voice.

The captain took his next step with limited information. He concluded that Ogilvie seemed calm and professional and was fit to drive, but Connolly was not. He summoned the K-9 team, which initially refused to enter the area and then relented, to come screen Ogilvie's SUV so they could let Ogilvie pass the retractable barrier. Fellow officers said Braun told them he believed both men were "hammered" and violating the Service's ten-hour rule, which prohibited agents from drinking within ten hours before reporting for duty. Some of the officers had wanted to perform a sobriety test on the agents, but Braun explained that that would be a "career killer." The officers understood that he was talking about his career, not Connolly's. Braun later denied making those comments.

There was no disputing, though, that the high-ranking agents' bizarre entry onto White House grounds represented a three-alarm fire for the Secret Service Uniformed Division. The officers had called Braun for help, Braun had called his boss for advice, and Braun's boss now called his supervisor, Deputy Chief Alfonso Dyson, to alert him to the scene on the White House's east side. Dyson oversaw all officers at the White House, and after getting a quick briefing, he called Connolly at about 11:19 P.M., moments after Ogilvie had dropped Connolly at his own government car. Dyson normally reported to Connolly, but that night Connolly was the one needing Dyson's counsel.

"I fucked up," Connolly told the chief.

Dyson twice urged Connolly to report this to his boss "before things get out of hand." Connolly agreed that he would. Both Ogilvie and Connolly drove to their respective homes, despite Braun's belief that Connolly was probably impaired. Neither reported the events of March 4.

But karma came back to haunt the pair of powerful agents. At least one of the officers working that rainy night when Ogilvie and Connolly showed up looking plastered had themselves been busted and demoted just a year earlier after an alcohol-fueled night out in the Florida Keys. That previous March, a 1 A.M. crash in Islamorada that involved two Secret Service officers prompted a deep-dive internal investigation. It revealed many of the officers on the trip had hit the local sports bar hard that night for shots of tequila. A supervisor ended up having to drag the men out of the bar, and at least one vomited all over their rented van. They were technically on duty at the time and supposed to be preparing to receive the Obama family for a few days of vacation early the next morning. Director Julia Pierson had stripped several of the officers of plum specialist assignments and bucked them back to post-standing duty at the White House as a result. Now, a year later, the officers of Florida Keys fame weren't going to let two senior agents in the Secret Service get away with such a brazen, drunken escapade.

An officer created a secret email account that Friday, March 6, and wrote a description of the incident that he and his colleagues rapidly forwarded from friend to friend in the Secret Service family. One version simply said two unnamed agents were suspected of driving drunk back to the White House, being involved in some kind of car crash, and blundering their way into an area cleared due to a suspicious package. A former agent caught wind of the incident and called me that Friday to find out if I had heard what happened after Donovan's retirement party. Over the weekend, many dozens of current and former Secret Service agents had shared and forwarded the email.

Retired agent Mike Novak, a longtime friend of Clancy's, was worried when another alum alerted him to the allegation and how widely it had been shared. Hundreds of current and former agents knew all the gory details, but one critical person absolutely did not: Joe Clancy. Novak, who had overlapped with Clancy when they worked at Comcast, wanted to protect his friend from embarrassment. Clancy was just one month into his role as permanent director. Novak called Clancy at about nine o'clock on Monday morning, March 9, at headquarters to clue him in.

Clancy listened and thanked Novak. He felt sure this had to be a bogus story, but he called Billy Callahan, the deputy director of protective operations, to ask him to check into it. Nobody had mentioned this incident in Clancy's morning briefings the previous week. Despite Dyson's reminding Connolly to report the incident to his boss, Obama detail chief Rob Buster, Connolly had done and said nothing, even when he and Buster met two days later to discuss the failure to immediately apprehend the suspicious package suspect. By midmorning Monday, Richard Coughlin, the deputy assistant director then overseeing the Office of Professional Responsibility, met with Clancy to alert him to the detailed story making the rounds over the weekend. This one shocked the director because it named the two agents. Clancy had worked closely with Connolly and supervised him on the detail. Both he and Ogilvie were highly experienced supervisors. The director felt he couldn't properly investigate this internally, based on Secret Service policy. He told Coughlin to notify the office of the Department of Homeland Security's inspector general, John Roth, and ask him to take over the investigation that night.

Two days later, I published a story breaking the news that Connolly and Ogilvie were being investigated based on allegations they had been intoxicated and involved in a possible car accident and had either crashed or bumped into a White House security barrier.

Many details weren't yet confirmed. I stuck to what I knew: the specific allegations that Clancy had received and that he wanted investigated— a possible "crash" involving two agents, allegedly drunk, as described in the mystery email:

> The Obama administration is investigating allegations that two senior Secret Service agents, including a top member of the president's protective detail, drove a government car into White House security barricades after drinking at a late-night party last week, an agency official said Wednesday.

But other news outlets reported a crash as a fact, not an allegation that Clancy wanted run to ground:

> Two senior Secret Service agents, including a top member of President Barack Obama's

protective detail, crashed a car into a White House barricade following a late-night party for retiring spokesman Ed Donovan and it's suspected they had been drinking, sources confirmed to CNN.

When the story published, though, the instant reaction among even hardened Secret Service alums was disgust.

"Hi, Carol," former CAT supervisor Dan Emmett wrote me.

I am sad, angry and essentially incredulous. After everything that the Service has gone through over the past three years this defies the imagination. The Service had the chance to rebuild its reputation with the American people but have, in all probability, set back the rebuilding process back by years. The public is fed up as well as the good agents who are forced to put up with this type of reckless, irresponsible lack of leadership.

Joe Clancy did the right thing by referring this to OIG/DHS and I am certain it will be an extremely thorough investigation. If Ogilvie and Connolly did what they are alleged to have done, they are done. If true, this is the height of irresponsibility, incompetence and total disregard for the Secret Service and the office of the Presidency.

At the White House, the reaction was barely concealed revulsion. Senior Obama aides there were sick of playing clean-up for the Secret Service's debacles. This misconduct had taken place on the White House grounds and implicated one of the president's highest-ranking protectors.

"I'm aware of those reports," White House press secretary Josh Earnest told reporters who asked about the incident at the press briefing the next day. "The allegations included in them are disgusting." Earnest said the administration and the Secret Service took the reports "very seriously" and then tersely referred additional questions to the Secret Service press office.

Clancy took a series of beatings on Capitol Hill over the March 4 incident, as his mid-March hearings on the Secret Service budget turned into inquisitions about Secret Service screw-ups. House Appropriations Committee chairman Hal Rogers scolded the new director at a hearing for his head-in-the-sand approach to the two agents' alleged drunk driving. "To say you're not investigating because you want the inspector general to investigate is hogwash," Rogers said. He also questioned Clancy's ability to change the Secret Service's arrogant, above-the-rules culture. "I don't sense at this moment that you have the determination to make that happen," Rogers said.

The quiet, always polite, and somewhat robotic Clancy began to resemble a tattered rag doll, though, as members took turns flaying him at a March 24 congressional hearing. Two of the Secret Service's strictest overseers—Representatives Jason Chaffetz and Elijah Cummings, the chairman and ranking member of the House Oversight Committee—had called the hearing, aghast at what had happened. But their outrage ratcheted higher after Clancy told them before the hearing that he couldn't provide key details about the incident and he wouldn't let his senior deputies answer the committee's questions.

"By refusing to allow the witnesses we invited to testify—with firsthand knowledge of the incident—Director Clancy is keeping Congress and the American public in the dark," Chaffetz said. "It is unclear why Director Clancy is choosing at the start of his tenure to be so unhelpful to Congress."

Democrats, the White House's natural defenders, didn't show Clancy any mercy either. Behind closed doors, Cummings told Clancy he couldn't take much more of the "merry-go-round" of misconduct at his agency. From the dais, he warned Clancy that the anonymous officers who created the email about the March 4 incident apparently didn't trust him to punish the agents involved, and others had disrespected him by leaving him in the dark about a brewing scandal. He said President Obama's life was in danger thanks to "an agency at war with itself." "I believe when the chain of command is broken, there is no command," Cummings said. "It's like a body without a head, and where there is no command, there is vulnerability and the vulnerability goes to the safety of the president of the United States."

Several lawmakers expressed shock upon learning that Clancy refused to share videotape of the incident with members, and that much of it had been essentially destroyed, overwritten rather than preserved. "I'm a little bit more than troubled by the willful ignorance here," Massachusetts Democratic representative Stephen Lynch said. "You don't ask questions and then you destroy evidence." At headquarters, employees seethed as they watched Chaffetz bash the polite, even docile Clancy, repeatedly interrupting and berating him before the television audience. The anger fueled an organic rebellion. Aneda Arriaga, a supervisor in administration, watched Clancy's testimony on her office TV, like many supervisors in headquarters. Just eighteen minutes into the hearing, a curious Arriaga opened the Secret Service's confidential "Master Cases Index" on her desktop computer and typed the name Chaffetz. A tiny file popped up for the current Oversight Committee chairman. It showed that Chaffetz had applied to become a Secret Service agent in 2003 in a western field office and been rejected. According to the record, the Service never interviewed Chaffetz and chose a "better qualified applicant" for the slot, a rejection known in the Service as "getting BQA'd."

The information was stored in a restricted Secret Service database and protected by law as private personnel information.

The news of Chaffetz's rejection spread quickly. Before lunchtime, Cynthia Wofford, a deputy assistant director over the Intelligence Division, heard about Chaffetz's application from co-workers. An agent in the Dallas office that evening looked up Chaffetz in MCI and emailed Clancy's chief of staff, Mike Biermann, asking him to call about "some information." By the end of that Tuesday, seven people had searched the Chaffetz file. By the end of the next day, Wednesday, thirteen more had accessed his records.

Midmorning on Wednesday, Wofford had stopped into the office of Clancy's deputy director Craig Magaw to share what she knew, but he shooed her away with his hand.

"Yeah, yeah, we know," Magaw said.

Clancy and Magaw were both scheduled to attend an important luncheon that afternoon: Clancy was hosting former directors of the Secret Service to get their advice on the agency's challenges. Before they went to the lunch, Magaw told Clancy about Chaffetz's rejected application. In a sign of how effectively the Service spread gossip, two of the former directors had already heard about Chaffetz's failed application for an agent job in 2003 from other retired agents. Different people remembered the particulars of who said what differently, but all remembered the Chaffetz matter coming up and Clancy acknowledging it. Former director Lew Merletti said he brought up Chaffetz's history with the Service at the lunch. Another person remembered former director Brian Stafford asking Clancy about the rumor.

"We're looking into it," Clancy replied. "I don't know if it's good or bad."

One of the guests said Chaffetz should consider recusing himself from oversight of the Secret Service if he had been turned down for employment at the agency. Clancy would later say he didn't remember the discussion at all. He was the only person attending the lunch who did not recall the subject coming up. After the luncheon, Clancy's chief of staff, Mike Biermann, came up to Clancy to let him know about the rumor circulating about Chaffetz.

"Yeah, I know," Clancy replied.

Over the next several days, a total of forty-five agents peeked at Chaffetz's file, and the vast majority had no legitimate work reason to do so. Agents also began forwarding by email a parody poster someone created that pictured Chaffetz sitting at the dais during a hearing.

The top caption read GOT BQA FROM THE SERVICE IN 2003.

The bottom caption read ELECTED TO CONGRESS IN 2009.

Several days after the hearing, on March 30, Ed Lowery, a newly promoted assistant director over training, got angry seeing that Chaffetz now planned to subpoena Secret Service employees. He sent the public affairs chief an email at 10 P.M. about Chaffetz's failed effort to become a Secret Service agent. "Some information that he might find embarrassing needs to get out," Lowery wrote. "Just to be fair." It was a time-honored Secret Service tradition: Sully your critics, using whatever dirt you could find.

Two days after Lowery suggested that someone should leak a congressman's legally protected personnel file, two media outlets published that precise information. **The Daily Beast** reported on the evening of April 2 that Chaffetz had been rejected for an agent job either in 2002 or 2003. I published a story the same evening saying multiple staff in Secret Service headquarters were sharing Chaffetz's personnel information about his rejection. I had the added benefit of a rare one-on-one call from a high-level source in the administration.

I had called the Secret Service for comment earlier in the afternoon, and now called back around 6 P.M. to tell them the **Post** story would publish very soon. I assumed the pleasant spokesman on duty would send me a standard "no comment" email. To my surprise, my cellphone rang, and I heard Secretary Jeh Johnson's deep voice after I answered. He had not been a fan of my stories about Secret Service screw-ups, and I knew from his aides that he hoped I would soon move on to another topic to cover. He hated anonymous leaks, too, and I'd been a beneficiary of a lot of them relating to the Service.

"Carol, I'm going to say something to you that you probably haven't heard from any of your sources," the secretary said sternly. "Everything I'm about to say is entirely **on the record.**"

Johnson told me that he and Clancy had both personally called Chaffetz moments earlier to apologize in separate phone calls, and said they were appalled by what appeared to be a privacy violation. Clancy had also just asked Inspector General John Roth to investigate how this presumably illegal leak had occurred. "If and to the extent the matters reflected in this report are accurate, then the United States Secret Service and the Department of Homeland Security owe the member of Congress an apology," Johnson told me. "If true, those responsible should be held accountable."

The chairman appreciated Johnson's heartfelt apology.

"Look, I'm embarrassed," Johnson told him. "This is wrong. It shouldn't have happened. We're going to dive into it. We're going to figure it out."

A line had been crossed. The Service's method for silencing a foe looked crass and brutish under a glaring light. Chaffetz felt creeped out by the experience. He barely remembered applying, but he wondered what else the Secret Service was capable of. "It's a little bit scary," Chaffetz said later. "Secret

Service agents diving in my background as a sitting member? These are people trusted with guns . . . for goodness' sake."

The incident infuriated his normally sunshiny wife, however. "I mean, how juvenile is that? Who are these people sitting in cubicles who do this?" Julie Chaffetz said. "I'm thinking: That's the best you've got?"

A few weeks later, Clancy issued a statement to all his staff asking them to stop blaming the media and the Congress and look inward about the reasons the Secret Service was under a microscope. "I understand that we are all human beings and sometimes we make mistakes," he wrote. "However, I do not consider the majority of recent misconduct to be mistakes. Each incident represented a lack of judgment, and that is something we can control."

A few months later, Roth reported the findings on the sharing of Chaffetz's personnel file. Roth found Lowery's venting email and published it in his report. Though there was no evidence that Lowery had leaked the information, his private suggestions looked terrible for both him and Clancy. The director had handpicked Lowery to be his assistant director just one month earlier, as part of what he described as a reform-minded team of new leaders to replace more than two-thirds of the previous senior management team.

Roth found that eighteen supervisors knew that Chaffetz's information was being improperly accessed and widely shared at the time. After interviewing everyone involved, he concluded that no one had notified Clancy of a widely known breach. He chided senior supervisors for letting Clancy down.

"These agents work for an agency whose motto— 'Worthy of trust and confidence'—is engraved in marble in the lobby of their headquarters building," Inspector General Roth wrote in his summary report. "Few could credibly argue that the agents involved in this episode lived up to this motto."

BUT ROTH'S REPORT opened another embarrassing can of worms for the Service. Both Magaw and Biermann read an early copy of the report and felt Clancy himself had not told the whole story—and that left them hanging. Clancy told the inspector general he didn't know about the rumors circulating and staff learning about Chaffetz's application until April 1, when **The Daily Beast** and **The Washington Post** started inquiring about it. But both Magaw and Biermann knew they had personally told Clancy on March 25. Magaw also knew Clancy had discussed the topic at the director's lunch that same day. Roth's agents had never asked Magaw about this point-blank, so he never volunteered it. Magaw approached Clancy privately after reading Roth's report to say this couldn't stand. The director's failure to mention their discussion let people blame Magaw for withholding information from the director when he hadn't.

Clancy called the former directors he was closest

to, Merletti and Stafford, to jog his memory. They
told Clancy he had indeed discussed the Chaffetz
information with them on March 25. Clancy called
Roth to say he had refreshed his memory and
needed to make an amendment. Clancy was frustrated, feeling he'd needlessly embarrassed the
agency. He was angry at himself for not preparing
for the interview with Roth. He simply hadn't
remembered the passing mention of Chaffetz at a
luncheon four months earlier.

Roth was furious, having already given the report to Congress and now poised to publish it on
September 30. As Clancy tried to explain, Roth
kept thinking: **These are trained agents. They prep
for interviews. They know the penalties for lying.
If you know the answer, great. If you don't remember, say you don't remember.**

Roth chose the only path he felt was fair. He
would be transparent, publish the report as it was,
and reopen the investigation. "I can't parse this out
with you now," Roth told Clancy. "We're going to
have to reinterview you."

The timing was, once again, horrible for the
Secret Service. Secretary Johnson and his chief of
staff, Christian Marrone, were planning a victory
lap for the Secret Service, a celebration of their
agents' and officers' massive and successful effort
shepherding and protecting Pope Francis on his
three-city tour of the United States while also providing security for 160 world leaders at the United

Nations General Assembly. Johnson had scheduled an October 5 press conference at Secret Service headquarters to sing the praises of the Service and the four other sister agencies who had devoted resources and staff to the all-hands-on-deck effort. But instead, after I wrote an October 2 story saying Clancy was changing his account of the Chaffetz leak, lawmakers and reporters were reassessing the director's honesty.

Representative Tom Cotton took to the House floor and said Clancy should resign or be forced out if he had intentionally misled the inspector general. "He was hired to clean up wrongdoing in the Secret Service, not perpetrate it and cover it up," Cotton said.

At the October 5 press conference, Johnson looked angry even though he was there for the Santa Claus role of heaping praise on a team in great need of it. "The Washington press focuses on IG reports, fence jumping and the like," Johnson said at his conference. "But we need to see the much larger picture . . . and the massive security effort the Service just pulled off.

"Far too often the press and public are captivated by episodes of bad news; as leaders, it is our responsibility to ensure that the public does not lose sight of the extraordinary and successful good work of our dedicated public servants, so that it is never taken for granted," Johnson continued. "Over the last two weeks the U.S. Secret Service was flawlessly successful in orchestrating one of the largest, if not the largest, domestic security operation in the history of this country."

A reporter asked Clancy about his contradictory statements, and he chalked it up to a memory lapse. "You have to consider I was interviewed four months after these events took place," Clancy explained. "My memory was incorrect." Few people, even agency critics, believed Clancy would lie. But it became clear as Roth reopened his probe that Secret Service agents had tried to avoid being forthcoming. In interviewing Magaw a second time, Roth's agents had only one question:

"Why didn't you tell us you notified Clancy?"

Magaw's answer was simple: "You didn't ask."

Clancy cleared up the mistake he made. Roth issued an addendum. But the director felt burned by the timing of Roth's report on the Chaffetz leak, as it had come right before his agency was due to receive some much-deserved applause. He and Roth met in his office on November 23 to clear the air.

"There was some suspicion that your office had intentionally timed the report," Clancy told him.

"I would never do that," Roth said. "The reports come out when we finish them."

Clancy nodded. That was good enough for him. Then he let Roth in on something that had eaten at him. Before the pope's visit in September, the director had gone to Rome with some advance agents to observe how the pope's security team shielded him and get used to their protocols. While visiting, some of the staff at the Vatican made jokes they thought were funny about the Secret Service agents needing to find prostitutes. Clancy, a devout lifelong Catholic, recoiled. Even on a trip he considered such an honor, he was haunted by the Secret Service's lingering tabloid reputation.

"That hurt," Clancy told him.

Roth nodded. He could see that it truly did. Father Joe had been chosen as director for the same reason so many others had been in the past: He was an insider with close ties to the president. But Father Joe's attempts to restore honor to the Service weren't working.

CHAPTER 26
CHAOS CANDIDATE

On the crowded floor of a massive auditorium in Louisville, Kentucky, on March 1, 2016, citizens of a deeply divided America mixed dangerously close to one another. Donald Trump, the leading Republican presidential candidate, was delivering a fiery campaign speech about punishing criminals and blocking immigrants from slipping into the country, and lamenting the passing of the "old days . . . when we were less politically correct." The crowd roared in approval.

While Trump basked in the applause, he was also getting fed up. As he spoke, small clusters of protesters had interrupted him several times. A few weeks earlier, Trump had complained about some of these noisy detractors and urged his fans to "just knock the crap out of them." Now, deep into his thirty-five-minute speech in this Kentucky convention center, Trump spotted a protester who had hoisted a mocking sign that showed Trump's face photo-shopped onto the body of a pig. Trump's fuse blew, sparking a firestorm in the crowd.

"Get 'em the hell out of here," Trump snarled into his microphone, pointing at the protester. "Get 'em out! Get 'em out!"

A scowling group of white men obediently rushed forward to surround the twenty-one-year-old Black woman carrying the sign and yank it out of her hands. For the next two minutes, Kashiya Nwanguma was threatened and shoved like a rag doll across the crowded floor of the Kentucky International Convention Center.

Matthew Heimbach, a self-professed neo-Nazi who had come to the event to see Trump and recruit members to his white supremacist group, pointed a finger in Nwanguma's face and shouted "Leftist scum!" As the men circled her, Nwanguma heard people snarling "Nigger" and "Cunt" at her. A man she didn't see stepped out from behind Heimbach and shoved her in the back with two hands. Trump continued to yell "Get 'em out" with gusto. Alvin Bamberger, a Korean War veteran in his seventies caught up in the frenzy, had stepped in to follow those orders, repeatedly shoving her in the back and pushing her toward the exits. The young woman, a track and field athlete studying at the University of Louisville, somehow stayed calm and had the presence of mind to take out her phone to film her attackers in action.

"Get out of here. We don't want you here!" Bamberger said as he shoved her once more.

"Stop pushing me," Nwanguma said.

Nwanguma, who had come to the rally alone to protest Trump's attacks on Muslims, had projected confidence and calm. But she found it painful later to watch the video of her body bobbing through the crowd, the jeers of those witnessing the assault, the absence of anyone stepping in to help. Only then did she realize how much danger she had been in. She had been lucky to escape with a few bruises.

"Protesting is an American tradition," she explained later. "When you don't believe in something, we have the right to say we don't believe in this. . . . No matter what all of the people around you believe, you should be able to go into a space [and] not be attacked for having a different belief."

On that day, neither Secret Service agents nor local police had come to Nwanguma's rescue. They had been busy in another section of the convention center, rushing to separate another protester from a man who had punched him in the stomach. That vision of a Black woman being shoved by angry white men harked back to the ugly civil rights wars of the 1950s and 1960s, when lines of angry whites cursed Black students trying to enter a public school. This Kentucky rally came to typify the explosive nature of the Trump campaign events. It was a cause of great stress, and also some embarrassment within the Secret Service.

Trump displayed an uncanny ability to tap into that part of the country's fury that simmered just barely below the surface. His swelling ranks of supporters were often white people, blue-collar workers and retirees from rural communities, who were angry at the downward slide of their value in modern American society. They had watched their own and their children's economic prospects dwindle, watched their towns shrivel from the closure of manufacturing plants and main street storefronts, watched their chance at high-skilled jobs drift beyond their reach. Many spoke with disgust of the "liberal elites," especially in the Obama White House, who they believed had elevated the rights of minorities, same-sex couples, transsexuals, and immigrants and spat upon a more traditional America, the one they imagined in the halcyon past.

Agents watched Trump stand amid that crackling anger and try to turn up the heat. His calls in Kentucky to "get 'em out" were not a one-off. In an Iowa rally in February, Trump had urged audience members to take matters into their own hands if they saw protesters threatening to throw tomatoes. "Knock the crap out of them, would you? I promise you, I will pay for the legal fees. I promise."

Three days after the shoving incident in Louisville, at a rally in Warren, Michigan, Trump complained again about protesters and asked for the audience's help. "Get him out! Try not to hurt him. If you do, I'll defend you in court."

Further increasing the risk of a violent situation, Trump's campaign team had a seat-of-the-pants style and, unlike past presidential contenders, suffered from a gaping lack of experienced hands to plan large events. The combination of the slipshod planning for his events, the confusion created by Trump insisting on having his own private security guards around him, and the toxicity and violent outbreaks at his rallies led some agents to dub Trump the Chaos Candidate.

Working detail agents fretted over the security risks that Trump created on the campaign trail, and they were annoyed that he continued to keep his personal security chief Keith Schiller at his side. The private security team Schiller led focused on removing loud protesters at events, but Schiller hovered close to the candidate like a personal bodyguard, and agents feared he would one day get in the way at the wrong time. At a March rally in Dayton, when a protester leaped the barricades and rushed the stage, agents rushed to cover Trump—and then Schiller rushed up a few seconds behind. He stepped into the middle of the path the agents would have used if they'd needed a quick exit to take Trump offstage. One agent later said of that incident: "JV trying to keep up in a varsity game."

The truth was that Secret Service agents had never witnessed a presidential race so contentious, so angry as the Trump campaign in 2016. At the Dayton rally, the twenty-one-year-old Ohio college student who rushed the barricades at a Trump rally was able to reach the corner of the stage, just feet from the candidate. Trump was visibly flustered, until agents were able to drag the student, Thomas DiMassimo, to the ground. DiMassimo said he had hoped to grab the microphone from Trump and send a message "that Donald Trump is a bully, and he is nothing more than that." In June, a more serious threat arose when a twenty-year-old British man was arrested at a Trump rally in a Las Vegas casino after police said he tried to grab an officer's gun out of its holster.

This general trajectory of Trump's campaign events—the candidate drawing crowds full of vitriol, and righteous supporters both armed and ready to rumble with mocking dissenters—was deeply concerning. Detail agents asked that barriers used to hold back spectators be pushed an additional six to ten feet back from the stage, to give them more time to surround and shield the candidate if someone rushed them. People were crashing through the barriers more frequently, something agents had rarely seen before. Director Clancy was worried too, calling the threat level for the 2016 candidates "elevated" compared to years past, with protesters "threatening harm to the candidates, being disruptive, and some just wanting to be heard." In July, the Secret Service called in its largest phalanx of reinforcements in history, a total of four thousand agents from the Secret Service and brother agencies, for the Republican National Convention in Cleveland.

Despite the chaos, members of the Secret Service were privately cheering Trump's political message about cracking down on criminals and immigrants. Many in the agency leaned conservative politically anyway because of their law enforcement roots, and often voted Republican. A good number had been quietly rooting against Hillary Clinton, sharing jokes about what a nightmare she would be in the Oval Office. As a First Lady and secretary of state, she had earned such a bad reputation in the agency that it was hard to separate the reality from the lore. Some agents who had been on her protective details over the years swore she had refused to speak to them, scolded them for poor route selection when driving her to an event, and called the director to lodge complaints about them. Trump, by contrast, was normally playing bro to the agents, joshing with them about the "crazies" who showed up to boo and hiss at his rallies.

There were notable exceptions in the agency, of course. One seasoned agent working frequently on Trump campaign events found Trump's behavior intolerable to watch up close; the man pleaded for a reassignment, never giving the real reason, so he could escape Trump's orbit. One of the Service's highest-ranking women supervisors, Kerry O'Grady, was aghast at Trump's behavior on his frequent visits to the Rocky Mountain states she oversaw as the agent in charge of the Denver field office. It wasn't his politics that made her skin crawl; it was his lack of a moral code. He cheered fascist slogans, ridiculed the weak, and incited violence at his rallies. At a rally in Greeley, Colorado, O'Grady was shocked to realize that a national reporter had hired a retired agent for protection because Trump had incited attacks against him and the press in general. After **The Washington Post** released a video recording on October 7 in which Trump bragged that he could grab women "by the pussy" without asking, O'Grady couldn't contain her building feelings. She had taken her protection duties seriously, making aggressive moves to safeguard Trump's life such as adding reinforcements at rallies and once recommending pulling him offstage at an event where massive crowds were throwing rocks and surrounding the building. But Trump represented everything she'd spent a lifetime fighting in law enforcement. His behavior branded him a predator and a bully—the kind of danger she was normally shielding the public from. That night, she wrote a private Facebook post that many agents would later call a dereliction of duty but which she considered the rational response to a dangerous candidate like none the Service had protected before.

O'Grady, a twenty-three-year veteran of the agency, wrote that she realized publicly endorsing Clinton could be a violation of the law that prohibited government servants from taking partisan positions. "But this world has changed and I have changed," O'Grady wrote. "And I would take jail time over a bullet or an endorsement for what I believe to be disaster to this country and the strong and amazing women and minorities who reside here. Hatch Act be damned. I am with Her."

Some male agents in Denver noticed and stored images of her post. Within days, copies were reported anonymously to the complaint hotline of the inspector general's office. The inspector general's team concluded that this was a relatively minor personnel matter and routed it to the Service to handle. Near the end of November, Wofford, O'Grady's direct supervisor, called her. Wofford said her boss, Assistant Director Ken Jenkins, had instructed her to contact O'Grady about her ill-advised post. O'Grady said she knew she had crossed a line and explained she had already taken down the post. She asked Wofford if she was in trouble. Wofford told her to consider the call a verbal counseling, a formal discipline used for minor infractions, but didn't spell out which policy O'Grady had violated. By that time, Trump was the President-elect, and the last thing the Service wanted was to poke the man who would be their new boss. In what had become a Secret Service pattern, the agency kept chugging along, glad to keep a potential controversy under the radar.

But O'Grady had trouble stifling her concerns

about Trump. The day after his inauguration, the day of the Women's March, she updated her profile picture to add an image of Princess Leia. The caption underneath read: A WOMAN'S PLACE IS IN THE RESISTANCE. Within hours, someone leaked screenshots of her earlier "bullet" post to a D.C.-based reporter, who called O'Grady for comment. O'Grady, who was authorized to speak to the press, explained off the record that Trump's "pussy" comment seemed to mock the crime of sexual assault and had triggered a flood of memories of an incident in which a male college student tried to rape her in her freshman year. O'Grady alerted headquarters to the reporter's call; her new boss said he'd check into it with Jenkins and called back to say the issue of her Facebook post had been "put to bed" and was no longer an issue. Then the reporter published the full story on January 24. In a matter of hours, the Secret Service turned on O'Grady with urgency and ferocity.

Agents across the country, especially male supervisors, hit the roof. One retired agent who had worked with O'Grady and admired her work ethic called me, nearly spitting into the phone. "She has got to go," he said. "She's not some baby agent. She is a GS-15 supervisor. She's the face of the Secret Service. And she's not going to take a bullet?" O'Grady met with her staff to alert them to the story and answer questions. Headquarters summoned her to Washington to be debriefed, saying they were concerned about her safety.

But when O'Grady arrived at the D.C. airport, she was surprised to find that an agent she didn't know was picking her up and taking her to the agency's internal affairs unit for an investigation. She had to turn over her gun. While she waited to go into an interview room, Tony Ornato, the head of Trump's detail and a colleague she knew well, emerged from that same room and glared at O'Grady. "Hey, Tony," she said, but he walked away without responding.

The investigators asked her a barrage of questions. What kind of phone did she use to talk to the reporter, work or personal? Had she made the call on government time? Supervisors claimed she'd lost the confidence of her staff.

On her first day in Washington, the board of the retired agents' association, a networking group for alumni, voted to kick O'Grady out of their club. "She engaged in conduct deemed by a majority of the Board to be detrimental to the Association of the U.S. Secret Service," the association wrote to members. Director Clancy issued an unusual and confusing notice to all staff later that night announcing that the Secret Service was investigating the agent at the center of a news story on a "bullet" remark. It was odd to describe one employee's personnel matter, but Clancy reported the Service had earlier looked into that Facebook post in November and "action was taken." He added that the Service would now investigate—again. O'Grady told friends she feared the agency, amid the publicity, was searching for something, anything, even a technical violation, to manufacture a case against her.

Her instincts proved right. Over the next month, she was flown to headquarters three times for interrogations; her office, gym locker, and computer were searched; she was given a polygraph test and psychological evaluation, both of which she passed. In the end, the Service charged her with three violations, none of which had anything to do with the post she had already been disciplined for. She was cited for (1) breaking the Service's policy barring staff from talking to reporters (though she was the designated public spokesperson for her district, the agency said she wasn't supposed to talk to national reporters), (2) storing alcohol on government property by having a flask in her office (though supervisors in headquarters kept alcohol in their offices), and (3) obstructing the investigation by seeking to have colleagues remove alcohol from her office and other supervisors' offices. They bucked her down two grades, from a GS-15 to a GS-13.

O'Grady would ultimately beat this downgrade, and the latent campaign against her. She believed Trump was pressuring the agency to fire her; she and her lawyer insisted to a judge they wanted the Service to turn over all communication between the White House and the Secret Service about her. The Service had long resisted any settlement talks, but they quickly settled the case after hearing this request. O'Grady retired.

O'Grady's suggestion that she didn't want to "take a bullet" was anathema to the Service's ethos of protecting whoever was duly elected. But agents and alums outraged at her anti-Trump sentiments weren't equally offended by agents who expressed racist views or personal and political disgust with Hillary Clinton. The fury at O'Grady was understandable in some ways. But something much deeper in the Service's DNA was fueling the caustic reaction, in which they were protecting a conservative in their own image. No supervisors complained about field office agents who had "Make America Great Again" hats on their desks. Supervisors hadn't raised the same harsh objections when friends on the job shared "Crooked Hillary" memes that depicted the former secretary of state with red eyes and a devil's pointy ears, or swapped crude jokes about her inability to satisfy her husband. The Secret Service was still overwhelmingly an agency of cops who preferred long prison sentences for bad guys rather than sentencing reform, who, like Trump, tended to speak dismissively about women, minorities, and immigrants. A large number of the Service's agents and officers, unlike so many other career civil servants in Washington, were pleased to see the man who spoke their language step onto the White House's North Portico on Inauguration Day to enter his new home.

———

THE SERVICE HAD given Trump the code name Mogul in honor of his success as a business owner and executive. But the real estate developer's arrival actually exacerbated two key management problems the Secret Service had been suffering from through the last term of President Obama: an overworked staff and an overstretched budget. The new president decided he would move to Washington, but his wife, Melania, and son Barron would stay in New York until the end of the school year. In addition, Trump signaled in his first weeks in the job that, contrary to his promise to save taxpayer money on his travel and "rarely leave the White House," he would be visiting his Mar-a-Lago resort on many weekends. On top of that, the Service had to increase the number of people they were protecting—to add eighteen members of Trump's family, from his wife to his grandchildren. The president had two grown children who were active parts of his business empire and frequently traveled internationally for their work. Within weeks of his arrival, the Service sought a $60 million increase in its budget just to keep up with the new expenses.

The accumulating costs worried John Kelly, the secretary of homeland security, under whose purview the Secret Service fell. The president's budget office was busy working on Trump's first budget proposal, the anticipated starting gun to signal the new administration's priorities. Trump knew what his base of supporters wanted him to do: take a big knife to all of it. Mick Mulvaney, the budget office director who had been known as a fiscal conservative in Congress, was eager to oblige, and endorsed a 30 percent cut in both the Environmental Protection Agency and the State Department. Everything would get chopped except the departments working to stop and prosecute illegal immigrants at the border. Kelly could tell the Service wasn't going to get the large influx of cash it needed, so he started looking for ways to cut special projects and operating costs. One big-ticket item in the Service's budget request was a $60 million project to replace the six-foot White House fence with a stronger, twelve-foot version. The Service labeled the new fence a security necessity, something they had been working to finalize ever since a fence jumper got inside the White House in 2014. Kelly asked his team to look at some cheaper options. At the same time, the secretary faced a roadblock in trying to pare back. Just as Donald Trump the developer had insisted on personally choosing the green marble for the bathroom floors when renovating the Plaza, the president had strong feelings about certain aesthetics on the White House grounds. Trump wanted the Service to redesign the fence. He didn't like the tightly spaced black rails with the pointy spears on top.

"Too much like a prison," Trump said.

The fence replacement project also called for strength testing and possible reinforcement of the complex's six vehicular entry gates. The president, whose travel habits were causing this careful examination of potential cuts, proposed a massive multi-million-dollar change. He wanted to dig up and replace all the lowered gates, because he hated the bump he felt when his limo drove over them.

Budget officials and Kelly tried to push off the plan; digging up and replacing the enormous vehicle gates was considered so cost-prohibitive, they hoped to delay and delay until Trump got tired of asking.

Instead, Kelly turned to reviewing the large number of security details—forty-one in all. The Secret Service was stretched so thin protecting all these people that some Trump aides getting protection occasionally had to ride in their agents' personal cars. Senior officials were told to give the Secret Service two hours' notice if they needed a ride, because they couldn't take a car out for the whole day. The Secret Service simply didn't have enough working vehicles to go around. He looked for details he could cut, and started with Treasury Secretary Steve Mnuchin. There was no credible threat against Mnuchin's life. He was getting the detail because of tradition; Treasury had been the first home of the Secret Service, and the Treasury secretary continued to enjoy a detail even after the agency was moved into the Department of

Homeland Security after 9/11. Kelly said it was time to rethink tradition. He was considering reducing or eliminating his own detail, and he suggested Mnuchin give up his. Mnuchin was aghast. He scurried to complain to Jared Kushner, and soon began urging that Trump and Kushner let him return the Secret Service to its rightful home in Treasury. "Mnuchin felt it was a God-given right," said one national security official. "He pulled out all the stops. There weren't even any known threats to him."

Kelly blocked Mnuchin's transfer idea, but he lost on the detail. Mnuchin kept it even as a female cabinet member, Education Secretary Betsy DeVos, was getting a stream of death threats and had to temporarily hire her own private security. The decision left the Service scrambling to find enough bodies to staff details for forty-one people, pulling agents from other assignments and rotating them out of their field offices for two-week stints, all to shield and follow every waking move of this expanded group of presidential family members and senior advisers. It also forced the Service to pay the Trump organization more money. Mnuchin at the time was a favored cabinet secretary of Trump's; he had moved into one of the most expensive suites in Trump's International Hotel in Washington while his home was being renovated and lived there for six months. The Franklin Suite normally cost $8,300 a night, but Mnuchin negotiated a discount. Mnuchin's choice of hotel generated a lot of income for Trump's business. On top of Mnuchin's bill, the Secret Service also had to rent a room next door to the secretary's for six months, which meant taxpayers paid $33,000 more to Trump's company.

Being stretched thin had led to humiliating security lapses in the Obama years, and it happened again in the early months of Trump's first year in office. Over the course of one March weekend, Trump's new security team would commit two major blunders, a mixture of embarrassing and dangerous. These back-to-back screw-ups, one of them largely kept secret, would test their relationship with the new Boss and raise doubts whether they were worthy of his trust and confidence. In the second week of March, Washington's fickle spring weather teased the city's residents with a balmy preview of summer. Temperatures rose into the high seventies, and downtown office workers flocked to outdoor cafés for lunch al fresco. But on the afternoon of Friday, March 10, the weather snapped back to bitter winter. Dark clouds rolled in, the wind picked up, and temperatures plummeted back to freezing. Secret Service officers working the afternoon and evening shifts on the White House grounds took refuge in their guard boxes and eagerly awaited their turn to rotate to a post inside the residence.

The rapid downturn in the weather mimicked the darkening mood inside President Trump's

White House. His domestic policy team and political advisers were reeling from several setbacks that Friday, his fiftieth day in office. Some top Republicans warned the White House that Senate conservatives were not likely going to embrace a GOP House bill to repeal Obamacare, one of the president's top objectives. Legal challenges against Trump's travel ban continued to mount. The Associated Press and **The Washington Post** broke the news that lawyers had warned the Trump transition team before and after the inauguration that Michael Flynn, the president's pick for national security adviser, would need to register as a foreign agent working for foreign governments.

After a late afternoon meeting with his secretary of housing, the president retired for the day. He asked for a favorite comfort meal to be brought up for dinner from the White House chef: meatloaf. He stewed in front of a television set in the executive residence that evening, flipping between cable news shows carrying mostly unflattering headlines about the stalled state of his agenda.

Standing outside the White House, a few hundred yards east of the entrance, another person was agitated that evening. A twenty-six-year-old engineer named Jonathan Tran walked along the north fence line several times, trying to figure out how to get to the other side. Tran feared he was being followed by a mysterious stranger as he approached Pennsylvania Avenue. He faced the north side of the Treasury building and a spiky fence that continued west as far as the eye could see and bordered the White House's North Lawn. Tran wore a hooded jacket and a backpack; he carried two cans of mace. Also stuffed inside the backpack were a laptop, a book by Donald Trump, and a letter for him. Tran, the son of poor Vietnamese immigrants, had studied electrical engineering and was the first of his family to go to college. But he had suffered a one-two punch in the summer of 2016: He had lost his job and his girlfriend, which plunged him into a deep depression. Untreated and isolated, he became delusional.

For months, Tran had been hearing voices warning him that the president was vulnerable to assassination. He believed people were listening to his calls and intercepting his emails. In his agitated state, Tran believed he had to alert the president to critical information he had about Russian hackers and help save his presidency. Tran, who had been living in his car and subsisting on junk food since losing his job, drove from San Jose to Washington to fulfill his mission in late February.

Tran hoped to speak with Trump when he arrived February 27 at the Hay-Adams hotel, where Trump's longtime ally Roger Stone was hosting a swanky party for the launch of his book, **The Making of the President 2016**. Milling about awkwardly in the mahogany-paneled reception room, Tran was disappointed to learn Trump would not be attending. "It's my fault," he told a conservative media editor he met at the book party. "The Russian dossier, it's my fault. I wrote it." According to the journalist Cassandra Fairbanks, Tran said that the CIA and FBI were following him, trying to keep him from telling Trump that he knew that the reports of Trump being videotaped in a "golden showers" incident were fabricated.

Several days passed, with Tran continuing to scheme about ways to see the president. On the night of March 10, Tran decided this was his last chance. None of the Uniformed Division officers spread around various posts on the White House complex that night noticed the thin, solitary fig- ure in a dark hoodie shuffling along Pennsylvania Avenue near Fifteenth Street. But with the plum- meting temperatures and on-and-off rain and sleet, several officers on the complex were inside their booths, trying to avoid the freezing cold.

Just after 11:20 P.M., Tran casually hopped over the five-foot-high fence on the north side of the Treasury Department, which bordered the White House lawn. The Treasury property was officially part of the White House compound and thus the Secret Service's responsibility. At least one sensor alarm sounded at the Secret Service's Joint Operations Center, letting the watch commander know there had been a breach somewhere on the Treasury com- plex. The JOC automatically relayed an alert to every guard booth and radio on the compound.

A Secret Service officer in the vicinity rushed

out to the fence line. But by that point Tran was walking south along the tree-lined western border of the Treasury property, something the Secret Service colloquially called the Moat, following East Executive Drive. At the end of the Moat, Tran scaled an eight-foot-high gate that stood between him and the East Grounds of the White House. Walking a few more yards east to the main visitor entrance for White House parties, he hopped another three-and-a-half-foot fence between him and the East Wing. He stopped to tie his shoelace before moving closer.

Some of the sensors designed to detect movement on this eastern flank of the White House appeared to be either turned off or broken. These sensors' newer technology made the alarms highly sensitive and had thus become a source of headaches for the Secret Service. The sensors generated false alarms as numerous contractors came and went in their work on a top-secret construction project on the East Grounds, so they were frequently deactivated while the work was going on. The classified project aimed to increase the president's safety in case of a massive explosion. But with the alarms malfunctioning and often shut off, the president was even more vulnerable.

In the dark and the rain, several officers debated whether the original alert of a breach at the Treasury fence was also a false alarm. "Nothing found," one officer radioed to the command center.

As the agents looked for signs of their mystery

intruder, Tran had already made it past three manned security posts on the East Grounds and reached the eastern entrance to the mansion. He looked in the windows and tried unsuccessfully to open a door. Then he rounded the corner, heading toward the South Portico, which boasted a half dozen different doorways and an ornate marble staircase, all leading to the president's residence. In the course of fifteen minutes, he had been able to elude a team of fifteen trained security professionals who had been alerted to a possible intruder and crossed two hundred yards of White House property without being stopped.

But then Officer Wayne Azevedo, stationed at the nearby Charlie 11 post on the South Grounds, saw a shadow move. He spotted Tran as he appeared to duck behind a pillar at the base of the portico. When Tran caught sight of an officer in black uniform, he turned and began walking briskly toward the South Lawn, away from the White House. Azevedo called out to him to stop.

"What are you doing here?" he barked.

"I am a friend of the president," Tran said. They were now face-to-face. "I have an appointment."

"How did you get in here?" Azevedo asked.

"I jumped the fence," Tran said.

With that, the officer reached for his handcuffs and told Tran he was putting him under arrest. Azevedo radioed for backup, not realizing his radio wasn't working. He then searched Tran's pockets and discovered he had a can of mace inside his jacket. In his backpack, officers would find another can of mace, his laptop, Trump's book, and Tran's letter for the president. In the letter he never got to deliver, Tran said he had important information about Russian hackers. He acknowledged that some described him as schizophrenic but asserted that "third parties" had intercepted his phone and email communications. Police took Tran to the main lockup at the D.C. jail.

On Saturday morning, Gen. John Kelly, the secretary of homeland security, learned about the jumper not from the Secret Service, but from the early morning news reports. He was more than annoyed, but he kept his composure, telling his chief of staff he wanted some answers quickly from the Service's acting director, Billy Callahan.

The general was up early that Saturday, preparing to head for a series of meetings with the president at Trump National Golf Club in Potomac Falls, Virginia, out near Dulles Airport.

The president had a fairly quiet morning that day. After a round of golf at Trump National, he summoned members of the press pool into the club to see that he was holding a luncheon "meeting" that included some of his cabinet members and their wives. One reporter asked Trump what he thought of yet another intruder getting within steps of the White House mansion.

"Secret Service did a fantastic job," Trump

declared about the jumper's arrest. "It was a troubled person. It was very sad."

Kelly sat at the opposite corner of the luncheon table, listening to the president's answer with his back to the visiting reporters. He pursed his lips. Kelly was still awaiting a fuller picture of what went wrong, but "fantastic" was definitely not the word Kelly would have used based on what he knew so far. The secretary had his hands full managing the fallout from the president's hastily announced travel ban, but he knew he had to get to the bottom of this breach. He was stunned that yet again a stranger had penetrated so deep onto the grounds, and he wanted to know why the officers on duty hadn't nabbed him immediately.

The Secret Service leadership, however, took comfort in the president's words. They declined to answer questions from reporters Saturday about whether all the alarms worked and how the jumper had crossed so much ground without impediment. "We're not going to have any more for you on that," spokesperson Catherine Milhoan said.

Out of the public eye, Kelly checked in with his chief of staff, Kirstjen Nielsen, who said the Service was dragging its feet, not giving her a full picture of what happened, saying they were still sorting through a few things. Kelly was their boss. He told Nielsen to summon Acting Director Callahan for a briefing immediately, and to bring the security tapes from Friday night. "Enough with the bits and pieces," he said. "Get 'em over here. I want to know what we knew, what we didn't, and what the hell happened."

Callahan told Kelly his team was still interviewing all the officers and commanders on duty that night and working on a PowerPoint presentation. They arranged to give Kelly a full briefing that coming Friday, St. Patrick's Day.

"Classic Secret Service," groaned Rich Staropoli, a former agent who was working for Kelly at DHS. "If you need to do a bunch of slides in a PowerPoint to tell me what went so horrendously wrong, you've got a problem."

The briefing day arrived. Kelly was horrified as he watched the tapes showing Tran's breach and his long walk around what was supposed to be the most secure eighteen-acre property in the world.

The worst part came as Kelly saw the shoddy state of the so-called cutting-edge technology the Service had deployed to prevent any intrusion on the White House. Nearly every piece of it had failed in some way that night. A crucial sensor that normally detects movement coming over the fence line was on the fritz, so it never sounded an alarm to the Joint Operations Center. One of the motion-activated lights that were supposed to flash when someone crossed the White House grounds didn't work. A camera in the eastern portion of the grounds where Tran entered wasn't functioning properly. When an officer spotted Tran seventeen minutes later, the radio on his shoulder wasn't working, so it never relayed his location to his fellow officers when he banged the radio switch to report that he had a possible suspect. They didn't know he had found someone or where he was, so they couldn't rush to him and provide backup.

Holy shit, this is bad, thought one of Kelly's aides who was watching nearby. Kelly put his hand to his forehead and asked Callahan how in the world all of these systems could have failed. Callahan explained they had run out of money to repair some of these devices, but they hoped to eventually get the funds and get them repaired or replaced. Callahan and his deputies explained this was not the end of the world, because the Service had several duplicative layers of security on the grounds to protect against any single failure. Kelly just sat back for a minute, saying nothing. In this case, he reminded them, none of those extra layers, neither the officers nor the canines, had worked. Kelly saw a White House that was unacceptably vulnerable, and a Secret Service leadership that didn't seem all that concerned. Callahan may not have worn it on his sleeve, but he did consider the breach a very serious one.

After the briefing, one of Representative Chaffetz's investigators got a call from a whistleblower inside the Service. "You might want to know something about that jumper," the source told the staffer. "He was on the grounds for more than fifteen minutes before we found him."

Chaffetz called and texted me to try to let me know, but I was on an airplane to San Francisco. When the plane landed, I turned on my phone and it immediately began buzzing with backed-up texts and calls from him and Secret Service sources. It was 3:45 P.M. on the East Coast. CNN had just broken the story. The March 10 jumper had somehow gotten onto the White House grounds undetected and lingered there for seventeen minutes.

The Secret Service issued a statement that afternoon, altering considerably their previous claim that they had successfully apprehended a jumper. The statement said surveillance cameras and alarms showed that Tran had jumped over the Treasury fence at 11:21 P.M., hopped two more fences on the White House grounds, and hadn't been found by an officer until 11:38 P.M. No longer was their performance fantastic.

"The men and women of the Secret Service are extremely disappointed and angry in how the events of March 10 transpired," the statement read.

THE FOLLOWING MONDAY, at Kelly's invitation, Chaffetz came to a closed Secret Service briefing to see the videotapes of the incident that the Joint Operations Center had collected.

Just as Kelly had, Chaffetz recoiled at watching Tran jump three barriers and seeing no officers rushing to the scene. He was surprised by Tran's relaxed demeanor. He rested against a fence. He tied his shoes. He pulled on a door handle on the East Wing. Still no officers came.

"Did you not have adequate staff on duty that night?" Chaffetz asked.

"No, sir," Callahan said. "We staffed it the way we always do."

Chaffetz called me later to share his reaction to the breach. He was careful not to discuss classified details about the technology the Service uses. I knew the Service had infrared and microwave sensors that ring the compound and motion sensors buried under the lawn, but he said he didn't want to be specific about what was deployed, what failed, and what worked that night.

Chaffetz sounded resigned. "It was painful to watch," he said. "Everyone was slow and pathetic and inadequate. This is by far the worst one and most inadequate and scary. They just didn't respond."

And then he took stock of the acting director.

"When I sat there looking at this individual, who had spent his entire career there, and he could not defend a single thing that happened, I had a visceral feeling," Chaffetz said. "I appreciate that he didn't try to excuse this. But it scared me to hear him say, 'This is the way we've always done it.'"

Callahan years earlier had proposed cutting back the number of officers on the White House complex at times when the president was gone. The Service was under pressure to save money, and

Callahan was looking for a logical place to apply the knife.

Wackrow said the failure on March 10 should have set off alarm bells throughout the Trump White House. It proved the Secret Service had failed to fix the problems that had been laid bare back in September 2014.

"The talking point from the Secret Service is that this is a success," Wackrow said of Tran's capture. "It was a success by default. Your success shouldn't be predicated on the attacker's failure. This is absolute negligence on the part of Bill Callahan and Joseph Clancy. . . . The fence is the same size, technology is obviously failing, the training must not be working. It's a fundamental failure on every level."

MIKE WHITE WAS BEAT.

That March 10 weekend started off badly for the Secret Service. The security level had been raised to Condition Red just before midnight on Friday because Tran had reached the East Wing while the president was sleeping upstairs. The breach prompted agents to swarm toward the president's bedroom on the second floor just in case. As the special agent in charge of Trump's detail, White had to quickly gather the essential facts and share them with the president.

That weekend only got worse for the Secret

Service, and for White as the bearer of bad news. White had a special touch, supporting his agents while also working well to find common ground with White House staff. It had been his calling card and helped explain why he'd been working on presidential protection so much longer than most. But in this moment, he couldn't come up with a way to justify what his agents had done.

On Saturday, March 11, while the president was praising the Service's "fantastic" response to Tran's fence jumping the previous night, Trump's eight-year-old grandson was feeling quite the opposite about the agents assigned to protect him.

That afternoon, Donald Trump III had fallen asleep in the back of his Secret Service detail's sport utility vehicle. Two agents, one from the Nashville office, another from the Atlanta office, had been driving him home from some activity. Donnie awoke to find one of the protective agents in the back of the truck with him, and another chuckling. The agent appeared to have snapped selfies with his famous young charge.

The boy felt both afraid and uncomfortable. When he got home, he told his mother, Vanessa Trump, "I don't like those guys. They were taking pictures of me."

His mother was stunned, but she focused first on asking questions to make sure Donnie was okay. When she got to talk to her husband, Donald Trump, Jr., later that weekend, she laid out what happened. The president's son hit the roof.

"What?" he said. "Are you serious?"

His mind raced, as Vanessa's had, wondering if the agents were some kind of deviants. She said their son reported only the selfies, no touching or anything else. Because the Service was so strapped covering all the president's extended family and extensive travel, the Trump family members didn't have a set group of agents they got to know. Instead the Service sent a rotating set of agents from various field offices every few weeks to shepherd each family member to school, work, social events, and other trips.

Vanessa and Donald Trump, Jr., had to wait until Sunday night to talk to a top supervisor about what had happened. The supervisor assured the president's son that he would alert headquarters and they would investigate immediately. "He called it in to headquarters. They told the agents, 'We want your phones. We want to polygraph you,'" one former agent said. "They were trying to figure out—did they send it somewhere?"

The two agents on the grandson's detail were called in for interviews with investigators at headquarters and relinquished their phones to prove they had not forwarded any selfies of the president's grandson.

White had been proud and pleased to have won the job he worked so many years for, and now had the title of special agent in charge of the president's detail. But for this veteran of presidential protection, it had come a little late.

Agents who work the president like to say that every year on "the show," the president's detail, is equal to four in normal human years. Stress ran high. White had joined Senator Obama's campaign detail as one of the first three supervisors in May 2007, then went straight to President Obama's detail and spent another eight years there. A favorite among Obama aides from the early campaign days, White had resisted leaving in hopes of becoming the special agent in charge. With President Trump's election, he was now the top dog. But White had spent nine years on a job that agents were supposed to leave in four. He was beat. Beat enough that he told friends he wanted out.

Now, after learning about the two family detail agents' silly hijinks, White prepared to have another awkward conversation with a boss he had known only about three months. On Monday morning, White found Sean Spicer outside his office and asked for some time alone with the president to brief him on a security personnel matter. The detail had just whisked Trump into a secure location inside his own home on Friday night after the jumper on the East Grounds. Now White had some more embarrassing news to tell Trump. He planned to share the worst part, then quickly pivot to explain what the Service had done to fix it.

Spicer said there wasn't a lot of free time in Trump's schedule.

"It's important, Sean," White persisted.

"Okay, I'll get you ten minutes," Spicer said.

In the Oval Office, White told it straight: Two idiots assigned to help protect Trump's extended family had been caught taking selfies with Trump's sleeping grandson. He made clear that there were consequences for the agents. They had been questioned by the agency's internal investigations unit and were being reassigned immediately. The Trump family would not see these two again.

Trump sat in his chair behind the desk, slack-jawed. He asked White to rewind to the beginning.

"Now tell me that one more time. What happened, again?"

White obliged.

Trump asked a question to be sure he understood. **These guys weren't pervs, right?**

No, White assured him. **They were just being idiots.**

Trump shook his head in disbelief. Then he stared back at White, squinting. "What the fuck is wrong with you guys?" he said.

WHILE TRUMP AND his son were furious with knuckle-headed agents' behavior with a family member, two other Trump family members were getting inappropriately—and perhaps dangerously—close to their detail agents.

At the same time as the selfie incident, a different kind of trouble was brewing in the household of Donald Trump, Jr. The president's son was spending more time away from home in late 2017, and his wife, Vanessa, was growing frustrated by the overwhelming logistical details she had to track and provide to the Secret Service agents who were assigned to watch her five young children. Donald Trump, Jr., had asked in September 2017 to give up his Secret Service protection, complaining he didn't like the hassle of it. Friends said he wanted more freedom, fewer watchful eyes. In March 2018, Vanessa filed for an uncontested divorce and would also opt to formally waive protection for herself. Secret Service agents reported that Vanessa Trump had started dating one of the agents who had been assigned to her family. The agent didn't face any repercussions, however. At that point, neither he nor the agency were her official guardians.

Meanwhile, Tiffany Trump, the daughter whom the president rarely mentioned as part of his family, had broken up with her boyfriend from college. In the aftermath, she began spending an unusual amount of time alone with a Secret Service agent on her detail. Service leadership became concerned at how close Tiffany appeared to be getting to the tall, dark, and handsome agent. It was prohibited for agents to have close personal relationships with the people they protected, as it could impair their objectivity and jeopardize the safety of their charge. He and she insisted that nothing untoward was happening, and he noted that being alone with Tiffany was required for his assignment. The concern was resolved when the agent later relocated to a field office in 2019.

It wasn't clear whether the president knew what was being said about Tiffany or Vanessa and Secret Service agents, but he sometimes acted as if he were the head of personnel decisions at the Service. Trump had twice complained to try to get the head of Melania's detail, Mindy O'Donnell, removed from her supervisory job. Like some fellow agents, Trump was bothered by the chunky heels she wore on the job.

"She's too short," Trump told advisers. "How do you run in heels?"

In the end, Mindy O'Donnell's days on the First Lady's detail were numbered for a reason other than the president's negative reaction to her height. She moved off the detail and took a new assignment in 2018 amid a personal soap opera. As she and her husband, a senior and well-respected supervisor, separated, allegations surfaced that she was having a romantic relationship with another agent on the family detail. The Service quickly replaced her without fanfare.

Trump was pleased to see Mindy O'Donnell gone. But he remained obsessed with getting over-weight agents removed from their posts when he saw them at the White House or working near him on presidential events. "I want these fat guys off my detail," Trump told advisers, who felt the president might be confusing officers with agents. "How are they going to protect me and my family if they can't run down the street?"

CHAPTER 27

TAKING A HIT FOR TRUMP

Early on the morning of Saturday, April 8, 2017, a line of more than two dozen souped-up golf carts were parked under a grove of trees on the lush grounds of the Trump International Golf Club in West Palm Beach. The carts had arrived in trailers driven up Interstate 95 from Miami—as a temporary necessity for the Christmas holidays when Trump decamped to his nearby Mar-a-Lago club to plan his new administration. But now they were a permanent fixture on the property. Donald Trump didn't walk his courses, but rather rode in a golf cart; Secret Service agents needed to do the same.

The carts had a few special features, to suit their unique mission. Most were new, unlike the club's carts kept in the nearby cart-barn and rented by members. These vehicles had more horsepower, so the agents driving them could outrun a man if need be. Many had large storage cabinets on the back, where agents on the elite Counter Assault Team could store their high-powered rifles and other emergency gear.

That Saturday at 9 A.M., the president's motorcade sped out of Mar-a-Lago, where he had been staying for the last two nights, and about five minutes later the cars pulled, one by one, up the palm-tree-lined drive. The detail leader followed the president into the club's entrance, then into the dining room for a quick breakfast before a round of golf. It was a perfect day, with temperatures in the low seventies and passing clouds. This was Trump's twelfth visit to this course in his first three months as president. For the past several weeks, White House press secretary Sean Spicer had been fielding persistent queries from the White House reporters about the frequent golf outings, and about Trump's seeming lack of focus on these critical early days of his presidency—or the bill to American taxpayers. The press corps bore down on Spicer, reminding him of Trump's repeated accusations on the campaign trail that Obama had wasted the public's time and money golfing, and Trump's promise that he would be "too busy working for you" to do likewise. But by April 8, only two and a half months into his presidency, Trump was on pace to hit his own golf courses ten times more often than Obama had golfed. Due largely to Trump's frequent jet-setting to his own resorts, the Trump family was on track to bill the taxpayer twelve times more for their travel than the Obama family had.

That morning, Trump and his Service protectors had deployed a relatively new tactic to deflect the nagging questions. They ditched the traveling press pool at a nearby library, where reporters had to sit in a conference room for hours and White House aides declined to say exactly what Trump was doing at his golf course. A White House spokesman said Trump was going to his club for meetings and to make calls that weekend. But he was of course golfing, in his trademark white golf shirt, black pants, and red "Make America Great Again" cap.

When he finished the round sometime after noon, Trump returned to the clubhouse for lunch. Club members applauded as he entered, and Trump smiled, then waved a warm hello to a friend he had asked to be the U.S. ambassador to Austria, Patrick Park. When Park and his party later got up to leave, one guest asked Trump if he'd be back to golf soon.

"Yes. I'll be here for Easter," Trump said. Someone mentioned that that was the following weekend. "Is Easter next week?" he asked. "Well, then, I guess I'll be back next week."

At Secret Service headquarters, the travel bills in his first few weeks were causing significant discomfort: The agency was going to burn through their $74 million annual travel budget for protective duties far too quickly. Trump's preference for visiting his own faraway properties wasn't abating.

Fearful of how they would cope, the Secret Service had asked the White House budget office in March for an emergency injection of another $33 million. An internal document explained that the increase was necessary because senior officials' travel was "extremely variable, difficult to predict and to plan for in advance as many protectees' travel plans are unknown with limited time to prepare." The Service budget request didn't mention that the Service had never made this claim before the forty-fifth president's arrival—nor that Trump was the person giving them limited time to prepare.

Still, the institution was genetically pro-grammed to find a way to say yes to the president. Working agents didn't see these trips as a choice, and didn't trouble themselves with how much their bosses and the taxpayers were paying for the president's travel habits. Compared to bills the Secret Service had shouldered over the years to protect presidents, renting golf carts for about $2,000 a visit didn't seem so high. The Service had just paid $64,000 to a contractor to test and service Trump Tower's elevators. Both had to be done. Agents were pleased to have found a work-around to protect the president's life as he played his umpteenth round of golf.

Indeed, the golf cart rental was a comparatively small cost to add to the $3.2 million it cost the U.S. military, the Coast Guard, and the Secret Service each time Trump decided to visit Mar-a-Lago and play a few holes. But no matter the Secret Service's desire to deliver for the boss, the costs for these trips were rapidly adding up. For Trump's critics, the golf cart bills would soon come to symbolize the pain the president was causing his own Secret Service.

In mid-April, reporters sniffed out a contract showing the Service had paid $35,000 to rent carts for Trump's South Florida clubs for the first three months of Trump's presidency. A **Palm Beach Post** columnist, Frank Cerabino, joined a flurry of pundits wagging a finger. "If this pace keeps up, it would cost more than a half million dollars for Florida golf cart rentals during his first administration," he wrote in an opinion column. "There's something unseemly about the Secret Service going to Trump's private golf courses to protect him while having to provide their own golf carts . . . The real story here could just be that the Secret Service is an easy mark. After all, the protection service is also paying for the maintenance on the elevator at the privately owned Trump Tower in New York. Who knows what's next? We may see agents replacing cracked barrel tile on the roof of Mar-a-Lago in the name of national security."

The cart rentals cast the president as a politician on an endless holiday—on the public's dime. Yet the Service's biggest physical and financial drain was paying to support all the agents and officers it needed on each trip—at least seventy for even a barebones visit. The Service had to pay for hotels, food, transportation, and overtime for the entire team. On top of the protective and counter assault teams that shadowed the president, advance teams had to prepare a security plan for each visit. Secret Service officers had to set up checkpoints at the entrances to any clubs he visited, create vehicle screening zones with bomb-sniffing dogs for any guests, and man magnetometers at the building entrance. Trump's weekend visits were becoming so routine, the agents and officers were logging tens of thousands of dollars in overtime each visit. The average weekend hop to Mar-a-Lago cost the Service about $400,000 to support its staff. If the president traveled every other weekend to golf, would the Service have enough left to pay for his packed schedule of travel around the country for official duties, and the even more expensive upcoming foreign trips to Saudi Arabia, Ireland, Paris, and Asia, much less for the travel of his family and the vice president?

President Obama's critics had excoriated him for his golfing trips and Hawaii vacations, noting that this travel had cost taxpayers an estimated $97 million over his eight years in office. Trump's travel, however, cost the government $13.6 million in just one month and quickly rose to $20 million in two months, according to a report by Congress's watchdog. If the forty-fifth president continued at this rate, Trump alone was on target to cost the U.S. taxpayer more than $600 million for his travel in one term.

———

BUT THE AMOUNT of jet-setting wasn't the only strain Trump had placed on the Secret Service. Another pressure had been building since just before the president's inauguration and was again entirely due to the president's choices, as well as his wife's. In December, President-elect Trump notified the Secret Service that he wanted the agency to treat Trump Tower, the location of Trump's luxury penthouse and corporate headquarters, as his personal residence. On top of that, Melania Trump shattered precedent by deciding she would choose to remain at Trump Tower with her son, Barron, for the next five months, saying she wished to let him finish out his current school year. (What the Secret Service didn't know was that Melania Trump was also using the delay for leverage and personal financial gain; she wanted to renegotiate her prenuptial agreement with Trump to sweeten the settlement she'd receive in a divorce and secure a future role for her son in Trump's company.) The law governing presidential protection allowed presidents to choose one personal residence—other than the White House—where the Secret Service would provide 24/7 protection, whether he was there or not. President Bush chose his ranch in Crawford, Texas; President Obama chose his family's residence in Chicago.

But Trump's choice created a security challenge unlike any the Secret Service had ever faced before:

to protect a fifty-eight-floor skyscraper in America's largest city, located on Fifth Avenue in midtown Manhattan, one of the busiest shopping districts in the world. Assessing and shielding the Trump family's three-story penthouse apartment from attacks created a protection price tag unlike any other the Service had encountered. The Service realized in March 2017 this wasn't going to be doable with the money they had for presidential protection, so they asked the White House budget office for a second emergency injection of $28.3 million to secure the property. The price tag dwarfed anything that had come before. Securing Obama's personal home in Chicago had cost hundreds of thousands each year. The Service also had to reassign roughly a third of the agents in the New York field office to Trump Tower duty, pulling them away from their jobs investigating financial crimes. New York City had to indefinitely close down a side street on the south flank of the midtown tower. The level of protection provided for Trump Tower wasted money and manpower the Service could ill afford, and the burden of shielding a skyscraper where the president almost never stayed only compounded as the bills kept rolling in for the glitzy places Trump was frequently visiting instead.

In April, Democrats in Congress began demanding investigations of Trump's travel costs and the burden it placed on the Secret Service. The increasing media focus on the trips was starting to worry prominent Republicans. In a public town hall in northeast Iowa, Republican senator Joni Ernst faced several questions about the president's frequent flyer status at Mar-a-Lago, including going there to host Japanese prime minister Shinzo Abe in February and Chinese president Xi Jinping just a few days before the town hall. Ernst was openly critical of the pattern, adding that she supported the president's agenda but that he had "certain flaws" as a person. "I do wish that he would spend more time in Washington, D.C.," Ernst said. "That's what we have the White House for."

Inside Secret Service headquarters, meanwhile, the acting director and chief financial officer worried about the president's proposed budget for the agency for the new fiscal year. Though Trump's travel was gutting the agency's coffers, the president proposed raising the Service's budget a paltry eight-tenths of one percent for the fiscal year starting in October. How would they stay in the black, with the president's pattern of travel, with the overtime meter running so fast, even with the extra injection of $60 million for travel and Trump Tower?

To make matters worse, the Service was lacking a permanent director at the time, a person to lobby the president directly. Director Clancy, a longtime leader of President Obama's detail, had announced a few weeks after the inauguration that he was leaving to give President Trump the chance to name his own director. Trump had a close and jovial relationship with agents on his detail, especially with the top supervisor who was about to become his special agent in charge, Tony Ornato. But there was no way any supervisory agents were going to second-guess the president on his choices. Kelly tried to recommend fewer trips, explaining to Trump that this travel was forcing the Service to cut back on other parts of its work, but Trump's only response was "Just work it out, okay?" Kelly knew he needed a new director but felt unsure about Callahan and his current team after the Tran incident. Callahan would withdraw his name from consideration and then take a few months of medical leave that April to receive treatment for cancer. Kelly recommended a retired Marine Corps general whom he knew well and trusted, Randolph "Tex" Alles. But Trump had resisted, saying he wanted to hire someone he knew—and besides, Alles didn't have "the look" Trump was hoping for. The president dithered. Finally, Kelly put his foot down, saying he was the secretary for homeland security, for God's sake, and he had to be the one to make this call. Begrudgingly, Trump officially named Alles to the job on April 25.

So into this challenging moment walked Alles, a director Trump never wanted in the first place. Many members of the senior leadership and protective detail agents resented him as well, because he wasn't "one of them." Alles was the first Secret Service director in at least a hundred years who had not come up through the ranks, a break in tradition that old-timers had ferociously resisted.

AS ALLES WAS getting acquainted with his job, the president kept traveling to his properties. As temperatures turned balmy in the nation's capital in late April and May, Trump simply changed his migration pattern. White House advisers braced themselves when they saw sunny forecasts for the upcoming weekend in the Washington area. It usually meant they'd have to generate "mini cabinet meetings" or set up work calls that weekend for the president to field at Trump's National Golf Club in Sterling, Virginia, so the president could golf without looking as if his only goal was eighteen holes. As summer arrived and Mar-a-Lago closed for the season, Trump headed north—to his five-hundred-acre golf club in Bedminster, New Jersey. Trump had avoided paying hundreds of thousands of dollars in New Jersey property taxes by growing hay and raising goats on a corner of the property, claiming a farmland exemption, but federal taxpayers would soon be paying millions to create a security bubble around the president at his private club that aides soon dubbed Camp David North.

The real Camp David, the historic mountainside compound in the Maryland foothills near Frederick, would have been a more economical choice—and one a century of presidents had made in seeking an escape from the pressures of the White House. Camp David was a forty-minute helicopter ride away, as well as being a naval base permanently protected by Marines and other Navy units, thus eliminating the need for most of the Secret Service officers and agents to fly in to stand guard as a human barrier around the property. But Trump, who had opted for marble bathrooms and gold leaf adorning his own homes, found the woodsy retreat in the Catoctin Mountains boring.

"Camp David is very rustic, it's nice, you'd like it," Trump said with a smidge of sarcasm, talking to a European journalist just before taking office. "You know how long you'd like it? For about thirty minutes."

The summer was also the season for Congress to start hammering out the final federal budget for the upcoming fiscal year. In a June hearing before the House Appropriations Committee, Alles hemmed and hawed when asked if he could really make do with the eight-tenths of one percent increase the president had proposed for the Secret Service annual budget—an increase of $18 million, less than what it cost to protect Trump Tower for one year. He eventually acknowledged he would prefer another $200 to $300 million so he could hire necessary staff and make critical investments in training and technology. Under questioning, Alles agreed it was "important" for the Service to build a mock-up White House at its training facility so protective teams could properly run drills for shielding the executive mansion from attack. Experts had deemed the multi-million-dollar training tool an urgent priority for the Service in the wake of the 2014 fence jumper failure, but the president had eliminated that allocation. Trump's budget request would give the Service the smallest increase of all agencies in the Department of Homeland Security; Immigration and Customs Enforcement would be boosted 29 percent and Customs and Border Protection by 9 percent. In the hearing, frustrated Democrats pointed out to Alles all the ways the president was shortchanging his agents and their zero-fail mission at a time when the Service was still in recovery, facing a new degree of burnout from Trump duty, and still losing employees faster than it could hire them. The session got messy when Democrats on House Appropriations asked Alles to justify $26 million to protect a tower where the president didn't live, and which his wife would soon depart.

"I know that we have a responsibility to Trump Tower, to protect Trump Tower when the president is there," said Representative Bonnie Watson Coleman, a New Jersey Democrat. "Now we have an additional and different responsibility here, I think, because the First Lady stays there and uses that as her primary residence. I believe that that is somewhat unprecedented to have the First Lady live someplace other than her husband."

"The Trump Tower has been designated as one of his residences," Alles replied, then added, "It is not unusual, I would say, and you would, we would understand this as parents, they wanted their son to finish the school year in New York, and the plan is to move down this summer, and that will alleviate some of the pressure up there in that area."

"Okay. Let me stop you," Watson Coleman said, sensing some potential good news. "So you won't be providing this twenty-four-hour security three hundred sixty-five days a year at the Trump Tower? You will only be providing it when the family, the president's family, are there?" she asked.

Alles paused, realizing he was about to disappoint.

"We will still, because the sons will be there," he said. "We will still be providing security."

The expensive security and road blockades had to continue, because the tower was the president's official residence. That Trump's sons worked there just added extra justification. The fact that the president would visit Trump Tower only three times in his first year in office didn't matter. Under the law, the Service had to maintain a constant security presence, and they weren't going to do a halfway job. Taxpayers suffered, but there was one winner from the Service's dutiful compliance with the law: the president's company. The Trump organization collected $6.3 million—roughly one-fourth of the $26 million the Secret Service spent securing the tower—as payment for rent and utilities for the space the government needed to secure the tower.

By August, just four months into the job, Alles realized he had to go to Congress to plead for more financial help. He needed lawmakers to remove the caps they had placed on the total salary and over-time he could pay agents in a year. Agents were running full throttle to cover the president's trips to his Mar-a-Lago, Bedminster, and Sterling, Virginia, properties as well as providing details for eighteen Trump family members. That required dashing to Dubai, Uruguay, Saudi Arabia, and Aspen with the president's grown children as they played and pro-moted the Trump organization. Alles didn't have the money to pay more than a thousand agents all the overtime they were owed. He began meeting with members of Congress to explain his dilemma, and his staff arranged an interview with a **USA Today** reporter to better spread the word of Alles's valiant fight for his team.

Alles told the reporter that protective agents' and officers' duties had dramatically expanded in the Trump presidency—what he called "the new reality." He said if the director was going to run his people this hard, he needed to pay them for work he was asking them to do and expected to keep asking them to do. He sought Congress's permission to increase what he could pay his people—by $27,000 each—at least through the duration of Trump's time in office. "We have them working all night long; we're sending them on the road all of the time," he said. "Normally, we are not this tapped out."

The president seethed when he saw a printout of USA Today's August 21 online story featuring Alles's interview, with the headline SECRET SERVICE IS GOING BROKE PROTECTING TRUMP. Trump saw his Secret Service director essentially blaming him for his protection team's empty coffers. "This is fucking terrible," Trump bellowed to an aide. "What the hell is he doing?"

Kelly, who had recently become Trump's chief of staff, quickly passed along word to Alles: Trump was pissed. Kelly backed Alles's goal, as he himself had been floored when he heard from his detail agents that they still hadn't been paid for work done during the campaign and inauguration. Alles had been trying to boost morale, to show the troops he was fighting for them. But Kelly felt the interview was a poor choice and was disappointed that his friend had accidentally created a public relations problem for the president. Now Alles's press aides scurried to issue a new statement on his behalf, amending and correcting his remarks to make the overtime problem appear like a modest and chronic "issue." "This issue is not one that can be attributed to the current administration's protection requirements but, rather, has been an ongoing issue for nearly a decade due to an overall increase in operational tempo," Alles said in the updated statement.

In truth, the financial problem could be attributed **directly** to the current administration, and more specifically to a president who made decisions without any concern for cost or consequences. In his eight months as president, Donald Trump had forced the Secret Service to shepherd him on trips to his resorts for golf trips on twenty-six out of thirty weekends. His family members had made roughly 650 out-of-town trips. The Service was working twelve times as many such trips with Trump and his family as they had with Obama and his.

As was his habit, President Trump didn't examine his own actions. He remained peeved at Alles despite the director's efforts to walk back his remarks. Trump privately groused about Alles's loyalty and experience, seeking to turn the tables. He suggested perhaps the Secret Service wasn't being managed very well if it was running out of money. He complained to his advisers that Alles didn't seem smart. In what had become his habitual way of showing displeasure, the president began to make fun of Alles's looks. Anyone who wasn't ready to duke it out for Trump and present well on camera earned a subpar rating from the president. "Have you seen his big ears?" Trump asked a cluster of senior advisers gathered around the Resolute Desk with him one day. "He looks like Dumbo the Elephant."

That August, Tex Alles had his hands full trying to hire new staff and pay the ones he had without further antagonizing the president. The deputies he had inherited, most of them former protective detail agents, considered him an outsider and often withheld information from him, for fear he might make changes they didn't like. Alles tried to prove his commitment to the front line, doing things staff hadn't seen a director do before. "He showed up at the White House and did a night shift with the officers. He'd show up at five A.M. and walk the grounds with them," said one administration official. But the protection agents, the people on Trump's detail, and those who had risen to senior jobs at headquarters didn't embrace him: "They still felt he wasn't one of them because he hadn't served watch."

THAT SAME MONTH, a new crisis arose. The State Department's regional security officer alerted the director by classified cable to some worrisome news: A woman who had been working as an investigator for the Secret Service in the U.S. embassy in Moscow for more than a decade—and who was frequently left alone in the agency's office—was almost certainly working as a Russian spy. In a routine five-year security check conducted on all foreign nationals working at the embassy, State Department investigators discovered that the soft-spoken woman had been meeting clandestinely, and frequently, with members of Russia's primary intelligence agency.

Alles's senior deputies assured him that this foreign national employee would never have had access
to anything sensitive or classified and couldn't have
done any damage to national security. Alles agreed
that the State Department should fire her. Normally
the Service would launch a thorough "Mission
Assurance" investigation in the wake of any security
breach, to determine the extent of the damage and
what factors had allowed the breach in the first
place. But that's not what they did in this case. The
embassy's regional security officer simply accepted
the Service's decision, and days later pulled her
clearance and terminated her. The Secret Service
closed its Moscow office soon after, as Vladimir
Putin ordered that America reduce its presence in
Russia and send home more than seven hundred
U.S. embassy workers by September.

But the story behind this suspected Russian spy
was more complicated. Embassy officials had first
flagged a concern about her contacts with intel
operatives six months earlier, and Secret Service
supervisors had done nothing about it. The Secret
Service's lead agent in Moscow had received the
State Department's warning—clues that indicated
she was in contact with the Federal Security Service,
or FSB, the successor agency to the KGB. That
Moscow agent alerted his boss, who supervised
Russia and numerous offices in Europe, Chris
Henderson, the special agent in charge of Paris. The
Moscow agent complained that Henderson never

responded. Henderson said he kept leadership apprised of important developments in the case. With no actual investigation, Alles's senior deputies told him they had reviewed the potential for the Russian employee to have done damage or to have stolen or accessed anything sensitive. There was none, they said.

The Russian woman may have done nothing other than be interrogated by FSB officers about her embassy work. On the other hand, she had worked at the office when the Russian government hacked White House emails in 2014. She had access to the Secret Service's email system. State Department security officials warned the Moscow agent that she could have compromised any electronic devices in the office. With no serious investigation, the Secret Service would never know whether she had shared sensitive material with an American adversary.

"You know the hostile work environment of the Secret Service, and the current director is looked upon as an 'outsider' because he was never a Secret Service agent," one agent told me about the way the Moscow case was handled. "The deputy director and [assistant directors] withhold a lot of information from the director to sabotage his agenda, just like they did to former director Julia Pierson. There was no protocol in place; neither was there any follow-up investigation to assess the amount of intel she took and shared with the FSB."

There was another reason for the Secret Service

to sweep this unpleasantness under the rug quickly. At that moment, Russia was a four-letter word inside the White House and a topic sure to draw the president's fury. The president was still fuming to all of his advisers and friends about a special counsel who had been appointed in May to investigate both Russian state efforts to interfere in the 2016 election to his benefit and also his campaign advisers' secret contacts with shadowy Russians. Trump regularly complained that the investigation was casting a cloud over his presidency, bellowing in one memorable exchange with his White House counsel and attorney general that he was "fucked." The president was not going to want to hear that a Russian spy had penetrated the U.S. embassy during his campaign for office.

Still, the failure to probe what information the foreign national accessed in the Moscow office struck former agency supervisors as bizarre. "You have a building full of professional cyber security investigators—and a need to know," said one former high-ranking Secret Service official. "They could have taken a look at what was she accessing. Internally, you would **want** to know that. Why didn't they look into it?" A year later, when **The Washington Post** found out about the Russian investigator and new details surrounding her firing, the Service began a quiet investigation—which mostly consisted of trying to find out who had leaked this information to the press. Some people familiar with the operation in Moscow complained that David Deetz, who was then the supervisor overseeing internal misconduct investigations, appeared to have a personal relationship with the female investigator from his time as the resident agent in Moscow. He left his job leading internal investigations the month after the **Post**'s report.

EPILOGUE

By June 2018, the president had just about had it with his Secret Service director. A delusional survivalist in Pennsylvania had threatened on Facebook to put a bullet in Trump's head and was now a fugitive—and believed to be armed and dangerous. Police went to arrest twenty-six-year-old Shawn Christy after he lodged his threat, but he fled into the woods and disappeared. Pieces of his backstory suggested to the Secret Service that he could be the real thing, the next John Hinckley. He had had a protective order for stalking vice presidential candidate Sarah Palin and arrests for threatening her lawyers, a signal of a volatile obsession with the spotlight. However, none of the many federal law enforcement agencies under Trump's command had been able to catch him. Trump asked the special agent in charge of his protective detail,

Tony Ornato, what in the world was the holdup. But Trump liked Ornato, a tough-talking agent who had served in the New York office, been at Trump's shoulder for the last year, and had the classic bodyguard look, so the president chose to blame Alles, the Secret Service director he never wanted.

On and off that year, the president's daughter Ivanka and her husband, Jared Kushner, had been asking Kelly and Nielsen whether Trump could just make Ornato the Secret Service director. The couple also felt closer to Ornato because he was someone they spoke to frequently about security arrangements and who tried to accommodate their requests. Ivanka and Jared were also at war with White House chief of staff Kelly. He had refused to overrule career experts who warned against giving Kushner the highest top-secret security clearance. Alles was a longtime friend of Kelly's, so the director became suspect in their eyes. Homeland Security officials tried to explain to Ivanka and Kushner that making Ornato director wasn't appropriate. Just because someone was a devoted and well-liked protective agent didn't automatically make them a good manager of a complex $2 billion organization. But as had been the case in previous administrations, President Trump and his family weren't looking for an executive to be a steward for the Secret Service and chart its strategic mission. They were looking for the comfort of someone with proven loyalty to them.

In meeting that summer, Trump unleashed his fury at Alles about the inability to track down and arrest his would-be assassin. His anger had been building that morning as he read news stories that were not, as he'd hoped, trumpeting news of his overflowing popularity as he campaigned for Republicans in the midterms, but reminding readers that a man who wanted to kill him was on the lam. Christy was reported to have eluded authorities as he sneaked out of his hometown in Pennsylvania coal country by stealing a school van. When Alles joined Trump in the Oval Office a few hours later, the president yelled so loud at his director that other advisers in the room physically braced themselves.

"Why can't you catch this guy?" the president screamed. "This is embarrassing to me."

Trump didn't seem to understand that the FBI, not the Secret Service, was the agency in charge of the manhunt. Alles tried to explain but Trump waved him off. He didn't care.

"Just find him!" the president yelled.

Local police would finally catch Christy hiding out in an Ohio streambed in October. But when Kelly resigned as chief of staff at the end of 2018, Alles's days were numbered. By this time, Nielsen had risen to become the new secretary of homeland security. In the early weeks of the new year, the new chief of staff, Mick Mulvaney, told Nielsen that it was probably time for Alles to find a new job.

Ironically, Alles had made strides in the unglamorous but important work of fixing one of the Service's worst problems: its slow, broken hiring process. For the first time in three years, the Service was on track to hire reinforcements faster than people left. Alles was nonetheless booted in April 2019, notified by Mulvaney that his tour of duty was over without any reason, at the same time the president removed Nielsen as secretary of homeland security and made several other leadership changes at the department. Trump wanted to make Ornato director, but Ornato said he had other plans and suggested to the president that he hire his good friend James Murray, a twenty-three-year member of the Service, a veteran of presidential protection who also oversaw Trump's transition and inauguration. Trump hired Murray after an interview lasting roughly ten minutes. The president soon after promoted his loyal detail leader Ornato to a political role that was unprecedented for the nonpartisan Secret Service. At the president's urging, Ornato took on the job of presidential political adviser, as the deputy chief of staff in the Trump White House.

Alles's departure marked a key turning point, the end of yet another failed experiment to try to change up the old way of doing things at the Service with an outsider. Alles had made progress in modernizing the Service's hiring process, but he had struggled to democratize the promotion system and to get the Service to move from survival mode to a strategic vision. The old guard resisted a disruption in the system that had suited and empowered them. Julia Pierson had learned that painful lesson when she attempted reforms and was grossly undermined by deputies who hoped to see her fail, only to have a string of gobsmacking security lapses in 2014 force her out the door.

Before he took office, Trump knew almost nothing about the suffering the Secret Service had endured after its budget was dangerously whittled down for years, part of a 2010 Republican effort to steadily trim the size of government. He didn't know about the staff burnout from the routine cancellation of days off, or that Service employees repeatedly ranked it as one of the most miserable places to work in the federal government. As he entered the Oval Office in 2017, Trump never took notice of alarming bipartisan reports warning that the Secret Service was "an agency in crisis," in desperate need of new blood to replace leadership that had grown adept at covering up problems rather than solving them and whose staff had dropped to its lowest level in a decade. He didn't heed the warnings that the Service would continue to suffer—and falter—unless the next administration ponied up hundreds of millions of additional dollars every year to add 280 more agents, replace its outdated technology, and revive its moribund training programs. In the wake of the unacceptable in September 2014—a limping veteran with a knife getting inside the White House and reaching the foot of the stairs leading to the president's personal quarters—the White House and members of Congress made solemn promises to build a sturdier foundation for the Secret Service so its agents could deliver on their mission.

That wasn't Trump's promise or concern, so he paid it no mind. "To him, the Secret Service means the members of his personal detail, agents who look after him and that he personally interacts with," said one agent familiar with Trump's interactions with fellow agents. "But he doesn't care about the Secret Service. If it doesn't involve him directly, he doesn't care about it at all."

FOR THE FINAL year of his presidency, Trump requested a less than 1 percent increase in funds for the Service, and to cover the cost of inflation, his budget called for cutting $62 million from the funds that pay for overtime, travel expenses, relocations for promotions, repairs to the Service's aging cars, and technology upgrades at the Joint Operations Center. This center was supposed to coordinate the response to intruders and attacks, but its faulty technology had contributed to the most humiliating breach on the White House grounds in Secret Service history.

In the four years since that breach, the Secret Service had, by several measures, reverted to its old self. The Service had modernized in some ways, growing more adept at identifying threatening characters on Twitter and on social media, where the president liked to engage his enemies. But for the most part, the Service had returned to its vulnerable, strained state of just striving to keep up. By the final year of Trump's presidency, the Service also had successfully fought off efforts to install an outsider and reform its two-decades-old system of promoting loyalty over competence and ducking strategic planning or self-critique. One agent who left the Service in frustration during the Obama years offered a blunt diagnosis of the situation, one I'd heard often in the years I was reporting this book. He sought me out after his departure and sent me a note thanking me for shedding light on the Service's woes. He lamented a culture in which "much was discussed but nothing was done."

"It is frustrating to me to see a job I truly loved and people I worked closely with being so poorly managed and led," he wrote. "In highlighting the challenges, which are great, most examination fails to identify the root cause of the problems. I can say with great confidence that it was not merely the 2013 government shutdown, nor was it the events of agents in Cartagena. It was a lack of strategic, professional management of an agency whose mission knows no pause. Most directly, the selection of supervisors and senior agency leadership has been disastrous."

The agent pointed to the Secret Service's corrupt promotion system, which so closely resembles La Cosa Nostra's that agents refer to being "made" when they win their first major promotion, normally orchestrated through horse trading among competing bosses. The agents scrambling to rise in the agency learn the importance of loyalty to their "family tree," the first supervisors and teammates who backed them, even if it requires later covering up for their misconduct or mistakes.

"Once you are selected and initiated into the club, your loyalty is to the hierarchy, regardless of the situation," the ex-agent wrote. "Newly made bosses have to become willfully ignorant to the deterioration in the effectiveness, morale and capability of the agents and the agency."

Finally, the Service's rewards system provides no incentive for bosses to make tough choices or long-term plans, he said. Managers relentlessly chase the next promotion, the mark of their loyalty. The rapid turnover in assignments—sometimes every eighteen months—discourages managers from taking the risk of making a decision that could go badly when it can be left to the next guy to solve. Agents often use the same phrase to describe how quickly people pass through their offices on their way to the next rung of the ladder: "He was here for a cup of coffee" and then he was gone. As senior leaders near retirement, they race to cash in on their prestigious Secret Service résumé, often relying on the same family tree they obediently covered for, to help them land lucrative private security jobs at Fortune 500 corporations and giant Wall Street firms.

"Many of the same managers who lead the charge that there are no real morale or attrition problems," he wrote, "just a lack of agents who put their jobs ahead of their families, are themselves scrambling to find retirement jobs before the brand, which they have devalued, can no longer get them over the wall."

That ingrained culture had formed and festered, beginning with the highly politicized final years of President Clinton's tenure. That culture was threatened with a shake-up for the first time during President Obama's second term, when cracks in the Secret Service's firmament were laid bare. And that culture stubbornly regained its hold by the end of President Trump's term in office.

As had happened so many times in Secret Service history, the agency mirrored to some extent the values and challenges of the president it served. But Trump pushed it further: he manipulated and politicized this force to a degree not seen since Nixon occupied the White House. While Donald Trump expressed interest in his detail agents' lives and offered his gratitude for their hard work, Trump saw the larger Secret Service as he did any other federal agency: another tool at his disposal, one that could help him achieve his political goals. He wasn't interested in the boring work of governing, to ensure the agency's long-term health, and instead the employees of the Secret Service took a major hit for Trump. Rather than get the boost of money the previous administration and members of Congress had pledged, the Service—which turned 155 years old in 2020—was stuck on the same hamster wheel, its staff racing to keep up with Trump's jaunts, its agents waiting months to get paid for their extra sweat, its essential security system repairs delayed yet again. Trump was dragging the Secret Service back and forth to his properties for his rounds of golf, but they were ultimately pawns in a larger pattern with a lucrative payoff for Donald Trump. Yes, his travel was forcing the Secret Service, Defense Department, and other federal agencies to take money out of their pockets to support the president's trips, and they handed a small portion of that over to the Trump organization. But something much bigger was under way and barely noticed. By traveling so often to his clubs, Trump was vacuuming up the money of not just the Secret Service and other federal agencies that secured his trips, but of everyone: scores of Republican politicians, corporate VIPs, special interest lobbyists, and foreign delegations, all of whom flocked to follow him, seeking an audience to curry his favor and paying his business for the special access.

AS TRUMP'S FOURTH year in office drew to a close, the Secret Service once again served as a pawn in the president's plan to show his own strength and rev up his most racist supporters for reelection. But Trump's desperate political theater crossed a line even for members of this agency, which was hardwired to obey without complaint, and exposed some long-buried political fissures. It happened as protesters of police brutality and systemic racism took to the streets in dozens of U.S. cities in late May, all in the wake of a cellphone video that showed a Minneapolis cop asphyxiating a Black man named George Floyd in broad daylight. Protests erupted in Minneapolis and quickly spread to Chicago, New Orleans, Atlanta, and Washington. On the night of May 29, the volume and aggression of Washington protesters who rushed the White House stunned the Secret Service. More than a dozen people knocked over temporary barricades to get closer to the grounds; one man jumped the fence on a corner of the complex. The Service activated Condition Red, and President Trump's detail rushed him, his wife, and his son to an underground bunker for a little over an hour, until officers felt sure there would be no breach of the compound.

The next morning, Trump tweeted that his Secret Service brought in reinforcements after Friday night. He boasted that his guards were itching to put the "professional" protesters down. "Big crowd, professionally organized, but nobody came close to breaching the fence. If they had they would have been greeted with the most vicious dogs, and most ominous weapons, I have ever seen," Trump tweeted. "That's when people would have been really badly hurt, at least. Many Secret Service agents just waiting for action. 'We put the young ones on the front line, sir, they love it.'"

Trump was talking tough again, but the tweet caused discomfort for the Secret Service bosses and started a rare crack in the Service's wall of silence on the topic of politics. A cluster of agents and officers in the rank and file complained among themselves: They wanted nothing to do with Trump's crude political theater. "That remark really pissed people off. We're not some brownshirt brigade here to do his bidding and attack protesters," said one agent. "We are here to protect democracy and our government."

The protests continued through the weekend, and the president fumed Monday morning at press reports he had gone "into hiding" from the protesters, rushed to the bunker on Friday night. Trump told his aides he had to show he could "dominate" these people rising up against the police's long history of abusing their use of force and chanting in the park in front of the White House. His wish was granted later that evening. To clear the park, the U.S. Park Police fired pepper spray gas and exploding rubber pellets into the crowd to forcibly drive them out, using Secret Service officers and agents to support their operation. Aides filmed Trump's triumphant walk from the White House to a nearby church, a kind of campaign ad to show-case his strength. Meanwhile, clergy, protesters, politicians, military commanders, and even police publicly condemned the president's tactics. Former defense secretary Jim Mattis broke his silence on Trump's presidency to announce his disgust that Trump had used military and police as a political tool to silence protesters calling out the country's racism.

But that use of overwhelming force was roiling the staff of the Secret Service, with Black officers and agents demanding that their supervisors answer some hard questions. Part of their anger stemmed from a suggestion by a white officer, Joe Vadala, who had proposed that the agency use fire hoses in the future to keep protesters away from the man-sion and reduce the risk of a breach. "Some said it was old school but 'Old School' works!" wrote Vadala, who had received awards for his life-saving reactions on the job. A flood of Black employees pelted the officer on the forum, insisting that his words were indicative of a Service aligned with the worst instincts of Donald Trump.

"There is no legal justification for ever using high-pressured hoses on American civilians ex-ercising their First Amendment right to protest," co-worker Rodney Grant wrote, reminding Vadala that they swore an oath to protect people's consti-tutional rights. "History informs us that such tactics were used during the civil rights movement to terrorize, abuse and intimidate African-American men, women and children engaged in peaceful protest."

"Can't believe anyone would think that hosing people was an okay suggestion," another wrote. "These types of 'Old School' thought processes is part of the reason we have the issues we have now."

The Service leadership tried to shut down the ruckus by scrubbing Vadala's suggestion from the forum, but anger kept building among many African American officers and agents about his hose proposal. It increased after the forcible clearing of Lafayette Square in front of the White House on Monday, June 1, a brutal sweep to allow a photo op for Trump to show his power over people protesting the police killing of George Floyd. Ten days later, the Secret Service director was scheduled to host a virtual town hall meeting to hear staff concerns about Floyd's death, a tender subject in many law enforcement agencies. More than a thousand officers and agents dialed in that Thursday on June 11 at 12:30 P.M. Director Murray opened the session by explaining this was a chance for an open conversation, and he soon expressed his horror at Floyd's death.

"What happened in Minnesota was horrific, it was heinous, it was inhuman," the director said. "It's antithetical to anything we've ever talked about in this job. . . . That's a fact and so the grief and the anger, and the outrage that came after it, is easy to understand."

A staff member asked if their superiors endorsed using harsh crowd-clearing tactics and munitions, which days earlier had been used to clear Lafayette Square. The staffer wanted to know the Secret Service's standards for those tactics and also how it would avoid engaging in police brutality. Others listened in keenly, wondering why the Secret Service, one of the most elite in law enforcement and one grounded in citizens' rights to free speech, had participated at all. Senior leaders on the call explained that Secret Service officers used force only to defend themselves and had shown admirable restraint amid the violence over the weekend of protests. "So when you see on TV groups throwing flashbangs or smoke grenades or other things, that's not us," the head of the officer corps, Chief Tom Sullivan, told those listening in. Left unsaid was that while the Park Police gave the order that Monday to forcibly remove the crowd, the Secret Service needed the protesters cleared in order to accomplish the president's goal of walking through the park.

One employee asked if officers on the White House fence line could take a knee in a show of solidarity with protesters pressing to end police brutality against Black people. Deputy Director Leon Newsome, the highest-ranking Black official in the Secret Service, said all employees had First Amendment rights, but they should work to ensure that expressing their views didn't interfere with their job. Murray, who had previously warned that the Secret Service needed to remain "agnostic and apolitical," reminded the group of their unique position. "That's certainly our right, but certainly much more problematic not just as a federal employee but specific to who we are and what we do in the Secret Service," the director said.

But conservative political views were more accepted at the Service than others, staffers groused after the meeting. Some in the Service were so overwhelmingly pro-Trump that supervisors had raised no complaint or concern when agents openly joked about bleeding-heart liberals and displayed "Make America Great Again" hats on their desks, a seemingly clear violation of the Hatch Act, which prohibits supporting candidates in the workplace. The Black employees now felt angry that the flexibility on political speech seemed to flow only one way.

Many minority officers felt Vadala's fire hose proposal reflected a deeper racism within the agency. One staffer asked why agents and supervisors who made racist comments had been promoted. Chief Operating Officer George Mulligan said racist and sexist behaviors were corrosive to the teamwork necessary to accomplish the agency's mission and, when reported, were thoroughly investigated. Carolyn McMillon, the head of the agency's Office of Equity and Employee Support Services, said the agency carefully vetted candidates for promotion to supervisor and considered any worrisome past conduct.

Several Black employees left the nearly two-hour town hall feeling moved by some of the conversation, but skeptical that things would change.

"The main people who needed to hear this message [weren't] on the call," one Black agent told some fellow agents.

"If this conversation isn't continued in the field, nothing changes," another responded.

"Dude in my office will still have his MAGA hat on his desk," said a third. "Glad I'm not easily intimidated."

SO MANY IN the Service felt worn down as Trump's time in office neared its final months. Few of the deep reforms prescribed after the security failures of 2014 had been fully implemented. The forty-fifth president was using the Service as a political weapon and shield, in his single-minded and failed quest for reelection. Quite the opposite of apolitical, the Service had become a presidential pawn once more. The new director, Jim Murray, had built a reputation for standing up for his staff, but President Trump had made that nearly impossible. Trump installed the head of his detail, Tony Ornato, in a temporary political position in the White House as his deputy chief of staff, making the president's political goals the central mission for a Secret Service employee. And while Ornato and Murray were close, the arrangement meant

Ornato effectively outranked the director. Though the lethal coronavirus arriving on American soil in January 2020 had been declared a national emergency in March, the president insisted on continuing to host rallies to energize his supporters and boost his own ego. Ornato had arranged for the Service to enable the president's authoritarian march across Lafayette Square on June 1 and coordinated the forceful removal of people protesting George Floyd's killing. Ornato had also been a key organizer of the president's campaign rallies out of town, putting the president's wishes ahead of the security of the people who protected him.

Trump's decision to travel—and his preference that his own staff not wear masks—would put not only him in danger. It would also increase the health risk for hundreds of Secret Service agents and officers who had to help secure his visits to Oklahoma, Arizona, Pennsylvania, and Florida, and even the White House's Rose Garden—for events that would later be deemed "superspreaders." Over the course of the year, roughly three hundred agents and officers would test positive for the virus, often infecting their family members, or have to quarantine following contact with an infected co-worker. President Trump contracted the virus, a security failure as well, and, after a short hospitalization and an experimental antibody treatment at Walter Reed National Medical Center, recovered.

No one in Secret Service management had blocked the frequent trips out in public on the grounds that they were unnecessarily risky for the president or for staff. Not even when an infected Donald Trump insisted his agents drive him to the street bordering Walter Reed so he could wave to supporters. The manipulation of the Service for political ends, which previous directors had warned against as the worst possible fate for the agency that protects democracy, had never been more brazen.

In the inner circle of the presidential detail, many agents were cheering for Trump's reelection. When election night finally came, Trump claimed the early lead but fell far behind by morning, with Biden the projected winner and Trump disputing it and alleging fraud. Four days later, on Saturday, November 7, Biden emerged the clear victor as final vote counts showed he won the crucial swing state of Pennsylvania and the networks declared him the presumed next president. Still, the Secret Service leadership declined to authorize the full protection detail that had always been provided to presidents-elect, a level of security approaching that of the president's own. The director and his team took their lead from the White House, where Trump had blocked the normal peaceful transition of power, a feature of American democracy that had long been the envy of other nations. Because of the president's insistence that he was the victim of some inexplicable fraud, Biden did not immediately receive the protective shield of a specially equipped armored car, a twenty-four-seven counterassault team, and a beefed-up detail with more veteran agents. The Service spread the word to confused agents that they simply had to wait until the results were truly official—when Trump conceded or when the votes were certified by the Electoral College. But many agents said this delay ignored the agency's own security training: Once he became the presumptive president-elect, Biden was automatically a bigger target for assassination.

A former Secret Service official who oversaw candidate protection said many agents leaned Republican, as he did, but they never let personal politics shape security choices. He called the delay disturbing: "If I were in charge, he'd get it all and Trump could fire me if he wanted. We don't do politics." Said another former presidential protector: "It appears the Service for some reason is picking a side. I don't know how the Service recovers from crossing this line."

The decision to withhold this extra security only compounded the Biden camp's fears that Trump had corrupted this elite band. What few realized was that clusters of agents, including some on Trump's detail, were openly rooting for Trump, a fact hiding in plain sight. On Facebook and other forums, some of these public servants who promised to be above party were promoting Trump's debunked conspiracy theories about rigged voting machines tossing Trump votes and a stolen election. Their views would harden over the coming weeks and shock colleagues, as they cheered a president trying ever more desperate plots to overturn the results.

ON JANUARY 6, the forces pulling the country apart erupted in violence on the Capitol grounds. That day, the president egged on his angry supporters gathered for his speech on the National Mall, urging them to march on Congress and block lawmakers from certifying a "stolen" election. "If you don't fight like hell, you're not going to have a country anymore," Trump said, telling his chanting followers they were all going to walk down Pennsylvania Avenue to the Capitol to give Republican lawmakers a message. "We're going to try and give them the kind of pride and boldness that they need to take back our country." The mob did as he asked. Thousands marched to the Capitol and quickly broke through the police barricades on its west lawn. After another hour of battling the police in their path, hundreds broke through the Capitol's windows and doors, in a chilling scene that resembled newsreels from a third world country. Inside the Senate chamber, where lawmakers had gathered to certify the election, a small Secret Service detail whisked Vice President Pence off the floor to a hideaway office. Only seconds later, an offshoot of the mob, chanting that Pence was a traitor, rushed up to a second-floor landing where Pence and his agents had just passed.

Despite the heroism of their brothers in arms that day, some Secret Service personnel again took to social media in the days after January 6, empathizing with and defending the mission of the armed rioters who breached the Capitol—the same ones who had endangered the Pence agents and pummeled Capitol Police officers with metal pipes and bats. One Secret Service officer called the armed protesters "patriots" seeking to undo an illegitimate election, and falsely claimed to her friends that disguised Antifa members had started the violence. One presidential detail agent reposted a popular anti-Biden screed that criticized Democrats for their relentless attacks on Trump. It read: "I tolerated #44 (Obama) for 8 years and kept quiet. Here is my issue with the whole, 'let us all be a United States again' that we heard from Joe Biden. We remember the 4 years of attacks and impeachments. We remember the resistance and 'not our president'. We remember the president's spokesperson being kicked out a [sic] restaurant. . . . We remember that we were called every name in the book for supporting President Trump."

Others shared the commentary of pro-Trump conspiracy leaders criticizing Democrats. One agent reposted the image of an upside-down American flag, a military signal for extreme distress, with the words of right-wing activist Raheem Kassam: "In less than 12 months they closed our businesses, forced us to wear muzzles, kept us from our families, killed off our sports, burned down our cities, forcibly seized power, and shut down our speech. Then they accused *us* of the coup."

Given all the ways the Secret Service had enabled Trump in the last year—from enabling his authoritarian march across Lafayette Square to the murmured support in the ranks for overturning Biden's election—it was understandable that the president-elect and his aides had doubts. Was the agency entrusted with Biden's life fully committed to the assignment? So serious was this concern about Trump's corrosive hold on the Secret Service that Biden transition advisers urged that the agency swap out all members of the Trump presidential detail before Biden's inauguration. Headquarters agreed to a compromise. They would bring back some of the senior agents whom Biden knew well from his vice presidential detail and make them supervisors on his new presidential team. Biden advisers, meanwhile, laid plans to replace Murray in the first half of 2021. The incoming team was disturbed by a director who would allow the Service to be used in an authoritarian photo op and in campaign events that jeopardized the public and their own workers' health, and let a top official cross over to a political role in the White House. When Trump lost reelection, Murray had even returned Ornato to the Secret Service fold, as he was not yet eligible for retirement, and promoted him to be an assistant director.

"The biggest tragedy is that Trump politicized a part of the Secret Service, who pride themselves on being apolitical," one newly departed agent explained. "That's the Trump effect."

Trump gave the Secret Service a parting gift on his way out, a result of him fomenting the armed insurrection at the Capitol and stoking alt-right extremists' dreams of overthrowing the government. The protection agency spent the final two weeks of his administration scrapping and rapidly rewriting its months of security plans for the inauguration of the forty-sixth president. Newly bracing for another violent assault, the Service directed a massive lockdown of the city unlike any other in modern history. Their effort, coordinated with the Pentagon, the FBI, and numerous law enforcement agencies, would encase the Capitol, the White House, and many of the monuments of the National Mall in eight-foot-tall black fencing, topped by razor wire in key spots near where Biden would pass. For several days before the inauguration, security teams blocked traffic from entering more than 350 square blocks of downtown Washington and adjoining neighborhoods, and later shuttered thirteen subway stations in the city's core. More than fifteen thousand National Guard soldiers were deployed to help secure an emblematic American ceremony, an event that was typically attended by hundreds of thousands of cheering spectators and now had to be treated as an active target of domestic terrorists.

ONE TRUMP ADMINISTRATION official who oversaw the agency and studied the Service's vulnerabilities up close regretted the political stain Trump had left but was more disturbed at how Trump and several presidents before him had let the agency down. The person told me it wasn't the staff's fault that sensors on the White House fence line didn't work, that the full replacement of an outdated White House fence hadn't been completed nearly six years after a humiliating breach, that overworked detail agents had to use their own cars for lack of a reliable government fleet, that their leaders hadn't fully equipped them for a bioweapon attack or a multi-layered assault on the White House.

"I still firmly believe they have to modernize—and not just when it comes to resources," the official told me. "Technology is the first thing. If anyone has seen the television show **24**, they would die if they saw what the Secret Service has. It's a joke. They would die."

Today, the Service remains spread dangerously thin. In addition to protecting a president and vice president and their families, and key senior leaders, the Service also protects hundreds of foreign leaders who visit the United States every year, investigates a broad range of financial crimes, assesses and investigates violent threats whether they are made in bars, in written letters, or on Twitter, researches the traits of school shooters to help communities prevent future attacks, helps local police track down missing and exploited children, and much more. This official told me they and their fellow senior national security advisers revere the commitment of so many of the Secret Service's soldiers on the front line, but they remain haunted that the agency hasn't been given the money, staff, or tools to do all its jobs. This neglect creates an opening for a serious attack on our democracy.

"Someone in the near future needs to sit down and figure out: What is their mission? Because they can't do the mission they have now," the person said. "These people are patriots. We're letting them down and we're leaving the country at risk."

It should haunt us all.

ACKNOWLEDGMENTS

First and foremost, I must thank the Secret Service agents and officers, past and present, who have given so much to our country over the decades and continue today to sacrifice their comfort and personal lives so that our democracy remains safe. I have watched them guard their post for hours in the falling snow, serve as the lone beacon of calm when a true crisis hit, and generally hold themselves to a superhuman standard. This book charts some of the agency's stumbles and struggles, but those events do not diminish the phenomenal, enduring contribution that the thousands of men and women of the Secret Service have made to the nation.

I am indebted to a group of security professionals who committed themselves so deeply to their mission that they dared to call out their agency's weaknesses to make it stronger and keep future presidents safe. In speaking to a reporter, they risked being fired at worst and vilified at best. My profound thanks to agent Bill Gage and so many other current agents and officers who still cannot be named. Each sought to help the Service remain true to its motto, to be "Worthy of Trust and Confidence." The American public owes them thanks as well.

I am grateful to the dozens of former agents who gave the Secret Service some of their best years and then graciously entrusted me with their memories to help create a more complete history. Special appreciation to the late Win Lawson and Bob DeProspero, who schooled me in the tension between a politician's desire to shake every voter's hand and an agent's need to assume each one holds a gun. I'm so much wiser thanks to the insights of Tony Ball, Gerald Blaine, Clint Hill, Tim McCarthy, Tim McIntyre, Ray Moore, Larry Newman, Joe Petro, Robin Philpot-DeProspero, and so many more. Thanks to Catherine Milhoan and Larry Berger for their professionalism to ensure each voice was heard. My deep thanks to former Secret Service director Julia Pierson, who had reason to turn me away after my stories about security blunders on her watch contributed to her firing. Instead, she was a rigorous analyst who pinpointed for me some causes for the agency's decline over her thirty-year career, including the insular culture that resisted her reforms and worked to conceal rather than fix what was broken.

On a personal note, I thank the centerpieces of my life. First to John Reeder, I could not have done this work or arrived here without your pep talks, forbearance, and love. You have been both my immovable rock and my gentle guide, depending on what I needed most. Elise and Molly, I set out to do this work for you, my smart daughters. But I marvel now at the support you have provided me, and the role models you have become with the exceptional standards you set for yourselves. Thank you for the joy and pride you have given your father and me.

To my mom, thank you for telling me I could do anything, and for being the best cheerleader. To Brooke and Henry, for knowing me the best and always being in my corner. To my late father, Harry, for teaching me the joys of hard work. To my extended Reeder and Reno clans, my bonus families.

My heartfelt thanks to good friends, who cheer and inspire me and make this whole ride a lot more fun. Thank you especially to Michelle Dolge, Julie Maner, Lisa Resch, Lisa Rosenberg, Kristi Teems, Liz Weiser, Kristin Willsey—and your big-hearted husbands. Thanks to my ornament group, book club, and college customs group for all the laughter and wisdom you've given me. Special gratitude for Mary Elizabeth DeAngelis and Paige Williams, friends and role models I was lucky to land alongside in my first reporting job.

I have been both humbled and delighted to work on this book with a brilliant editor, Andy Ward of Random House. He paved a path for me by betting on a news reporter who had never written a book and then throwing his consummate talents into framing the story of this once elite corps. My profuse thanks to Amelia Zalcman for the care she devoted to this opus, and to Sam Nicholson for smart edits that make it shine.

This book would not have come into being without a force of nature, my literary agent and friend, Elyse Cheney. She said I simply **had** to tell this story. Later, she wisely urged me to expand the book's ambitions and reveal the broader lessons behind the Service's rise and fall.

I sometimes can't believe my luck to work as a reporter at **The Washington Post,** my professional home and the springboard for this project. Thanks to **Post** owner Jeff Bezos for literally keeping the lights shining on our democracy, to publisher Fred Ryan for his steady hand at the helm, and to our former executive editor Marty Baron for his dedication to the most difficult reporting. Marty was the Papa Bear to so many **Post** investigations, and he breathed life into this one. My deepest gratitude to national editor Steven Ginsberg for his flawless instincts and unfailing advocacy for his staff; to editors Peter Wallsten and Anne Kornblut, who first saw the possibilities of digging into this topic; to editor Matea Gold, who encouraged me always to keep learning more; to Cameron Barr, Dan Eggen, and Dave Clark for smart ideas and support; and to Sam Martin and Liz Whyte for safeguarding my research.

I've benefited from the sage advice and generosity of so many authors who went before me, including Steve Coll, Anne Hull, David Maraniss, Dana Priest, Susan Schmidt, Joby Warrick, Del Wilber, Paige Williams, and Bob Woodward. I thank the stellar colleagues in my **Post** family for saddling up with me to chase a good story and improving my work: Yasmeen Abutaleb, Devlin Barrett, Leonard Bernstein, Bob Costa, Alice Crites, Aaron Davis, Josh Dawsey, David Fahrenthold, Amy Gardner, Anne Gearan, Tom Hamburger, Shane Harris, Rosalind Helderman, Peter Hermann, John Hudson, Greg Jaffe, Michael Kranish, Michelle Lee, Nick Miroff, David Nakamura, Ellen Nakashima, Jonathan O'Connell, Damian Paletta, Ashley Parker, Beth Reinhard, Phil Rucker, Robert Samuels, Ian Shapira, Lena Sun, Craig Timberg, Matt Zapotosky, Katie Zezima, and so many more. With journalists like these, nothing will stay hidden for long. Thanks to the amazing team at NBC and MSNBC, where I'm honored to be a contributor. Their smart, savvy hosts, including Hallie Jackson, Rachel Maddow, Stephanie Ruhle, Katy Tur, Nicole Wallace, Andrea Williams, Brian Williams, and Ali Velshi, shine a light, day in and day out, on the best breaking journalism, making sense of important truths for a broader audience.

So many people help bring a book to life. There is no one better to join you on a book journey than Julie Tate, whose exhaustive research and fact checking deserves its own Pulitzer Prize. At Random House, I am lucky to have London King, Madison Dettlinger, Barbara Fillon, and Ayelet Gruenspecht spearheading the publicity that brings this work to a larger audience, Emily DeHuff copyediting my words, and Kaeli Subberwal keeping me on track. I'm grateful for the team at Elyse Cheney Literary Associates, including Allison Devereaux, Danny Hertz, and Claire Gillespie. Warmest thanks to Marvin Joseph for a magical portrait; Alicia Majeed for her styling mastery; Dee Swan for her consultation on book covers; Maryanne Warrick for her interview transcription; and Quinn Scanlan for early research.

NOTES

1. PROTECTING LANCER

5 **Cheers went up as Kennedy told the crowd:** Remarks at the Pulaski Day Parade, Buffalo, New York, The American Presidency Project, October 14, 1962.

7 **Palm Beach police arrested him:** "'Bomber' Planned to Kill Jack at Mass," Associated Press, December 20, 1960.

8 **The Service struck a deal with the federal government:** James Rowley testimony before the Warren Commission, July 18, 1964.

12 **After attending the speech:** Jay Sekulow, **Witnessing Their Faith: Religious Influence on Supreme Court Justices and Their Opinions** (Sheed & Ward, 2005), p. 165.

12 **In September 1901, Czolgosz traveled to Buffalo:** 1994 White House Security Review, Secret Service History, books.google.com/books?id=86628a9v-mo C&pg=PA165#v=onepage&q&f=false.

16 **Lincoln liked what his Treasury secretary outlined:**

Thomas J. Craughwell, **Stealing Lincoln's Body** (Cambridge, Mass.: Belknap Press of Harvard University Press, 2008), p. 44.

17 **But still the Treasury Department often tasked:** Stephen Mihm, **A Nation of Counterfeiters** (Cambridge, Mass.: Harvard University Press, 2007), p. 344.

19 **The Service's investigation of the KKK:** Philip Melanson, **The Secret Service: The Hidden History of an Enigmatic Agency** (Carroll & Graf, 2002), p. 20.

19 **President Grant's attorney general ordered Whitley:** Charles Lane, **Freedom's Detective: The Secret Service, the Ku Klux Klan and the Man Who Masterminded America's First War on Terror** (Hanover Square Press, 2019), pp. 181–84.

20 **The scandal badly diminished the Service's clout:** Melanson, **The Secret Service: The Hidden History of an Enigmatic Agency,** p. 22.

20 **At its height, the agency had had:** Melanson, **The Secret Service,** p. 22.

23 **Theodore Roosevelt, the first president to have:** Joseph Bucklin Bishop, **Theodore Roosevelt and His Time: Shown in His Own Letters** (Scribners, 1920).

26 **Coffelt had been one of the best-liked guards:** Sarah Booth Conroy, Blair House Remembrance," **The Washington Post,** November 2, 1990.

26 **He wrote a private note:** Harry S. Truman, "Letter to Dean Acheson," November 2, 1950, shapell.org/manuscript/harry-truman-assassination-attempt/.

2. TEMPTING THE DEVIL

28 **Kennedy derided the idle jet-setter class:** Memo to secretary Evelyn Lincoln, John F. Kennedy Presidential Archives.

29 **"I traveled over three hundred days":** J. Paul Landis,

speech about Kennedy Secret Service at Cleveland Polka Association Meeting, May 31, 2012, youtube.com/watch?v=wENV85zx_S0.

30 **But congressional resistance:** Robert S. Allen and Paul Scott, "House Group Studies President's Protection," **Sarasota Herald-Tribune,** May 14, 1964.

31 **The prank endeared him:** Philip Meyer, "JFK Liked Crowds, Scared Guards," **The Akron Beacon Journal,** November 23, 1963.

32 **"The Secret Service and FBI were beside themselves":** "JFK's Pacific Swim, August 1962," pophistorydig.com/topics/jfks-pacific-swim-1962/.

32 **With dripping pant legs:** Kenneth P. O'Donnell and David F. Powers, **"Johnny, We Hardly Knew Ye":** **Memories of John Fitzgerald Kennedy** (New York: Open Road Integrated Media, 2013), youtube.com/watch,?v=KEHEw-dop00.

32 **Within fifteen minutes:** "JFK's Pacific Swim"; "Kennedy Caps Visit with Dip in Pacific," **Los Angeles Times,** August 20, 1962.

33 **"If anyone is crazy enough":** Pierre Salinger, **P.S.: A Memoir** (New York: St. Martin's Press, 2001), p. 155.

33 **"You guys don't want anything to ever happen to me":** Vince Devlin, "Former Secret Service Agent Kept Watch over Presidents and Their Families," **Missoulian,** April 29, 2007.

34 **But alone in the residence:** Caroline Kennedy, **Jacqueline Kennedy: Historic Conversations on Life with John F. Kennedy** (New York: Hachette Books, 2011).

35 **You're going to see a lot of shit:** ABC News interview with Tim McIntyre, youtube.com/watch?v=30Hl4EEO9Qo.

40 **The judge agreed:** Transcript of the Remarks of the Vice President, Broom County Courthouse Steps,

Binghamton, New York, September 30, 1960, presi
dency.ucsb.edu/ws/index.php?pid=25517.

40 **He checked again:** "Report of the House Select Committee on Assassinations of the U.S. House of Representatives," part D, p. 431.

42 **"Oh, yeah," Milteer said:** House Select Committee
on Assassination, Report, Volume 3, 919. Exhibit JFK
F-450; accessed August 12, 2020, history-matters.
com/archive/jfk/hsca/reportvols/vol3/pdf/HSCA_
Vol3_0919_3_Rowley.pdf.

43 **But otherwise, the agents would do nothing:** Testimony of Inspector Tom Kelley before the Warren
Commission, accessed August 13, 2020, mcadams.
posc.mu.edu/russ/jfkinfo/hscakell.htm.

43 **In 1962, at Kennedy's request:** Patricia Sullivan, "Robert I. Bouck, 89," **The Washington Post,** May 8, 2004.

43 **An author before he became president:** Philip Zel-
ikow and Ernest May, preface to **The Presidential
Recordings: John F. Kennedy: The Great Crises,** vols.
1–3 (New York: W. W. Norton, 2001), pp. xvii–xxiv.

43 **After hearing about the threat:** House Select Committee on Assassinations, "Final Report: I. Findings—D. Agencies and Departments of the U.S.
Government Performed with Varying Degrees of
Competency," p. 232.

45 **He asked police to clear overpasses:** Warren Commission Report, chapter 8, "The Protection of the President," archives.gov/research/jfk/warren-commission
-report/chapter-8.html.

3. THREE SHOTS IN DALLAS

46 **"Going with Mrs. Kennedy will be terrific":** Pierre
Salinger, **With Kennedy** (New York: Doubleday,
1966), p. 3.

48 **At six foot one, with a pale complexion:** Douglas B. Roberts, "MSU Leader's Dad Was Secret Service Agent in Car Behind John F. Kennedy in Dallas on November 22, 1963," **Michigan Live,** November 22, 1963.

48 **"If I don't mingle with the people":** William Manchester, **The Death of a President** (Boston: Back Bay Books, 1967), and Gerald Blaine, **The Kennedy Detail: JFK's Secret Service Agents Break Their Silence** (New York: Gallery Books, 2011).

49 **The Tampa advance agent, Jerry Blaine:** "50 Years Later, JFK's Visit to Tampa Still Resonates," **Tampa Bay Times,** November 22, 2013.

50 **After greeting a crowd of thousands:** "Time Capsule: JFK's Visit to Tampa, November 18, 1963," **Tampa Bay Tribune,** November 12, 2013.

50 **Women screamed upon seeing the president:** "Time Capsule: JFK's Visit to Tampa, November 18, 1963," **Tampa Bay Tribune,** November 12, 2013.

51 **"Floyd, have the Ivy League charlatans":** Manchester, **Death of a President.**

51 **"It's excessive, Floyd":** Blaine, **Kennedy Detail.**

54 **So a reporter in the group:** Richard Mackie statement to the Warren Commission.

55 **The Cellar didn't have a license:** Christopher Evans, "Remembering the Cellar," **Fort Worth Star-Telegram,** May 25, 1984.

55 **He and Mackie personally welcomed:** Ibid.

55 **"The firemen are guarding the president":** Ibid.

57 **"Mrs. Kennedy is organizing herself":** Philip Potter, **The Sun,** (Baltimore) November 23, 1963, p. 1.

57 **There, two thousand members and guests:** Louisville Courier-Journal, November 23, 1963, p. 18.

58 **"Yep, that's right":** Blaine, **Kennedy Detail.**

58 **Landis wasn't the only new guy:** Ibid., p. 142.

59 **An impromptu crowd of two thousand:** Paul Landis, statement to the Warren Commission, November 27, 1963, mcadams.posc.mu.edu/russ/m_j_russ/Sa-landi .htm.

60 **Crowds stood four and five people deep: Warren Commission Report,** chapter 2, "The Assassination," archives.gov/research/jfk/warren -commission-report/chapter-2.html#motorcade.

61 **The husband nudged his wife:** Warren Commission, Testimony of Barbara Rowland, April 7, 1964, mcadams .posc.mu.edu/russ/testimony/rowland_barb.htm; mcadams.posc.mu.edu/russ/testimony/rowland_a .htm.

61 **"I don't know. I don't see any smoke":** Warren Commission, Testimony of Paul Landis.

62 **Mrs. Kennedy wailed:** Warren Commission, Testimony of Roy Kellerman.

62 **Landis hadn't connected the first two shots:** Warren Commission, Testimony of Paul Landis.

62 **Kellerman, now flecked with that blood:** Warren Commission, Testimony of Roy Kellerman.

63 **He shouted into the radio:** Manchester, **Death of a President.**

63 **Greer punched the accelerator:** Warren Commission, Testimony of Roy Kellerman.

63 **Agent George Hickey grabbed the AR-15:** Warren Commission, Testimony of George W. Hickey, Jr.

64 **Hill felt sure the president was dead:** Warren Commission, Testimony of Paul Landis.

65 **He clambered over the seat divider:** Warren Commission, Testimony of Rufus Wayne Youngblood, mcadams .posc.mu.edu/russ/testimony/youngblo.htm.

65 **Like an echo:** Blaine, **Kennedy Detail.**

65 **It can happen all the time:** Win Lawson interview, C-SPAN, November 5, 2003.

65 **Just moments later, a young woman's voice:** Jimmy Breslin, "A Death in Emergency Room One," **New York Herald Tribune,** November 23, 1963.

65 **"Dr. Jones, the president's been shot":** Rick Jervis, "Doctor Who Treated Kennedy Relives Final Moments," **USA Today,** August 7, 2013.

66 **Some detail members rushed back:** Warren Commission, Testimony of Roy Kellerman and Emory Roberts.

66 **She shook her head:** Warren Commission, Testimony of Paul Landis.

67 **"Jerry, we have had an incident":** Warren Commission, Testimony of Roy Kellerman, jfkassassination.net/russ/testimony/kellerma.htm.

68 **In the hospital passageway:** Warren Commission, Testimony of Clint Hill.

68 **"It's about as bad as it can get":** Clint Hill, **Five Presidents: My Extraordinary Journey with Eisenhower, Kennedy, Johnson, Nixon and Ford** (New York: Gallery Books, 2017).

68 **Most patients like this don't survive:** Warren Commission, Testimony of W. E. Perry, April 9, 1964, mcadams.posc.mu.edu/russ/testimony/perry_w.htm.

69 **Mrs. Kennedy stood up from her chair:** Warren Commission, Testimony of Paul Landis.

69 **"It's too late, Mac":** Breslin, "A Death in Emergency Room One."

73 **Mrs. Kennedy sat in the back:** O'Donnell and Powers, "Johnny, We Hardly Knew Ye."

73 **He thought of the Kennedy children:** "Cleveland-Area Man Who Was on JFK's Secret Service Detail Talks About Dallas," **Akron Beacon Journal,** November 17, 2013.

73 **If I'd only been on the rear steps:** Hill, **Five Days in November.**

74 **Back at Parkland Memorial Hospital:** Manchester, **Death of a President.**

74 **Two weeks after her husband's funeral:** Mary Barelli Gallagher, **My Life with Jacqueline Kennedy** (David McKay, 1969).

4. NO TIME TO GRIEVE

76 **"Fifty odd coincidences":** Jim Bishop, **A Day in the Life of President Kennedy** (New York: Random House, 1964).

76 **"Do you suppose I could get":** "Popular Reading?" **Warren Times-Mirror,** August 1, 1962.

77 **He simply didn't want to be the cause:** "149.8 Million Whittled from Kennedy Money Bill," **The Greenville News,** April 2, 1963.

77 **Their chief stepped forward:** William Manchester, **The Death of a President** (Boston: Back Bay Books, 1967), p. 389.

78 **"They paid no attention to me":** Manchester, **Death of a President.**

78 **A helicopter airlifted President Johnson:** Ibid., p. 405.

79 **"There was no feeling that he blamed anyone":** Gerald Blaine, **The Kennedy Detail: JFK's Secret Service Agents Break Their Silence** (New York: Gallery Books, 2011).

81 **He rose quickly in supervisor jobs:** "Former Secret Service Chief James Rowley, 84, Dies," **The Washington Post,** November 2, 1992.

81 **The president liked to tell the story:** Ibid.

82 **"Please, Mrs. Kennedy":** Clint Hill, **Five Days in November** (New York: Gallery Books, 2014).

83 **Johnson confided that he had initially decided:** Manchester, **Death of a President.**

84 **Hill clenched his jaw:** Clint Hill, **Five Presidents: My Extraordinary Journey with Eisenhower, Kennedy, Johnson, Nixon and Ford** (New York: Gallery Books, 2017).

85 **Kirkwood wouldn't mention:** Christopher Evans, "Remembering the Cellar," **Fort Worth Star-Telegram,** May 25, 1984.

85 **Despite their efforts:** Drew Pearson, **Washington Merry-Go-Round: The Drew Pearson Diaries** (Lincoln, Neb.: Potomac Books, 2015).

86 **"I have praised the Secret Service":** Ibid., p. 211.

87 **"We didn't say anything":** Evans, "Remembering the Cellar."

88 **But another blow to the Service:** Richard Dudman, "Ex-Chief Criticizes Performance of Secret Service in Dallas," **St. Louis Post-Dispatch,** December 8, 1963.

89 **"and why that agent in the front seat":** Ibid.

90 **The team was then also asked to examine:** Mary Ferrell Foundation, **Notes on Warren Commission's Creation,** maryferrell.org/pages/Walkthrough_Formation _of_the_Warren_Commission.html.

92 **IBM had computerized millions:** Planning Document: United States Secret Service, "Plan to Meet Requirements for Expanded Protection of the President and Vice President of the United States," Aug 27, 1964.

93 **"I think we fell far short of the mark":** Silvio Conte Oral History Interview, John F. Kennedy Presidential Library, October 18, 1977, accessed August 13, 2020, jfklibrary.org/asset-viewer/archives/JFKOH/Conte %2C%20Silvio%20O/JFKOH-SOC-01/JFKOH-SOC-01.

93 **"There were a number of times when he slipped":** Robert S. Allen and Paul Scott, "House Group Stud-

ies President's Protection," **Sarasota Herald-Tribune,** May 14, 1964.

95 **But President Theodore Roosevelt:** Philip Melanson, **The Secret Service: The Hidden History of an Enigmatic Agency** (Carroll & Graf, 2002), p. 33.

96 **"I won't even go to the bathroom":** Conversation with James Rowley, President Lyndon Johnson tapes, May 13, 1964, accessed August 13, 2020, millercenter.org/the-presidency/secret-white-house-tapes/conversation-james-rowley-march-2-1964 and millercenter.org/the-presidency/secret-white-house-tapes/conversation-james-rowley-may-13-1964.

96 **The president grew even more hostile:** Ibid.

99 **His final answer for the history books:** Warren Commission, Testimony of James Rowley, June 16, 1964.

100 **Somehow, he didn't break:** Conversation with James Rowley, President Lyndon Johnson tapes, May 13, 1964.

102 **Mr. Rowley tried to tell us:** Warren Commission, Testimony of C. Douglas Dillon, September 2, 1964.

103 **"If I were Chief Rowley":** Conversation with McGeorge Bundy, Lyndon B. Johnson tapes, September 27, 1964.

103 **"All of the Secret Service men":** Warren Commission, Testimony of Ralph Yarborough.

5. ONE LAST DAY ON THE TRAIL

107 **But that morning, Cornelia Wallace heard:** Stephan Lesher, **George Wallace: American Populist** (New York: Da Capo Press, 1995), pp. 479–82.

107 **"I don't think I'm going to go":** "George Wallace: Settin' the Woods on Fire," PBS documentary, pbs.org/

wgbh/amex/wallace/filmmore/transcript
/transcript1.html.

107 **"One more day of campaigning"**: "George Wallace: Settin' the Woods on Fire."

107 **He scolded his wife:** Dan T. Carter, The Politics of Rage: George Wallace, the Origins of the New Conservatism, and the Transformation of American Politics (Baton Rouge: Louisiana State University Press, 2000), p. 435.

107 **They headed to the airport:** "George Wallace: Settin' the Woods on Fire."

108 **"segregation now, segregation tomorrow"**: Governor George Wallace inaugural speech, January 14, 1963, accessed August 13, 2020, digital.archives.alabama. gov/digital/collection/voices/id/2952.

109 **"I have a dream that one day"**: Martin Luther King, Jr., "I Have a Dream," Washington, D.C., August 28, 1963, accessed August 13, 2020, americanrhetoric. com/speeches/mlkihaveadream.htm.

112 **And as King had done:** "George Wallace: Settin' the Woods on Fire."

112 **"Somebody's going to get killed"**: Time, May 1972.

112 **The unemployed twenty-one-year-old:** "Now, Arthur Bremer Is Known," The New York Times, May 22, 1972.

113 **Nevertheless, Bremer chose his outfit:** George Wallace shooting, Prince George's County Police investigative files.

113 **"I've decided Wallace would have the honor"**: Arthur Bremer, An Assassin's Diary (Pocket Books, 1973).

113 **Bremer could not recall his mother ever hugging him:** "Now, Arthur Bremer Is Known."

113 **"No English or History test"**: Bremer, Assassin's Diary.

114 **Bremer got a job after high school:** George Wallace shooting, Prince George's County Police investigative files.

114 **He ran up to a woman he didn't know:** Joan Pemrich statement, George Wallace shooting, Prince George's County Police investigative files.

114 **Bremer pleaded for her to reconsider:** Pemrich statement, George Wallace shooting, Prince George's County Police investigative files.

115 **Bremer wrote how easily he could have killed:** Bremer, Assassin's Diary.

116 **"Three men in reflective orange overalls":** Ibid.

117 **Dozens of Canadian police:** "We Confronted Nixon!" New Canada, vol. 3, no. 3, July 1972.

118 **At one point, Bremer saw Secret Service agents:** Bremer, Assassin's Diary.

119 **"Another security breakdown":** Ibid.

119 **"Their faces were one inch from the glass":** Ibid.

120 **Walking up to the Wheaton stage:** Lawrence Dominguez statement, George Wallace shooting, Prince George's County Police investigative files.

121 **"I imagine the coach":** Dan Fesperman, "20 Years into Life Sentence, George Wallace Still Struggles with Pain," The Sun (Baltimore), May 14, 1992.

121 **But several agents:** Agent Jim Taylor statement, George Wallace shooting, Prince George's County Police investigative files.

122 **Farrar directed his cameraman to film him:** Lesher, George Wallace, p. 480.

122 **But the agent walked away:** Statement of television producer Fred Farrar to investigators, George Wallace shooting, Prince George's County Police investigative files.

123 **"I think it's best we cancel":** "Wallace Shunned 1972 Security Tip," The New York Times, October 2, 1975.

124 **"It was a very calm crowd"**: Cornelia Wallace interview, "George Wallace: Settin' the Woods on Fire."

124 **Wallace began his speech:** William Grieder, "Wallace Is Shot, Legs Paralyzed; Suspect Seized at Laurel Rally," **The Washington Post,** May 16, 1972.

124 **Their job was to scan:** Robert Innamorati statement, George Wallace shooting, Prince George's County Police investigative files.

124 **One of the agents was:** Secret Service records submitted to investigators, George Wallace shooting, Prince George's County Police investigative files.

125 **"Keep an eye on that guy":** John Davey statement, George Wallace shooting, Prince George's County Police investigative files.

125 **Capizzi felt uneasy:** Daniel Capizzi statement, George Wallace shooting, Prince George's County Police investigative files.

125 **Prince George's County Police corporal:** Aaron Kraut, "George Wallace's assassination attempt: FBI agent reflects, 40 years later," The Washington Post, May 9, 2012.

126 **The governor pecked campaign worker Dora Thompson:** Madelyn Saunders statement, George Wallace shooting, Prince George's County Police investigative files.

126 **As the point man:** Bill Breen statement, George Wallace shooting, Prince George's County Police investigative files.

126 **A few others in the crowd piggybacked:** Daniel Capizzi statement, George Wallace shooting, Prince George's County Police investigative files.

126 **"That's all right":** Neil A. Hamilton, **The 1970s** (New York: Facts on File, 2006).

127 **Other agents filled in:** James Taylor statement, George Wallace shooting, Prince George's County Police investigative files.

127 **In that hardly noticeable span:** Madelyn Saunders statement, George Wallace shooting, Prince George's County Police investigative files.

128 **Agent Nick Zarvos spun backward:** Video of Wallace shooting, accessed August 13, 2020, youtube.com/watch?v=GUeywO7-ZXw.

129 **"I thought they'd shoot him again":** Cornelia Wallace interview, "George Wallace: Settin' the Woods on Fire."

129 **When Secret Service agents and police officers lifted her:** Erin Edgemon, "Blood-Stained Clothes Worn by George Wallace in May 15, 1972 Shooting Held in State Archives," Alabama.com, May 15, 2014.

6. THE PRESIDENT'S SPIES

130 **He had just started a meeting:** Author's review of Richard Nixon's presidential calendar, accessed August 12, 2020, nixonlibrary.gov/sites/default/files/virtuallibrary/documents/PDD/1972/075%20May%201-15%201972.pdf.

130 **He pulled his boss into a side room:** Author's review of Richard Nixon's presidential daily diary, accessed August 12, 2020, nixonlibrary.gov/virtuallibrary/documents/PDD/1972/075%20May%201-15%201972.pdf.

132 **Nixon hoped to tarnish the senator's political star:** Carl Bernstein and Bob Woodward, "Woodward and Bernstein: 40 Years After Watergate, Nixon Was Far Worse than We Thought," *The Washington Post*, June 8, 2012.

133 **"Why don't we just do it":** Nixon White House tapes, May 15, 1975, accessed August 13, 2020, nixontapes.org/wallace.html.

134 **"You tell him to just keep his spirit":** Nixon White

House tapes, May 15, 1975, accessed August 13, 2020, nixontapes.org/wallace.html.

134 "Well, he's liable to be out there": Nixon White House tapes, May 15, 1975, accessed August 13, 2020, nixontapes.org/wallace.html.

134 He welcomed their guests: Nixon remarks on reopening of the Blue Room, American Presidency Project, May 15, 1972.

135 "Didn't he ask for it?": Nixon White House tapes, May 15, 1975, accessed August 13, 2020, nixontapes. org/wallace.html.

136 Kleindienst insisted that police: Nixon White House tapes, accessed August 12, 2020, nixontapes.org/ mp3/024-097.mp3.

138 Colson said he needed him: Fred Emery, Watergate: The Corruption of American Politics and the Fall of Richard Nixon (New York: Crown, 1994).

138 Rowley instructed an agent: Dan T. Carter, The Politics of Rage: George Wallace, the Origins of the New Conservatism, and the Transformation of American Politics (Baton Rouge: Louisiana State University Press, 2000), p. 440.

138 A pornographic comic book: James T. Wooten, "Milwaukee Man Held as Suspect," The New York Times, May 16, 1972.

138 "In America, here one": Ibid.

139 The plan to plant evidence died: Carter, Politics of Rage, p. 440.

139 "He doesn't like to have to explain": Maxine Chesire, "Senator Gives Up Guards," The Washington Post, June 8, 1972.

141 On June 17, 1972, D.C. police arrested: Alfred E. Lewis, "5 Held in Plot to Bug Democrats' Office Here," The Washington Post, June 18, 1972.

142 **That man, James McCord:** Bob Woodward and Carl Bernstein, "GOP Security Aide Among Five Arrested in Bugging Affair," **The Washington Post,** June 19, 1972.

144 **"I want one who's our boy":** Author listened to the recording of the Nixon tapes housed at the Richard Nixon Presidential Library and Museum.

146 **"You apparently don't get the picture":** Clint Hill, **Five Presidents: My Extraordinary Journey with Eisenhower, Kennedy, Johnson, Nixon and Ford** (New York: Gallery Books, 2017), p. 389.

146 **Hill would always feel protective:** Ibid., pp. 390–91.

146 **At 3:15 P.M., Haldeman called Newbrand:** George Lardner, "President Nixon Ordered Spy Placed on Sen. Kennedy's Secret Service Detail," **The Washington Post,** February 8, 1997.

148 **Nixon and his close friend Bebe Rebozo:** Jack Anderson, "Merry-Go-Round," **The Washington Post,** July 16, 1973.

148 **One of the president's legal assistants bragged:** Ibid., November 9, 1973.

151 **The president had whipped up the crowd:** Chief Blackmore, 1983 interview with Harry Farrell, fliphtml5 .com/kixm/owrc/basic/51-60, p. 38.

152 **"We know that":** Harry Farrell, "How Nixon Incited 1970 San Jose Riot," **San Jose Mercury News,** May 22, 1994.

153 **Both spectators and reporters at the event:** Stanford Daily News, October 30, 1970, and October 30, 1972.

153 **"We wanted some confrontation":** H. R. Haldeman, **The Haldeman Diaries: Inside the Nixon White House** (New York: G. P. Putnam's Sons, 1994), p. 205.

154 **On September 6, The Washington Post reported:** Bob Woodward and Carl Bernstein, "Nixon Wiretapped Brother," The Washington Post, September 6, 1973.

154 **A day later, the Senate's Watergate Committee:** "Did Nixon Wiretap His Brother?" UPI, September 7, 1973.

155 **The papers called it the Saturday Night Massacre:** "The Watergate Story: A Timeline," The Washington Post, accessed August 13, 2020, washingtonpost.com/wp-srv/politics/special/watergate/timeline.html.

157 **It was polite code for his new task:** "The Secret Service: New Boss for a Troubled Team," Time, November 26, 1973.

158 **Wong warned Butterfield:** Bob Woodward, The Last of the President's Men (New York: Simon & Schuster, 2016), p. 79.

158 **"Goddamn it":** Ibid., p. 77.

159 **"Yes," he gulped:** Alicia Shepard, "The Man Who Revealed the Nixon Tapes," The Washington Post, June 14, 2012.

160 **Fifteen days later:** "The Watergate Story," The Washington Post, accessed August 12, 2020, washingtonpost.com/wp-srv/politics/special/watergate/part3.html.

7. A CASUAL WALK TO CHURCH

166 **Nancy Reagan had been floored:** Nancy Reagan, My Turn (New York: Random House, 1989).

170 **Starting at about 9 A.M., Nixon gave a pained farewell speech:** Transcript of Nixon's Farewell Speech to Cabinet and Staff Members in the Capital, The New York Times, August 10, 1974.

171 "My personal mood was very emotional": Richard Keiser interview with Richard Norton Smith for Gerald R. Ford Oral History Project, November 15, 2010.

174 Buendorf was walking immediately behind: Ron Nessen notes about the shooting, September 5, 1975, accessed August 12, 2020, fordlibrarymuseum.gov/library/document/0151/1671504.pdf.

175 "So I'm looking down": Larry Buendorf interview for Gerald Ford Oral History Project, June 22, 2010, accessed August 13, 2020, geraldrfordfoundation.org/centennial-docs/oralhistory/wp-content/uploads/2013/05/Larry-Buendorf-.pdf.

178 "It didn't go off!": 1994 Secret Service security assessment, accessed August 13, 2020, prop1.org/park/pave/list.htm.

178 the agents who interviewed her: Leroy F. Aarons, "The Emergence of Sara Jane Moore," The Washington Post, September 28, 1975.

179 Then she headed to the St. Francis hotel: Vincent Palamara, Who's Who in the Secret Service (TrineDay, 2018), p. 102.

179 A local police officer pulled the gun: Geri Spieler, Taking Aim at the President: The Remarkable Story of the Woman Who Shot at Gerald Ford (New York: Palgrave Macmillan, 2008).

179 "I felt very bad I was not there": Richard Keiser, Interview with Richard Norton Smith for Gerald R. Ford Oral History Project, November 15, 2010.

180 Uniformed officers and agents at the White House: Mel Ayton, Hunting the President: Threats, Plots and Assassination Attempts—from FDR to Obama (Washington, D.C.: Regnery History, 2014), p. 128.

181 Parr was mesmerized by the central character: Jerry Parr, In the Secret Service: The True Story of the Man

Who Saved President Reagan's Life (Carol Stream, Ill.: Tyndale House, 2013).

183 They had mapped out every step: Del Wilber, **Rawhide Down: The Near Assassination of Ronald Reagan** (New York: Henry Holt, 2011), p. 61.

183 This "routine" visit would require: Parr, **In the Secret Service.**

185 With his right hand, Reagan waved: CBS video of the shooting, March 31, 1981.

186 Agents of Parr's era practiced a series of drills: Parr, **In the Secret Service,** p. 215.

188 Inside the limo, Reagan groaned: Ibid., p. 216.

188 **God, don't let me run over Timmy:** Wilber, **Rawhide Down,** p. 83.

189 "We're going to Crown": Ibid., p. 89.

191 "Get an ambulance": Ibid., p. 91.

192 Forcing himself to speak slowly: Nancy Reagan, **My Turn,** p. 1.

193 "Maybe he's insisting on seeing": Wilber, **Rawhide Down,** p. 104.

193 The First Lady reached over: Ibid., p. 105.

193 "George, if this traffic doesn't open up": Nancy Reagan, **My Turn,** p. 2.

193 "No, no, you can't do that": Ibid., p. 2.

193 He was glad he had thought: Wilber, **Rawhide Down,** p. 105.

194 A thought flashed through his mind: Parr, **In the Secret Service,** p. 221.

199 "I prayed all the prayers I knew": Notes from unpublished interview with the late John Simpson, provided by Del Wilber.

200 They consulted with Delahanty: "F.B.I. Confirms Malfunctioning of Explosive Bullet That Struck Reagan," **The New York Times,** April 4, 1981.

200 **"He's in the car!":** CBS video of the shooting, March 30, 1981.

201 **A worried co-worker drove Carolyn Parr home:** Parr, **In the Secret Service,** p. 229.

202 **He had resigned:** Ibid., p. 230.

202 **"I think you saved the president's life":** Ibid., p. 236.

8. BATTENING DOWN THE HATCHES

204 **"After viewing the video tapes":** T. R. Reid, "Secret Service Checking Limousine Position," **The Washington Post,** April 1, 1981.

204 **"The Secret Service did an absolutely marvelous job":** Ira Allen, "Washington News," UPI, April 2, 1981.

208 **"I am not overly intelligent":** Maureen Santini, "He Would Have Died to Keep the President Alive," Associated Press, May 15, 1985.

210 **"We'd never heard a supervisor say that":** Victor Vargas, **The Man Behind the Suit,** Arizona State University documentary.

211 **"You need to get some rest":** "Reagan's Close Call," **Newsweek,** April 1981.

212 **Deaver glanced at him and felt a chill:** Michael K. Deaver, **A Different Drummer: My Thirty Years with Ronald Reagan** (New York: Harper, 2003).

9. NIGHT OF THE LONG KNIVES

227 **"I realize that is the popular perception":** "Head of Secret Service Says Its Job Is Now Tougher," **The New York Times,** November 30, 1981.

230 **He had led Reagan's detail:** "Simpson Named to Head Secret Service," UPI, December 2, 1981.

230 **He sought to favor:** Stephen Hunter and John Bain-

bridge, Jr., **American Gunfight: The Plot to Kill President Truman—and the Shoot-out That Stopped It** (New York: Simon & Schuster, 2007).

235 **And though she knew it was irrational:** Nancy Reagan, **My Turn** (New York: Random House, 1998).

236 **"If it makes you feel better":** Ibid.

10. A HAPPY SERVICE, A RISING THREAT

240 **His father, who became a U.S. senator:** Information accessed August 11, 2020, from michaelkranish.com/Michael_Kranish/Bush_Family_History.html.

242 **When the Bushes knew they'd be staying:** Doro Bush Koch, **My Father, My President** (New York: Grand Central Publishing, 2006).

243 **"That's unbelievable":** Ibid.

245 **What better place to find cheering supporters:** Lisa Zagaroli, "Hamtramck Welcomes President's Plan for Economic Aid to Poland," Associated Press, April 18, 1989.

248 **Later, just weeks after Bush was elected:** John Daughetee statement to the Oakland Police Department, August 1989.

250 **"I almost killed President Bush":** "Robbery Suspect Says Voices Told Him to Kill President," Associated Press, August 9, 1989.

253 **seeking a personal audience:** " 'Kuwait Will Endure,' Bush Vows," **Los Angeles Times,** September 28, 1990.

256 **Osama bin Laden was the millionaire son:** **The 9/11 Commission Report: Final Report of the National Commission on the Terrorist Attacks Upon the United States** (New York: W. W. Norton, 2004), p. 56.

257 **"We have to do something to take them out":** Lisa

Anderson, "Witness Details Bin Laden Terrorism," **Chicago Tribune,** February 7, 2001.

259 **Another top Bush adviser translated this:** Chase Untermeyer, **When Things Went Right: The Dawn of the Reagan-Bush Administration** (College Station: Texas A&M University Press, 2013).

260 **He and fellow leaders of al-Qaeda:** U.S. intelligence report, "Fatwa to Attack U.S. Interests in Saudi Arabia and Movement of Explosives to Saudi Arabia," January 8, 1997.

260 **In his Sudan exile:** SSI Special Report, **Desert Shield and Desert Storm: A Chronology and Troop List of the 1990–1991 Persian Gulf Crisis** (Carlisle, Pa.: U.S. Army War College, 1991).

261 **He had grand plans to kill Americans:** Osama bin Laden, "Jihad Against Jews and Crusaders," accessed August 11, 2020, fas.org/irp/world/para/docs/980223-fatwa.htm.

11. A ROCK STAR PRESIDENT

262 **The Star's January 23 edition:** "My 12-Year Affair with Bill Clinton: Mistress Tells All," **Star,** January 23, 1993.

263 **"They can't run a story like this":** John J. Goldman, "Clinton Lied in Denying Affair, Woman Insists; Rebuttal: Gennifer Flowers Offers Tapes as Proof of a Liaison. She Refuses to Discuss Apparent Discrepancies in Her Story," **Los Angeles Times,** January 28, 1992.

264 **"I'm not prepared tonight to say":** "Governor Clinton's Interview with Steve Kroft," **60 Minutes,** January 26, 1992.

264 **"I saw a side of Bill":** Goldman, "Clinton Lied in Denying Affair, Woman Insists."

264 **But though Clinton was indeed lying:** Peter Baker

and Susan D. Schmidt, "FBI Taped Aide's Allegations," **The Washington Post**, January 22, 1998.

269 **He didn't have any sweat on his face:** William C. Rempel and Douglas Frantz, "Troopers Say Clinton Sought Silence on Personal Affairs; Arkansas: The White House Calls Their Allegations About the President's Private Life 'Ridiculous,' " **Los Angeles Times**, December 21, 1993.

269 **"I can't fool you guys, can I?":** David Brock, "His Cheatin' Heart," **The American Spectator**, December 1993.

270 **"You don't know what that outfit":** Michael Isikoff, **Uncovering Clinton: A Reporter's Story** (Crown, 1999).

270 **Bruce Lindsey, Clinton's campaign aide:** Ibid.

271 **But also, as governor, he had commandeered:** Brock, "His Cheatin' Heart."

271 **At the same time, the governor of Arkansas:** The **Boston Herald**, February 4, 1992, p. 8.

273 **Bush's team flew in that morning:** "Bush Campaign Speech," C-SPAN, October 25, 1992.

275 **"It's no secret that the governor loves":** Robert Rankin, "Clinton's Penchant for Mingling," **Philadelphia Inquirer**, November 24, 1992.

275 **Retired agent Dennis McCarthy:** Marlene Cimons, "A President and His Protectors: Clinton Is a Challenge for the Secret Service, but Agents Are Used to It," **Los Angeles Times**, January 12, 1993.

276 **He wanted to be sure no one was listening in:** Rebecca Borders, "Hell to Pay," **The American Spectator**, January 1997.

277 **The item claimed the First Lady had a wicked temper:** Bill Zwecker, "Hot Rumors," **Chicago Sun-Times**, February 19, 1993.

278 **"It occurred to us at the time":** Borders, "Hell to Pay."

284 "**The pigs are here**": politico.com/magazine/story /2015/04/clinton-white-house-the-residence -excerpt-116706_Page4.html#.WVp4xoTyt0w

288 "**It was a challenge**": John Feinstein and Red Auerbach, **Let Me Tell You a Story: A Lifetime in the Game** (Back Bay Books, 2005) p. 191.

293 **Nobody in the Clinton White House:** "Transcript: William Jefferson Clinton," **Fox News Sunday**, September 24, 2006.

293 **Chief of Staff Mack McLarty dispatched:** Carl Bernstein, **A Woman in Charge: The Life of Hillary Rodham Clinton** (New York: Vintage Books, 2008).

294 **Perry told friends:** Brock, "His Cheatin' Heart."

295 **On Tuesday, the Los Angeles Times reporters:** William C. Rempel and Douglas Frantz, "Troopers Say Clinton Sought Silence on Personal Affairs; Arkansas: The White House Calls Their Allegations About the President's Private Life 'Ridiculous,'" **Los Angeles Times**, December 21, 1993; Brock, "His Cheatin' Heart."

295 "**We lied for him**": David Brock, "His Cheatin' Heart," The American Spectator, December 1993.

297 **She was then negotiating with Congress:** Bernstein, **Woman in Charge.**

299 **Now she and her lawyers spelled it out:** Paula Jones complaint, U.S. District Court for the Eastern District of Arkansas, May 1994.

299 "**Kiss it,**" **he said:** Ibid.

300 "**Please,**" **Clinton had said:** Bernstein, **Woman in Charge.**

12. THE INTERN

308 "**I'm expecting one**": The Starr Report: The Official Report of the Independent Counsel's Investigation

of the President (Washington, D.C.: Public Affairs, 1998).

309 **"I'll bet it's Monica":** Ibid.

313 **Midway through:** Monica Lewinsky Grand Jury Testimony, August 6 and August 20, 1998, accessed August 12, 2020, washingtonpost.com/wp-srv/politics/special/clinton/stories/mltestimony.htm.

314 **Lewinsky instead performed oral sex:** "Narrative Pt. III: Continued Sexual Encounters," **The Washington Post,** accessed August 12, 2020, washingtonpost.com/wp-srv/politics/special/clinton/icreport/6narritiii.htm.

314 **Then Lewinsky let herself out:** Ibid.

317 **The president later confided in Lewinsky: Starr Report.**

319 **"This is about the office of the presidency":** John M. Broder and Stephen Labaton, "Shaped by a Painful Past, Secret Service Director Fights Required Testimony," **The New York Times,** May 30, 1998.

319 **"The director of the Secret Service, a taxpayer-funded agency":** Tim Weiner, "Secret Service Tells Its Agents to Keep Quiet About the Past," **The New York Times,** December 17, 1997.

319 **Seymour Hersh speculated that something more must be:** "Secret Service Warned About Going Public," **The Washington Post,** December 18, 1997.

319 **They asked that he retract his claims:** Ibid.

322 **Clinton grew increasingly anxious:** "Narrative Pt. III."

322 **A new conservative website:** George Lardner, "The Scandal's Producer and Publicist," **The Washington Post,** November 17, 1998.

324 **"I've got nothing to hide": Starr Report.**

324 **A member of the group discouraged the officer:**

Susan D. Schmidt, "Clinton, Lewinsky Met Alone, Former Guard Says," **The Washington Post,** February 11, 1998.

326 **Merletti told Kelleher they had to meet with Starr:** Jim Lichtman, "Trust and Confidence, Part 1," ethics stupid.com, April 11, 2016, accessed August 12, 2020, ethicsstupid.com/personalities/trust-and -confidence/.

328 **"I certainly do. It's my fault":** "Mike Wallace, Interviewer: 'You and Me,'" NPR, November 8, 2005.

328 **"The sound of a gunshot":** Ken Gormley, **The Death of American Virtue: Clinton vs. Starr** (New York: Broadway Books, 2011), p. 425.

328 **"It's as if he couldn't":** Gormley, **The Death of American Virtue,** p. 426.

330 **Merletti, when later questioned by an FBI agent:** Ibid., p. 667.

331 **"The argument was pure craziness":** Louis J. Freeh, **My FBI: Bringing Down the Mafia, Investigating Bill Clinton, and Fighting the War on Terror** (New York: St. Martin's Press, 2006), pp. 266–67.

334 **"Sir, my focus is the safety and security of the president":** Larry Cockell, grand jury testimony transcript, July 17, 1997, p. 42.

13. SCRAMBLING ON 9/11

339 **Bush's brief stop at the school:** "Fact Sheet: President Bush—Putting Reading First," September 10, 2001, The American Presidency Project, accessed August 12, 2020, presidency.ucsb.edu/ws/index .php?pid=79074.

342 **"A plane has hit the World Trade Center":** Garrett M. Graff, "We're the Only Plane in the Sky," **Politico,** September 9, 2016.

343 **As the leader of the detail:** " 'We're Under Attack': Native Pittsburgher Escorted President on 9/11," WPXI.com, September 7, 2011.

344 **a fresh new horror came into focus:** Declassified USSS statement for 9/11 Commission report, "Actions of TSD (Technical Security Division) Related to Terrorist Incident," September 12, 2001.

345 **"We need to turn all the planes away":** Nelson Garabito, 9/11 Commission interview, March 11, 2004; Terry Van Steenbergen, 9/11 Commission interview, March 30, 2004.

347 **News stations were replaying tape:** "A White House View of 9/11," LBJ Library, September 3, 2013.

348 **"Oh my God! There's more explosions":** "September 11, 2001: As It Happened," CNN, September 11, 2001.

348 **"We gotta get out of here!":** Graff, "We're the Only Plane in the Sky."

349 **"You can't do it in front of second-graders":** Ibid.

349 **"We need to get him secure":** Ibid.

350 **DON'T SAY ANYTHING YET:** Allan Wood and Paul Thompson, "An Interesting Day: President Bush's Movements and Actions on 9/11," May 15, 2003, globalresearch.ca.

350 **"We need to get you to Air Force One":** Graff, "We're the Only Plane in the Sky."

351 **Card proposed a compromise:** Ibid.; "A White House View of 9/11," LBJ Library, September 3, 2013.

352 **But she could see that this aircraft had charted a course:** Brian Ross, "Flight 77 to the White House," ABC News, October 24, 2001.

353 **The Intelligence Division agents:** Former assistant Secret Service director Danny Spriggs in interview at Newseum, April 11, 2017.

353 **A JOC officer told him:** Danny Spriggs, declassified 9/11 Commission statement.

353 **Spriggs had begun his phone call:** Truscott interview with USSS Inspection Division, October 1, 2001.

356 **"We have an aircraft, moving very fast":** The 9/11 Commission Report: Final Report of the National Commission on the Terrorist Attacks Upon the United States (New York: W. W. Norton, 2004).

356 **"The plane is turning":** Ibid., p. 39.

356 **It's one of our jets:** Ross, "Flight 77 to the White House."

359 **"How the hell could a plane hit":** 9/11 Commission Report, p. 35.

360 **Scott then walked over to the West Wing:** James O. Scott, memo of September 12, 2001, interview with USSS Inspection Division, October 1, 2001.

361 **"Sir, we have to leave immediately":** Vice President Richard B. Cheney interview, "9/11: The President's Story," TLC, September 12, 2016, accessed August 14, 2020, youtube.com/watch?v=N-75OeMabLY.

361 **Neither Scott nor other key members:** "The Underground White House," White House, accessed August 14, 2020, whitehouse.gov1.info/tunnel/.

363 **"Today, we've had a national tragedy":** President George W. Bush remarks at Emma E. Booker Elementary School, September 11, 2001, accessed August 14, 2020, americanrhetoric.com/speeches/gwbush911 florida.htm.

363 **"Poof, he was gone":** Tom Bayles, "The Day Before Everything Changed, President Bush Touched Local Lives," **Sarasota Herald-Tribune,** September 10, 2002.

364 **The Service had asked that they be placed there:** "A White House View of 9/11," LBJ Library, September 3, 2013.

364 **Bush's fellow passengers learned the grim news:** Ibid.

367 **Together they grabbed their cat:** "President George W. Bush: The 9/11 Interview," National Geographic Channel, September 11, 2011, youtube.com/watch?v =ke_OgE_V6tQ.

14. "YOU DON'T BELONG HERE"

369 **"Nineteen men armed with knives":** "Transcript: 9/11 Panel Releases Its Final Report," FDCH E-Media, July 22, 2004.

370 **In 1998, he led a tabletop exercise:** Richard Clarke interview with 9/11 Commission, March 2003.

370 **At the Secret Service, Director Stafford instructed his staff:** Becky Ediger, Deputy Special Agent in Charge, statement to 9/11 Commission.

373 **"That was driving decisions":** Susan B. Glasser and Michael Grunwald, "Department's Mission Was Undetermined from Start," The Washington Post, December 22, 2005.

373 **"Creating a cabinet office doesn't solve the problem":** Ari Fleischer, White House press briefing, March 19, 2002.

374 **Without a tear, O'Neill said so long:** Glasser and Grunwald, "Department's Mission Was Undetermined from Start."

381 **"Director Stafford, recently one of the major national news magazines":** House Judiciary Committee hearing on the Department of Homeland Security, July 9, 2002.

15. "HE PREDICTED ALL OF IT"

395 **The compound was quiet:** White House Statement, December 12, 2006.

403 **Baserap's survey found overwhelming agreement:** Survey, executive summary, by Officer Charles Baserap.

16. "HE'LL BE SHOT SURE AS HELL"

409 **By 2004, he represented just six hundred thousand people:** Jeff Zeleny, "Once a Convention Outsider, Obama Navigated a Path to the Marquee," **The New York Times,** August 27, 2008.

410 **"I stand here knowing that my story":** Barack Obama, Address to Democratic National Convention, July 27, 2004.

412 **Michelle shared her fears in blunt terms:** "How He Did It," **Newsweek,** November 17, 2008.

412 **Just six months earlier, Michelle had met: Vogue,** June 2005.

412 **That December, at the end of their beach talks:** "How He Did It."

413 **And he had to get professional protection soon:** Peter Slevin, **Michelle Obama: A Life** (New York: Penguin, 2015), p. 236.

413 **"I don't lose sleep over it":** "The Obamas on Security," CBS News, interview with Steve Kroft, February 9, 2007, accessed August 14, 2020, youtube.com/watch?v=nyUsDOeFo24.

415 **"Our world will become unbearable":** Alex Spillus, "Obama Gets Protection; Secret Service Guards Him Amid Fears of Plot," **London Daily Telegraph,** May 5, 2007.

417 **Unfortunately, some:** "American Morning," CNN, May 4, 2007.

418 **"Obama will die":** "Hyphoid Logic," accessed August 14, 2020, vyoma108.blogspot.com/2008/02/threats-against-barack-obama-americas.html.

418 **On April 22, while Clinton and Obama were still:** Daryl Johnson, **Right-Wing Resurgence: How a Domestic Terrorism Threat Is Being Ignored** (Lanham, Md.: Rowman & Littlefield, 2012).

422 **"deliberate attempt to embarrass the agency":** David Johnston, "Obama Secret Service Agent Tied to Sex Joke," **The New York Times,** May 15, 2008.

423 **Late that Saturday night:** Statement of Karen Neb, female with Adolf, FBI agent affidavit, September 24, 2008.

425 **A day after FBI agents told a federal judge:** Kristen Wyatt and Lara Jakes Jordan, "Fed Official: Colo Men No True Threat to Obama," Associated Press, August 25, 2008.

427 **The Service had installed two van-sized sheets:** Paul Thompson, "Bulletproof Glass Shield for Obama Victory Speech As Security Is Stepped Up for President Elect," **Daily Mail,** November 5, 2008.

428 **Agents estimated that in the months:** Ron Kessler, **In the President's Secret Service** (New York: Crown, 2010).

429 **More than two thousand people joined Stormfront:** Eve Conant, "Rebranding Hate in the Age of Obama," **Newsweek,** May 4, 2009.

17. SULLIVAN'S CREW

442 **She hadn't reached the lecture halls:** Peter Slevin, **Michelle Obama: A Life** (New York: Penguin, 2015).

18. THE NIGHT BULLETS HIT THE WHITE HOUSE

450 **On the rooftop of the White House:** Carol D. Leonnig, "Secret Service Fumbled Response After Gunman

Hit White House Residence in 2011," **The Washington Post,** September 27, 2014.

458 **The Park Police did not obtain a warrant:** USSS Spot Report: Oscar Ramiro Ortega-Hernandez, November 17, 2011.

19. "I WOKE UP TO A NIGHTMARE"

469 **"See logistics below":** USSS Inspection Report: Cartagena.

470 **Of the 175 Secret Service personnel in town:** Department of Homeland Security Office of Inspector General: USSS Cartagena Review and USSS Inspection Report: Cartagena.

471 **The men presumed it was the Pley Club:** DHS Office of Inspector General: USSS Cartagena Review.

472 **Stokes had about four or five beers:** USSS Inspection Report: Cartagena.

472 **She told him it would cost:** DHS Office of Inspector General: USSS Cartagena Review.

472 **"I have goose and some mixers":** USSS Inspection Report: Cartagena.

473 **In the thirty-plus years since CAT was formed:** Dan Emmett, **Within Arm's Length: A Secret Service Agent's Definitive Inside Account of Protecting the President** (New York: Macmillan, 2014), pp. 102–10.

473 **And during that time:** foxnews.com/politics/ exclusive-secret-service-agents-partied-like-rock -stars-on-obamas-vineyard-vacation.

474 **He grabbed a pole:** USSS Inspection Report: Cartagena.

475 **The American men kept ordering more vodka:** Interview with Dania Londono Suarez, **Today,** May 7, 2012.

475 **"If he gives me a 'little gift'"**: USSS Inspection Report: Cartagena.

476 **She wanted to be clear how much**: USSS Inspection Report: Cartagena.

476 **"No problem, baby"**: Carol D. Leonnig and David Nakamura, "Woman Describes Night in Secret Service Scandal," The Washington Post, May 5, 2012.

476 **By this time, he had tossed down**: USSS Inspection Report: Cartagena.

477 **Bongino and Huntington stood by**: Videotapes of agents entering Cartagena hotel, obtained under Freedom of Information Act by Malia Litman.

477 **Bongino carried Luciana piggyback**: USSS Inspection Report: Cartagena.

477 **She well knew the hotel policy**: USSS Inspection Report: Cartagena.

478 **Huntington looked at her, startled**: USSS Inspection Report: Cartagena.

478 **"No, let's go, bitch"**: Leonnig and Nakamura, "Woman Describes Night."

478 **He watched Suarez through the peephole**: USSS Inspection Report: Cartagena.

479 **She grabbed a pillow from Bongino's bed**: DHS Office of Inspector General: USSS Cartagena Review.

479 **Every now and again, he could see his shadow**: DHS Office of Inspector General: USSS Cartagena Review.

480 **When she explained her dispute**: USSS Inspection Report: Cartagena.

481 **The local police sergeant then handed the wad of cash**: DHS Office of Inspector General: USSS Cartagena Review.

481 **he passed another CAT member**: USSS Inspection Report: Cartagena.

482 At 9:15 A.M. Thursday: USSS Inspection Report: Cartagena.

482 Over the phone, the Caribe security director: USSS Inspection Report: Cartagena.

483 "This is very, very serious": USSS Inspection Report: Cartagena.

492 Within hours: David Nakamura and Joe Davidson, "U.S. Secret Service Agents Recalled from Colombia," The Washington Post, April 13, 2012.

20. SULLIVAN'S STRUGGLES

496 He paused, his face tightening: Remarks by President Obama and President Santos of Colombia in Joint Press Conference, April 15, 2012, obamawhitehouse. archives.gov/the-press-office/2012/04/15/remarks -president-obama-and-president-santos-colombia -joint-press-confer.

504 "Even one is concerning": Director Sullivan briefing book, May 18, 2012.

510 Two agents implicated in Cartagena: Agent statements to U.S. Secret Service investigators, USSS Inspection Report: Cartagena.

511 Sullivan said the Service had worked with the intelligence community: Hearing of the Senate Homeland Security and Governmental Affairs Committee, "Secret Service on the Line: Restoring Trust and Confidence," May 23, 2012.

511 Senator Collins gave Sullivan her own read: Hearing of the Senate Homeland Security and Governmental Affairs Committee, "Secret Service on the Line: Restoring Trust and Confidence," May 23, 2012.

512 "He kept saying over and over again": Ed O'Keefe, "Secret Service Director Apologizes as Senators Detail

New Misconduct Allegations," The Washington Post, May 23, 2012.

21. OUTED

533 **Investigators initially feared:** "Country Reports on Terrorism 2015," United States Department of State Publication Bureau of Counterterrorism and Countering Violent Extremism, released June 2, 2016.

533 **Prieto had been read into some:** Department of Homeland Security, Office of Inspector General, Report of Investigation, April 29, 2014.

22. A NEW SHERIFF IN TOWN

539 **About thirty-two agents:** USSS Inspection Report: Cartagena.

544 **On October 19, Senator Johnson issued a press release:** "Johnson Memo on Cartagena Revelations Indicate Inconsistencies with Congressional Testimony," White House Statements, Office of Senator Ron Johnson (R-WI).

23. A LISTING SHIP

560 **The conversations gave the impression:** USSS Inspection Report: Barraclough.

24. "HE'S IN THE HOUSE"

581 **Gonzalez parked his 1996 Ford:** USSS Spot Report: Gonzalez.

582 **A cavalry scout:** Carol D. Leonnig, Spencer S. Hsu, and Annys Shin, "White House Intruder Was Armed

with a Knife," **The Washington Post,** September 21, 2014.

582 **At his home near Fort Hood:** Michael M. Phillips and Jeffrey Sparshott, "Accused White House Fence Jumper Had Earlier Arrest Record," **The Wall Street Journal,** September 22, 2014.

582 **As he set off for the White House:** Spencer S. Hsu, "White House Fence Jumper Had Ammunition, Machete in Car, Prosecutors Say," **The Washington Post,** September 22, 2014.

583 **Around 7:05 P.M., President Obama stepped out:** White House Pool Report, September 19, 2014.

584 **Malia and Sasha, along with a school friend:** White House photographer Pete Souza, photographs from September 19, 2014.

592 **White House still suffered from a manpower shortage:** USSS Inspection Report materials: Gonzalez.

594 **she didn't have time to properly lock the doors:** USSS Inspection Report: Mission Assurance.

594 **Gonzalez yelled from outside:** United States Department of Justice, Government's Sentencing Memorandum, Omar Gonzalez, June 1, 2015.

598 **Gonzalez said he had to alert the president:** USSS Inspection Report: Gonzalez.

598 **Gonzalez suddenly became manic:** USSS Spot Report: Gonzalez.

25. CLANCY'S TURN

624 **"Only a director from outside":** David Francis, "Obama Taps Insider as Secret Service Chief After Being Prodded to Pick an Outsider," **Foreign Policy,** February 18, 2015.

628 **To protect their own officers and the public:** Depart-

ment of Homeland Security, Office of Inspector General, Report on Gonzalez, May 6, 2015.

628 **He backed up and drove forward twice:** "Video Shows March 4 Secret Service Incident," **The Washington Post,** March 24, 2015.

635 **Two days later, I published a story:** Carol D. Leonnig, "Secret Service Agents Investigated After Car Hits White House Barricade," **The Washington Post,** March 11, 2015.

635 **"Two senior Secret Service agents":** Kevin Liptak, Michelle Kosinski, and Chris Frates, "Report: Drunk Secret Service Agents Crash into White House Barrier," CNN, March 12, 2015.

637 **"I'm aware of those reports":** Ibid.

638 **"It is unclear why Director Clancy is choosing":** Carol D. Leonnig, "Secret Service Chief Questioned over Handling of White House Incident," **The Washington Post,** March 24, 2015.

638 **"I believe when the chain of command is broken":** Susan Crabtree, "Chaffetz Airs Video of March 4 Secret Service Incident," **Washington Examiner,** March 24, 2015.

640 **The information was stored:** Carol D. Leonnig and Jerry Markon, "Secret Service Official Wanted to Embarrass Congressman," **The Washington Post,** September 30, 2015.

641 **The bottom caption read:** Ibid.

643 **"If and to the extent the matters reflected":** Carol D. Leonnig, "DHS Asked to Probe Secret Service over Release of Chaffetz's Rejection," **The Washington Post,** April 2, 2015.

645 **"These agents work for an agency":** Leonnig and Markon, "Secret Service Official Wanted to Embarrass Congressman."

647 **At the October 5 press conference:** Carol D. Leonnig, "Secret Service Gets Some Much-Needed Praise," **The Washington Post,** October 5, 2015.

26. CHAOS CANDIDATE

650 **Donald Trump, the leading Republican presidential candidate:** Avi Selk, "The Violent Rally Trump Can't Move Past," **The Washington Post,** April 3, 2017.

651 **"Get out of here":** James Wilkinson, "Korea War Veteran Who Was Caught on Camera Shoving Black Woman at a Trump Rally Says He 'Sincerely Regrets' His Actions and Denies He Is Racist," **Daily Mail,** March 10, 2016.

652 **"Protesting is an American tradition":** Jose Del Real, " 'Get 'Em Out!' Racial Tensions Explode at Donald Trump's Rallies," **The Washington Post,** March 12, 2016.

653 **"Knock the crap out of them":** "Trump: 'Knock the Crap' out of Tomato Throwers," **The Washington Post,** February 1, 2016.

653 **Three days after the shoving incident:** Del Real, " 'Get 'Em Out!' " **The Washington Post,** March 12, 2016.

654 **The combination of the slipshod planning:** Fred Barbash, "That Unusual Trump 'Incitement' Ruling Wasn't Just About One Rally but a 'Multitude,' " **The Washington Post,** April 3, 2017.

654 **He stepped into the middle of the path:** Kenneth P. Vogel, "Trump Private Security Force 'Playing with Fire,' " **Politico,** December 19, 2016.

655 **Trump was visibly flustered:** Martin Savidge and Dana Ford, "CNN Exclusive: 'Trump Is a Bully,' Says a Man Who Rushed Stage," CNN, March 14, 2016.

663 **In addition, Trump signaled in his first weeks:** Har-

riet Sinclair, "Trump Slammed Obama for Taking Vacation, But He Just Booked 17-Day Golf Retreat," **Newsweek,** August 3, 2017.

667 **the Secret Service also had to rent a room next door:** David A. Fahrenthold, Joshua Partlow, Josh Dawsey, and Carol D. Leonnig, "Secret Service Paid Trump's D.C. Hotel More than $33,000 for Lodging to Guard Treasury Secretary," **The Washington Post,** April 30, 2020.

670 **According to the journalist Cassandra Fairbanks:** Caleb Stephen, "White House Jumper Bizarrely Told Journalist Just Days Earlier That He Was Responsible for Trump 'Golden Shower' Dossier," **Intellihub,** March 14, 2017.

673 **"Secret Service did a fantastic job":** "Secret Service Arrests Man on White House Grounds," CBS News, March 11, 2017.

677 **"The men and women of the Secret Service":** USSS Press Release: "White House Fence Jumper," March 17, 2017.

27. TAKING A HIT FOR TRUMP

688 **That morning, Trump and his Service protectors:** Julie Hirschfield Davis, "Was Trump Golfing? White House Shrouds Time at His Clubs in Mystery," **The New York Times,** March 19, 2017.

688 **A White House spokesman said:** Kevin Liptak, April 8, 2017, twitter.com/Kevinliptakcnn/status/850755377306193922?s=20.

688 **"Yes. I'll be here for Easter":** Shannon Donnelly, "Exclusive: President Trump to Return to Palm Beach for Easter Weekend," **Palm Beach Daily News,** April 10, 2017.

690 **"If this pace keeps up"**: Frank Cerabino, "Trump Palm Beach: Golf Cart Rental for President Has Us in the Rough," **Palm Beach Post**, April 17, 2017.

691 **The average weekend hop**: "Secret Service and DOD Need to Ensure That Expenditure Reports Are Prepared and Submitted to Congress," United States Government Accountability Office, January 2019.

691 **President Obama's critics**: "New Obama Travel Costs Bring Eight-Year Total over $96 Million," **Judicial Watch**, December 29, 2016.

691 **Trump's travel, however, cost the government**: "Secret Service and DOD Need to Ensure."

692 **(What the Secret Service didn't know)**: Mary Jordan, **The Art of Her Deal: The Untold Story of Melania Trump** (New York: Simon & Schuster, 2020).

694 **Trump had a close and jovial relationship**: Chandelis Dister, "Trump Names Secret Service Official as New Chief of Staff for Operations," CNN, December 7, 2019.

696 **Trump had avoided paying**: S. V. Date, "The Golfer in Chief Is Also the Goatherd in Chief, Saving Him Tens of Thousands," **Huffington Post**, August 15, 2019.

696 **but federal taxpayers would soon be paying**: Peter Overby, "Trump's Third Home Away from Home to Cost Taxpayers Millions," NPR, July 19, 2017.

697 **"Camp David is very rustic"**: Michael S. Rosenwald, "Mar-a-Lago 3, Camp David 0. With Trump as President, Is the Rustic Md. Retreat Doomed?" **The Washington Post**, February 20, 2017.

698 **"I know that we have a responsibility"**: House Homeland Security Committee Hearing, "How Can the United States Secret Service Evolve to Meet the Challenges Ahead?," June 8, 2017.

700 **By August, just four months into the job**: Drew Har-

well and Amy Brittain, "Secret Service Asked for $60 Million Extra for Trump-Era Travel and Protection, Documents Show," The Washington Post, March 22, 2017.

700 "We have them working all night long": Kevin Johnson, "Exclusive: Secret Service Depletes Funds to Pay Agents Because of Trump's Frequent Travel, Large Family," USA Today, August 22, 2017.

701 "This issue is not one that can be attributed": "Report: Secret Service Out of Money, Can't Pay Hundreds of Agents to Protect Trump and His Family," Fox59.com, August 21, 2017.

702 In his eight months as president: Karen Yourish and Troy Griggs, "Tracking the President's Visits to Trump Properties," The New York Times, accessed July 21, 2020, nytimes.com/interactive/2017/04/05/us/politics/tracking-trumps-visits-to-his-branded-properties.html.

702 The Service was working twelve times as many: Walker Davis and Linnaea Honl-Stuenkel, "The Trump Family Is Taking 12x More Protected Trips than the Obama Family," Citizens for Responsibility and Ethics in Washington, April 10, 2020.

EPILOGUE

713 As he entered the Oval Office: Carol D. Leonnig, "New Breaches Revealed in Report That Says Secret Service Is 'in Crisis,' " The Washington Post, December 3, 2015.

713 and whose staff had dropped to its lowest level: USSS Protective Mission Panel, Executive Summary provided to the Secretary of Homeland Security, December 15, 2014.

INDEX

ABOUT THE AUTHOR

CAROL LEONNIG is a national investigative reporter at **The Washington Post,** where she has worked since 2000. A three-time Pulitzer Prize winner and co-author of the number one **New York Times** bestseller **A Very Stable Genius,** Leonnig is also an on-air contributor to NBC News and MSNBC. A Maryland native, she lives in Washington, D.C., with her husband and their children.